Nestor Makhno and F
in Ukraine, 1

Nestor Makhno and Rural Anarchism in Ukraine, 1917–21

Colin Darch

First published 2020 by Pluto Press
345 Archway Road, London N6 5AA

www.plutobooks.com

Copyright © Colin Darch 2020

The right of Colin Darch to be identified as the author of this work has been asserted
by him in accordance with the Copyright, Designs and Patents Act 1988.

British Library Cataloguing in Publication Data
A catalogue record for this book is available from the British Library

ISBN 978 0 7453 3888 0   Hardback
ISBN 978 0 7453 3887 3   Paperback
ISBN 978 1 7868 0526 3   PDF eBook
ISBN 978 1 7868 0528 7   Kindle eBook
ISBN 978 1 7868 0527 0   EPUB eBook

Typeset by Stanford DTP Services, Northampton, England
Simultaneously printed in the United Kingdom and United States of America

For my grandchildren

Historia scribitur ad narrandum, non ad probandum – Quintilian

Contents

Maps

Abbreviations

GPU   State Political Directorate (Gosudarstvennoe Politicheskoe Upravlenie)

GRAZ   Group of Russian Anarchists Overseas (Gruppa Russkikh Anarkhistov za Granitsei)

KADA   Crimea-Azov Volunteer Army (Krims'ko-Azovs'ka Dobrovol'cha Armiia)

KP(b)U   Communist Party (bolsheviks) of Ukraine (Komunistychna Partiia [bil'shovykiv] Ukrainy)

NEP   New Economic Policy (Novaia Ekonomicheskaia Politika)

RKP(b)   Russian Communist Party (bolsheviks) (Rossiiskaia Kommunisticheskaia Partiia [bol'shevikov])

RPA(M)   Revolutionary Insurgent Army (makhnovists) (Revoliutsionnaia Povstancheskaia Armiia [makhnovtsev])

RVS   Revolutionary Military Council (Revoliutsionnyi Voennyi Sovet)

SRs   Socialist Revolutionary Party (Partiia Sotsialistov-Revoliutsionerov)

TsIK   Central Exeutive Committee (Tsentral'nyi Vikonavchyi Komitet)

UNR   Ukrainian National Republic (Ukrains'ka Narodnia Respublika)

VRS   Military-Revolutionary Soviet (Voenno-Revoliutsionnaia Sovet)

VTsIK   All-Russian Central Executive Committee (Vserossiiskii Tsentral'nyi Ispolnitel'nyi Komitet)

Acknowledgements

My interest in *makhnovshchina* dates back to the late 1960s, and the research for this book was carried out intermittently over the many years since then by visits to, or through correspondence with the following libraries, archives and research centres. I owe an enormous debt of gratitude to the librarians and archivists who have assisted me both personally and by providing me with photocopies or microfilm of necessary documents: the Bibliothèque de Documentation Internationale Contemporaine (BDIC), Nanterre; the Bibliothèque Nationale, Paris; the British Library, London; the Bundesarchiv, Koblenz; the Canadian Mennonite Bible College Library, Winnipeg; the Centre Internationale des Recherches sur l'Anarchisme, Lausanne; Columbia University Library, New York City; the Deutsche Bücherei, Leipzig; what was then the Gosudarstvennaia Biblioteka SSSR im. V. I. Lenina, Moscow; the then Gosudarstvennaia Publichnaia Biblioteka im. M. E. Saltykova-Shchedrina, St. Petersburg; the Hoover Institution on War, Revolution and Peace, Stanford University; Indiana University Library, Bloomington; the Internationaal Instituut voor Sociale Geschiedenis, Amsterdam; the Library of Congress, Washington DC; the National Library of Canada, Ottawa; New York Public Library, New York City; the School of Slavonic and East European Studies, University of London; the Schweizerische Landesbibliothek, Berne; the Bodleian Library, Oxford; the University Libraries of the University of Birmingham, the University of Bradford, the University of Helsinki, the University of Michigan in Ann Arbor, the University of Toronto and the University of Wisconsin; and the YIVO Institute for Jewish Research, New York City.

I want to acknowledge and thank the people who, over a long period of many years have given generous, willing and unstinting assistance in the research, writing, correspondence and, of course, conversation that have led to this book. It's possible that some may have forgotten assisting me. Their help included granting me access to unpublished memoirs and other documents, responding to factual and other queries, criticising draft chapters and helping with translation. I must mention especially Ivan Antypenko of Philadelphia; Paul Avrich; Delice Baker-Duly who provided Swedish translations many years ago; G. N. Britten; the late E. H. Carr; the late Richard Caulk; Georgi Derluguian; Irina Filatova for several points of clarification; M. Fransiszyn; Daniel Guérin; Zenon Jaworskyi; Viktor Kachun; Annemarie Kinfu who provided German translations; Michel Kovetzki; the late A. L. Morton; Richard and Rita Pankhurst; Sean Patterson; Victor Peters; Michael Petrowsky; Mark Plant; the Very Rev.

N. Pliczkowski; Jenny Sandler, who drew the maps; Alexandre Skirda; the late Teodor Shanin; Iuri Shevchenko of the University of Khar'kov for assistance with routes and distances; Vladimir Shubin (no relation of Aleksandr Shubin) for critical comments; Yehuda Slutsky for sharing his work on the Ukrainian pogroms; the late Volker Stitz; Lucien van der Walt; Leo van Rossum; Gottfried Wellmer who provided German translations; Dr. Olex Wintoniak of *Dniprova Khvylia*; the late Michael Wolfers; and Jason Yanowitz. Last, my special and enduring thanks go to Gary Littlejohn, who supervised with good humour and patience my now-superseded doctoral dissertation on *makhnovshchina*, and has also read through this manuscript and made many valuable suggestions; to Leo Zeilig, without whose enthusiastic encouragement a version of this work would still be lying in the bottom of a drawer; and to first Hilary Davies, Tom Rampling and Toni Ongala, and later Agnes Nkhoma-Darch for their many years of extraordinarily patient support. My thanks to the four anonymous reviewers of my original proposal, and to Pluto Press for their ongoing support – specifically to David Shulman, for his patience, and to Robert Webb. Some of the people mentioned above will almost certainly find themselves for various reasons in more or less strong disagreement with my argument and my conclusions, which now differ significantly from my earlier views on the Makhno rebellion. Nonetheless, I am grateful for their help.

Needless to say, I alone am entirely responsible for the interpretation as well as for all errors and omissions of whatever kind in this book.

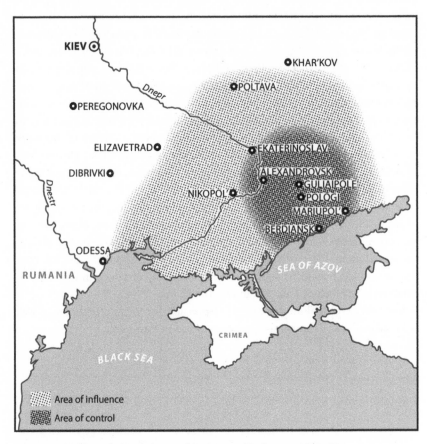

Map 0.1   Makhnovshchina's Areas of Activity and Influence, 1918–21

The heartland of *makhnovshchina* was based around Guliaipole, Ekaterinoslav and Aleksandrovsk, but the movement's influence extended intermittently over a much wider area. (Cartographer: Jenny Sandler).

1
The Deep Roots of Rural Discontent: Guliaipole, 1905–17

Nestor Ivanovich Makhno was born far from the centres of power, in the provincial Ukrainian town of Guliaipole, in Aleksandrovsk district, Ekaterinoslav province, probably in 1888, the fifth child in a family of former serfs.[1] We know little for certain about his childhood and adolescence, and what we do know comes not from contemporary documentation but from later testimonies,[2] including Makhno's own. Some may have fed into each other, and some are the objects of condemnation,[3] while Makhno's own account was written in exile long after the events. The outline of the story of his youth is known but does not help us to understand how this half-educated provincial rebel, with no experience of soldiering, was able to become both an anarchist revolutionary and a successful commander within as well as apart from the Red Army.

After the emancipation of the serfs in 1861 his father, Ivan Mikhnenko, continued to work for his former master. When his wife was pregnant with Nestor, their fifth child,[4] Ivan got a job with the Jewish merchant Kerner, who owned a factory, a shop and nearly 500 hectares of land.[5] Before Nestor was even a year old, Mikhnenko died.[6] The family lived in a shack near the market square, on the edge of town. They were too poor, in a semi-rural community, to afford to keep pigs or chickens, and Makhno's earliest memories were of deprivation and struggle.[7]

Guliaipole, a provincial town like many others, was located on the river Gaichur, near the railway line to Ekaterinoslav.[8] After the Stolypin agrarian reforms of 1906,[9] the number of estates in the area grew to around 50, many owned by German colonists.[10] Facilities included banks, a post and telegraph office, churches, a police station, a hospital, the *volost'* administration building and several schools. Small-scale industrialisation had created a semi-proletariat, peasant workers at most a generation away from the land. Millworkers came seasonally from Poltava or Chernigov in the north, to live in barracks outside the town. Others laboured in factories, foundries or flourmills, or worked as domestic servants.[11] German settlers, Jews and Russians lived in the area, but the population remained overwhelmingly Ukrainian.[12]

Makhno's childhood and adolescence seem to have been unexceptional in this peri-urban provincial environment. When he was eight years old, he attended elementary school in Guliaipole for a couple of years and held a series of jobs as a farm boy, and then as an apprentice in a dye factory. By the time he was 14, according to one testimony, he had become a skilled dyer,[13] and he later worked in the Guliaipole iron foundry.[14] His contact with foundry workers may have had some influence on the formation of his political outlook and union activism, for metal-workers were known for their political militancy.[15] Years later Makhno admitted that growing up poor fuelled his resentment against the better-off:

> ... I began to feel a kind of anger, of malice, even of hatred, for the landlords and above all for their progeny; against the young idlers who passed me by, all plump, hale and hearty, well-dressed, smelling of perfume, whereas I was dirty, in rags, barefoot and stinking of the dung heap ...[16]

Aleksandr Shubin has pointed out that these circumstances were 'almost ideal' for fostering resentment: 'poverty and a desire to escape it, to assert himself so as to take revenge on those who were responsible ...'[17]: the later rapid growth of the insurgency that Makhno led is at least partially explicable in such terms. Makhno's attachment to his mother, Evdokiia Matveevna, was strong, and her struggles fed into his anger towards the privileged. For years he harboured a grudge against a policeman who had once slapped her, and after his release from prison in 1917 he came close to shooting the man.[18] The question remains, however, why it was that Makhno, out of the millions of youths in similar circumstances, went on to seize the historical moment between 1917 and 1921 and lead a massive uprising of the rural poor?

It seems probable that differences in the narratives around Makhno's youth are determined to some extent by political positioning. He was supposedly hot-tempered,[19] and there is anecdotal evidence that as a youth he was considered indolent and surly, qualities that led, in at least one case, to his losing a job.[20] Indolence and surliness, of course, are plausible manifestations of resentment towards the wealthy. What is certain is that by his late teens, after the revolution of 1905 and irrespective of the psychological or personal circumstances that led him to it, Makhno became politically active. He seems initially to have been sympathetic to Menshevik ideas, and helped to distribute their literature. Despite this initial sympathy for the Mensheviks, he soon joined an anarchist-communist group – his older brothers were already members[21] – and quickly became a participant in insurrectionist actions of 'propaganda of the deed', such as an attack on a post office, and robberies or 'appropriations'.[22] The anarchist-communists wanted a society organised around loose confederations of producers' associations, in which agricultural and industrial labour would co-exist. Distinctions between inferior and superior work, between workers by hand and workers by brain, would vanish. This disappearance of the division of labour would result in a communal society in which all would work from free will.[23]

The conditions in which anarchist-communist ideas took root were by no means static, even in the Ukrainian provinces. Rapid urbanisation and industrialisation in the Russian Empire in the late 1800s and early 1900s were driving social change in both the cities and in the countryside. It has elsewhere been argued that government policy and institutional obstacles to easy movement into large cities meant that much industrialisation remained strongly linked to the countryside.[24] Hence, the provincial city of Ekaterinoslav experienced massive population growth in this period: there were 47,000 people living there in 1885, around the time of Makhno's birth, but by 1897 this had more than doubled to 113,000, and in 1910, before the outbreak of war, had again doubled to 212,000 inhabitants.[25] Similar social and economic transformations took place in the rural areas generally, affecting the outlook of the peasantry in important and complex ways.

In the early twentieth century, the majority of Russian peasants were still organised around the *dvor* (household), a loose family unit that was the nucleus of peasant society in the sense that the family's lives were integrated with the farming enterprise that provided food and even a surplus.[26] In Teodor Shanin's words:

> The family provides the essential work team of the farm, while the farm's activities are geared mainly to production of the basic needs of the family and the dues enforced by the holders of political and economic power.[27]

The other key social structure was the *obshchina* or peasant commune, a mechanism for distributing strips of land to families according to capacity and need. This was done though a 'patriarchal village assembly' called a *skhod*, made up of male heads of household and some village elders, who would decide when 'repartition' had become necessary, as well as when it was time for planting and harvesting. Most peasant farmers neither hired labour (which was provided by family members) nor worked for hire (as their needs were met by family production). Despite its democratic deficiencies, the *skhod* controlled many aspects of social and economic activity, as well as providing some security for the *obshchina*'s members.[28] However, architects of the emancipation of 1861 were concerned not to prejudice the interests of landowners, so liberated serfs were required to purchase allotments from their former oppressors, sometimes losing as much as a quarter of their land in the process.[29] Despite the romanticism about the character of the commune in the writings of some Slavophiles, they were far from being static and could also become centres of conflict: they were far from being 'rustic haven[s] of equality, stability and brotherly love'.[30] In times of unrest and revolution, violent clashes over land and other issues were frequent, particularly between peasants who had remained in the communes (*obshchinniki*), and peasants who had left in order to engage in private commercial farming (*otrubshchiki*), who were seen as exploiters.[31]

Access to schooling, access to transport networks, a growth in male labour migration,[32] and military service for young men all began to impact on the so-called traditions of rural life, including the *obshchina* itself. Rural people could buy clothes and books, as well as manufactured goods.[33] They engaged directly with the state through the judicial system, pursuing justice and resolving conflicts through the courts in diverse ways.[34] Through the networks established by these processes, radical political ideas spread quickly among the younger members of the community, although the older generation – in positions of relative power as members of the local administration, the police force, or the bureaucracy – supported 'tradition', including the subjugation of women.[35]

Revolutionary unrest broke out in January 1905 all over the Russian Empire, and continued intermittently until 1907. In Ukraine it was most marked by peasant revolts on the right bank, although there were also strikes and violence in Khar'kov and Ekaterinoslav, and by the end of 1905 soviets had appeared in many Ukrainian cities. In the context of these revolutionary events, the varied processes of modernisation, and the state's resistance to them during the so-called 'Stolypin reaction' from 1906 to 1910, the Guliaipole anarchist-communists saw their immediate task as a violent struggle against the police, the most obvious local manifestation of state violence. This was a continuation of tactics adopted during 1905. Southern anarchist groups such as the *Chernoznamentsy* (followers of the Black Flag) had energetically bombed, robbed, blackmailed and sabotaged, but with little impact. Many such activists were youths of Makhno's generation: few were members of the intelligentsia. All the groups were numerically tiny, probably totalling less than 6,000 people for the whole Russian empire.[36] After the defeat of the 1905 revolution, the sectarianism and pressure from the state significantly weakened the anarchist movement. Many militants were dead, in jail, or exiled, and survivors were isolated.

The Guliaipole organisation called itself the 'Peasants' Group of Anarchist-Communists', and through a propagandist named Vol'demar Antoni maintained links with an anarchist-communist group in Ekaterinoslav.[37] The dozen or so core members were mostly peasants, with a larger fringe of hangers-on. They held political classes in each other's homes or in the open air. They used codenames and had a probation period for new members. They were tactically and organisationally unsophisticated, but appear to have been genuinely driven by political conviction in the notion of freedom for the people.[38] Relations between the Guliaipole and Ekaterinoslav groups were close, influenced by an army deserter called Aleksandr Semeniuta. Most of their expropriations and assassinations were carried out between September 1906 and July 1908.[39]

According to one account the other members did not trust Makhno because he was habitually drunk, aggressive and talkative, often picking fights.[40] Some testimonies claim that he was careless: a saucepan that he used to mix explosives once blew up on his mother's stove.[41] On the other hand, Aleksei Chubenko says Makhno attended meetings daily, and carried out missions efficiently and selflessly.[42]

The first robbery took place on the evening of 5/18 September 1906,[43] when three armed men appeared at the home of a local merchant called Pleshchiner and demanded money. He handed over cash and jewellery. On 10/23 October, another group carried out a similar robbery, demanding 'money for the starving'.[44] They spent the money on a duplicating machine, producing leaflets and tracts attacking the Stolypin reforms, and calling for mass struggle against the *kulaki*. The third expropriation targeted the manufacturer Mark Kerner, the 'Croesus of Guliaipole' and the former employer of Makhno's father. He was robbed by assailants who got away with cash and a silver ingot. Kerner later testified that there were seven members of the gang and that they seemed nervous, for he noticed that their hands were shaking. Two days later, on 15/28 November 1906, the expropriators sent Kerner a letter expressing regret that they had taken so little money from him. The 'detachment of armed workers', as they styled themselves, told Kerner that they knew he had informed the police and warned that if investigations continued his home would be bombed.[45] Makhno was certainly under police surveillance by this time – in 1917, when Makhno gained access to the police archives of Guliaipole, he discovered that at least one member of his anarchist group had been a police spy.[46] In late 1906 he was arrested for the first time, on suspicion of the murder of a rural police constable, but was released immediately.[47]

After the attack on Kerner the anarchist gang lay low for the rest of winter and through spring. In August 1907 they attempted a fourth expropriation, this time in the Gaichur settlement, a suburb of Guliaipole near the railway station. Four armed men with their faces covered burst into the house of a merchant named Gurevich late at night. They demanded money in the name of the anarchist-communists – the first time the group had identified itself during a robbery. Unfortunately for the expropriators, Gurevich's nephew refused to be intimidated and raised a hue-and-cry. The four seized a post-office wagon near the railway station and galloped away, shooting as they went.[48] Undeterred, on 19 October/1 November 1907 they tried again, this time ambushing a post-office cart which they raked with gunfire, killing a postman, a village constable, and a horse.

The local police failed to identify the robbers, but immediately after the last ambush the anarchists' luck turned for the worse. A prisoner in Ekaterinoslav jail told the police that he knew the names of the ambushers – a fellow-prisoner had confided that he had taken part in the attack. The assault had been the brainchild of Vol'demar Antoni, who had provided the assailants with weapons. The witness Zuichenko later denied that he had participated, but did admit that he was an anarchist and an agrarian terrorist, and that he had in the past set fire to the properties of *pomeshchiki* (landlords).[49] Makhno and Antoni, claimed Zuichenko, knew and trusted him and had confided in him.[50] More evidence was soon forthcoming with witnesses confirming that Makhno, Anton Bondarenko and Prokopii Semeniuta had all taken part in the ambush and that Semeniuta had been involved in the earlier robberies.[51] In late 1907, the police arrested Makhno again on suspicion of having committed political murders and expropriations. Again, they could prove nothing, and soon released Makhno, this time – ironically enough – on the surety of a local factory-owner.[52]

Recklessly, the anarchists continued their activities. On 10/23 April 1908 Ivan Levadnyi, Naum Al'tgauzen,[53] and two or three others set off from Guliaipole towards Bogodarovsk settlement in Aleksandrovsk district, 40 kilometres away. Later in the day a merchant called Levin was robbed of cash and gold by five armed men with soot-smeared faces. On 13/26 May another merchant was the victim of an attempted robbery, during which his daughter was shot and wounded. The expropriators escaped but with no loot. On 9/22 July the group attacked the government wine-shop in Novoselovke, near Guliaipole, and shot and killed a shop-assistant.

By 28 July/10 August the police were ready to move. They raided a meeting at Levadnyi's house, and shots were exchanged. Prokopii Semeniuta and a police constable were killed.[54] The police subsequently arrested six anarchists, who were all sentenced to administrative exile.[55] Antoni served a one-month prison term.[56] The detective in charge was a local named Karachentsev. To expose the group and its activities, he resorted to the standard weapon in the armoury of the Tsar's security forces, the *agent provocateur*, infiltrating the group with his men, who played an active part in the assaults and robberies. The anarchists exposed and executed at least one of these agents. From information provided by the others, Karachentsev compiled a list of members, identifying the leader and supplier of weapons as Vol'demar Antoni.[57]

Karachentsev lacked hard evidence against other members of the group and decided to take direct action. He had heard that Aleksandr Semeniuta was in hiding in Ekaterinoslav and tracked down other anarchists hiding in the city, arresting Lisovskii, Levadnyi, Zuichenko and Al'tgauzen. Levadnyi broke under interrogation and described the whole series of robberies and killings, starting with Pleshchiner and continuing through the ambush of the postal wagon up to the shooting of the police constable. Al'tgauzen confessed to having participated in the robberies of Shindler and Kerner.[58] Much later Makhno held Al'tgauzen responsible, as an *agent provocateur*, for the downfall of the group, but at the time he was indicted with the others.[59] Zuichenko confessed and

Karachentsev then arrested more anarchists, including Shevchenko and Mariia Martynova, Lisovskii's lover.

Zuichenko's testimony provided Karachentsev with the evidence he needed to bring the suspects to trial. Antoni, the group's first leader, had fled to Belgium but had maintained his contacts with the group, acting as a supplier of weapons and explosives. After Antoni's flight, Aleksandr Semeniuta had become the dominant figure in the organisation. Zuichenko described the group's meetings, which took place most often at Levadnyi's house, where they planned the expropriations. He revealed that they had planned to assassinate Karachentsev, and to shift their centre of activity to Ekaterinoslav, which was why Semeniuta had moved there.

After this success, Karachentsev telegraphed Guliaipole with instructions to arrest Nestor Makhno along with four other anarchists. Throughout August 1908 a series of confrontations, confessions, accusations and counteraccusations took place as group loyalty dissolved and individuals tried to save themselves by betraying others. Through it all Makhno – who seems by the sparse evidence available to have been committed and principled – refused to admit anything.[60] On 1/14 September the police intercepted a note from Makhno to Levadnyi, telling him to 'take the matter into [his] own hands'.[61] The prosecutor later made much of this. Makhno explained it simply as an exhortation to Levadnyi not to attempt to shift his guilt onto the shoulders of others. The authorities produced another note from Makhno at the trial, referring in guarded terms to the planning of a possible escape attempt.[62] But by now the police had found more witnesses in Guliaipole. Shevchenko's brother was willing to testify that he had been hiding bombs in the courtyard, and that the group had held meetings at his house. He claimed that he had seen them in possession of sums of money as well as weapons.[63]

By this time Semeniuta had escaped abroad and sent Karachentsev a letter, addressing him as a 'spotted devil', and inviting him to come to Belgium, 'where there is freedom of speech, and one can talk freely'.[64] In the autumn of 1909 Semeniuta came back to Guliaipole to seek revenge for the death of his brother Prokopii, and ambushed Karachentsev outside a local theatre, shooting him dead and escaping.[65] Later on, in 1911, he returned again, accompanied by a young anarchist woman. An informer spotted the pair and told the police, who surrounded the house. In the gun-battle that followed Semeniuta refused to surrender and shot himself; the young woman was wounded.[66]

At a preliminary hearing three of the accused retracted their earlier statements, alleging that they were made under duress. Makhno denied membership of any kind of association and repeated his explanation of the note to Levadnyi. But Zuichenko again confessed to everything and betrayed them all. One of the accused was hanged on 17/30 June 1909 by order of a court martial and another died of typhus in the prison barracks.[67] Antoni and one of the others had escaped abroad. The arraignment accused Makhno and some others of several expropriations, under articles of the penal code that carried the death penalty. The prisoners stayed in custody in Aleksandrovsk for a year while investigations were completed. During the winter they managed to contact comrades who were still at large and planned an escape during a transfer to Ekaterinoslav. The attempt was abandoned in freezing sub-zero conditions.[68]

Makhno's case was heard by the Odessa District Court Martial,[69] convened in Ekaterinoslav in March 1910, and he was found guilty and sentenced to death by hanging. He lived as a condemned prisoner for fifty-two days, until the authorities commuted his sentence, partly thanks to his youth (he was not 21 until October), and partly thanks to his mother's efforts on his behalf.[70] Of all these anarchist comrades who took part alongside Makhno in the post-1905 insurrectionist actions, the only one who survived to assume a role in the Makhno insurrection after 1917 was Nazarii Zuichenko.[71]

In July 1911 Makhno started a term of twenty years hard labour in Butyrka Prison in north-west Moscow.[72] The years that Makhno spent in prison changed his life. It was in jail that he met Petr Arshinov, the man who was to 'confirm him in the faith of Bakunin and Kropotkin', support him throughout the civil war and follow him into exile.[73] A native of Ekaterinoslav, Petr Andreevich Arshinov was two years older than Makhno, and had been a Bolshevik before his conversion to anarchism in 1906. He had worked as an itinerant metal-worker on the railways, and had contributed to the Bolshevik newspaper *Molot*. Arshinov received a death sentence for his anarchist activities, but escaped to France, and subsequently to Austria-Hungary. The Austrian police caught him trying to smuggle subversive literature into Russia and extradited him. After a second trial he was sentenced to hard labour, and in 1911 joined Makhno in Butyrka.[74]

When the two men met, Arshinov had already experienced the hard life of the professional agitator and political exile. A resourceful man, he had gone to some lengths to improve his education, and he now worked to improve Makhno's. His younger fellow-prisoner, commented Arshinov, 'showed great perseverance, and studied grammar, mathematics, literature, cultural history and economics. Prison was the school where Makhno learned the history and politics that were to help him in his subsequent revolutionary activity'.[75] He concentrated especially on three subjects – history, geography and mathematics. He used the prison library, and devoured both illegal and legal literature, reading Kropotkin, the poet Lermontov and many others. Nor was he above picking the brains of better-educated fellow-prisoners.[76]

In 1912, Makhno wrote later, he experienced a 'deep inner crisis'. This convinced him that he must find his salvation through individual effort and that socialist intellectuals mostly only wanted to be 'masters and leaders':

In the end ... I no longer felt the slightest respect for the so-called 'distin-guished politicians' or their opinions. I reached the conclusion that as far as vital, concrete problems were concerned these men were nothing but children like me.[77]

He decided that everybody was equally deserving of respect, and that 'those who consider themselves superior do not deserve the attention that they receive'.[78]

Makhno was neither an easy companion nor a model prisoner and was often in trouble. He spent time in irons, or in the solitary confinement cells, where he contracted the pulmonary tuberculosis that eventually led to his death in exile.[79] He had already spent time in the prison hospital in Ekaterinoslav with typhoid fever, and in Moscow his health continued to deteriorate. Despite his illness, however, he was always on the lookout for opportunities to escape.[80] His fellow-inmates, with whom he argued constantly about politics, sarcastically dubbed him *skromnyi*, or 'the modest one'.[81] The years in Butyrka left Makhno with an enduring hatred of prisons, and later, at the height of his power, when his forces captured a town he would release the prisoners and blow the jail up or set fire to it.[82]

Two major events marked the years that Makhno spent in prison. The outbreak of war in 1914 divided the political prisoners in Butyrka, as it divided their comrades outside, into two camps. Makhno read in *Russkie Viedemosti* that Kropotkin had taken a pro-war position, and despaired.[83] He conducted vigorous polemics from the defeatist position, opening one tract with the words, 'Comrades! When will you stop being such scoundrels?' Some of the Socialist Revolutionary Party (SR) prisoners were indignant enough at this to want to hold an enquiry into the authorship of the anonymous pamphlet.[84] The second event was the overthrow of the Tsar in February 1917, and the assump-tion of power by the reformist Provisional Government. This led in March, under pressure from the Soviet of Workers' and Soldiers' Deputies, to a decla-ration of general amnesty for all agrarian, military or terrorist crimes.[85] Both Makhno and Arshinov were released under this amnesty. Makhno's sudden lib-eration after more than seven years in prison seemed to him to be as sudden as a 'crash of thunder'[86] – and this is the key moment, the moment when the real story begins, when the story of a single dissatisfied, semi-urbanised peasant youth starts to become the story of a revolutionary mass movement seeking a form of political democracy that would challenge top-down decision-making to give those without power or property, in the hinterlands of empire, control over the governance of their lives.

At the time Makhno was a penniless 28-year-old, newly released from jail, and without professional skills.[87] His eyes had been damaged by the years in prison, and he wore dark glasses in sunlight.[88] Arshinov stayed in Moscow, where he was briefly active in the Moscow Federation of Anarchists, but

Makhno was persuaded by his mother and his remaining anarchist comrades in Guliaipole to come home.[89] He lacked experience in practical politics, but his prestige in Guliaipole as a returning political prisoner was high, and according to his own account the local anarchists and their sympathisers greeted him enthusiastically.[90] The handful of published documents from this early period show him convening a meeting of a local committee, asking that the value of food rations for families of serving soldiers be publicised, reporting on the theft of a horse, attempting to organise the collection of statistical data on population and land, and dealing with issues of soldiers in reserve regiments released for fieldwork.[91] Makhno became 'a completely ordinary Soviet functionary'[92] working in an office and dealing with bureaucratic questions.[93]

Vasilii Golovanov, who is a sympathetic and imaginative chronicler, argues that at this moment it is possible to see Makhno as a tragic figure, a man who sacrificed his chance of happiness to struggle for a political ideal.[94] The interlude between Makhno's arrival in Guliaipole in February or March 1917, and his flight from the town a year later, in April 1918, offers us a glimpse of the paths Makhno might have followed had he not chosen – or been compelled to choose – to become a guerrilla commander. It is a period that has (still) attracted relatively little scholarly attention, as Timoshchuk pointed out in 1996.[95] To begin with, it seems, Makhno even hoped to settle down and live a peaceful domestic life. He went back to work at the Kerner factory,[96] and after a few months, in November 1917, he married a young local woman, Anastasia Vasetskaia, apparently at the insistence of his mother.[97] According to one account, Vasetskaia had written 'warm letters' to him when he was in prison, and they soon had a child. But Makhno's chances of domestic happiness were short-lived: his comrades in the 'Black Guards' threatened Vasetskaia and forced her to leave Guliaipole with the baby.[98]

The February revolution – the abdication of the Tsar and the coming to power of Kerensky's Provisional Government in Moscow – had released the pent-up energy of the Ukrainian masses. Makhno was returning to a country that was undergoing a massive realignment of forces. In late March a group of intellectuals led by Mykhailo Hrushevs'kyi[99] formed the *Ukrains'ka Tsentral'na Rada* (Ukrainian Central Council). Its initial, modest objectives were to coordinate the national movement and to demand from the Provisional Government the right to print books and newspapers in Ukrainian and to teach it in schools.[100] It later supported the idea of a federal framework (while more radical left parties, including the communists, worked for revolutionary transformation). However, with the *Rada*'s unilateral declaration of Ukrainian autonomy in June 1917, 'the genie' in Plokhy's words 'was out of the bottle'.[101]

In Guliaipole, some of Makhno's old comrades had survived, but there were many faces that he did not know.[102] He decided that he was not going to miss an opportunity to help create, as he put it, '…the means whereby to do away with the old regime of slavery and to conjure up a new one wherein slavery would not exist and wherein authority would have no place'.[103] Police persecution had decimated the original anarchist group, but the handful of remaining members had reconstituted themselves as a new organisation in May 1916, and Makhno's return saved the group from collapse.[104] He frequently spoke at rallies, helped to print leaflets and organise public demonstrations, and agitated for 'Free Soviets' and for the non-recognition of Kerensky's government.[105]

Makhno understood that the group lacked structure and spoke vigorously in favour of coordinated action. One speech, quoted in full in his autobiography (presumably from memory) summed up the development of his political ideas, and attacked sectarianism within anarchism. He referred to the 'destructive phase' of the revolution and argued that coordination was required to get rid of government institutions, as well as all forms of private ownership. This included taking over factories in the towns. At the same time, it was necessary to 'draw closer to the peasant masses so as to assure ... the constancy of their revolutionary enthusiasm'. 'Our group', he claimed, 'is the only one which has remained in contact with the peasant masses' since the 1905–6 revolution. The anarchists in Aleksandrovsk and Ekaterinoslav had been decimated, and were unreliable. The first task, therefore, was to organise a Peasant Union, and to elect an anarchist at its head.[106]

Makhno's political positions were accompanied by rudimentary preparations for armed struggle – he had learned harsh lessons from the 1906 events. He believed that the best chance of success lay in forging close connections with the peasant masses, in seizing control of non-revolutionary organs and in establishing institutions to exercise power. Political isolation would be fatal, as it had been during the Stolypin reaction: the old anarchist 'insurrectionist' tactics would not work:

> I determined to jettison different tactical requirements assumed by the anarchists in the years 1906–1907. During that period in fact, the principles of organisation were sacrificed to the principle of exclusiveness: the anarchists huddled in their circles which, removed from the masses, developed abnormally, were lulled into inactivity and thus lost the chance to intervene effectively in the event of popular uprisings and revolutions [107]

Some purists, to whom any form of organisation that was not spontaneous was anathema, objected to this position, arguing that propaganda was the only legitimate activity. Makhno believed, however, that peasants would understand that the anarchists did not want to impose opinions, but merely to present them.[108]

At the time the effective government of Guliaipole was military: a Serbian regiment, supported by a Russian machine-gun detachment, was garrisoned there. One of the officers had been elected president of the 'obshchestvennyi *komitet'* (the communal committee), an organ of the Provisional Government that could not enforce its will in the provinces. Makhno quickly realised that he had an excellent opportunity to step into the power vacuum before the SRs[109] or other parties. At a meeting of the *skhod* Makhno attacked the idea that the Social Committee could be chaired by someone from outside the community, unaccountable for his actions. He proposed that the different sections of the town should choose representatives to study the question.[110]

At the end of March representatives reconvened to discuss the election of a new structure. An SR proposed the formation of a Committee of the Union of Peasants and Makhno seized on the suggestion as a pretext for presenting a proposal of his own. He contemptuously dismissed the political parties for gambling with the future,[111] and urged the peasants to concern themselves with the immediate consolidation of revolutionary gains through communal ownership of land, mills and factories. On this basis they could build a new life for themselves without worrying about such irrelevancies as the Constituent Assembly.[112] The meeting set up a Union of Peasants, with 28 members, and chose Makhno to chair it – he later claimed that his unanimous election to the chair happened 'despite my pleas to the contrary. In point of fact I was extremely busy at that time, setting up the office of our group'.[113] Within a few days the Union had enrolled all the peasants in Guliaipole except for landlords. Makhno and the secretary of the Union toured the district, setting up branches in nearby villages. Impressed by the revolutionary mood of the peasantry, Makhno returned determined to channel the impulse for social change into an anarchist direction.

The period from Makhno's release in early March until the end of May was critical. He saw the weaknesses in past tactics adopted by anarchist-communist groups and persuaded many of his comrades that his heterodox ideas on organisation were not only essential in practice but justifiable in theory. After he had established a broad base of support in the Union of Peasants, and had neutralised the *obshchestvennyi komitet*, he became the most powerful political figure in Guliaipole. His analysis of the situation and the measures it demanded were accurate. He worked unceasingly to recruit new members into the Union, and at propagating anarchist ideas. He was not above using force to attain his ends. At least one of his opponents died violently, and when the anarchists gained access to local police archives and discovered the names of informers and provocateurs, they planned several executions.[114]

This was a period of political confusion, with the old institutions, in Trotsky's telling phrase, awaiting only a swish from the broom of history,[115] and events in a small Ukrainian town attracted little interest in Moscow. It was unlikely that local news would have reached the capital in time for any action to be taken. It was difficult enough for the Provisional Government to keep abreast of developments in the major cities of European Russia, and impossible to control them.[116] The local bourgeoisie was too weak to prevent Makhno from consolidating power or to stop him guiding the revolutionary enthusiasm of the peasants. The processes of modernisation and the impact of war had rendered the old social and political structures obsolete, and they were collapsing. In Guliaipole at least, Makhno was ready to hand with a plan for a new edifice, and at first he met with little opposition from other left parties such as the SRs, who accepted the broad outlines of a revolutionary strategy based on the Union of Peasants.

In Kiev, several developments took place that affected Makhno's chances of success in the aftermath of the fall of the autocracy. By April the *Rada*'s demands had grown: they wanted national autonomy within a federation of Russian republics, and summoned an All-Ukrainian National Congress to discuss it.[117] Conferences and congresses followed, as new Ukrainian newspapers and political parties emerged. A numerically small group of Ukrainian liberal intellectuals in Kiev dominated most of this activity.[118] Although the *Rada* was reformist in its social policies – and included in its membership Social Democrats such as the writer and intellectual Volodymyr Vynnychenko – it was at this point only a government-in-waiting. It had little support and still believed in a federal solution via a Constituent Assembly. The *Rada* had few supporters in the villages, and peasants were indifferent to the nationalists and their organisations, understanding that the *Rada*'s objective was to replace the Russian and foreign bourgeoisie with a more liberal Ukrainian one. 'Get off the rostrum! We'll have nothing to do with your government!' they shouted at one unfortunate nationalist who tried to arouse their feelings against the *katsapy* in Guliaipole.[119]

Makhno knew that he needed to mobilize not only the peasantry but also the proletariat in support of his idea of an autonomous regional revolution. Throughout May he worked feverishly to consolidate his political position in the various committees and unions of Aleksandrovsk and Guliaipole. The significance of what Aleksandr Shubin has termed 'Makhnovist syndicalism' should not be ignored when characterising the Makhno insurgency as primarily a peasant movement.[120] Between March and December 1917 Makhno led the local Union of Metalworkers before handing over to a deputy, Mishchenko. During this period he organised the supply of goods for factory workers, made union membership compulsory, negotiated wage increases at the Kerner metallurgical plant and pushed for an eight-hour working day – all in conditions of capital flight and economic collapse.[121] Makhno regarded trade union organisation as an essential step towards anarchist self-government and as a tool for solving complex social problems, and at the beginning of June he turned his attention to the workers, concentrated in a few small factories in the towns. He received an invitation to a meeting at which the Aleksandrovsk anarchists hoped to form a single federation for their area.[122] Makhno seized the chance, ignoring what he believed was a purely formal division between the anarchist-communists and the anarchist-individualists, and helped to set up the federation. He discovered that some workers had already reached the same conclusions that he had on industrial questions, and helped to organise a general strike to demand wage increases of 80 to 100 percent. Makhno was duly elected to chair the trade union and the benevolent fund. The strike was a great success, with the employers granting the wage increases.[123]

For several months, Makhno had lost contact with his comrades in the Russian anarchist movement. He had written to Moscow a couple of times – once to Kropotkin after the latter's return from exile – but received no replies. Although things were going well enough in Guliaipole and its environs, Makhno was suspicious of urban anarchists, who took few initiatives. The peasants were refusing to pay rent to the landlords, and were demanding the expropriation of the large estates, yet the anarchists in Petrograd and Moscow seemed uninterested, although on the face of it such developments should have augured well for their ideas. In August Makhno attended the Ekaterinoslav provincial Congress of Soviets as a peasant representative. The only result was a lengthy debate and a decision to classify the Union of Peasants a 'soviet'.[124]

In late August the Executive Committee of the Petrograd Soviet issued an appeal to revolutionaries in the countryside to form Committees for the Defence of the Revolution.[125] This request was made just as Kornilov – appointed by Kerensky as supreme military commander – began to threaten the peasantry's revolutionary gains.[126] Kornilov's attempted coup against Kerensky in late August failed, but the news of the outbreak of counter-revolution in late August stimulated a renewal of class struggle in Guliaipole – and again Makhno showed that he was equal to the opportunity. The moment provided the anarchists of Guliaipole with the means for mobilising the mass of poor peasants against the landowners and the local capitalists, to deliver what they hoped would be the final blow against the old order. At the height of the crisis Makhno set about expropriating the estates. He seized deeds and certificates of ownership from landowners and *kulaki*, using the documentation as the basis for a property inventory. At a meeting of the local soviet, the peasants decided that the listed land and livestock should be divided equally, and *kulaki* and *pomeshchiki* should be permitted to keep a share.[127] Meanwhile, the villagers set up a Committee for the Defence of the Revolution as requested, and Makhno became its chair. He viewed the new committee as primarily executive in function, and used it to disarm and dispossess the bourgeoisie, the colonists, the *kulaki* and the landowners.

Makhno believed that the Kornilov counterrevolution was the most immediate of several threats, and that the Provisional Government and its member parties also constituted a danger. It was essential that the power of the capitalist class should be broken as soon as possible. This line met with an enthusiastic

response from the peasants, from whom the impulse for expropriation origi-
nated. Makhno was to write later of this period that '... an instinctive anarchism
showed through all the designs of the toiling peasantry of Ukraine at that time,
revealing an undisguised hatred for all state authority coupled with a desire to
free themselves from it'.[128] The process of seizing the land, factories, mills and
livestock was generally peaceful, although attempts to hide wealth met with
violent retribution. The expropriation marked the beginning of a real change
in social relations in the area, and the Provisional Government's local representatives became sufficiently alarmed to visit Guliaipole in an attempt to advise
caution, but the peasants warned them off. Makhno now had little patience with
organs of bourgeois power. The anarchist-communists, together with the metalworkers' and carpenters' union, called a regional Congress of Soviets, aiming
to formally deprive the *obshchestvennye komitety* of all but advisory functions.
This, Makhno argued, would permit the anarchists to operate without hin-
drance, and would accustom the peasants to the idea of a libertarian society.[129]

Meanwhile, in Russia, on 7–8 November 1917 (old style 25–26 October),
Lenin and the Bolsheviks 'came to power'.[130] The events in Petrograd seemed
to the peasants of Guliaipole to be a copy on a grander scale of the social revolution that they had already initiated in their region in the preceding months.
'During the October days', wrote Makhno,

> ... the proletariat of Petrograd, Moscow, and other large cities, as also the
> soldiers and peasants in the towns, under the influence of the anarchists,
> Bolsheviks and left SRs, were only ... expressing with greater precision the
> objectives for which the revolutionary peasantry of numerous Ukrainian
> regions had been struggling since August, but in conditions that were favour-
> able from the urban proletariat's point of view.[131]

The revolutionary convulsions that seized the major Russian cities throughout
the year did not mean that it was inevitable that 'Petrograd' would simply be
followed by the rest of the country. The initial response in Guliaipole to the
news of the October revolution was one of intense interest, although it was not
immediately clear exactly what had happened. The slogans 'land to the peasants'
and 'factories to the workers' seemed unobjectionable, but Makhno was
unhappy, for example, with the idea of elections to a Constituent Assembly.[132]
Chronologically, 'Great October' was a step that the Ukrainian peasantry had
by-and-large already taken – even though the revolution in Guliaipole had not
gone as far as Makhno wanted. The policy of expropriation had aroused the
enthusiasm of the poor peasants, but they seemed less keen on forming anarchist communes. Nor were land-seizures completed or unopposed by October.
The peasants were still felling acres of forest and seizing grain, in the face of
disciplinary action by Cossack troops.[133] In December the local nationalists

attempted to call in Ukrainian troops from Aleksandrovsk against Makhno, but the commander had other priorities and the move failed.[134] Makhno had been successful in establishing himself and his group as the dominant political force at the local level, but he was unable to initiate the social revolution that he wanted to see through political action alone. It was time to turn to violence.

Some time in October/November, the anarchists started arming themselves. A Black Guard detachment of 60 members was established, and with Marusia Nikiforova began to accumulate weapons and ammunition by attacking trains, police stations and warehouses.[135] Belash admits that at this time they 'did not yet have a military unit as such', although they did have access to some rifles.[136] In November an incident occurred that made the anarchists aware of their vulnerability. They received news that Nikiforova had been arrested in Aleksandrovsk by the local commissar. Despite threats, the commissar refused to release her; the anarchists then took steps to organise a proper *revkom*, release the weapons from private hands, and initiate the voluntary mobilisation of the 'Black Guards' (*Chernaia Gvardiia*).[137] As the news of the Bolshevik seizure of power broke, Nikiforova was rescued, and *makhnovshchina* took its first steps towards becoming a militarised movement.[138]

The divided Ukrainian Bolsheviks did not follow the Russian example and come to power in Kiev. In some places – in Lugansk and other towns of the Donbass – they did gain control and refused to recognise the *Rada*. In other areas, including Khar'kov and Ekaterinoslav, they collaborated in piecemeal fashion with both Ukrainian and Russian left parties and did acknowledge the *Rada*. Relations between the *Rada* and the Bolsheviks in Kiev were hostile, but despite this, the Bolsheviks briefly joined the so-called 'Small *Rada*', a committee that sat in continuous session and made important decisions when the full *Rada* was in recess. However, the launch of a White counterrevolution in the southeast complicated this struggle between the Bolsheviks and the *Rada*. The day after the Bolsheviks took over in Petrograd, Alexei Kaledin, a Cossack general, declared an independent Don Cossack state. In December 1917, Lenin assigned Vladimir Antonov-Ovseenko to the task of crushing the revolt, and by January the Bolsheviks were at war with the nationalists of the *Rada* as well. Makhno's detachment, which by this time consisted of several hundred fighters, fought alongside the Bolsheviks.[139] In the early days of this incipient Red versus White civil war there was rapid movement along railway lines, but casualties were light and small forces could still control large areas.

When Makhno had visited Ekaterinoslav for the Provincial Congress, he found the city a microcosm of the confusion in Ukraine as a whole. The Bolsheviks and Left SRs dominated the Soviet. The *Rada* controlled some armed battalions. Some sailors from Kronstadt on their way to the southeast to fight Kaledin were billeted in the town. There was even a bourgeois 'neutralist' faction.[140] On 10 January 1918, after Makhno had returned to Guliaipole with some weapons for his comrades, Soviet forces entered Ekaterinoslav on the way to Kiev. They were moving along a narrow front that missed Guliaipole altogether, but it was not possible to remain neutral. The anarchists and poor peasants of Guliaipole recognised the negative attitude of the *Rada* towards their local revolution, and decided to support the Bolsheviks, forming a class alliance between the workers and the poor peasants against the nationalist petty-bourgeoisie and the conservative elements backing them.

When Makhno's detachment reached Aleksandrovsk, the Bolsheviks were in control and Makhno busied himself releasing prisoners and trying in vain to blow up the prison.[141] Soon afterwards the partisans received news that several train loads of Cossacks were passing through to join Kaledin. Makhno and his forces seized the Kichkas Bridge over the Dnepr at Ekaterinoslav to prevent their passage. After some negotiations, Makhno appropriated the Cossacks' weapons, but left them their horses and let them go. This seizure of arms – a mixture of Russian, German and Austrian rifles and pistols – provided the basis for Makhno to organise his own army, and to disperse rival centres of power in Guliaipole.[142] By spring 1918, his forces numbered 5,000 men.[143] The Bolsheviks, however, arrested the unarmed Cossacks at Aleksandrovsk, confiscated their horses, and sent the soldiers back to Khar'kov.[144] This incident was the first of several that increased Makhno's suspicion of Bolshevik intentions. Since Soviet forces had arrived there had been more arrests than under the *Rada*. Makhno resigned his command and returned to Guliaipole with his detachment.[145]

By this time the anarchists in Guliaipole were running out of money, which they resolved by the simple expedient of exerting pressure on the local bank. They believed, however, that reliance on such outmoded economic procedures as money-exchange was hindering the implementation of anarchist social organisation. A delegate went to Moscow and other cities to arrange direct exchange of commodities with interested groups of workers; surplus grain for manufactured goods. Some Moscow trade unions showed interest and sent their officials to Guliaipole to complete a deal. The villagers duly sent grain off to Moscow, where the workers dispatched a consignment of textiles and other items in return, only to be held up by the Bolsheviks in Aleksandrovsk. The peasants were outraged at this interference with their almost-successful anarchist economic experiment, and threatened to march on Aleksandrovsk and disperse the Soviet. The Bolsheviks released the goods.[146]

It was only in February 1918 that a system of anarchist communes was organised on expropriated estates on anything like a significant scale – just as the Austro-German invasion of Ukraine was about to destroy the hope of social revolution. Some agrarian communes had been established earlier in the villages, during the autumn months. In his memoirs Makhno describes the communes with frustratingly little specific detail. He mentions that there were four communes in a radius of around ten kilometres of Guliaipole, and 'lots of others in the region as a whole'.[147] It remains unclear what the anarchists were able to accomplish in this first short period of experimentation before the invaders arrived, and we must rely largely on Makhno's own account. Livestock and agricultural equipment were seized along with the estates of the *pomeshchiki*, although the former landlords were allowed to keep a couple of horses, one or two cows and a plough.[148] The 'peasants' (Makhno does not categorise them), together with ex-soldiers, immediately set to work on 'springtime farm chores'. Work in the fields, as well as such domestic tasks as preparing and cooking meals, was undertaken communally, but Makhno claims that individuals could absent themselves whenever they wanted, provided that they informed their 'nearest workmates'. Similarly, although meals were taken communally, 'each individual, or even an entire group was free to make what provision it chose for ... food, provided always that all of the other commune members had prior notification'. Schooling was organised along the lines developed by the Spanish anarchist Francisco Ferrer.[149] Makhno offers no commentary on how effective these arrangements were, nor does he describe what problems arose and how they were solved.[150] He spent two days a week 'helping out ... during the spring planting', and working 'at the electricity station'.[151]

This vague description of the way the communes operated was written years afterwards, when Makhno had every reason to portray the experience in a positive light. Later authors have been less complimentary. The anarchists killed a local landowner, Klassen, and then organised a model commune on his abandoned estate:

> ... it was a kind of prototype for the future ... In this 'commune' they did not work so much as organise drunken orgies, although Makhno tried ... to moderate his ... friends. He worked in a commune two days a week, but failed to establish proper discipline ... after that the word 'commune' in the sense used by the *makhnovtsy* started to cause horror among the townspeople.[152]

This kind of social experiment could not survive for long in the prevailing conditions. There were too many outside forces interested in Ukraine, with its fertile soil and its concentration of mines and metallurgical industries, including the *Rada* in Kiev and the Bolsheviks, whose nationalities policy emphasised the right to self-determination while advocating the close association of states. Ukrainian Bolsheviks were divided between leftists who feared that independence would weaken both Russian and Ukrainian proletariats, and rightists from the industrialised left bank who supported national self-determination.[153]

The period from March 1917 until February 1918 was the period of Makhno's greatest social and *political* achievement. Most accounts concentrate on his *military* exploits in 1919 and 1920, when he was operating as an insurgent leader rather than leading an attempt to realise anarchist practices. The claim that *makhnovshchina* was a revolutionary movement of the toiling masses rests fundamentally on an analysis of its special accomplishments in the socio-political sphere: there were other peasant revolts, other *atamany*. Such an analysis must focus on 1917, and on the period between November 1918 and June 1919, when Makhno operated without military interference. But the available evidence fails to demonstrate that he was able to accommodate to the needs of a complex modernising economy based on industrialisation and urbanisation.

2

The Turning Point: Organising Resistance to the German Invasion, 1918

During the period of relative peace after the fall of the Tsar, Makhno and his comrades had an opportunity to put anarchist ideas into practice. This moment ended in February and March 1918 when the Germans and Austrians invaded Ukraine. There was never to be another prolonged period with such potential: *makhnovshchina* was to be transformed into a militarised insurgency, and Makhno to become a partisan guerrilla leader. In mid-1918 he was forced to flee Guliaipole, making a journey around Russia that 'played a crucial role in shaping [his] views'.[1] It was a turning point: the locally-based anarchist project to establish democratic behaviours, through which peasants and workers could decide their own lives, was overwhelmed by the immediate need to organise armed resistance against foreign occupiers. In the longer term, struggles against other, later threats to local autonomy were continuously to consume the anarchists' energy.

The Ukrainian republic that emerged in 1917 sued the Central Powers for peace in February 1918, ending the state of war – and reducing the country to a mere 'nation-building project approved by the Germans'.[2] The German army moved into Ukraine on 18 February, and quickly drove the Bolsheviks out.[3] One senior officer wrote later that

> ... it is the strangest war ... they put a handful of infantrymen with machine guns and a cannon on the [railway] track and head off for the next station, which they capture, then arrest the Bolsheviks, bring in more troops by rail, and then set off again.[4]

By 1 March they had occupied Kiev and reinstated the *Rada*.[5] The Austrians – latecomers who needed food supplies more than the Germans – insisted on control of specific areas, such as the port city of Odessa. The army commands eventually agreed on a demarcation of zones of influence on 28 March, with Germany allotted the lion's share of territory. Austria gained control of half of Volhynia, Podolia, Kherson and Makhno's province of Ekaterinoslav,[6] although it was the Germans who controlled the collection and distribution of resources.[7]

In March, the Bolshevik government in Moscow signed a peace treaty with-drawing Russia from the war.[8] Survival depended on ending the fighting, but the price was high. Russia lost Finland, Poland, the Baltic countries, Bessarabia – and Ukraine was already gone.[9] Although resources provided to Germany and Austria were denied to Russia, Lenin and Trotsky nonetheless needed to secure a workable peace with the Central Powers.

With only 20,000 troops at the Bolsheviks' disposal, they were heavily out-numbered in Ukraine – and their soldiers were more interested in land than in war. The Bolshevik insistence on defending Ukraine against overwhelming odds fed anti-communist feeling, but in the end the resistance to German occu-pation amounted only to a series of holding actions by demoralised communist troops.[10] The south-eastern periphery of the Russian empire fragmented into a patchwork of autonomous Soviet republics – the Don, the Crimea, the Kuban, Odessa – over which there was no effective unified military command. Furthermore, the Ukrainian Bolshevik movement split into factions over its relationship to the Russian party.[11]

The *Rada* succeeded in isolating Ukraine from Bolshevik rule, but at the price of exposing the population to military occupation.[12] Indeed its power 'rested chiefly on German bayonets'.[13] On 15 March the *Rada* asked the Germans to 'liberate' eastern Ukraine – the provinces of Khar'kov, Ekaterino-slav, Tauride, Poltava and Kherson, which were still under Bolshevik control. The Germans seized their chance and pushed on towards the Black Sea coast and the Donbas, meeting with only sporadic resistance from Red Guards.[14] Central authority had disappeared, and neither the *Rada* nor the Bolsheviks had established effective, centralised administration. The countryside was par-celled up into fiefdoms run by local *atamany* or by spontaneously emerging local popular structures, anarchist in character if not in ideology.[15] The Soviet of Peasants' Deputies that had nominally been running Khar'kov province – for instance – had issued proclamations against land seizures, but they continued unabated nonetheless.[16] A rapid and uncontrollable process of devolution of power to the local level was taking place.[17]

Even in these chaotic conditions, by the end of April Ukraine was fully under foreign military occupation and was forced to supply the Central Powers with the huge quantities of grain, animals and poultry that they demanded.[18] German estimates foretold large wheat surpluses in the next harvest in June and July;[19] they were not unduly concerned about the possibility of peasant resistance to the expropriation of food supplies.[20]

Anarchists were active not just in Guliaipole but also in Ekaterinoslav, driving around in armoured cars in front of the Red Guards. German accounts, unsympathetic and disapproving, describe a situation of chaotic criminality. The soldiers found an ordinary town with inns, hotels, parks, schools, museums and white-painted churches – but with its middle-class inhabitants disguised as

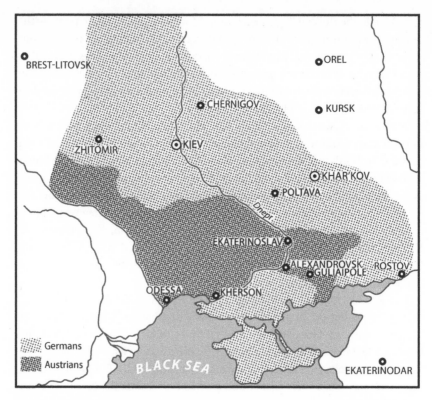

Map 2.1   The Occupation of Ukraine by Germany and Austro-Hungary, 1918
The area occupied by the Germans stretched all the way north to the Baltic Sea.
(Cartographer: Jenny Sandler)

workers, unshaven and wearing caps and overalls, fearful of Bolsheviks and anarchists.[21] The anarchists had opened the jail and released the inmates.[22] While the Bolsheviks looted shops and emptied banks, the anarchists visited the bourgeoisie in their homes and tortured them until they revealed where their wealth was hidden. In such a narrative, apart from the cruelty, there was little difference between revolutionaries and burglars.[23]

The 'southern anarchists' issued a declaration in March, urging their comrades to fight the Germans, not in defence of some ideal 'fatherland' but rather for a 'world federation of free communes'.[24] In Guliaipole, the anarchists expressed contempt for the *Rada* and for nationalists in general, 'chauvinists in cahoots with the anti-revolutionary bourgeoisie', part of a nation-wide network of 'informers, spies and provocateurs'.[25] Local SR leaders, petty landowners and former army officers generally regarded the anarchists as thieves and brigands, and pointed to other regions where land redistribution had taken place in an orderly fashion, and where anarchists had not seized control. While the parties squabbled, the Germans reached Aleksandrovsk, about 85 kilometres from

Guliaipole, meeting limited opposition from Red Guards and Left SRs. All the same, the ease with which the Germans drove back revolutionary forces demoralised even the most optimistic of the anarchists.

Discussions took place in Guliaipole between various local structures – the Revolutionary Committee, the Soviet of Workers' and Peasants' Deputies, the trade unions and the anarchist group. Makhno insisted that a joint communiqué be issued explaining the gravity of the situation to the workers, and appealing for volunteers to defend the revolution. He later wrote that young and old alike 'poured into' the local soviet to enlist.[26] Guliaipole raised six companies of 220 men each, one apparently recruited entirely from the Jewish community. The anarchist group formed a detachment of a few hundred men armed with rifles, revolvers and sabres. About half had horses. A local doctor began to organise a field hospital and medical teams. Makhno asked for weapons from a nearby Red Guard reserve commander, taking him on a tour of one of the communes. Apparently impressed, the commander allotted some artillery, 3,000 rifles and several carloads of ammunition to the *makhnovtsy*,[27] but the anarchists discovered that the artillery pieces lacked automatic sights.[28]

The Guliaipole detachments seemed battle ready. Makhno tried unsuccessfully to contact Bolshevik headquarters to obtain the needed gunsights, but the SRs had cut the telephone lines. Shortly afterwards, the SRs issued a proclamation calling on the peasants to welcome and help the 'fraternal armies' of Germany, Austria and the Central *Rada*. Rumours were reaching Guliaipole confirming that the advancing armies were destroying villages whose inhabitants resisted, but were providing those who cooperated with sugar, textiles and even shoes. The faint-hearted among the townspeople of Guliaipole began to weaken, and Makhno heard another rumour that a delegation had gone out to try to appease the advancing Germans. He responded with a proclamation dramatically headlined 'The traitor's soul and the tyrant's conscience are as black as a winter's night'.[29] The anarchists launched a campaign (aimed at the SRs) against the persecution of 'anarchism or its anonymous defenders', summarily shooting one of the fiercest critics, a military officer called Pavel Semeniuta-Riabko.[30] At the same time Makhno was conciliatory, continuing to negotiate with the SRs. His anarchist comrades were unconvinced, and Makhno consoled himself with the thought that this showed independent thinking.[31]

Makhno was then summoned to meet Aleksandr Egorov, the commander of the Southern Front, but in the confusion could not find him.[32] He was then diverted by a summons to one of the communes, where drunken sailors were terrorising the inhabitants. After dealing with the problem, he caught the train for Verkhnii Tokmak to find Egorov. As we have already noted, Makhno tended to deal with every small crisis in person and single-handedly.[33] This trait had near-catastrophic consequences, when his undisciplined supporters were facing an approaching German army, and local landowners were mounting vigorous opposition to the anarchists. It was precisely at this crucial moment that Makhno left the front-line on what turned out to be a fool's errand.[34] Mid-journey Makhno heard that the headquarters had moved: even the commander of the Bolshevik reserves had lost contact. He considered returning to Guliaipole, but decided to continue his journey, chasing the elusive headquarters eastwards and trying to keep in touch with Guliaipole by telegraph. On 15 April he received a message from his comrade Boris Veretel'nikov urging him to return.[35] There was great confusion, and suspicion that an attempt was to be made on his life, and the Germans were expected hourly. Makhno immediately turned around and set off homewards.[36]

Things were falling apart, and the journey was difficult; when he reached the village of Tsarekonstantinovka he received a desperate appeal from Veretel'nikov:

> On the night of 1st April, on a forged instruction bearing your signature, the anarchists' detachment was recalled from Chaplain and disarmed ... The wretched traitors, by a subterfuge, forced the Jews to perform this ignominious task ... come quickly ... rescue us.[37]

The *Rada's* troops had occupied Guliaipole without resistance and disarmed the anarchists. One former anarchist comrade 'strode in at the head of the *haidamaky*', ripped the anarchist banner from the wall and trampled on the portraits of Kropotkin and Bakunin.[38]

Makhno and Marusia Nikiforova (*atamansha* of the Aleksandrovsk anarchists)[39] tried to recruit retreating Red Guards for a counter-attack on Guliaipole.[40] Although two armoured cars were available, the Bolsheviks were unwilling, and all that could be rallied was a detachment of mixed cavalry and infantry from Siberia. Makhno and Nikiforova planned an operation to rescue the imprisoned anarchists and recover their weapons. Then a third message from Veretel'nikov arrived: pressure from the peasantry had resulted in the release of the anarchists. The bourgeoisie and most Jews had fled. The anarchists were preparing to go underground, and Veretel'nikov now advised Makhno *not* to return.[41] Makhno heeded this advice and decided to call off the counter-attack. He had been distracted, events had overtaken him, and he had lost touch with the centre and source of his power, Guliaipole. Reluctantly he joined the general eastward movement towards Taganrog, in the hope of collecting any followers that he could find along the way.[42]

The Germans were losing patience with the *Rada*: on 24 April a senior official wrote that '... cooperation with the current government ... is impossible ... The Ukrainian government must not interfere with the military and economic activities of the German authorities ...'.[43] There followed a list of demands that the *Rada* would clearly never accept. On 26 April the German commander, General Hermann von Eichhorn, placed Kiev under martial law,[44] and two days later Pavlo Skoropadskii was proclaimed *Hetman* of Ukraine, reviving an eighteenth-century military title.[45] Skoropadskii – a wealthy, conservative officer – consented to German demands: to recognise Brest-Litovsk; to form a Ukrainian puppet army; to dissolve the soviets and land committees; to adopt legislation on the compulsory delivery of grain; and to sign a free-trade agreement with Germany. He agreed to restore property rights, permit private ownership of land, and preserve the large estates 'in the interests of agriculture'.[46] The Hetmanate relied upon the professional administrators of the old Tsarist state apparatus: its police force, the *Dershavna Warta* or State Guards, were noted for their brutality. General Erich Ludendorff commented that 'we [had] found a man with whom it was very easy to get along',[47] and German officials began planning a puppet Ukraine modelled on British dominions, with a government of dependable local notables.[48]

In Taganrog, crowded with refugees and deserters, the authorities were trying to control anarchist activity. Nikiforova was arrested for her activities in Elisavetgrad and Aleksandrovsk, but an investigating commission acquitted her.[49] The Bolshevik military commander Vladimir Antonov-Ovseenko even endorsed her revolutionary spirit.[50] But hers was not an isolated case: the Cheka moved against anarchists in other towns and cities such as Petrograd and Samara,[51] charging that these fierce critics of Brest-Litovsk were hooligans and thieves. Lenin commented in *Pravda* on 28 April that anarchists opposed both socialism and communism and that 'to put [them] down ... *requires an iron hand*'.[52]

Late in the month, Makhno and his band held an impromptu conference in Taganrog and discussed the disaster at Guliaipole. Makhno was worried that Jews would be blamed for the fall of the town, but the meeting agreed that the Jewish company was not to blame.[53] The German occupiers were largely indifferent to both the peasants' feeling for the land and the intellectuals' feeling for the nation, but it was only as resistance grew that the *makhnovtsy* began to be carried along on a wave of dissatisfaction not especially of their own making.[54] The meeting agreed to wait for the harvest in June and July before attempting any armed resistance: it would then be easier to mingle with the peasants in the fields. They planned to collect weapons and organise cells of five to ten fighters for a terrorist campaign against German officers and *pomeshchiki*. In the meantime, Makhno would travel around Russia to assess the situation and contact Russian anarchist groups.[55]

Heading east towards Rostov-on-Don, Makhno set off on a two-month journey that would take him as far as Moscow and – reputedly – to a meeting with Lenin. Rostov was under pressure from the Whites along the eastern coast of the Sea of Azov, and from the Germans and Austrians in the west. The local anarchists had all but disappeared, and as soon as he could, Makhno moved on to Tsaritsyn, 400 kilometres northeast and far away from both Whites and Germans. He was able to ride a train with some Red Guards, as there was still some rapport between anarchists and Bolsheviks in the field, and indeed some Red Guard commanders were anarchists.[56] But even with Red Guards, travelling was risky: north of Rostov, Makhno was arrested while helping to requisition food. Fortunately, he had documents proving he had been chair of the Revolutionary Committee in Guliaipole.[57] In Tsaritsyn, Makhno unwisely intervened in a local dispute,[58] and then, at the beginning of May, fled on a riverboat, travelling up the Volga to Saratov, 400 kilometres further north.[59]

As in Tsaritsyn, in Saratov the anarchist movement was in bad shape. News finally reached Makhno that the *Rada* had been replaced by the pseudo-monarchical Hetmanate, supported by Germans and landowners. For Makhno, the news confirmed that while the Bolsheviks were responsible for Brest-Litovsk, the Left SRs shared responsibility 'for not breaking their coalition with Lenin's government ... [and] for not ordering armed struggle ... against the occupation of Ukraine'.[60] Gangs of sailors roamed the town and an anarchist 'Detachment of Odessa Terrorists' was refusing to be disarmed.[61] Again Makhno decided to move on, and set off southwards towards Astrakhan. Here the local Soviet was strong and confident, preaching Bolshevism to the Muslim population of the Volga Valley.[62] Makhno got a job with the Soviet, hiding his anarchist affiliation, and was assigned to an agitation section. Meanwhile he secretly contacted the local anarchist group, which printed one of his poems in their newspaper under his prison nickname, *Skromnyi*, which some anarchists still remembered.[63] It was his first publication.

The libertarian content of his agitation work aroused suspicion, and yet again he was compelled to move on, doubling back through Tsaritsyn and Saratov, sailing up the Volga by steamboat.[64] Makhno read newspaper stories about the repressive and brutal *hetman* regime, and decided it was not yet time to return home. He got a ticket to Moscow by producing his identity card as chair of the Guliaipole *revkom*, and set off by train. The journey was slow, and all kinds of rumours were circulating. There was a delay of over 24 hours in Tambov[65] before the train reached Moscow.[66] Makhno's arrival went unnoticed; he had published no theoretical articles and had been working far from the capital.

In June 1918 Bolshevik fortunes were at a low ebb. The Reds were threatened by the Germans in the west and the south, the Whites in the Caucasus and the Czech Legion and the Whites across the Urals. The Mensheviks and Right SRs had been expelled from VTsIK on 14 June, primarily because of their involvement in the so-called 'democratic counter-revolution'. The Bolsheviks lacked an effective army and were running short of food. The railway workers in Moscow were restless, and on 19 June shooting broke out at a union meeting. A split with the Left SRs over the treaty of Brest-Litovsk was imminent. The 5th All-Russian Congress of Soviets opened in Moscow on 4 July and the SRs, outnumbered three to one by the Bolsheviks, demonstrated noisily against the German occupation: two days later SRs disguised as Chekists assassinated the German ambassador in Moscow.[67] In Kiev on 30 July, a Left SR assassinated General von Eichhorn, commander-in-chief of German forces in Ukraine. The SRs then turned against the Bolsheviks themselves, killing two leaders in Petrograd and seriously wounding Lenin in Moscow in August. The regime reacted by unleashing a campaign of terror in the autumn, allowing the unarmed and disorganised urban anarchists no room for manoeuvre. The Cheka's role was not to judge but to strike: all types of anarchist were crushed.[68]

Makhno, arriving in Moscow as the crisis was peaking, was shocked by anarchist attitudes, quibbling over points of theory while the Bolsheviks entrenched themselves. Moscow was 'the capital of the paper revolution', producing only slogans and manifestos.[69]

Map 2.2   Makhno's Journey to Moscow and Back, 1918

Makhno's journey to Moscow by train, riverboat, and in places on foot, led him all over the south between April and June, and allegedly culminated in a meeting with Lenin himself. (Cartographer: Jenny Sandler)

He visited leading anarchists and found them demoralised – even Arshinov was not interested in returning to Ukraine, and others, such as the poet Lev Chernyi, were actively cooperating with the regime. For three weeks Makhno spent his time at meetings, reading and making contacts. He attended the All-Russian Congress of Textile Unions, as well as gatherings of Left SRs.[70] He was especially eager to meet Kropotkin, the elder statesman of Russian anarchism, then aged 75.[71] He had been bitterly disappointed when Kropotkin supported the war in 1914, but still admired the old man. In 1917, when the anarchists of Guliaipole received news of Kropotkin's return from 40 years in exile, 'an indescribable joy' had seized the group and they had sent off a letter asking for practical advice.[72] Later, when Kropotkin was in need, the *makhnovtsy* sent some food to him in Dmitrov.[73] Makhno went to see Kropotkin in Moscow in a reverent frame of mind, expecting answers to questions; however, when the two met, the outcome was inconclusive. Kropotkin, the *ideinye* anarchist, insisted that only Makhno could solve his own problems, remarking 'one must bear in mind, dear comrade, that there is no sentimentality in our struggle – selflessness and strength of heart on the path to the goal one has chosen will conquer everything'. Makhno later wrote that this comment stayed in his mind and sustained him through his long struggle.[74]

In the posthumously-published second volume of his memoirs, Makhno describes meetings with both Sverdlov and Lenin while he was in Moscow, probably sometime between 14 and 29 June 1918.[75] Makhno's account is the only known evidence for these encounters,[76] but as Louis Fischer wrote in the 1960s, Lenin often talked to peasants as a way of 'taking the pulse'.[77] Aleksandr Shubin, writing more recently, agrees: 'the description of the conversation in Makhno's memoirs is quite plausible'.[78] Nevertheless, some caution is required; there are other errors in the volume.[79] As the English translator observes, in writing the memoirs

Makhno was not interested ... in serving the needs of professional historians ... He portrays ... himself as a supporter of some form of Ukrainian autonomy ... [but] the emphasis on his nationality may be a later interpolation.[80]

According to Makhno, he wandered into the Kremlin complex, and managed to find the building he was looking for, where he was directed to Sverdlov's office.[81] The conversations, reconstructed from memory years later, are stilted and formulaic, exchanges of pleasantries followed by obvious questions about the class character of the Ukrainian peasantry. Lenin asked Makhno what he understood by the slogan 'All power to the Soviets' – the role of the soviets was a key point of difference between anarchists and Bolsheviks. Shubin has written that 'while soldiers went to their deaths for *Power to the Soviets*, singing the International under the red flag, *Soviet Power* was becoming stronger behind them. It became clear that *they were not the same thing*.[82] The peasants, said Makhno, took the slogan 'All power to the Soviets' to mean that power over their affairs must rest with the workers themselves at the local level. The other main bone of contention was the Bolsheviks' general lack of interest in the peasantry. Makhno claimed that Lenin told him that if there were other anarchists like him, the Bolsheviks might be willing to work with them to set up 'free producer's organisations'.[83]

On 29 June 1918 Makhno left Moscow on a slow train for the south, with a false passport and disguised as a Ukrainian officer. Arshinov was at the station to see him off.[84] The trip was a risky one, and at one point he was arrested by the Austrians; he walked the last 25 kilometres to Guliaipole.[85]

The Hetmanate's policy of restoring estates to the landlords was an important driver of peasant discontent, but recent research has shown that 'most of peasants' complaints ... focused on the actions not of returning landlords, but of the occupying soldiers'.[86] The Germans and Austrians continued to requisition foodstuffs and livestock without compensation. For example, at a horse fair in June, a German detachment took whichever animal seized their fancy, and when the peasants resisted, imposed a fine of 75,000 roubles on the host village for attacking a German officer.[87] There were many other incidents. Commissions set up to assess damage to the seized estates forced the peasantry to pay compensation to their former landlords, and each community was responsible for payments by individual members.[88] As repression intensified, peasant opposition to the Germans and Skoropadskii moved from the passing of congress resolutions to armed insurrection.[89] The first armed detachments were formed in Kursk, Kiev and Chernigov provinces in early May, and attracted vigorous and brutal repressive action from the occupying forces. The scale of these guerrilla actions escalated quickly, especially in Podolia, Khar'kov and Ekaterinoslav.[90]

Among minority victims of the widening violence were both Germans and Jews. Many German colonists in Ukraine were Mennonites, commercial farmers who had arrived in the Russian Empire in the late-eighteenth century, settling in religious communities in Ekaterinoslav, Tauride and Kherson. They initially welcomed the arrival of the German and Austrian troops, and before the invaders withdrew in the autumn of 1918, set up self-defence (*Selbstschutz*) units to resist the *makhnovtsy* and other partisan groups. This was a political error, creating popular hostility towards the Mennonites, and a violation of their non-violent principles.[91] The *makhnovtsy* were responsible for attacks on Mennonite communities from late 1918 onwards, of which the most savage occurred in Eichenfeld in November 1919. Mennonite memoirs of the period typically list the names of martyrs and enumerate pillaged villages, farms and settlements.[92] However, as Sean Patterson has argued, pointing to the 'resentment associated with land hunger and poverty', such a Mennonite meta-narrative fails to engage with

> ... the breakdown of neighbourly relations between Mennonites and Ukrainians where roots of the conflict may be glimpsed. This was a process that began before the arrival of Makhno ... and even before the German occupation ... With the collapse of order in the countryside the situation escalated ...[93]

Mennonites were not the only victims. Peasant units were often anti-Semitic and would plunder Jewish houses, while leaving other homes intact. They also collected taxes.[94]

Makhno's return from Russia went unnoticed. He slipped into the village of Rozhdestvenka, 20 kilometres from Guliaipole, and went into hiding.[95] Many comrades were under arrest, and the Austrians had burned his mother's home and shot his brother Emel'ian, a wounded veteran.[96] On 4 July he issued a 'proclamation', couched in broad terms, exhorting the peasants to expel the invaders and establish a free society. Cautiously, he made ten copies, and circulated them to known sympathisers in the Guliaipole region.[97] The response was disappointing: he received a note telling him not to come back, adding that 'the Jews' were hunting out revolutionaries, just as they had 'betrayed the revolution' to the Austrians in April. Makhno sent back a warning against anti-Semitism, but the reply repeated the same accusations.[98]

The dominant narrative recounted here describes the embryonic insurgency in the period from April 1918 to the end of the year, before Makhno became a major protagonist in the Ukrainian struggle. However, it derives principally from a sequence of mutually-reinforcing sources: primarily chapters 3, 4, and part of 5 of Arshinov's 1923 book; the second and third volumes of Makhno's own memoirs, edited by Volin and published posthumously in the 1930s; and Viktor Belash's text, as edited by his son in the 1990s. There are identifiable errors in Makhno's text, and there is still relatively little published primary documentation.[99]

Makhno planned to organise Guliaipole into zones, each with a nucleus of committed revolutionaries, who would gather their most energetic and fearless neighbours into guerrilla squads. These would selectively ambush Austrian patrols – and landowners – in isolated areas. Such 'rapid and unexpected blows' would eventually demoralise the occupying forces sufficiently to permit an assault on the garrison at Guliaipole. Unfortunately, his followers launched several feeble attacks, which the Austrians and Hetmanite authorities easily repulsed. The disorganised raids precipitated a wave of arrests and house searches. Makhno's presence was revealed, and he beat a hasty retreat to Ternovka, 80 kilometres away, using the false passport issued to him in

Moscow.[100] In Ternovka – for whatever reason – Makhno found the fighting spirit that Guliaipole's inhabitants had lacked. He set about organising platoons, and warned of the dangers of launching attacks too early.[101] The Red Guards had abandoned some weapons during their retreat in the spring, and the tiny squad was adequately armed.

Reconnoitring Guliaipole, Makhno found that Austrian punitive detachments were requisitioning grain, and fighting had broken out. In general, the Germans failed to restrain the Austrians and *pomeshchiki* from demanding land, grain and 'compensation' all at once, and the landlords were beating and imprisoning the same peasants who had driven them from their estates only months before. The Germans saw the supply of raw materials from Ukraine as essential: 'we are justified to use our troops there' wrote Ludendorff, 'it would be a mistake to do otherwise'.[102] But many local men had returned from the front carrying arms, and the Germans had little understanding of the political forces at play. They lacked a clear policy and failed to exploit Ukraine's resources effectively. The rivalry with the Austrians was an irritant, and even the German Foreign Office and the Supreme Army Command were unable to agree on policy matters.[103] As late as September a German officer, Lt.-Col. Bach, wrote that 'the bands of partisans [are] not political organisations, but only gangster bands, people too lazy to work'.[104]

In Ternovka, Makhno began to raid country estates, and the Austrians sent a punitive detachment, forcing Makhno to flee westwards towards the Dnepr, where he recruited some demobilised Ukrainians.[105] He then set off back to Guliaipole to resume operations. The evidence for this period is sparse and, in Timoshchuk's words, 'of a romantic and legendary character'. These 'terrorist actions of Makhno' can be seen as 'ordinary armed robberies', which were reported as having been 'decisively suppressed' by the *Warta* and the military.[106]

Makhno's return coincided with the arrival of various anarchist intellectuals who attached themselves to the movement and subtly changed its character. One outcome of anarchist emigration to Ukraine was the establishment in Khar'kov in autumn 1918 of the 'Nabat' Confederation of Anarchist Organisations.[107] With a network of branches in Ukrainian cities, it was dominated by Volin (V. M. Eikhenbaum), Petr Arshinov and Aron Baron, and attempted to bring anarcho-syndicalists, anarchist-communists and individualists together, while simultaneously allowing them considerable autonomy.[108] The newly-arrived comrades started telling Makhno how to conduct his affairs, arguing that an uprising was impractical and he should wait for Bolshevik help. But Makhno was afraid of losing the initiative if he delayed.[109] He had recruited about 100 followers, but still lacked the strength to raid Guliaipole itself; he had already attempted unsuccessfully to blow up the Austrian headquarters.[110]

It was mid-September before he had built up sufficient military strength to move closer to Guliaipole. His campaign opened with a stroke of good fortune:

on the way to Guliaipole he disarmed a troop of *haidamaki*, capturing horses, uniforms and weapons. Disguised, his men then came upon and routed a militia detachment.[111] Guliaipole itself was garrisoned by Austrian troops and in a state of alert. The Austrians took brutal reprisals against anyone who helped the partisans, shooting some and exacting fines on others. The repression, together with Makhno's growing popular reputation gained him more recruits, some with weapons. Eventually, he attacked the Austrian garrison with 400 fighters, capturing the post office and the railway station. It turned out that most of the Austrians were out on patrol at the time: nonetheless, the raid was a morale-booster.[112]

The *makhnovtsy* knew that they could not defend the town against Austrian regular troops and withdrew north-westwards when they heard that two troop trains were approaching. They gathered in a wooded area near Dibrovka (Velikaia Mikhailovka, also known as Bol'shaia Mikhailovka), where Makhno encountered Fedor Shchus', a former petty officer in the Imperial Navy, now leading a small band.[113] Shchus' agreed to join forces,[114] and later became a valued commander.[115] Meetings were held to discuss the successes of Denikin's Volunteer Army in the Kuban and the Caucasus: Makhno warned that this force might prove to be their most dangerous enemy.[116] While the partisans met, the Austrians and *haidamaki* were preparing to attack. On 30 September they set up roadblocks around Dibrovka, isolating Makhno in the forest with a group of 30 men and a machine-gun. According to one account the Austrians had a battalion of about 500 men in the village, reinforced by 200 *haidamaki* and auxiliaries, with reinforcements on the way.[117]

The *makhnovtsy* attempted a surprise counter-attack. Some partisans approached the main square undetected, and Shchus' led a machine-gun detachment to the far side of the town. The Austrians, surprised, allegedly fled in panic when the insurgents opened fire from both sides of the square – but archival sources indicate that they had already departed, and 'the gang of the anarchist Makhno terrorised the population ... engaging in battle with the Warta'. The booty was insignificant, just 'the armament of a small Warta squad'.[118] Nonetheless, it was at this point that Makhno earned the honorific *Bat'ko*,[119] a moment that Golovanov argues acquired a 'sacred meaning' that is 'undoubtedly a key to the whole mythology of Makhno'.[120] While the *historical* status of the engagement at Dibrovka as a military operation against Austro-Hungarian units is therefore questionable, its *symbolic* importance as a *personal victory* for Makhno – who escaped the encirclement and gained the loyalty of his followers – remains undeniable.[121]

The German general staff were annoyed by the unrest, and the Commander-in-Chief in Kiev ordered that Makhno's band should be eliminated.[122] On 5 October the Austrians bombarded Dibrovka with artillery, wounding both Makhno and Shchus' and forcing out both the insurgents and many residents.

The remaining peasants were abandoned to the swift reprisals of the Austrians and the *haidamaki*, who burned their houses down. The next night, when the partisans were a day's march away, they saw a glow in the sky from the blaze.[123] Later, in what rapidly became a 'devastating vendetta', the *makhnovtsy* took revenge on the Mennonite colonists who had collaborated with the Germans and the Hetmanate. Later, monetary and other indemnities were imposed on them; horses, carts, food and weapons were seized for military purposes.[124]

By the autumn of 1918 the Central Powers were losing the war on the Western Front, and their grip on Ukraine loosened. In October the Austro-Hungarians left Guliaipole, and the insurgents marched in.[125] Makhno's power in the area now seemed secure, and he tested his strength by sending a message to the Hetmanate's commander in Aleksandrovsk, demanding the immediate release of five Guliaipole prisoners, including his brother Ssava. The authorities refused, but assured Makhno that no harm would come to the prisoners.[126]

Makhno believed that an organised army was necessary to defend political gains, but as an anarchist, he also believed that no person had the right to command another. At an extraordinary conference held in late 1918 in Guliaipole he proposed a solution: the reorganisation of the various partisan bands as 'federal' units of a standing army with its headquarters in Guliaipole. Through such a reorganisation, and by maintaining a tight cohesion among the units and the staff, argued Makhno, the federal principle could be guaranteed, and they could organise effective common defence.[127] He envisaged units of combined cavalry and *tachanki* that could cover large areas at speed. Some insurgents argued against these ideas, on the grounds that there were no professional commanders in the movement with the experience necessary to conduct operations on a large scale.[128] The command staff consisted of Makhno himself as commander-in-chief, Viktor Belash as chief of staff and, additionally, a Bolshevik and a Left SR.[129] Makhno began to conduct conventional operations and in late October led a raid to the right bank of the Dnepr, collecting large supplies of arms.

He established three fronts; at the railway junctions of Chaplino-Grishino to the north, from Tsarekonstantinovka to Pologi in Mariupol' region, and at Orekhov in the Tauride. Pologi was an important railway junction between Chaplino and Berdiansk, connecting Aleksandrovsk and Ekaterinoslav to the Sea of Azov. The railways had continued to function, transporting troops and military cargo, as well as metal ores, coal and other commodities. From October onwards, the *makhnovtsy* began to raid the trains for booty. The departure of the Germans and Austrians created a surge of refugees, including former collaborators, along the lines of rail. One memoir tells of Makhno himself appearing at Pologi station in November:

The railway station was brightly illuminated, and soldiers paced up and down on patrol ... Makhno himself was strolling about among the refugees and observing the crowd ... people recognised him and pointed him out ... [but] no-one even thought of delivering him to the Austrians.[130]

Eventually the refugees were allowed to depart for Berdiansk unharmed.[131]

Without German support, Skoropadskii's position was deemed untenable. Symon Petliura, Volodymyr Vynnychenko and other former members of the *Rada* had been forming a new, radical nationalist government, the Directory, since late summer, and they triggered a revolt in November. Their army entered Kiev on 14 December 1918.[132] Makhno had doubts: Vynnychenko might indeed be creating a new government in Ukraine, he told his supporters,

... but I ask you, comrades, where among the toilers in the revolutionary towns and villages of Ukraine are to be found such fools as to believe in the 'socialism' of this Petliurist-Vynnychenkovist Ukrainian government ... ?'[133]

Despite this, the *makhnovtsy* adopted, with reservations, a policy of armed neutrality towards the Directory. Makhno believed that it had compromised itself politically by including Petliura, who had collaborated with the Central Powers during the invasion. Vynnychenko's democratic socialism might have made a military alliance acceptable to the anarchists, but the Directory's opportunism and lack of a mandate were deal-breakers: politically the *makhnovtsy* believed that the Directory was worse than the *Rada*.[134] While not seeking a fight, the *makhnovtsy* were ready should the need arise.[135]

On 26 December the Directory abolished the Hetmanate's police system (the *Warta*), and recognised trade unions and the right to strike.[136] It declared itself to be the Revolutionary Provisional Government of Ukraine, accusing the bourgeoisie and the landowners of bringing ruin on the country.[137] However, it struggled to control its Galician military units and could not compete effectively with a rival Bolshevik 'provisional government-in-exile', set up in Moscow in November 1918 under Georgii Piatakov, 'to mask the intervention and the split in the Ukrainian [communist] movement'.[138]

* * *

It is unclear how strong Makhno's forces actually were in late 1918. One source indicates that he commanded 300–400 infantry and 150 cavalry, with another 2,000 armed partisans in reserve. Timoshchuk argues that this is an underestimate, citing Denikin's estimate of five to six thousand fighters, and a report in a Ekaterinoslav newspaper that '10,000 well-armed and equipped *makhnovtsy*' had helped to restore Soviet power in Pavlograd and Guliaipole. Moreover, he comments, the higher number 'seems more likely, since at the end of December the *makhnovtsy* played a major role in the capture of Ekaterinoslav'.[139]

In late December the Red Army,[140] under the command of Vladimir Antonov-Ovseenko, began to advance into Ukraine from the north.[141] Antonov's superior officer, the Latvian commander-in-chief of the Red Army, Ioakim Vatsetis (*Latvian: Jukums Vācietis*) was more concerned with the threat of P. N. Krasnov's Don Army, to the southeast of Voronezh, and too close to Moscow for comfort. He refused to give Antonov more than the minimum of troops and weapons, and ordered him to attack behind Krasnov's lines to the southeast, away from Ukraine.[142] Nevertheless, Antonov's offensive from the north gathered momentum. His forces consisted of two ill-disciplined, under-manned and badly armed divisions of fewer than 4,000 men.[143] Antonov devised a strategy hinging upon the capture of three key cities: Khar'kov, key to the Donbass; Kiev, capital of Ukraine and the seat of nationalism; and Odessa, a port city crucial to the expected Anglo–French intervention. These were towns with an industrial working class sympathetic to the communist cause.

Antonov was desperate for men and began to recruit partisan groups with a record of anti-German or anti-White activity. He ordered these bands to foment rebellion and to organise themselves in readiness for the expected Allied intervention.[144] After the formation of the Ukrainian Soviet Government at Kursk on 28 November Antonov's position seemed stronger, as he was now, at least technically, working for the Ukrainians. Early in December he assumed real command of the two partisan divisions that had been assigned to him. Both units were under strength, disorganised and demoralised. Antonov energetically set about building his army, a task that required considerable resourcefulness. Throughout December he moved his troops forward into Ukraine, into position for the attack on Khar'kov. He was determined that Vatsetis should not deny him the opportunity to establish Soviet power in the south.

Oddly enough, Makhno had sent a message early in December to local Bolsheviks offering to cooperate against the Directory, but his offer had been refused, ostensibly because his forces were mere anarchist bandits.[145] The *makhnovtsy* were now turning westwards towards Ekaterinoslav, a move that brought them into contact with the forces of the Directory.[146] To the nationalists, the *makhnovtsy* were just another peasant gang that might possibly be usefully recruited. Ignorant of Makhno's politics, they interrogated him; what did he think of the Directory? What was his idea of Ukraine's political future? Would an alliance not be in the interests of both groups?[147] Makhno was uncompromising, and despite having no allies he refused to have anything to do with the Directory. Ukraine could only be free if the peasants and workers were free. Between the workers' movement and the movement of the bourgeoisie only an armed struggle was possible.[148]

After the negotiations broke down, the *makhnovtsy* moved onto the offensive against Ekaterinoslav. The town had fallen to the nationalists early in December and a week or so later they moved against the local soviet and dispersed it, arresting some Left SRs and communists.[149] There were Bolshevik detachments in the suburb of Nizhnedneprovsk on the left bank of the river, and they demanded that their comrades be released.[150] The Nizhnedneprovsk committee offered Makhno the command of their workers' detachments for an attack on the city, with a total of about 15,000 men.[151]

On 27 December Makhno launched his attack, employing a ruse of the kind that came to be considered typical of his style of warfare. There are various stories of *makhnovtsy* disguised in wedding dresses, or hiding in coffins at funerals, which are unverifiable and quite possibly fictional.[152] Workers were still riding in and out of the city from the suburbs by train, uninspected. The *makhnovtsy*, with their guns tucked under their greatcoats, boarded an early morning train for the centre of Ekaterinoslav. The trick succeeded, and the insurgents quickly captured the railway station, while fierce fighting broke out in the city.[153] The communists captured the bridge into Ekaterinoslav with the loss of only six men. An unexpected bonus came with the defection of a Petliurist artillery officer and his guns and gun-teams to the insurgents' side.[154] The fighting continued in great confusion for three days, until the partisans were in control of most of the city. Makhno opened the jail and released all the prisoners; he also formed a governing soviet and issued a decree against looting.[155] As Danilov and Shanin have pointed out, Soviet historiography represented the *makhnovtsy* as 'engaged *exclusively* in looting captured cities ... and passenger trains' while the evidence shows that all the armies – whether German or Austro-Hungarian, Ukrainian nationalists, Bolsheviks and Whites, or peasant insurgencies – needed to survive, and so all robbed and plundered.[156] There are other stories of the *makhnovtsy* engaging in wanton acts of destruction, burning libraries and archives, and deliberately shelling a city's buildings with cannon.[157] However, Makhno was aware that such conduct was incompatible with maintaining popular support and consistently punished it.

The troops of the Directory recaptured Ekaterinoslav after only a day. The insurgents withdrew eastwards across the Dnepr back to the area around Sinel'nikovo, where they dug in.[158] A period of cautious non-belligerence followed. Neither side was strong enough to mount a full-scale attack on the other, although intermittent clashes over supplies continued to occur in other areas. Meanwhile, the arrival of Antonov's army, theoretically under the orders of the Ukrainian Soviet government, split the Directory into a nationalist faction and one (including Vynnychenko) that supported a proletarian revolution as well as a Ukrainian state.

At the end of 1918 Ukraine was like a beehive that had been disturbed.[159] Nevertheless, it was a period of relative freedom in the interior of the area under the control of the *makhnovtsy*. They reached an agreement on a *modus vivendi* with the Bolsheviks: Antonov was more interested in seizing cities and towns in northern Ukraine. The communists were concentrating on urgent military and political problems rather than local administration – so for a few months the peasants of Guliaipole and its environs again had an opportunity to govern themselves. They returned to the system of communes that they had adopted in 1917–18. Anarchist commentators are careful to distinguish these working communes, or free communes, from other types such as the Bolshevik exemplary communes. These sympathetic accounts are obviously open to charges of bias: according to Volin, for example, the Makhnovite partisans exerted no pressure on the peasants, but confined themselves to propaganda in favour of free communes.[160] Arshinov asserts that 'these were real working communes of peasants who, themselves accustomed to work, valued work in themselves and in others'. But his account provides little detail:

> The peasants worked in these communes ... to provide their daily bread ... The principles of brotherhood and equality permeated the communes. Everyone – men, women and children – worked according to his or her abilities. Organisational work was assigned to one or two comrades who, after finishing it, took up the remaining tasks together with the other members of the commune. It is evident that these communes had these traits because they grew out of a working milieu and that their development followed a natural course.[161]

One commune near Prokovskoe was named after Rosa Luxemburg. It grew from a few dozen members to over 300, but the Bolsheviks broke it up in June 1919, after the split between Makhno and Trotsky.[162] Another, 'Commune no. 1', was located about seven kilometres away. Similar communes clustered close to Guliaipole, in a radius of about 20 kilometres. A pamphlet entitled *Osnovye polozheniia o vol'nom trudovom Sovet (proekt)* (Basic Statute on the Free Worker's Soviet: Draft) outlined the role of the soviets, which were to be independent of political parties.[163] They were to operate within a socio-economic system based on real equality, consisting only of workers, and could not delegate executive power to any member.[164] Even if the anarchist communes were truly voluntary, one difference distinguished the earlier period from the later. Makhno had learned the lesson of the Austro-German invasion. He knew that if the revolution in his area was to remain in peasant control, he needed an army to protect it. He had also learned to choose his enemies. He could distinguish between those to whom he could ally himself (the Bolsheviks), those he could ignore or take advantage of (the Petliurists) and those against whom he should struggle uncompromisingly (the Whites of General Denikin).

Meanwhile, aided by strikes that closed down public utilities, and by the panic which seized the defending nationalists, the Bolsheviks captured Khar'kov in January. Antonov, who had been agitating for the creation of a separate Ukrainian Front for some time, at last got his way. On 12 January the Bolsheviks reached Chernigov in the west, and by the 20th they controlled Poltava. On 16 January, the Directory declared war on Soviet Russia, hoping in vain for assistance from French forces in Odessa, and two days later communist troops led by the sailor Pavel Dybenko attacked Ekaterinoslav, eventually driving the nationalists out for a second time on 27 January. By 5 February Kiev had been abandoned to the Bolsheviks. For civilians, these latest occupiers represented a marked improvement. 'Compared not only to the *makhnovtsy* but even to the Petliurists,' wrote one citizen, 'the men of the Red Army created an extraordinarily disciplined impression.'[165]

3

Brigade Commander and Partisan: Makhno's Campaigns against Denikin, January–May 1919

January is the coldest month in Ukraine, with temperatures below zero and the *bora*, a northeasterly wind, bringing heavy snowfalls. January in 1919 was not only cold[1] but was also marked by a continuation of the political and military realignment of forces – as described in the previous chapter – in the struggle to secure Ukraine in the coming spring. This was a process in which Makhno, and his followers, aimed to play a key role. On 4 January, despite the fact that Russia and Ukraine were at least on paper now separate countries, the Revolutionary Military Council (*Revoliutsionnyi Voennyi Sovet* or RVS) unilaterally took the important military decision to constitute a Ukrainian Front, with Soviet forces having already captured Khar'kov the day before over ineffectual protests from the Directory in Kiev.[2] On 16 January Petliura mounted a coup to gain control of the Directory, and, ignoring earlier diplomatic feelers to Moscow and under pressure from his French sponsors, declared war on Soviet Russia.[3]

By this time Denikin's Volunteer Army consisted of over 80,000 men, of whom perhaps 30,000 were tied down in the rear, protecting his communication and supply lines from partisan raids.[4] From the first weeks after Skoropadskii's downfall and the withdrawal of the armies of occupation of the Central Powers, cavalry units of the Volunteer Army had begun probing along the Don and the Kuban rivers into Makhno's region. Denikin anticipated that the partisans would be engaged in fighting the Petliurists, but in fact, after the brutal struggle for Ekaterinoslav, that front was quiet, and the White cavalry met with unexpectedly stubborn resistance from the outgunned partisans. In January the *makhnovtsy* moved many of their troops to the southeast and gained control of much of the area eastwards towards the Sea of Azov. The front stretched for over 90 kilometres to the north and northeast of Mariupol', protecting the anarchist 'liberated zone' and even cutting into the Donbass.[5]

As the Whites increased in power and influence, the idea of an alliance between the partisans and the Bolsheviks, on the face of it in the interests of both sides, began to emerge.[6] The Red Army did not come into actual contact with the insurgents until February, when Dybenko's division arrived from the north at Sinel'nikovo, east of Ekaterinoslav. In fact, according to F. T. Fomin, a former member of the Cheka who was then at the front in charge of counter-espionage for the Bolsheviks, the first contacts had taken place earlier in the winter. Gusev, then Makhno's chief-of-staff, visited Fomin in his railway carriage at Khar'kov station, and asked him to pass a proposal for a formal alliance to the Ukrainian RVS. In exchange for weapons and supplies the Bolsheviks would gain the advantage of a coordinated command over a vital sector of the front.[7] Gusev claimed that the insurgent forces numbered about 10,000, but communist intelligence estimated only 4,000 infantry and about 3,000 unarmed men.[8] A few weeks later, in mid-February, the Soviet estimate of Makhno's strength was only 6,700 men.[9] Whatever their actual numbers, Makhno's forces were stretched thin, and even in a war of movement could not have withstood a determined assault by Denikin's numerically superior forces. Indeed, in late January and early February, the *makhnovtsy* only just managed to defend Guliaipole in a series of increasingly desperate actions against the Whites.[10]

The RVS, chaired by Antonov, discussed the proposed alliance. Denikin's advance presented a serious threat, and the RVS could not afford to turn away help. One opinion was in favour of breaking up the anarchist army and incorporating the troops into other units as reinforcements, thus minimising the anarchists' disruptive influence. The second view, which prevailed, was that the Red Army could safely absorb the insurgents as an integral unit, so long as political commissars were assigned to them.[11] The decision to conclude an alliance on these terms – permitting Makhno's forces to stay together – was a key moment in determining the events that followed.[12] As we shall see, the distinction between *military* and *political* integrity was understood quite differently by the two sides.[13] Indeed, by relying on Makhno's brigade to hold an important sector of the front, the RVS risked exactly the kind of rupture in the heat of battle that in fact occurred in June 1919. By assigning political commissars – who were often low calibre cadres – to Makhno's units, the Bolsheviks also risked alienating the *ideinye anarkhisty* who exercised a strong influence on the insurgent army. In addition, the *makhnovtsy* received the Bolshevik commissars with hostility, as representatives of city-dwellers who stole grain.[14]

Throughout the negotiations, the *makhnovtsy* remained politically active. In January they had captured 100 railway wagons of wheat, totalling 90,000 *pudy*, from Denikin, and sent them (with some coal as a bonus) to the workers of Moscow and Petrograd, a major propaganda coup that was even reported in *Izvestiia*.[15] On 23 January the anarchists convened their first regional congress at Greater Mikhailovka, to discuss, among other things, counter-measures against the twin threats of Petliura and Denikin.[16] Such congresses, it must be remembered, were considered to be the highest form of democratic authority in the political system of the Makhno movement, and involved peasants, workers and soldiers, who would take decisions back to village and local meetings.[17]

Makhno took the opportunity presented by this congress to establish firm control over various local, small-scale *atamany* such as Fedir Shchus, who had been arbitrarily robbing and murdering people in the area, and with whom he had been in conflict.[18]

In early February Makhno accepted Antonov-Ovseenko's command.[19] The Bolsheviks assigned his units to serve as the Third Brigade in the Trans-Dnepr Division under Dybenko and alongside Grigor'ev, an *ataman* known for his vicious pogroms.[20] *Ataman* Grigor'ev came from a family of kulaks in Podolia, and had fought in both the Russo-Japanese and Great Wars, rising to the rank of captain.[21] He was cunning and dangerous, although 'untrained and unskilled' as a commander. His political views were opportunist in the extreme: he supported in turn the *Rada*, the Hetmanate, the Directory, and then, after January 1919, the Bolsheviks.[22] In 1918 he started to gather local partisan groups together, and by February 1919 controlled a force of 23,000 men with machine-guns and artillery. After he turned against the Directory, the Red Army's commanders reached a tactical agreement with him and like Makhno, he retained control of his troops, under Red Army command. The most striking difference between the two partisan leaders was one of ideological consistency. Grigor'ev had few scruples about who he aligned himself with; he was an adventurer, anti-Semitic, xenophobic, and a hater of landlords.[23] Makhno, on the other hand, was driven by a political philosophy, which guided his practice: he punished anti-Semitism, he refused to cooperate with the White Guards, he was guardedly hostile towards Ukrainian nationalism. He cooperated with the Bolsheviks but mistrusted them. Perhaps the Red Army commanders should have anticipated problems mainly from the unpredictable Grigor'ev, but in the event, both of the *atamany* proved dangerous in equal measure, and the military situation in April and May 1919 was too confused to allow Bolshevik strategists time to analyse their allies.

Antonov may have feared the possibility of an alliance against Soviet power by the two unruly guerrilla leaders, but this turned out to be both politically and temperamentally unworkable. In fact, the *makhnovtsy* joined the Red Army on conditions that were unfavourable to the Bolsheviks. The insurgents were to keep their internal organisation, their black flags and their title of *povstantsi*.[24] They were to receive arms and supplies on the same basis as nearby communist units. In return, they had to accept the assignment of commissars to each regiment.[25] The last two points were the cause of bitter recriminations, and eventually of the first rift between the mutually suspicious new allies.

Part of the difficulty in bringing the two forces together was that Makhno's ideas of insurgent organisation were an attempt to resolve the contradiction between anarchist principle and military necessity. The two key points were mobilisation and discipline. Nominally, all Makhno's soldiers were volunteers, and they were all eligible for positions of command, either by election or by appointment. But so-called 'voluntary mobilisation' was also practised, and the evidence is mixed as to why and how the rural and peri-urban poor joined up with Makhno.[26] Possible motives include but are not limited to an ideological commitment to anarchism, a desire for loot and land, adventurism, or simply a desire to get rid of an outside authority that was seen as exploitative.

The most difficult idea to swallow for the Bolsheviks was that of 'freely accepted discipline'. At least theoretically, the troops voted on every regulation, and if passed, each rule was rigorously enforced 'on the individual responsibility of each insurgent and each commander'.[27] However, direct orders were to be obeyed immediately: a few years later, during his trial in Poland, Makhno angrily insisted that his men would 'unhesitatingly' carry out their orders.[28] Bolshevik military policy, on the other hand, had evolved from a position based primarily on political considerations, to one in which the problems of fighting to defend the revolution were of first importance. During the war against the Central Powers the Bolsheviks had denounced the militarism of the Tsarist regime. They had urged the peasant soldiers to rebel against the authority of their officers, who belonged to the class enemy. This tactic successfully undermined the Imperial Army, a weapon in the hands of the autocracy. The Bolsheviks infected it with revolutionary defeatism, both by agitation among the troops and by exploiting the soldiers' concrete experience of their commanders' cynical incompetence. By March 1918, when Trotsky became People's Commissar for War (*Narkomvoen*), all that remained of the Imperial Army was Vatsetis' division of Latvian riflemen.[29] The sentiments of the masses were a mixture of an emotional belief in pacifism and their trust in the Red Guards and the partisan detachments. For example, whether anarchist, SR, or Bolshevik, most revolutionaries believed that officers should be chosen by their troops. Trotsky abandoned these democratic and anti-authoritarian ideas in favour of centralisation and tough discipline. There were good reasons for the reversal, but it gave partisans like Makhno the advantage of appearing more consistent and more faithful to the Russian revolutionary tradition. The *makhnovtsy* made maximum use of this point in their propaganda.[30]

Trotsky believed that the peasants were the least reliable members of the Red Army. They deserted in droves, and their morale was often fragile. 'The chaos of irregular warfare expressed the peasant element that lay beneath the revolution', he wrote in 1929, 'whereas the struggle against it was also a struggle in favor of the proletarian state organization as opposed to the elemental, petty-bourgeois anarchy that was undermining it'.[31] However, Trotsky was quite prepared to recruit former Imperial officers for their military expertise, so long as the army contained a core of proletarians on whose support the Bolsheviks could politically depend.[32] He placed political commissars alongside the officers, from company level up to the commander-in-chief. Orders were valid only if both officer and commissar agreed. Thus, the Bolshevik leadership, with the support of small numbers of worker-soldiers, hoped to provide an example of dedication and enthusiasm, combined with iron discipline – the certainty of death in the rear – to hold the new army together. But the incorporation of units such as Makhno's into the Red Army as regular troops presented difficult practical problems, and there were regular clashes. When the first commissars arrived in the Makhnovite regiments they discovered a general lack of organisation and discipline. The 3rd Brigade's commissar reported from Guliaipole that, 'the headquarters as such do not exist. There were a few men, headed by the Brigade commander, who ran the whole brigade [...] everything was in a state of uncertainty and chaos'.[33]

Meanwhile, Makhno continued to consolidate his political base. A second regional congress was held in Guliaipole from 12–16 February[34] at which Makhno refused his nomination as presiding chair, citing the pressure of military events at the front.[35] Both Nabat and the Left SRs were represented, and speeches were made condemning attempts by the Bolsheviks to monopolise the soviets.[36] Importantly, the congress established a Military-Revolutionary Soviet (*Voenno-Revoliutsionnaia Sovet* or VRS) with ten members, of whom seven were anarchists, as its executive arm.[37] The congress retained, at least in theory, the right to dissolve the VRS.[38] After heated debate, the congress also resolved that a 'general voluntary and egalitarian mobilisation' should be called, which placated anarchist objections to enforced conscription, and also had the effect of creating a militia force with a centralised command structure, recruited village by village.[39] Makhno's comrade Petr Arshinov claimed that the decision resulted in a greater influx of volunteers, but he admits that most of them were turned away because there were no guns for them.[40] Indeed, by May, the troop strength had reportedly grown to as many as 55,000 men, of whom only about 20,000 or so were actually armed.[41]

On 19 February the order creating the Trans-Dnepr Division out of Makhno's, Dybenko's and Grigor'ev's units was finally issued. Makhno's troops – the 3rd Brigade – consisted of the 7th, 8th and 9th Rifle Regiments, and the 19th and 20th regiments.[42] The immediate benefit for Makhno was that he received several thousand Italian rifles, ammunition and funds to pay his soldiers.[43] Nevertheless, conditions for the Reds remained precarious: one political commissar reported that his troops had no equipment or uniforms, there were no billets, there were no medical staff even though a typhoid epidemic was raging, and nobody had been paid for months.[44] At the time Makhno was skirmishing to the southwest of Guliaipole, and he received orders to make contact with the Donbass units to his left.[45] The Red Army's primary military task in the south was to consolidate its advanced positions, and to destroy the White forces in the Donbass.[46]

In general, the spring of 1919 was a period of moderate success for the Red Army, as it pushed the Whites eastwards out of the Donbass. In March,

Makhno's brigade was ordered to cut off the White forces in the Berdiansk sector, as well as those operating further west from Melitopol'.[47] The *makhnovtsy* had already moved to secure the key railway junction at Pologi, on the line connecting Berdiansk to its hinterland. The station was defended by a White force of 500 men, with another 1,500 covering the approaches. The fighting, with artillery and armoured trains deployed, lasted for six days at the beginning of February and ended with a pincer movement executed by the *makhnovtsy* and Red Army detachments.[48] The defenders did not combine well, and were later even accused of cowardice,[49] but in any event, the insurgents captured significant amounts of weaponry and materiel.[50] The Red commander Pavel Dybenko commended Makhno's 'brilliant leadership' in personally leading the attack.[51] The subsequent advance towards Berdiansk was slowed by White resistance at the railway station of Velikii Tokmak, southeast of Aleksandrovsk, but the insurgents finally captured it on 10 March.[52]

For the time being at least the anarchist forces were popular with the Soviet authorities on military, if not on political grounds. Antonov issued an order emphasising the need to 'maximize on Makhno's success' in making contact with the enemy and driving them from the Berdiansk and Mariupol' area. He ordered the movement of troops and arms from the Crimea to reinforce Makhno's group for the assault.[53] The 3rd Brigade launched a 'decisive and energetic attack' that carried them as far as the junction of the Mariupol'-Platanovka railway, where they quickly destroyed the defending force.[54] The commissars noticed the effect of the partisans' success on the morale of other units. The political inspector of one Trans-Dnepr regiment reported that there was a glut of volunteers, but – again – no weapons for them. He suspected that they were motivated by the prospect of easy loot; 'all are drawn to Makhno, whose popularity is inconceivable'. He suggested that the political situation could be corrected after the military one was more firmly under control.[55]

The insurgents continued their advance towards Berdiansk. On 16 March *Pravda* reported that 'our forces' – that is to say, the insurgents – were moving south, and *Izvestiia* reported around the same time that the insurgent forces were driving back some of the best regiments of the former Imperial Guard.[56] Berdiansk was defended by the local Krims'ko-Azovs'ka Dobrovol'cha Armiia (Crimea-Azov Volunteer Army, or KADA) which, according to a local memoir, dismissed the Makhno threat as inconsequential – since they were just bandits, while KADA was made up of 'proper soldiers'.[57] But their confidence was misplaced: Makhno's advance began to create an atmosphere of panic in Berdiansk town, which at that time had a population of around 30,000, mainly made up of Russians, but with Greeks, Jews, Italians, Bulgarians and Turks as well.[58] Ticket prices on departing steamships were sold for highly speculative prices as 'bankers, merchants, homeowners, and the staff of foreign consulates' tried to secure passage to safety.[59] However, Makhno's forces, under the command of

Kalashnikov, held off on the outskirts of the town while the terrified citizens fled as best they could, only entering the centre of Berdiansk on 28 March.[60]

The story of the capture of Berdiansk was subsequently to feed into a meta-narrative of the cruel behaviour of the *makhnovtsy* towards the population at large, a narrative that included but was not limited to accusations of carrying out pogroms and massacring German Mennonite settlers at various times.[61] In Berdiansk, the panic-stricken evacuees would not have been so frightened, according to this logic, unless they had something to hide from revolutionary justice, and so deserved whatever fate befell them – the same logic of the French anarchist Émile Henry's remark that 'there are no innocent bourgeois'. Later, Soviet sources would claim that people were stabbed to death or blown up with grenades for having collaborated with the Whites.[62] Given the horrific atrocities that were common occurrences everywhere during the civil war, this seems plausible, even if unproven; nevertheless, the numbers killed, and the extent of the cruelty exercised by the conquerors of Berdiansk, both remain the subject of dispute.[63]

By the end of March, the Bolshevik commanders were arguing about the best way to deploy Makhno's troops. On 22 March, Dybenko telephoned Anatol Skachko, the commander of the Khar'kov group, to inform him of his intention to replace the anarchists at the front with newly-formed units despite what he called Makhno's 'inspired leadership'.[64] Four days later Skachko received orders to push the insurgent brigade forward in an attempt to capture Taganrog on the Sea of Azov and to turn the White flank and rear in the Bakhmut region to the northwest.[65] But on 28 March Denikin attacked the Soviet 8th Army northeast of Makhno's sector, and drove it northwards almost to Lugansk. Simultaneously, Makhno had again occupied Mariupol' on the coast, and was driving forward towards Rostov.[66] He was yet again short of supplies, partly because Dybenko had, on his own initiative, advanced into the Crimea.[67] There was in fact ongoing confusion in the command structure. Vatsetis ordered that the 3rd Brigade should be transferred across to the Southern Front, and despite Antonov's protests the move was carried out.[68] Makhno's units, between Mariupol' and Taganrog, came under the different command for operational matters, however the discipline and organisation remained in Antonov's hands. Supplies were to be provided by the Ukrainian government.[69]

There was still a lot of suspicion between the two groups, justifiably or not. In the second half of March Makhno received intelligence reports that his people were under surveillance, that his popularity was regarded with suspicion and that there might even be an assassination attempt in the offing. Makhno subsequently met Dybenko in a Berdiansk hotel and raised the issue with him. Dybenko denied all knowledge of the plan and assured the *bat'ko* that he remained in the good books of the command. There was much slandering of honest revlutionaries, he added, and Makhno was not the only target.[70]

On 31 March, the Ukrainian 2nd Army and the 13th Army counter-attacked against the Whites, initially with some success, in an attempt to occupy the whole of the west bank of the Don and thus release troops for other fronts. In response, Denikin's cavalry commander Andrei Shkuro attacked to the west in an attempt to outflank the Soviet right, where Makhno's brigade was still pushing forward along the coast to Rostov from Mariupol'.

Political problems continued, however, to distract from the military difficulties that faced the Red Army. At one level, Makhno's successes were still being lauded in such newspapers as *Pravda* and *Izvestiia*, and his popularity was at its height. Nevertheless, the problem of the situation of the commissars continued to worry the Bolsheviks.[71] On 2 April the political commissar of the Trans-Dnepr Division complained that anarchist and Left SR agitation was making his work difficult. The fighting units of the Guliaipole garrison were anti-communist and included many non-party elements. There was a shortage of arms and of uniforms, and the partisans who comprised most of the fighting units were tired and demoralised. What he needed, nonetheless, were more political workers and more political literature.[72]

At a broader policy level, the Bolsheviks were also having considerable difficulty developing a policy towards the local peasantry that would secure food supplies. In April 1919 the Central Committee of the Komunistychna Partiia (bil'shovykiv) Ukrainy (the KP(b)U), passed a decree 'On the Tasks of the Party in the Struggle against Kulak Gangsterism'. This implemented committees of poor peasants (*kombedy*, or in Ukrainian *komnezamy*) on the Russian model.[73] Kulaks were excluded from the village committees completely, and middle peasants were only allowed to vote but not to stand for election.[74] However the *kombedy* had no real incentive to assist the food committees (known as *prodorgany*), since any surplus that was extracted from the rich peasants went to the cities, and not into support for the rural poor. This applied equally to grain and to animal feed.[75] The Bolsheviks had already tried this tactic in Great Russia, under a decree of 11 June 1918, but had absorbed the committees into the rural soviets at the end of the year. In the new decree the Ukrainian Central Committee pledged itself to send as many experienced political workers as possible to the villages, and to publish more peasant-oriented political literature.[76] In Ukraine the differentiation between wealthy peasants (kulaks) and poor peasants was sharper than in Russia, and to the Bolsheviks another attempt must have seemed worthwhile.[77] However, Lenin noted at the 8th Party congress that it was a mistake to apply Russian policies uncritically to the 'borderlands'.[78] Nonetheless, the *kombedy* survived in Ukraine into the New Economic Policy (NEP) period, and some delegates at the 8th All-Russian Congress of Soviets were still defending their activities as late as December 1920.[79]

Despite the praise for and recognition of the military contribution of the *makhnovtsy*, the Soviet authorities regarded Makhno's activities with deepening suspicion. The RVS received information that Makhno had allegedly sent a delegate to Ataman Grigor'ev to negotiate terms for an alliance against the Bolsheviks. The town soviet of Ekaterinoslav had arrested the man. The situation, complained the Ekaterinoslav Bolsheviks, was 'absolutely impossible', and they urged the RVS to take urgent steps to liquidate the *makhnovtsy*, who were preventing communist work.[80] By mid-April 1919, several months after the incorporation of Makhno's units into the Red Army, the political position in the 3rd Brigade was still discouraging for the communists. Their decision to keep the insurgent units separate, after their acceptance of the unified command, now came back to haunt them in more ways than one.

Particular difficulties arose around the system of assigning commissars to each unit at all levels. For one thing, the insurgents saw no reason for them: 'Why do they send us commissars? We can live without them! And if we do need them, we can elect them from amongst ourselves'.[81] The assigned commissar for the brigade was stuck in Mariupol', unable to take up his post. The 7th Regiment was disorganised, and its commissar had been replaced because of his inactivity. The 8th Regiment was keener, but the commissar had been killed in action. In the 9th Regiment the commissar had been obliged to introduce 'comradely discipline', and there were no organised party cells. The Pravda Section, formerly the 1st Liubetskii Regiment, had neither commissars nor political workers and was reportedly infected with anti-Semitism. The 1st Don Cossack Regiment was newly formed, and the artillery had little political organisation.[82] The commissars were demoralised and complained of widespread pilfering among the troops. Drunkards had been sent to the front, members of the Cheka had been found decapitated or shot in the fields. In one town the partisans had dragged a wounded communist from his hospital bed and beaten him badly. One of Makhno's aides-de-camp, Boris Veretel'nikov, had gained a reputation for persecuting Bolsheviks and for refusing to supply them with food. One commissar described the partisans as 'the dregs of Soviet Russia'.[83] Another urged the RVS to send the best possible political workers to Makhno's sections. The work with Red Army men was good, with mobilised troops it was 'rather bad' and in the Makhnovite units it was lacking altogether. The commissar pointed out that some of his co-workers were hard drinkers, who themselves needed close supervision. They might easily make things worse, if left together with irresponsible soldiers. The refusal of political workers to go to the Makhnovite sections when assigned, he concluded, only encouraged 'banditry and anti-Semitism'.[84]

From the Bolshevik point of view these *military* difficulties were symptoms of a worsening *political* situation. Opinion was divided: there were suggestions for various kinds of 'reform', and recognition that given the threat posed by the Volunteer Army, it was unlikely that Makhno would take up arms against the Bolsheviks, and therefore he could continue to be 'used'.[85] The Ukrainian

Commisar for War (*Narkomvoen*), Nikolai Podvoiskii, however, wanted ideas on how to 'put the 'gangs' of Grigor'ev and Makhno into regular order. Alternatively, he wanted to know how to disband them and disperse the troops among reliable units. But nobody could suggest a practical method for dispersing armed regiments against their will without using much larger numbers of troops. Additionally, to mingle anarchists with Red Army units was to run the risk of spreading what Trotsky called the 'infection' of their radical ideas, their *partizanshchina*. In the end the Bolsheviks stuck to their decision to allow Makhno's units to stay together. In this way Antonov was left to deal with the intractable problem of political discipline. Indeed, Khristian Rakovskii, chair of the Ukrainian *Sovnarkom*, even argued that the *atamany* could not possibly be as terrifying as they seemed when surrounded by their supporters.[86]

Makhno's movement had attracted some qualified support from southern anarchist groups, of which the most important was the Nabat Confederation of Anarchist Federations,[87] dominated by the intellectuals Aron Baron and Volin.[88] The confederation was suspicious of Makhno, however, who they saw as overly pro-Bolshevik, and even tended to sympathise more with Girigor'ev.[89] From 2 to 7 April 1919 the Nabat Confederation held its first congress in Elisavetgrad. The congress strongly opposed anarchist participation in the soviets, which it described as organs of deadening centralism 'imposed from above'. No army based on conscription, claimed the Nabat intellectuals, could be regarded as a true defender of the revolution. Only a partisan army 'organised from below' could do the job.[90] This contradiction between a volunteer army and a conscripted one was always a problem for Makhno. His formula of 'general voluntary and egalitarian mobilisation' meant in practice that able-bodied men were liable to be drafted. But the Nabat Confederation continued to take a strongly voluntarist line on the question:

> A state army of mobilised soldiers and appointed commanders and commissars cannot be considered a true defender of the social revolution … it is a main stronghold of reaction and is used to suppress the uprisings that have broken out all over the whole country today, expressions of dissatisfaction with the policies implemented by those in power.[91]

By early April the alliance between the Red Army and the partisans was in danger of falling apart. Administrative confusion in the Bolshevik chain of command only made the situation worse. To Antonov's irritation, the High Command demanded that he better control Makhno and Grigor'ev, while simultaneously sending telegrams directly to the *atamany*. 'To deal with Makhno and Grigor'ev as my equals puts me in a false position', he complained to Rakovskii.[92] Indeed, military pressure from the Volunteer Army combined with Makhno's intransigence over political questions continued to make his position almost impossible.

On 10 April Makhno convened a third Congress of Regional Soviets in Guliaipole, in order to discuss policy questions. Delegates from 72 districts attended.[93] Despite the seriousness of the military situation for the Red Army and for the revolution in general, the Congress apparently felt no compunction about adopting and endorsing an anarchist platform, which the Bolsheviks inevitably viewed as a provocation. The platform rejected the dictatorship of the proletariat, denied the legitimacy of the All-Ukrainian Congress of Soviets and advocated the liquidation of Bolshevik soviets.[94] The anarchists ordered agitation for 'anti-state socialism', ignoring their earlier agreement with Antonov's RVS. The predictable reaction of the Bolshevik military authorities was to ban the Congress. Dybenko sent a telegram to Makhno ordering him to disband the session, on pain of being declared an outlaw.[95]

The delegates responded with a lengthy and heavily sarcastic manifesto headed *Kontr-revoliutsionnyi li?* (Are We Counterrevolutionary?)[96] This document attacked the legalism of Dybenko's declaration:

Can there exist laws made by a few people calling themselves revolutionaries, laws that enable them to outlaw *en masse* people who are more revolutionary than they are themselves? [97]

The partisans pointed out that they had held their first two congresses (in January and February) before Dybenko had even arrived in Ukraine. It was they, not the authorities of the Red Army, who had a mandate from the toiling masses.[98] Dybenko's threat was a hollow one, for Makhno was still engaging Shkuro in a key sector of the front. Indeed, while these heated exchanges over the revolutionary legitimacy of the congress in Guliaipole were taking place, Dybenko was continuing to issue detailed orders on the tactical disposition of the regiments of the 3rd Brigade. The broad objective was to liquidate Shkuro's breakthrough in the Grishino sector by securing the important railway junctions, while maintaining a general eastward advance and holding down the left flank of the 13th Army to the north.[99]

Shkuro was a Cossack cavalry commander, at his best in a war of movement. He had gained experience of partisan warfare in the northern Caucasus in 1918, and had a reputation for brutality.[100] His style of fighting was similar to Makhno's – he was a self-described *partizan* – and he was aware of the value of flamboyance and terror in warfare. His cavalry was known as the Wolf Pack, after the wolf skin caps that they wore for effect.[101] His corps consisted of a division of Kuban Cossacks, a Circassian cavalry division, an infantry division, and three gun batteries – over 5,000 men and 12 artillery pieces.[102]

Makhno had occupied Mariupol' on 30 March, but the collapse of the 9th Division to his left, and his shortage of supplies, placed his position in imminent danger.[103] The Red Army command was in a state of confusion. On 12 April Skachko informed Dybenko that Makhno's brigade was to remain under his command as the anchor on the left flank. He ordered him to counter-attack to stop the breakthrough between Makhno's left and the 9th Division's right.[104] Dybenko, who was in the Crimea, was complaining about a shortage of supplies, especially uniforms. He promised Skachko that he would send artillery, rifles and ammunition to Makhno's brigade.[105]

But stop-gap measures could not have solved the problem of weapons and uniforms: more radical steps were needed. Shortly afterwards the Ukrainian army was divided into three to improve its efficiency, with its headquarters in Ekaterinoslav.[106] Makhno's own solution to the supply problem was simple and direct: he seized supply trains and prevented the Bolsheviks from collecting food or from setting up any kind of administration in his area.[107] This kind of interference in Ukraine could have had – and often did have – serious consequences for the Bolsheviks in Russia. Military defeats and the failure to collect food from supposedly friendly areas placed the regime in danger. By June, A. G. Shlikhter, who was in charge of collecting food in Ukraine, could report the dispatch of only 12,377 tonnes of grain to Russia. In March Lenin had asked for over 800,000 tonnes.[108]

On 16 April, despite Dybenko's promises of help, Makhno had to evacuate Mariupol' under strong pressure from the Whites.[109] Vatsetis and Antonov mistrusted each other and they were unable to solve problems through cooperative action. On the same day, the commander-in-chief ordered Antonov to send another brigade from the Trans-Dnepr Division to support Makhno, 'whose attack in the direction of Taganrog is slowing down and almost failing'.[110] The next day, after Vatsetis had heard the news of Makhno's reverse and of the loss of Mariupol' and Volnovakh, he ordered an additional infantry division and a cavalry regiment to reinforce the 3rd Brigade, not counting the brigade ordered on the previous day. Vatsetis calculated that the 13th Army, the 8th Army, and the 3rd Brigade totalled 41,000 infantry and cavalry with 170 heavy guns, opposing 38,000 White Guards. With reinforcements from the 7th Rifle Division the Red Army total rose to 46,000, an advantage of 8,000 men.[111] But Antonov was convinced that only he fully understood what was possible and what was not on the Ukrainian Front. His reaction to Vatsetis' orders was irritable and uncooperative. 'You exaggerate our strength', he replied to the commander-in-chief, 'We have been weakened by constant fighting; we are poorly supplied; the troops want to go home'.[112] Food, clothing, ammunition, artillery, horses, even political workers, were nowhere to be found. On top of his other tasks he was now expected to move reinforcements that existed only on paper to a unit that was no longer his responsibility.

Lenin was concerned: on 18 April he cabled Rakovskii that Dybenko's attack into the Crimea was an unnecessary adventure, and that Dybenko might replace Makhno for a counter-attack towards Taganrog and Rostov.[113] The next day he told Trotsky's aide G. Ia. Sokol'nikov that he was disturbed by the slackening-off of operations against the Donbass and asked him to formulate practical directives to speed things up again.[114] Sokol'nikov replied that there were three causes of delay: disorganisation in the army, Denikin's acquisition of reinforcements and the weakness of Makhno's brigade on the flank. He recommended the reorganisation of the 9th Army to the east of Lugansk, and the prioritisation of the Southern Front.[115] Lenin informed Antonov directly that he should regard the Donbass as the most important objective, and to immediately give solid support to the Donbass-Mariupol' sector. He brushed aside Antonov's protests in advance: 'I see ... that there are quantities of military supplies in the Ukraine ... they must not be hoarded'.[116] But Antonov had been ordered to move troops westwards, past hostile Ukrainian nationalist and Polish forces, to relieve pressure on Soviet Hungary; to move troops eastwards to relieve the Southern Front; and to establish control over Ukraine to secure coal and grain supplies to Russia.

His forces were not the disciplined and well-organised formations depicted by Trotsky. Makhno's and Grigor'ev's units were by no means the only partisan forces in Ukraine: in fact, in Ekaterinoslav province, where Makhno was in control and formally in alliance with the Red Army, there were fewer rebellions against the Bolsheviks than there were in northern Ukraine, where no single *ataman* wielded power.[117]

Antonov agreed that Makhno's failure to resist Shkuro was partially the result of his autonomy, but he was not as critical of the insurgents as was Trotsky.[118] On 1 May, in a memorandum to the Central Committees of the Russian and Ukrainian parties, Trotsky argued for the reduction of partisan units to half their strength, to turn them into regular troops: Makhno had been ineffective under sustained enemy attack, and his forces had to be absorbed into regular formations. Criminal elements should be purged, discipline established and the system of elected commanders abolished. Antonov's approach of allowing a special status for the partisan units was 'opportunism'.[119]

From mid-April onwards it was clear to the Bolshevik commanders that they had misjudged the *atamany*'s potential, and over-estimated the effectiveness of their own command structure. This judgement was based on direct observation: Skachko, for example, had visited Grigor'ev's 'headquarters' in March, filing a scathing report that described the filth, disorganisation and drunkenness, and recommended that Grigor'ev himself be 'eliminated'.[120] Grigor'ev also had grandiose ideas about his own importance. On 10 April, after the capture of Odessa from the French on the 6th, he sent telegrams to Rakovskii, Antonov,

Dybenko, Makhno and other commanders boasting of his own courage and his troops' loyalty during the attack.[121]

A week later, at considerable personal risk, Antonov went to visit Grigor'ev at Aleksandriia in an attempt to bring him and his unit under effective control. He wanted to persuade Grigor'ev to join forces with Makhno's brigade for a swift offensive towards the Donbass. He was unable to convince him that the plan was a good one.[122] On 23 April Antonov met Grigor'ev again, and considered exerting pressure on him to attack southwards into the Donbass. To send the volatile *ataman* to such a crucial sector of the front was too risky, however, and it was equally impossible to leave him in the rear, close to Makhno's anarchist partisans. Antonov decided to send him to Bessarabia, to campaign against Romania in support of Soviet Hungary. In an emotional interview he convinced Grigor'ev, releasing more reliable troops and resolving his dilemma.[123]

Meanwhile Makhno was being particularly pugnacious. Grain requisition detachments (*prodovol'stvennye otriady*) were unable to operate in his area, and he had lost patience with the Bolshevik commissars in the 3rd Brigade, and arrested them, breaking the February agreement. His troops were wavering under the White attacks, and Antonov could ill afford to antagonise him. He therefore decided to visit Guliaipole himself, with two purposes in mind: to see for himself this 'under-sized, young-looking, dark-eyed man, wearing a Caucasian fur cap at an angle', and to assess him and his unit.[124] On arrival he noted that three secondary schools had been set up, several medical posts to treat the wounded and a workshop for repairing military equipment. There was also adult education underway focussing on political agitation.[125] The visit gave Antonov an opportunity to try to solve the two problems of Makhno's relations with Grigor'ev, and of his treatment of the commissars. Antonov was, by his own account, satisfied with the way Makhno ran his headquarters and with the fighting qualities of his men. He telegraphed to Khar'kov that he had stayed with Makhno for the whole day, and was convinced that there was no anti-Soviet conspiracy, and that the *makhnovtsy* were 'a great fighting force', and potentially 'an indestructible fortress'. The newspaper propaganda campaign needed to stop at once.[126] Still, Makhno had much to complain of – he was short of arms, ammunition, clothing and money. He had received 3,000 Italian rifles, but so few bullets that they were already used up.[127] His grumbles were justifiable – although the 3rd Brigade was under bombardment from land and sea, they had only two 3-inch guns in good condition and lacked machine-guns and cartridges. Yet when Dybenko had raised this point, headquarters accused him of placing the brigade's welfare before that of the division as a whole.[128]

Antonov was sympathetic, and issued orders for supplies to be sent to Makhno forthwith. On the question of the arrested commissars he was adamant. Makhno unexpectedly backed down, and released the imprisoned political workers, on condition that they must no longer work as spies for the Bolsheviks.[129] Even more comforting for Antonov to hear were Makhno's assurances that he did not have close relations with Grigor'ev, who he suspected of counter-revolutionary intentions. He admitted that he had indeed sent an envoy to Grigor'ev's camp, but only to discover what his plans really were. Shortly after this surprisingly friendly visit to Makhno, another senior Bolshevik arrived in Guliaipole. Lev Kamenev, deputy chairman of the Russian *Sovnarkom*, was on a mission to Ukraine, primarily to sort out the administrative problems that were preventing food supplies from moving northwards. As he was to discover, the problems were, in fact, much more than merely administrative.

4
Betrayal in the Heat of Battle? The Red–Black Alliance Falls Apart, May–September 1919

Lev Kamenev's visit to Guliaipole in May 1919 is well-documented, thanks to an account by his secretary, Vladimir Shapiro-Sokolin, who accompanied him. This text exists in four versions, written years apart and published or preserved as manuscripts in different archives.[1] The best-known was published in the Soviet journal *Proletarskaia Revoliutsiia* in 1925 under the initials 'V. S.' and has been widely cited, but it was only in 2017 that the author was definitively identified.[2]

The anarchist leadership – including Marusia Nikiforova – received Kamenev warmly with a guard of honour.[3] Kamenev wrote later that he was duty-bound to report that 'all the rumours about separatist or anti-Soviet plans by Comrade Makhno's insurgent brigade are ill-founded'. Indeed, he continued, in Makhno 'I saw an honest and courageous fighter who, under difficult conditions … gathers his strength and fights bravely against the White Guards and the foreign intervention'.[4] Kamenev complimented the insurgents on their liberation of the region from Skoropadskii and their defence of it against Denikin and Petliura.

There were still concerns. Kamenev was worried, among other issues, about the 'great evil' of anti-Semitism that he noticed among the fighters. Another problem was the failure of the insurgents to recognise that strategic resources – such as 'equipment, bread, coal, metals and oil' – needed to be distributed among fronts and sectors *by the centre* according to the needs of the moment: 'your sector … is only a thousandth part of the entire front … we must have everything in common'.[5] As long as local commanders interfered with the distribution plan for bread and coal, they were playing into the hands of the Whites. Kamenev pointed to the export of manufactured goods from Mariupol' without any consideration of what the centre needed. 'Makhno', he added optimistically, promised to 'make every effort to drive this consciousness into the heads of all who follow him'.[6]

Makhno was also suspicious. Before the delegation arrived he had privately expressed misgivings to Viktor Belash, wondering about possible 'dirty tricks', and cautioning Belash to be 'ready for anything'.[7] This was not unreasonable: voices among the Bolsheviks had argued a few days earlier for the sacking of both Makhno and Grigor'ev as commanders and the bringing of their forces under full Red Army discipline.[8] Kamenev was unwilling to accept the legitimacy of Makhno's VRS, which seemed to him to usurp the functions of the RVS of the Ukrainian Soviet Republic. The anarchists argued that the toiling masses of the region had created the insurgent VRS, and it could only be dissolved by them – or, they added pointedly, against their will by the counter-revolution. The Soviet RVS, on the other hand, was a creation of the Bolshevik Central Committee, and could be dissolved by fiat.[9]

At the end of the visit, Kamenev and Makhno embraced, and Kamenev assured the *bat'ko* that they spoke a common revolutionary language.[10] Arshinov later asked, rhetorically, whether this friendliness masked 'an irreconcilable hostility' to the anarchist project.[11] Nevertheless, Kamenev's visit was a high point in amicable relations between the anarchists and Bolsheviks in Ukraine, adherents of two irreconcilable revolutionary doctrines.

At a practical level Kamenev's real worry was food, not legalities, and he persuaded Makhno to stop obstructing military and civil supply operations. His assessment of the Ukrainian situation was realistic: 'whoever commands a large army will receive grain'.[12] However, he also realised that as long as Podvoiskii and Shlikhter could not cooperate over grain collection, agreement with Makhno was pointless. Makhno's wagons were guarded by soldiers from the insurgent forces as well as from the *Narkomprod* (the army supply organisation). Podvoiskii admitted to Kamenev that he had not even attempted to control the supply sections of semi-autonomous commanders such as Makhno.[13]

Meanwhile, fighting was continuing unabated: Shkuro's cavalry incursions were taking their toll, and he had broken through the Red Army's lines in early May. Makhno's brigade was down to four reserve regiments and seven artillery pieces. Two of his regiments had been defeated at Kuteinskovo.[14] The 8th Army was forced to pull back to protect the rear, abandoning Lugansk on 5 May. Lenin was enraged: 'There has not been a single accurate and factual answer from you ... as to which units are moving to the Donbass, how many infantry, cavalry or artillery, and which stations the leading trains are at', he told Rakovskii, Antonov and Podvoiskii. 'The fall of Lugansk shows that they are correct who accuse you of independence ... it is you who will bear the responsibility for disaster if you are late with serious help for the Donbass'.[15] Lenin conceded, however, that diplomacy was needed with Makhno, at least until Rostov could be captured. His consequent insistence on making Antonov personally responsible for Makhno's troops was complicated by the fact that Makhno's forces were deployed to the Southern Front.[16] Lenin had little respect for his commanders in Ukraine, or, indeed, for local peculiarities: 'In Ukraine at the present time, every gang chooses a political title ... and there is a gang

for every region'.[17] He expected Antonov to behave like a general, and simultaneously treated him like a mere subordinate. Two days after his first set of
instructions, he made both Antonov and Podvoiskii 'personally responsible for
Makhno's group' and demanded a speed-up of the movement of supplies to the
Donbass and 'the swift capture of Rostov'.[18]

Lenin's dismissal of Makhno as a mere gangster with a political title ignored
the reasons why the Ukrainian peasantry opposed the Bolsheviks and their
policies. The Ukrainian Central Executive Committee (TsIK, or *Tsentral'nyi
Vikonavchyi Komitet*)[19] was more realistic in its proclamation of 8 May, in
which it recognised the hardships that Ukrainian peasants were experiencing
and explained the measures adopted by the Soviet government in land and
food policy, as well as the objectives of the *kombedy*. Nonetheless, the *kombedy*
worked badly in Ukraine, where rich and middle peasants sometimes made up
a majority opposed to communist measures. The hopes of middle peasants that
they would get land from the large estates or even control of some manufacturing were dashed, and they were resentful.[20] In the spring of 1919, Ukraine 'was
seething and bubbling',[21] but the *kombedy* survived there longer than in Russia.
The party decreed in May that middle peasants could join, but the attempt
to win support came too late. Grigor'ev's revolt was by no means an isolated
manifestation of discontent,[22] although it was the largest and most dangerous,
mainly because of the leader's 'outlaw charisma'.[23]

The Ukrainian TsIK's proclamation blamed the nationalists, the Whites
and the forces of the intervention, which had set 'Ukrainians quarrelling with
Russians, Jews with Poles, Poles with Ukrainians, workers and peasants in the
towns with workers and peasants in the villages ...'[24] From late April, the area
under Grigor'ev's control became increasingly restless, as peasant soldiers looted
and pillaged, shot commissars and committed pogroms in a chain reaction
of impatient violence. Grigor'ev's troops, tired of the Bolshevik commissars,
were easily swayed by nationalists, SRs, or even anti-Semitic monarchists. The
ataman had mixed feelings about the Red Army, and was preparing to revolt
while continuing to offer assurances of loyalty to the cause of communism.
Kamenev was the first to discover that these assurances were valueless, when
his repeated attempts to contact Grigor'ev to discuss supply problems revealed
large-scale troop movements towards Ekaterinoslav.

On 10 May Antonov finally contacted the *ataman* and learned about the
rebellion at first hand. Grigor'ev transmitted the text of his Universal, in which
he renounced the authority of the Bolsheviks, and insisted that he would
continue to advance on Ekaterinoslav.[25] Antonov informed him that he would
be isolated, but Grigor'ev insisted he had the partial support of the 1st and
2nd Armies, and of the population. He claimed to be in touch with Makhno, a
prospect that would have alarmed Antonov, as the two groups were still close to
each other at Ekaterinoslav.[26] The Bolsheviks took immediate steps to avert the

possibility of the two forces merging. On 12 May Makhno received a telegram from Kamenev demanding that he take a stand against Grigor'ev's revolt: 'Either you will march with the workers and peasants of whole of Russia or you will, in effect, open the front to the enemy – there can be no hesitation!'[27]

Some *makhnovtsy* suspected that the Bolsheviks might have actually provoked the revolt, to justify breaking up autonomous partisan bands.[28] Makhno ordered his combat units to take energetic steps to defend the front,[29] and then sent a message to Kamenev, affirming that he would 'remain unchangeably true ... to the revolution of the workers and peasants' but not to the communist structures of government. Without 'precise information about Grigor'ev ... [and] what he is doing or for what reasons' Makhno continued, he would not take a position. At the end of the message Makhno wrote that he would continue to 'set up free worker-peasant unions, which will have all power to themselves' and to oppose the Cheka and other 'organs of oppression and violence'.[30] The message was clear: Makhno would not take sides under pressure. In fact, Grigor'ev had implied to Antonov that Makhno was willing to support him, but he was clearly anxious: one message read: 'Bat'ko! Why do you look to the Communists? Kill them! Ataman Grigor'ev'.[31]

The matter was settled politically when Makhno's proclamation, *Kto takoi Grigor'ev* [Who is this Grigor'ev?], was published and circulated, both as a leaflet and in the newspapers *Nabat* and *Put' k Svobode*.[32] It attacked Grigor'ev as an anti-Semitic predator and a traitor to the revolution, while blaming the Bolsheviks for his popularity: '[the party] created the anger in the masses from which Grigor'ev profits today'.[33] Indeed, Bolshevik policies towards the peasantry in Ukraine were heavy-handed and badly administered. The Bolsheviks had little rural support, and had aligned themselves against the rich and middle peasants in a situation of acute military peril, when they were in dire need of food supplies. They encouraged class antagonism and sent grain requisition units and the Cheka to intimidate the rural masses. By May, conditions in the villages were so bad that an administrative breakdown had become nearly inevitable.[34]

The impact of the loss of Grigor'ev's brigade (and of the troops needed to suppress the rebellion) on the military capability of the Red Army was devastating. It came when White cavalry were breaking through the lines, when Makhno's commitment was wavering, and when food and coal supplies were precarious. In addition, Grigor'ev's behaviour towards the population under his control was brutal. He was responsible for pogroms that were vicious even for that time and place – it is likely that his victims numbered about 6,000, in as many as forty different villages'.[35] The full weight of Bolshevik propaganda turned against him, denouncing him in newspapers, proclamations and leaflets, and accusing him of multiple crimes. Voroshilov, a capable officer who was then Ukrainian Commissar for Internal Affairs, was appointed military commander with special responsibility for the rapid destruction of Grigor'ev's gang. His command was autonomous, and the creation of yet another independent army in Ukraine complicated the Bolsheviks' severe problems of supply and administration.

Grigor'ev's revolt had serious consequences. It helped to create conditions for Denikin to press home his military advantage and drive the Bolsheviks out of Ukraine. This in turn helped to isolate the Hungarian Soviet revolution, ending Bolshevik hopes of seeing communists in power in Central and Western Europe. At the local level, it prepared the ground for a split between Makhno and the Bolsheviks, who lost trust in partisans and their political intentions. Although the revolt was not immediately eliminated, it quickly dwindled in strength to a few thousand men, engaged in harassing Red Army units and in destroying communications links and railway tracks:[36] the end of *grigor'ev-shchina* was announced prematurely on 23 May.

While this violent realignment of forces was taking place in the rear, the military situation at the front was also worsening. On 14 May Makhno's brigade, as part of the 2nd Army and alongside the 8th and 13th Armies, had begun the long-awaited attack on the Donbass, liberating Lugansk. Units of the 2nd and 13th Armies advanced deep into Denikin's rear areas, seizing the region around the important railway station of Kuteinskovo. To counter this threat to his left flank, Denikin moved Shkuro's corps from the front of the Red 9th Army to that of the 13th Army.[37] He aimed the blow carefully, striking at the sector where the *makhnovtsy* secured the right flank of the 13th Army. Makhno's forces had been weakened by the assignment of Dybenko's division, which had been on the 2nd Army's strength, to Voroshilov for his campaign against Grigor'ev, and between 16 and 19 May Shkuro's units broke through in Makhno's sector. The 13th Army reported on 22 May that Shkuro's cavalry had taken the villages of Maksimil'ianovka and Aleksandrovka, and that Shkuro was using tanks in the centre and on the left. Initial attempts to counter-attack had failed.[38] In a single day, White cavalry breached the front to a depth of 45 kilometres. Denikin exploited this success energetically against the under-armed and vacillating partisans, and within three days had opened a gap 35 kilometres wide and over 95 kilometres deep in Makhno's sector. By the end of May the rout had exposed the right flank and rear of the 13th Army, throwing the whole front into retreat from Denikin's coordinated attacks.[39]

Trotsky mistrusted insurgent groups, and expressed himself in extreme terms. On 17 May, four days after arriving in Ukraine, he called for 'a radical and merciless liquidation of the partisan movement'.[40] He dismissed Skachko and ordered Voroshilov to take over the 2nd Army, to reinforce it with troops from Khar'kov and to discipline Makhno's units. This was to be done by removing the anarchist leaders and 'restoring order' among the rank and file.[41] On 26 May Lenin instructed Kamenev, in response to a demand by Stalin for coal for the Baltic fleet,[42] to start loading coal from Mariupol' for Petrograd, authorising him to deal with Makhno in case he objected.[43] Trotsky believed that Makhno's anarchism was only *kulak* banditry in fancy dress, and told his commanders that it would be better to lose Ukraine to Denikin, whose anti-Soviet, reactionary views were clear to even the most unsophisticated peasant, than to Makhno, whose movement developed among and aroused the support of the masses.[44] To collect grain *and* coal *and* control Makhno on top of everything else, he told Lenin, would require 'a trustworthy Cheka battalion, several hundred Baltic fleet Ivanov-Vosnesenskii workers, and about thirty serious party workers'.[45]

While Trotsky abused Makhno politically, Vatsetis was trying desperately to plug the gap in the line, ordering an infantry brigade and an artillery division transferred to the command of the 2nd Ukrainian Army to take Makhno's position.[46] On 27 May the Red Army was forced to evacuate Lugansk, which they had captured only two weeks previously. In Moscow, Lenin watched these attempts to stave off disaster with dismay. 'Makhno rolls away westwards, opening the flank of the 13th Army', he telegraphed, 'Antonov and Podvoiskii … bear criminal responsibility for each minute of delay'. He demanded that the two commanders should stop sending 'meaningless and boastful telegrams', and should immediately reinforce the sector on a massive scale.[47] But Voroshilov knew that catastrophe was not to be averted by such measures.[48] He and Mezhlauk needed to strengthen the 2nd Army, which by the end of May consisted of little except Makhno's brigade, already in retreat. They argued briefly for the creation of a new 'Donbass front' but both Lenin and Trotsky rejected the idea.[49] There was some indication that even the 8th and 13th Armies were 'infected with the Makhnovite cancer'.[50]

Arshinov and others later accused Trotsky and Bolshevik commanders of deliberately starving the insurgents of weapons, making it impossible for them to defend themselves so that they might be more easily neutralised. There was also a propaganda campaign against them.[51] Recognition in January that the only possible source of supplies was the Red Army had been an important motive for the alliance in the first place.[52] Arshinov argues that the plan went wrong because the Bolsheviks did not realise how strong the Volunteer Army was, and were not expecting such powerful and well-coordinated blows. In support of this view he cites the visits to Guliaipole by Antonov and Kamenev at the beginning of May and the promises to have ammunition sent from Khar'kov: two weeks later, no shells or cartridges had arrived.[53] However, this would have been a high-risk strategy, and it is unclear that the Bolsheviks had the organisational capacity to pull it off. The inadequate supply system and the muddled chain of command hampered the Red Army throughout the campaign in Ukraine. Some former Tsarist officers, who had been brought in to serve in the Red Army, were spies and saboteurs who deliberately created confusion.[54] Without assuming that Bolshevik intentions towards the *makhnovtsy* were benevolent, these factors help explain supply failures.[55] In addition, the repeated calls for reinforcements in Makhno's sector – from Bolsheviks to Bolsheviks – belie any willingness to see the Insurgent Army annihilated.

Matters reached a head on 29 May. Makhno's headquarters sent Antonov a cable announcing that they had decided to create an 'independent insurgent army', under the command of 'Comrade Makhno': this army – eleven infantry regiments, two cavalry regiments and two strike groups – would continue to be 'operationally subordinate' to the Southern Front. They demanded an end to insulting language directed at their units.[56] On the same day the Bolsheviks ordered Makhno's arrest.[57] The insurgent VRS then decided to call an extraordinary Congress of Workers', Peasants' and Insurgents' Delegates for 15 June, to discuss the military crisis created by the White breakthrough and the political crisis in relations with the Bolsheviks. Despite the clash with Dybenko in April over the third congress, the tone of the telegram announcing this 4th congress pulled no punches. 'The Executive Committee of the VRS ... has reached the conclusion that only the working masses themselves can find a solution, and not individuals or parties'. The telegram was addressed to 'the districts, towns and villages of the provinces of Ekaterinoslav, Tauride and adjacent regions; to all units of *Bat'ko* Makhno's 1st Insurgent Division; to all Red Army troops in the same region'.[58]

The reaction of the Bolshevik commanders to Makhno's resignation of his command, followed by the summoning of another anarchist congress – both at a moment of military crisis – was decisive and harsh, as the uncertainty around the rumoured 'disbanding' of the insurgent units started to create panic.[59] Denikin was moving from success to success; on 1 June he captured Bakhmut, northeast of Guliaipole.[60] Simultaneously, the All-Ukrainian Congress of Regional Executive Committees passed a resolution 'On Makhno', which accused him of seeking the protection of the Soviet flag and of then attacking the political organisation of the Red Army and of the Soviet Government, while consolidating power for himself. Any attempt to convene a regional congress without the knowledge of Provincial and Regional Executive Committees would 'lead to severe consequences'. The Congress categorically condemned Makhno's actions and moved that '*Sovnarkom* should ... take ruthless and resolute measures'.[61]

Trotsky needed little encouragement. On 4 June he issued Order no. 1824, stating that the congress was forbidden, participation would amount to treason and that all delegates were subject to immediate arrest, as was anybody who publicised the event.[62] Two days later, on 6 June, Trotsky reiterated his ban on the congress in even stronger terms, declaring that any fighter who deserted to attend the congress was a traitor and would face the firing squad.[63]

Makhno did not receive a copy of Order no. 1824 for a few days, possibly because he was engaged in defending Guliaipole, which was captured by Shkuro's Cossacks after heavy fighting on 6 June. The *makhnovtsy* retreated to the railway station at Gaichur, a few kilometres away, with the staff, a few soldiers and a battery.[64] From Gaichur, on 8 June, Makhno addressed a long letter of resignation to Voroshilov, Trotsky, Lenin and Kamenev.[65] He protested that despite the 'deeply comradely' sentiments of Antonov and Kamenev, Soviet newspapers continued to represent him as a gangster and an accomplice of Grigor'ev. The Bolsheviks accused the partisans of all manner of crimes. They had allegedly abandoned their communications equipment to the advancing Whites, who then not only had access to Red Army messages, but also sent insulting telegrams directly over the wire.[66] In early May the *makhnovtsy* published, with derisive comments, a letter from Shkuro suggesting an alliance.[67] The Bolshevik press unscrupulously used this letter and the fact of its appearance in the insurgent newspaper to suggest that negotiations were actually taking place.[68] Finally, Makhno denied that he or his staff had *themselves* called the congress, which was convened by the workers and peasants, as was their inalienable right.[69]

Makhno was particularly irritated by Trotsky's article 'Makhnovshchina', which appeared in issue no.51 of *V puti* for 2 June, accusing the insurgents of undermining Soviet power without mentioning their role in the fight against Denikin.[70] 'I am fully aware of the central state authorities' attitude towards me', wrote Makhno in his letter, adding that such hostility led, 'with fatal inevitability' to the emergence of an internal front within the working masses. Such a situation constituted an 'unforgivable crime against the workers', and it was his duty to leave the post he had occupied.[71]

This moment constituted a turning point in relations between the *makhnovtsy* and the Bolsheviks, a moment in which the hostile view of the hard-liners led by Trotsky came to dominate the cooperative approach of Antonov and Kamenev, who had first-hand experience of the insurgency.[72] Antonov was a 'weighty voice in defence of the Makhnovist army as an ally of the Bolsheviks in the fight against Denikin', especially in his memoirs.[73] His report to Rakovskii on 2 May – a series of 19 bullet points with four concluding recommendations – pointed out that the *makhnovtsy* were 'imbued' with revolutionary spirit, lived modestly, were open to other viewpoints and did not agitate against Soviet power.[74] Trotsky, however, saw the partisan forces as an invasive foreign body within the Red Army, a body that he constantly demanded either transform itself – or be transformed – in conformity with the army's other constituent parts. For Makhno, this was an autocratic position, since his forces were the *actual* 'Red Army', created by Ukrainian peasants to protect their interests. They would avoid confrontation with the Bolsheviks and the shedding of 'brotherly blood', but would never dance to Trotsky's tune. The only body that could order them to lay down their arms was an all-Ukrainian congress of free workers.[75]

Despite the conciliatory tone of Makhno's letter, he played his hand badly by insisting on resigning his command and arguing that the impulse for the congress did not come from him. He had previously arranged with loyalist commanders that the bulk of his forces would remain under Red Army control – showing his intention not to weaken the front. His commanders would wait for his summons to re-join the insurgent forces. In this way he apparently hoped to make a clean break with the Bolsheviks and to avoid accusations of abandoning the front to the counter-revolution, while ensuring that he retained long term control of his army. In any event, he escaped arrest and departed with a cavalry detachment for Aleksandrovsk. In campaigning to cure the Red Army of the 'partisan infection', it seems that it was Trotsky who risked the patient's life: the Bolsheviks immediately began to arrest and shoot *makhnovtsy*, and took the opportunity to destroy the anarchist communes.[76]

Now that Makhno was gone, Red Army commanders acted swiftly to absorb the units that he had left behind. Some were ordered to Pavlograd to establish contact with Dybenko's forces. A new commander was appointed for the Guliaipole sector.[77] By 15 June the Ukrainian *Narkomvoen* reported that *makhnovtsy* units in the Grishino sector had been dispersed, and the partisans integrated into regular units.[78] As the Red Army retreated from Ukraine in disorder, other heads were doomed to roll. On 16 June Antonov-Ovseenko was removed from his command, and on 21 June the Ukrainian front was formally abolished by the Ukrainian TsIK.[79]

The break between the partisans and the Bolsheviks in the spring of 1919 had a ripple effect, marking the end of a period of relative freedom for anarchists and leftist intellectuals in Ukraine. The Red Army was under pressure from White Guards, and the political authorities were in no mood to tolerate criticism, least of all from anarchists, whom they held responsible for the looming catastrophe. They began to take severe measures. On 11 June they seized Mikhailev-Pavlenko, an engineer, while he was in action against Denikin on an armoured train. They accused him of having distributed notices about the convening of the banned regional congress. The Khar'kov Cheka sentenced him to be shot, alongside six peasants guilty of the same offence.[80] The Bolsheviks captured Iakov Oserov, Makhno's chief-of-staff, and condemned him to death with others including members of the insurgent VRS.[81] In mid-June 1919 they banned the newspaper *Odesskii Nabat* for publishing an article called 'The Truth about Makhno' that criticised the Bolsheviks.[82]

The Bolsheviks could do little more than try to minimise their losses and gather strength for a counter-offensive. Denikin was attacking in a two-pronged thrust along the length of the front and his renewed advance northwards began with successes on the right bank. The Volunteers aimed at Khar'kov and central

Russia, while the Army of the Caucasus struck at Tsaritsyn and the central Volga region.[83] Equipped with British tanks, aircraft, arms and ammunition, and counselled by British advisors, Denikin's forces began to sweep aside everything in their path. In the east the Caucasians advanced to within 65 kilometres of Astrakhan; in the west the Volunteer Army captured Odessa without heavy losses. The capture of Odessa – and of Kiev – boosted White morale, but Denikin's forces in north-western Ukraine were now in contact with the armies of the Directory and the Galicians around Kiev. Despite a community of interest, the two sides could not agree to cooperate against the Bolsheviks and fighting broke out between them, weakening Denikin's flank. General Wrangel, on the Volga front, managed to take Tsaritsyn despite Voroshilov's and Stalin's massive counter-offensive, and in August pushed forward to within 100 kilometres of Saratov.[84]

The factors that contributed to the Bolshevik rout included the weather and a typhus epidemic.[85] Another key reason for the 'catastrophic position on the Southern Front' was the absence of the peasant insurgent armies of Grigor'ev and Makhno in the field. Unsurprisingly, political work deteriorated as the military circumstances worsened.[86] The White generals made good use of their superior cavalry and of the railway system, gaining a tactical advantage that they exploited in probing for weaknesses. Denikin's successes in Ukraine also permitted him to deny the economic resources of the Donbass to both the Bolsheviks and the Ukrainian nationalists in the north-west.[87]

The White leadership did not agree on the wisdom of committing so many troops to Ukraine. Wrangel still favoured moving extra forces to the Volga, to contact Kolchak's army, and others argued for the consolidation of the area already conquered before continuing the advance – which the Red Army was unable to hold back.[88] The Bolsheviks began to evacuate as many men and as much materiel – especially rolling stock – as they could save. Nevertheless, despite the bleak military prospects for the revolution, political factors weighed against Denikin's long-term success. His acknowledgement of the inept Admiral Kolchak as Supreme Commander of the White Armies was a mistake, although it did produce the impression of political and military unity among anti-communist forces. The ill-timed and ill-fated secret order no. 08878 of 3 July 1919 for the 'Drive on Moscow' was also an error that overextended White forces in the months that followed.[89] The directive ordered a thrust northwards along the line of rail Kursk-Orel'-Tula to Moscow, and flanking drives via Voronezh-Riazan and even as far north-westwards as Saratov and Nizhnyi Novgorod. The longest of these thrusts would have had to cover more than 1,200 kilometres.[90]

By July, the White armies were poised along a 1,300-kilometre front that stretched from the Dnepr to the Don. With 100,000 men under arms, the Whites matched the Bolsheviks in strength, but were stretched along the long

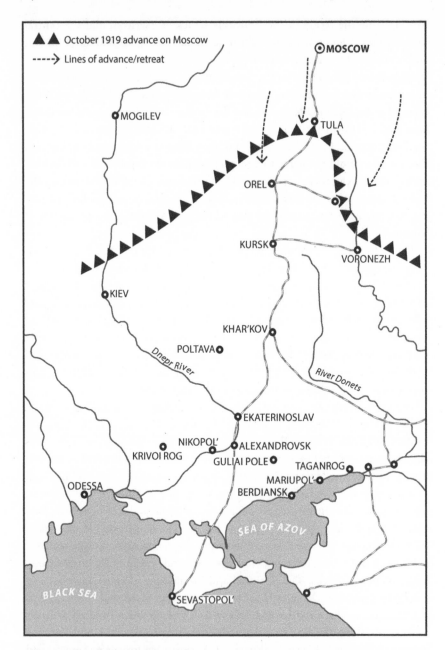

Map 4.1   Denikin's Advance on Moscow, 1919

The Volunteer Army under General Denikin advanced to within a few hundred kilometres of Moscow, and threatened to capture Tula, where the main Russian armaments
factory was located. (Cartographer: Jenny Sandler)

front.[91] In the south, the Dnepr River protected Denikin's left, but movement northwards inevitably exposed the flank. In addition – on their own initiative and ignoring the Moscow Directive – White commanders began to cross to the right bank to seize towns and cities. Shkuro captured Ekaterinoslav (on the river), and White units pushed westwards along the coast of the Black Sea towards Odessa, which they captured on 23 August. Meanwhile, other forces moved north-westwards to take Poltava and Kiev, which also fell on the 23rd.[92] However, White successes masked a vulnerability caused by the speed and spread of the advance. Denikin made mistakes, including his failure to consolidate behind his lines, which had a cumulative impact. His generals were undisciplined, and the Volunteer Army and the Don Cossacks lost contact with each other. His forces managed logistics poorly, along vastly extended lines of supply.[93] The Reds were not in much better shape: they were hampered by basic disagreements over strategy, by poor control and by doubtful support among the population in some areas. They did not win, in the end, entirely by military skill, but rather because they managed to trap the Volunteer Army in a salient at Orel', between the Latvian infantry on the right and Budenny's Red Cavalry on the left.[94] The Volunteers were eventually rescued by bad weather, but the momentum of the advance was lost.[95] Makhno's contribution to all this is discussed in the next chapter.

In the centre, north of Khar'kov, the Whites stood still from July until September, apart from a raid on Tambov and Voronezh.[96] In July, over Trotsky's objections, Vatsetis was replaced by Sergei Kamenev, a commander 'distinguished by ... a quick strategic imagination'.[97] Trotsky believed that an attack on the Don would drive recruits into the White Army: better to concentrate on the Donbass, where the support of the industrial working class and the dense infrastructure of roads and railways would help the Reds to capture and keep territory.[98] Kamenev and his supporters in the VTsIK, however, had discounted these social and political factors and opted for a classic military plan.[99] Lenin was furious at the setback: 'tell the Commander-in-Chief that this will not do. Serious attention must be paid to this ...' he demanded testily on 10 August.[100] On 23 July, Kamenev ordered a strike in the east, from the Volga towards Tsaritsyn and Rostov. The attack was launched in mid-August, but Wrangel stopped the Reds at the gates of Tsaritsyn. A secondary attack in the centre reached Kupiansk, to the east of Khar'kov, by the 25th. When these attacks faltered, the danger of encirclement by counter-attacking White units arose, and after a rapid retreat the Red Armies found themselves by 15 September back where they started.[101]

But the problems brought about by over-extension and rapid advances manifested themselves most perniciously behind White lines. It was Denikin's failure to confront the corruption and brutality of his own soldiers in the territory he controlled, as much as his military weaknesses, that created the conditions in which the intervention of the few thousand anarchist partisans of *makhnovshchina* sparked off other peasant insurrections and tipped the balance against him.[102] Denikin's political outlook was limited, although like Makhno he was the son of a serf.[103] He was an experienced officer and was considered capable of large-scale strategising, unlike Kornilov. However, he was also a Great Russian chauvinist, used to thinking in terms of a 'united, great and indivisible Russia', and ignorant of nationalist or anti-White feeling in the borderlands. His base of popular support in such industrial cities as Khar'kov, with its 'bolshevised' factory workers, was limited to the urban middle class. He regarded the Makhno movement as barbaric, destructive, the antithesis of what the Whites stood for, an existential threat to Russian history, tradition and culture.[104] Golovanov has described the conflict between Denikin and his enemies as 'a terrible, tragic incompatibility ... two cultures, two lifestyles ... [that] clashed and fought' with no understanding or empathy.[105] Believing in grand abstractions such as freedom, justice and the rule of law, Denikin refused to take overtly political decisions, hoping instead to keep a coalition of conservatives and liberals together on a platform of simple anti-Communism.[106] He left 'politics' to the shady intriguers who followed his camp, relying heavily, for example, on his unpopular advisor, I. P. Romanovskii, who was distrusted by his officers.[107]

However, it was the behaviour of his soldiers, and most especially those in the garrisons behind the lines, that cost him any chance of popular support.[108] His commanders, former Imperial officers, were used to wild living and easy money.[109] The flow of financial and material aid from the Allies helped to create a thriving, speculative black market in White areas. Nurse's uniforms, lingerie, summer kit for British officers, good quality cloth, were all goods which ended up sooner or later in the hands of those with ready money or with influence to peddle.[110] Illegal or arbitrary arrest was common. One of Denikin's generals ran a protection racket to cream off the profits from gambling operations, and White officers resorted openly to the armed robbery of terrified civilians. Corruption was accompanied by brutality. A diary by a White officer, captured by the *makhnovtsy*, described prisoners being killed by being tied to hand-grenades; others were mutilated and tortured on red-hot iron sheets.[111] Denikin's chaplain wrote that 'depravity has reached the point of absolute shamelessness [...The army] is nothing but a gang of thieves'.[112] The population of Guliaipole was specially targeted: ' ... it was the officers' revenge against the revolution ... peasants were shot, houses were destroyed and hundreds of wagon-loads of food ... were sent to the Don and the Kuban ... Nearly all the Jewish women in the village were raped'.[113]

The Bolsheviks were galvanised into intense political activity. In Kiev they held meetings, conferences and street demonstrations, and produced wall-newspapers, while the regular newspapers proclaimed a crisis: those who were not for the Bolsheviks were against them. The party proclaimed its slogans – 'All against Denikin!', 'All to fight the Ukrainian counter-revolutionaries!', and now 'All to fight the bandit Makhno!' The Bolsheviks claimed that the *makhnovtsy* were objectively helping Denikin, even though they were fighting against him. One poster showed a giant Red Army soldier with a dwarfish Makhno hooked onto the end of his bayonet.[114]

Accounts differ as to whether Makhno now sought recruits, and whether they were available. According to Arshinov, Denikin's repressive policies, both in restoring the old order and in forbidding any manifestations of Ukrainian nationalism, drove large numbers into the ranks of the *makhnovtsy*.[115] Many peasants were war-weary and unwilling to believe propaganda or to take up arms, but the brutality of the White occupation compelled them to flee, and Makhno's detachments provided a place of refuge.[116] Initially, Makhno had attempted to make a stand at the Kichkas Bridge across the Dnepr, about 12 kilometres southwest of Aleksandrovsk, but the Whites outnumbered him. Around 17 June he heard that several members of his headquarters had been shot, including anarchists and Left SRs. Makhno and a group of 600, together with a detachment of 250 under Shchus, retreated on 24 June across the Dnepr to the right bank. Belash – contradicting Arshinov – testifies that Makhno refused all requests from units that wanted to join forces with him, on the grounds that it would weaken the front against Denikin, which was facing severe difficulties.[117] The Red 14th Army, which had been created from the remains of the Ukrainian 2nd Army at the time of the dissolution of the Ukrainian front, was cut off to the south, in the region of Krivoi Rog. It was trying to push north under the young commander I. E. Iakir, who eventually managed to rescue several divisions from the closing trap and march them nearly 500 kilometres northwards.

While these processes were unfolding, the question of relations with the Grigor'ev movement remained an unresolved problem for the *makhnovtsy*. Both groups were operating in roughly the same territory, with Grigor'ev blocking Makhno's line of retreat westwards. But there were also problems of a political character. Aleksei Chubenko recounts that a group of anarchists went by car to talk to Grigor'ev and report back. When they arrived at the village where Grigor'ev's group had been based, they found a large crowd gathered around the bodies of 161 Jewish people who had been killed in a pogrom: 'when we saw this picture, we understood completely … we saw that [Grigor'ev] could never be our confederate'.[118]

Makhno began to consider eliminating Grigor'ev and absorbing his troops into the insurgent army.[119] Accounts differ about what actually happened.[120] One version says Makhno called a congress of insurgents from the provinces of Ekaterinoslav, Kherson and the Tauride, to discuss a programme of action for the partisans of Ukraine. Both Grigor'ev and Makhno were scheduled speakers. The conference met in the village of Sentovo, near Aleksandriia, on 27 July 1919, in the presence of about 20,000 peasant soldiers. Grigor'ev spoke first, asserting that the Bolsheviks were the real enemies of the working masses. They had to be driven from Ukraine by any means, even if it meant making common cause with Denikin. He himself was ready to make such an alliance with the Whites. After the Bolsheviks had been finished off, it would be possible to review the situation afresh.

In Makhno's eyes this speech sealed Grigor'ev's fate. Speaking next, he declared that the only possible kind of struggle against Bolshevism was a revolutionary one, and that to join forces with counterrevolutionary generals was criminal adventurism. To advocate such a course of action was to behave as an enemy of the people. Makhno demanded that Grigor'ev should account for the pogrom that he had organised in May in Elisavetgrad, and for his other anti-Semitic speeches and actions. 'Such scoundrels as Grigor'ev are a disgrace', declared Makhno, 'they cannot be allowed among the ranks of honest revolutionary toilers!' At this point gunfire broke out between the two groups of leaders and within a few minutes, Grigor'ev and his aides were dead.[121] Aleksei Chubenko claimed that he fired the fatal shots.[122]

After Grigor'ev's death, Makhno, Chubenko and other anarchist leaders addressed the assembled partisans, taking full responsibility for killing the *ataman*, and offering them the chance to join the insurrectionary army. The next day, on 28 July, the general assembly passed a resolution that set out in full the political reasons for the executions: Grigor'ev's counter-revolutionary 'policy, acts and aims' and his string of brutal pogroms. The resolution ended by declaring that the *makhnovtsy* believed it was 'their revolutionary duty to take upon themselves the historical consequences of this assassination.'[123]

The consolidation of Makhno's and Grigor'ev's forces in Kherson, and the nationalist threat presented by the Petliurists and the Galicians in the west, alarmed the Bolsheviks. On 3 August the Central Committee of the KP(b)U passed a resolution on the 'Kulak Counterrevolution', warning of the dangers of unification.[124] The soldiers of the Red Army were demoralised and disillusioned by the Volunteer Army's successes, and regarded their officers with suspicion. In late July units in the Crimea mutinied, at the instigation of *makhnovtsy* who had retained their posts within the Red Army. They deposed or executed communist commanders, and moved northwards to join the main insurgent force. Groups of Red Army deserters also arrived from Novi Bug.[125] The Red Army brigade in Dolenskaia, on the left flank of the 12th Army, went over to Makhno in early August.[126] By the middle of the month Makhno, although on the defensive, was in control of most of the area north of Nikolaev.[127] The cavalry detachment that he took with him when he left his command in the Red Army had swelled to between 15,000 and 20,000 men,[128] and Makhno reorganised his forces into four brigades of infantry and cavalry, an artillery division and a machine-gun regiment with 500 guns. Fedor Shchus' commanded the cavalry, numbering about 2,000 men. A special cavalry squadron of 150 to 200 men accompanied the *bat'ko* on his raids and expeditions.[129]

Sources differ as to the strength of and the degree of organisation within the Insurgent Revolutionary Army of Ukraine (*makhnovtsy*). It is instructive to compare the accounts of Volin, Arshinov and Belash with an intelligence report compiled by a Ukrainian National Army officer.[130] The report was written in October, and covered ideology, advisers, troops, logistics and Makhno's attitude towards the Ukrainian National Republic (*Ukrains'ka Narodnia Respublika* or UNR). This was after Makhno's forces had been fighting the Whites for several months, and we know that a major reorganisation had taken place at the beginning of September. According to the report, the *makhnovtsy* had no uniforms and did not wear badges of rank, and military organisation was loose. Although some of Makhno's aides attempted to introduce conventional structures into the army, the *bat'ko*'s control remained absolute, arbitrary and impulsive.[131] Although figures of up to 50,000 men were put about, reported the officer, the actual fighting strength was nearer 5,000. To this he added another 3,000 transport, education and political workers, and a huge camp-following. The 1,500 cavalry were divided into two regiments, the remainder of the fighters into eight infantry regiments, including two units that had deserted from the Red Army. Transport included all kinds of wagons, with camels, mules and horses. The units had machine-guns, but there were only about 35 artillery pieces, without an adequate supply of shells. Herds of cattle and sheep tailed along behind the army.[132] By contrast, Belash describes a highly mobile army that at its height consisted of

> ... 40,000 infantry, 10,000 cavalry, 1,000 machine guns and 20 artillery pieces ... served by another 13,000 [non-combatants] ... the convoy consisted of 8,000 britzkas and *tachanki* for the infantry, another 2,000 carriages for the staff, communications and medical, 1,000 carriages with machine guns, 1,000 with artillery supplies and 500 carrying food ...[133]

The insurgents were under increasing pressure from Denikin's forces attempting to outflank them on the right.[134] The partisans pushed the *denikintsy* back a few kilometres in a counter-offensive, but the attack lost its momentum because of a shortage of ammunition. The area was not completely free of Bolshevik troops pushing northwards to make contact again with the main body of the Red Army.[135] The RVS in Odessa had already resolved that their first task was to try to eliminate the gangs of Makhno, Zabolotny, Zeleny and the other *atamany* who occupied the territory between the main lines of rail.[136] The rate of desertion was high, and rumours abounded: the Trans-Dnepr division reported that it was untrue that a group of sailors had gone over to Makhno, and that some fighters had even 'shot their friends rather than let them fall into Makhno's hands'.[137]

Makhno's retreat westwards and northwards into Kiev province lasted several weeks, and covered a distance of nearly 600 kilometres; it was later to assume epic proportions in the historiography of Makhno's apologists. The rallying cry was 'All who care for freedom and independence, stay in Ukraine and fight Denikin'. Sources claim that the army swelled 'not by the day but by the hour' with a 'mass of volunteers from cities and towns'.[138] Volin, who took part in the withdrawal and was a member of the VRS, left a vivid picture of the conditions under which it took place, some of the details of which confirm the account of the UNR intelligence officer mentioned above. The weather was hot and dry, and the column 'moved slowly, with thousands of cattle, with wagons of every kind, with its own food supply'.[139] Constantly harassed by the White Guards, the column was protected by cavalry and led by the main fighting force in *tachanki*, 'each drawn by two horses [with] the driver on the front seat and two soldiers behind … A huge black flag floated over the first carriage'.[140] The incessant harassment by Denikin's cavalry, who willingly accepted hand-to-hand combat, took its toll. For over a month the insurgents moved westwards, engaging daily in small, costly actions.[141] In late August, when Denikin's troops received reinforcements from Odessa and Voznesensk, Makhno's army and supply-train were driven away from the lines of rail, first destroying some armoured trains.[142] Now, the retreating insurgents were forced to move from village to village along dusty country side-roads.

Bolshevik intelligence reports revealed the confusion that reigned in August. Various small-scale peasant uprisings broke out, and Jews, commissars and even the wives of commissars were executed. Peasant women laced milk with poison and served it to Red Army soldiers.[143] The Reds dragged wounded *makhnovtsy* from infirmaries and shot them.[144] Agitation 'of a Makhnovist character' against the commissars was successful among Red Army soldiers, and the *makhnovtsy*, whenever possible, disarmed Red Army detachments, searched out the commissars, and offered the rest the chance to join the insurgency. The peasants were dissatisfied because the *makhnovtsy* requisitioned 'everything': the Cossacks, the communists and the Petliurists were seen as robbers too. One report mentions the involvement of Latvians, Serbs and a few Chinese.[145] Nevertheless, the insurgents attempted to establish some principles of behaviour. An order dated 5 August began by emphasising that there was no place in the struggle for the pursuit of personal gain, and that the 'rich bourgeois class' and the Soviet punitive detachments were the real enemy. Military discipline was necessary, and drunkenness was a 'serious crime'. Insurgents were to behave in a 'polite and comradely' manner to civilians.[146] On 1 September, the insurgents called a meeting of unit representatives to discuss restructuring the army for rapid mobility in partisan warfare. A new VRS with thirty members was elected, with military control and cultural-educational departments. The name 'Revolutionary Insurgent Army of Ukraine (Makhnovist)' was adopted and a staff headquarters was established, with Viktor Belash responsible for organisation and management.[147]

In early September the Whites again seized the initiative, advancing rapidly northwards along a broad front. On the left too, White units pushed the Red Army back from Kiev north-eastwards towards Chernigov, on the other side of the Dnepr, hard up against the positions of the Polish Front. The main push ran along a line running due north from Khar'kov through Kursk, Orel' and Tula, home of the vitally important armaments factory, the *Tul'skii Oruzheinyi Zavod*. The Volunteer Army led the assault under General V. Z. Mai-Maevskii, whose reputation for reckless courage was matched only by his drunkenness and debauchery.[148] The thrust at the centre soon threatened to become a rout as the exhausted Red units fell back. Their field commander, Vladimir Selivachev, died – apparently of typhus – on 17 September.[149] Lenin complained constantly: 'in reality, we have stagnation, almost collapse.'; 'Denikin will triple his forces, get tanks'; 'it simply means destruction.'[150] On 20 September the Volunteer Army captured Kursk; a few days earlier cavalry units under General Shkuro had taken Voronezh.[151] By this time Bolshevik units were deserting to the White side en masse.

In mid-September, Makhno's column arrived in the area to the south-east of Uman' near the junction of the rivers Iatran' and Siniukha. 'Caught in a ring of enemies, trapped in a hopeless situation, the *makhnovtsy* fought desperately': they were running out of ammunition and artillery shells, and were being pushed back towards Uman'.[152] The Directory occupied the city of Uman' itself, to the north-west. To the south-east were White forces under the General Iakov Slashchev.[153] Slashchev recognised Makhno's military qualities: Makhno, he wrote, moved quickly and energetically, and even imposed 'a rather severe discipline'. Actions against him were 'always serious'.[154]

The Whites had largely ignored the Petliurists during the final drive towards Moscow. The *makhnovtsy* were uncertain what to do about the Petliurists.[155] To take on another enemy needlessly might well have resulted in the annihilation of both the insurgent and the nationalist armies: Belash wrote that 'we were happy with any ally against Denikin'.[156] The *makhnovtsy* – short of ammunition and with 8,000 wounded men – decided to ask the Petliurists to agree to remain neutral and to admit the wounded partisans to hospitals in Uman' for treatment.[157] At this point, after a catastrophic encounter with the left wing of the retreating Red Army, Petliura's Galicians decided to try to make an alliance with Makhno.[158] They made contact on 14 September, and the next day Makhno visited Uman' to conclude the treaty.[159] He wanted to barter some artillery shells for rifle ammunition, but this was refused. Strict military neutrality was to be observed and political disagreements were to be put to one side. Liaison officers were exchanged, and the wounded insurgents were transferred to the hospitals.[160]

Both sides regarded this agreement as entirely disposable. The insurgent propaganda section soon began to distribute leaflets among the nationalist soldiers, attacking Petliura as an enemy of the people and defender of privilege.[161] The nationalists, for their part, opened negotiations with Denikin and Makhno's apologists later accused them of permitting the encirclement of partisan positions by the Whites.[162] Possibly they could not have prevented it, for the Galicians came under attack from Denikin's forces soon afterwards.[163] By 25 September Makhno's army, free of its wounded, found itself surrounded by Denikin's regiments in an area of about ten square kilometres of wooded steppe around the village of Peregonovka.[164]

5

The Long March West and the Battle at Peregonovka

The White attempt to encircle and liquidate Makhno's forces ended in failure with the engagement at Peregonovka in late September and Makhno's break-through to the east behind the White lines. As we have seen in the previous chapter, by the end of August the exhausted *makhnovtsy* had abandoned the lines of rail along which they had been retreating, to shift deeper into the countryside, still moving westwards from village to village.[1] The *denikintsy* had been reinforced by fresh troops, and the insurgents had reorganised for greater mobility, but were running short of ammunition: two out of every three skirmishes were raids to capture supplies.[2] The White encirclement aimed to prevent Makhno from making contact with the nationalist forces of the Ukrainian Directory, a source of supply for ammunition, and to keep them away from Elisavetgrad, on the right bank 300 kilometres south of Kiev. From Elisavetgrad, the way east was wide open. At the same time, the *denikintsy* gained access, this far west, to the north–south line of rail and supply running from the port of Odessa through Voznesensk.[3]

This was a critical moment for the anarchist movement in Ukraine, but its significance for the *political* outcome of the revolution in broader terms may be disputed. In a book on Makhno published in 2011, Viacheslav Azarov wrote that his text was intended to analyse the process of

> ... social construction in the Free Region, and the struggle between the two concepts of the '*soviet*', anarchist and Bolshevik. *Consequently, the heroic pages of the Makhno epic – the retreat to the west of the Insurgent Army ... the decisive battle of Peregonovka ... all remain outside its scope.*[4]

This is an important point of emphasis and focus. To highlight the *military aspects* of Makhno's activities is to risk losing sight of the *political* claim – that *makhnovshchina* was an example of anarchist socio-political practice in action.[5] To highlight Makhno's *personal* characteristics – his alleged cruelty or his excessive drinking – is to miss the point that at its peak the movement he led, broadly anarchist in its ideology, attracted the active support of tens of thousands of men and women, and controlled much of southern Ukraine. Like the

Antonov rebellion in Tambov province, it was necessary for Makhno to articulate 'a political program [... as] part of the larger project of providing structure and organization'.[6] In the absence of such a programme – in Makhno's case, as Azarov points out, the struggle for 'power of the Soviets' against 'Soviet Power'[7] – it is hard to see how the movement would have attracted followers. The point is made in the movement's draft declaration of late 1919, which argues that 'the meaning and significance of the events in Ukraine should not be focussed on our army as such, *but on the broad popular movement that is unfolding in Ukraine* and whose defensive fighting force is the army'.[8] This text, the *Proekt Deklaratsii Revoliutsionnoi Povstancheskoi Armii Ukrainy (Makhnovtsev)*, was approved by the Military Revolutionary Council at a meeting on October 29, 1919 and is an important source for the programmatic thinking of Makhno and the *makhnovtsy*.[9] The document was a draft for discussion, produced in a hurry, and edited over a period of a month or so by Volin, in August 1919.[10] It was never submitted for adoption and ratification to a general congress.

The key concept in the draft declaration is that the Soviets should be constituted as the principal – but transitional – structure for the democratic expression of the 'voices' of *all workers*, regardless of their relative class position or their adherence to any particular political organisation or party. Rather, the declaration argues, forms of social organisation must be left to the creative initiative of 'the people':

> ... providing the people with a full opportunity to freely forge forms of economic and social life will naturally and inevitably lead to the establishment by the overwhelming working majority of the people of socialist forms of community. We find that these forms can only be found and forged by the working masses themselves, provided they have completely free and independent social and economic creativity. We therefore consider it impractical and even fatal to impose our beliefs on the working masses with political force or any kind of dictatorship; we consider it would be disastrous for us to lead the masses by controlling them from above.[11]

The role of the Soviets, or whatever other forms of deliberative bodies might be created, is left undefined:

> ... free peasants and workers naturally create – everywhere at local level – their socio-economic organisations ... In order to broadly unify mutual relations, all these organisations – production, professional, distribution, transport, and others – naturally create structures from the bottom up, in the form of economic councils that fulfill the technical task of regulating social and economic life on a large scale. These councils can be *volost*, city,

regional ... organised as needed on a free basis. They are by no means polit-ical institutions ...[12]

The declaration rejected a codified legal system or a fixed judicial or administra-tive apparatus, arguing that bureaucratic organisation leads to the destruction of justice 'at its root'.[13] Even the soviet itself, as a relatively formal structure, was seen as a transitional form that would be superseded. In the context of the civil war, these theoretical positions mostly remained unrealised in practice: never-theless, the movement strove towards their realisation, and their revolutionary potential was taken seriously, in one way or another, by large segments of the left-bank rural population. A later 'Declaration of the *Makhnovtsy*', prepared in 1921, marked a shift in important aspects: it declared a 'dictatorship of labour' and a system of trade unions led by anarchists, foreshadowing the thinking of the 'Platformists' in the 1920s. Makhno was promptly accused of 'bonapartism' by his comrades.[14]

Some accounts of the Makhno insurgency place what even Azarov calls the 'decisive battle' at Peregonovka at the centre of the narrative, together with the rapid advance eastwards in the following weeks. In this perspective, Peregon-ovka was the key moment when the anarchists saved the revolution. Arshinov had no doubts:

> ... the *complete defeat* of the Denikinists in their struggle against *makhnovsh-china* in southern Russia [sic] *determined the fate of their entire campaign against the Russian revolution*. It is necessary to emphasise the historic fact that the honour of having *annihilated the Denikin counter-revolution* in the autumn of 1919 belongs almost entirely to the *makhnovtsy*. If not [for them] the Whites would have entered Moscow ...[15]

This line has been influential among historians sympathetic to *makhnovsh-china*. Malet quotes from an obituary of Makhno asserting that 'it is certain that Denikin's defeat owed more to the peasant insurrection under the black Makhnovist banner than to the successes of Trotski's regular army'.[16] In Palij's opinion, the defeat 'decided Denikin's fate'.[17] Skirda states flatly that the battle 'determined the outcome of the civil war'.[18] Shubin follows the line, describing the 'sudden blow inflicted ... near Peregonovka' as having been 'devastating',[19] and quoting a remark attributed to a White officer that 'none of us knew that *at that precise moment* nationalist Russia had lost the war'.[20]

In the broader historiography of the revolution and civil war, this narrative earns Makhno his place: after Peregonovka, the rampage eastwards cut Deni-kin's lines of supply and halted his advance on Moscow. Chamberlin argues that Denikin's policies had allowed the landlords, police chiefs 'and other decidedly unpopular figures' to reappear, and he had 'thrown almost all his reliable troops on the front'. Hence, Makhno was able 'to play a most devastating role' behind Denikin's lines.[21] Mawdsley cites White officers to the effect that the removal of regiments from the frontline to deal with Makhno allowed the Red Army to turn the White flank at Orel' and launch a counter-attack.[22] Lincoln agrees, pointing to the destruction of the armoury at Berdiansk by Makhno in early October as a heavy blow, denying the Whites the artillery shells needed for the assault on Orel'.[23] Pipes says that the diversion of White regiments to fight Makhno 'had a very detrimental effect on the battle for Orel and Kursk, *which decided the Civil War*'.[24] A few voices disagree: Figes, quoting Trotsky, argues that 'the *entire fate of the Soviet regime* hinged on the defence of Tula' where Russia's main armaments factory was located.[25] Litvinov believes that *even in the absence of a breakthrough at Uman'*, the Bolsheviks 'would have managed to organise the defence of Tula and Moscow'.[26]

The engagement was small-scale, with perhaps six to eight thousand troops involved on Makhno's side, against 12 to 15 thousand White Guards. Casualties were 'at most, several thousand' and the *makhnovtsy* captured 23 guns and 100 machine-guns and took a few hundred prisoners.[27] For this reason Vasilii Golovanov urges caution, pointing out that the engagement was actually a 'quite modest' event, and that 'everything that happened after the battle at Peregonovka indicates that we do not really know Makhno's role in Denikin's defeat'.[28] White Guard memoirs – with the exception of two or three first-hand participant accounts[29] – recognise the battle's importance but tend towards modest assessments. Denikin conceded that Makhno's 'bold step' in attacking the White cavalry regiments allowed him to advance eastwards 'with unusual speed'. Within a couple of weeks, the uprising had spread 'over a vast territory between the lower Dnepr and the Sea of Azov ... The situation became serious and necessitated exceptional measures'.[30] This is some way short of admitting 'annihilation'. Slashchev, the White commander on the spot, conceded that the *makhnovtsy* broke the line and destroyed two regiments, but found it hard to consider this 'a fateful historical victory'.[31] With the exception of Kubanin, Soviet texts on the civil war are generally silent about the moment, although some published contemporary documents do mention collaboration between the *makhnovtsy* and Petliura's troops.[32] Kubanin, writing in 1927, points out that the anarchists were trapped, and could not trust Petliura, who wanted to keep the peace with the Volunteer Army.[33] There are of course first-hand accounts from various sources,[34] and Skirda has published a narrative synthesis.[35]

General Slashchev, the commander of the White forces confronting Makhno, faced a dilemma. If he attacked the *makhnovtsy* head on, it was likely to be a costly operation. If he waited for a better opportunity, Makhno's raids behind his lines would become more frequent. One of his detachments was 'completely exhausted by uninterrupted battles' and another was 'under-strength and demoralised'. The raids of the *makhnovtsy*, in Slashchev's judgement, were threatening to cause panic in the White ranks.[36] In clashes between the two sides, the *makhnovtsy* were constantly mauled by the better-disciplined White cavalry. The Whites were energetic and obstinate opponents and (unlike the Red cavalry), willingly accepted hand-to-hand combat, charging at their enemies 'at full speed'.[37]

By the time Makhno halted near Uman' and agreed with the Petliurists to hand over his wounded, a breakthrough to the left-bank was his only chance of surviving encirclement.[38] By 20 September the Whites had intelligence that he was looking for such an opportunity.[39] To prevent this, White units needed to maintain contact with each other on the flanks, strategically exploiting their superior numbers.[40] Their failure to do this – in an extremely fluid situation – gave Makhno a temporary tactical advantage in numbers over one regiment, and presented him with a chance that he was not slow to exploit.[41]

Initially the Petliurists were ranged to the northwest of the insurgents, with the Whites along a front to the southeast, around the small settlement of Golta. From 19 to 21 September there were minor clashes around the villages of Peregonovka, Kruten'koe, Pokotilovo, and Podvyskoe. Peregonovka changed hands several times. On 22 September Slashchev began the operation to encircle and eliminate the *makhnovtsy*. The First Simferopol' Officers' Regiment – which did much of the subsequent fighting – advanced in the centre on the line Kruten'koe-Tekucha. On the right, units under General Skliarov advanced towards Uman', and on the left flank were two infantry divisions and a regiment of Cossacks. The Simferopol' regiment concentrated in Peregonovka, with the *makhnovtsy* occupying high ground east of Kruten'koe and Rogovo, profiting from Skliarov's movement towards Uman'. During the advance, the Simferopol' regiment lost contact with Skliarov, with disastrous consequences.[42]

The fighting took place in a hilly area divided by ravines and by the confluence of the wide river Syniukha to the east, with its tributary the Iatran' to the west. On each side of the rivers lay patches of dense woodland. The village of Peregonovka lay due south of Rogovo, on the Iatran', with Kruten'koe to the west with forest behind it. The Siniukha could only be crossed at Novoarkhangel'sk to the north, or at Ternovka to the south. The area between the rivers was to become a death trap for the 1st Simferopol' Regiment.[43] From 21 to 25 September fighting continued, with both sides sustaining losses. The Whites repeatedly found themselves under artillery bombardment from the *makhnovtsy*, but persisted in their advance, dislodging the insurgents from the high ground and driving them from the forest near Peregonovka and Kruten'koe. By the 25th, partly because of poor coordination by the Whites, which permitted the insurgents to fall upon the exposed flanks of individual units, the *makhnovtsy* had regained some ground.

By 26 September Skliarov had occupied Uman', opening a gap of over 40 kilometres between Uman' and Rogovo (on the Iatran' north of Peregonovka).

Makhno exploited this mistake to the full.[44] During a brief lull in fighting, he regrouped and concentrated his forces on the right bank of the Iatran'. This manoeuvre consisted of moving troops northwards and eastwards from Semiduby and other villages to position them opposite the Simferopol' Regiment's weak right flank.[45] According to the White accounts, the *denikintsy* repulsed partisan attacks for two days, but on the night of 25-6 September they observed enemy movement. The Simferopol' commander reported that his troops were exhausted and isolated in a highly dangerous position facing massed enemy forces. The only response from Uman' was an expression of thanks for the regiment's heroism, and a request to hold out for another twenty-four hours, so that the encirclement could be completed.[46]

Meanwhile Makhno had delivered a morale-boosting speech to his troops, also tired and discouraged, ill-clad, ill-fed and running out of ammunition. The 600-kilometre retreat, declared the *bat'ko*, had been a strategic necessity, and now 'the real war was about to begin'. That evening a brigade of *makhnovtsy* made a feint near Kruten'koe, skirmishing with the Whites and pulling back westwards, thus creating the impression that a breakthrough was not imminent. Then, under cover of darkness, the whole insurgent army began to move to the east.[47] In the early hours on 26 or 27 September the *makhnovtsy* exploded some ordnance to lighten their baggage train and as a signal to attack on all fronts.[48] Makhno personally moved to the eastern sector, on the right bank of the Iatran', where his forces were concentrated, and pressed home an attack.[49] The *makhnovtsy* were under serious pressure from the Whites until Makhno took charge and led a cavalry attack against the exposed White flank.[50] Arshinov describes the *insurgents* as 'outnumbered', which although true strategically was not so tactically. He implies that the Whites received reinforcements during the fighting, but Al'mendinger complains that his right flank remained exposed and unsupported, and that coordination was poor.[51] By mid-morning, the battle was hanging in the balance:

> ... the outnumbered and exhausted *makhnovtsy* began to lose ground [... it] seemed that the battle and with it the whole cause of the insurgents was lost. The order was given for everyone, even the women, to be ready to fire on the enemy ...[52]

Slashchev, who had tried to set a trap for Makhno, was now about to fall into a trap himself. The Whites, professional soldiers, were guilty on numerous occasions of under-estimating their peasant enemies,[53] and even invented a fictional German staff officer, Colonel Kleist, supposedly the operational genius behind Makhno's successes. Slashchev commented on this rumour that, true or not, 'Makhno was able to conduct operations, showed remarkable organisational skills, and was able to influence a large part of the local population, which supported him and replenished his ranks ... Makhno was a very serious opponent and deserved special attention ...'[54] In the 1920s, articles by Soviet military specialists agreed that Makhno's forces survived owing to 'the manoeuvrability of the units, their ability to disperse quickly, and also serious miscalculations by the Red Command'.[55] At the other extreme, it has been claimed with national Ukrainian pride that Makhno invented a kind of *blitzkrieg*.[56] He learned military skills against the Austro-Hungarians in 1918: he understood that a war of manoeuvre was the most effective way of conducting guerrilla operations in the wide open steppe. Forest cover was scarce, and his units could easily be isolated, with no hope of reinforcements.[57] Engaging the enemy only when he had tactical advantage in numbers, Makhno's use of massed *tachanki* – four-wheeled carts with machine-guns mounted on them, pulled by two or sometimes four horses – enabled him to concentrate sudden withering fire on enemy units before a cavalry attack.[58] His commanders, some of whom had been non-commissioned officers during the war, were encouraged to take bold, independent initiatives. These tactics were effective in combat away from large settlements; but the *makhnovtsy* were less effective at securing captured towns when confronting conventional armies. They avoided

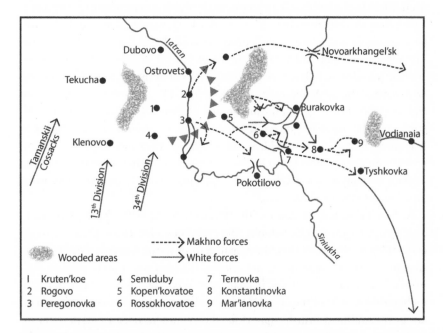

Map 5.1   The Engagement at Peregonovka, September 1919

The cavalry and *tachanka* engagement near the village of Peregonovka, in which the insurgents took tactical advantage of wooded terrain and the confluence of wide rivers, resulted in a breakthrough eastwards by the *makhnovtsy*. Based on maps published by White participants in the 1960s. (Cartographer: Jenny Sandler)

large-scale positional engagements unless compelled to do so, and were often defeated in such actions.[59]

The White machine-gun companies on the right were pushed back by insurgent infantry into the forest northeast of Konen'kovato, which was impassable for horses or heavy equipment. Emerging from the woodland, the Whites encountered more insurgents, this time with artillery support. Under continuous cavalry attack, and themselves running out of ammunition, the Whites continued to retreat towards the Siniukha, at the same time signalling desperately for support.[60] They were making for the southern ford at Ternovka, which was held by other White units, but they were also 'moving over trackless country, across large ploughed fields' and did not know exactly where they were. As it turned out, they were too far north.[61]

After retreating about 20 kilometres in hot conditions and with heavy losses, the Whites reached a bend in the river Siniukha to the north of Burakovka. Attempts to cross under fire failed, and some men drowned.[62] The units began to move southwards towards Ternovka, but were stopped by cavalry outside Burakovka, and prepared to stand their ground. At this point they discovered a dike across the river, and about 100 men succeeded in escaping to the left bank, from where they moved, still under pursuit, towards Konstantinovka. However, by this time there were more *makhnovtsy* blocking their way forward, and about 60 men under a Captain Gattenburger covered the escape of carts with the wounded to Novoukrainka, to the southeast. All the members of Gattenburger's rear-guard were killed.[63] Makhno's assessment of this action was generous: he described the 1st Simferopol' as 'distinguished by its extreme steadfastness and determination'.[64] A significant amount of materiel was captured: 20 field guns, over 100 machine-guns, and 600 prisoners, of whom 120 were officers.[65] According to Belash, the Whites suffered 6,000 casualties in the northern sector, with 4,000 others killed by the local peasantry while attempting to flee; perhaps as many as 5,000 Whites were taken prisoner.[66] Captured horses were distributed to the local peasants.[67]

As they had feared, the defeat of the Whites opened Makhno's path to the east, back to the Dnepr and Guliaipole. The remaining obstacles were a few weak garrisons left behind as Denikin prepared to push for Moscow. For Denikin, anarchism was a 'tragic farce', and *makhnovshchina* was 'purely popular and robber, but in no way political' in character[68] – but he still put a price of half a million rubles on Makhno's head.[69] Winston Churchill, pursuing a campaign in favour of continued British support for the Whites, advised Denikin to try to 'make use' of the 'Green Guards', whose numbers were growing, but he made no attempt to do so.[70] His soldiers believed that another Makhno-Red Army alliance would be an unbeatable combination, and that if that alliance were forged, the war would be over.[71] General Wrangel, more politically astute than Denikin, attempted to persuade his commander to take steps to face the threat behind the lines, but Denikin shrugged him off: 'we will finish [Makhno] off in the twinkling of an eye'. Wrangel records that this attitude filled him with 'doubt and apprehension'.[72]

* * *

The outside world, including the Bolsheviks, came to hear of the battle only indirectly. The 12th Red Army was aware that Petliura's forces had been in the Kazatina, Zhmerinka and Vapnarkia regions in Kiev and Podolia provinces in late September and early October, and that there was a loose agreement with Makhno against Denikin. In a reference to the battle, a later Bolshevik intelligence report noted that 'according to our information, Petliurist troops together with Makhno's fought a battle against the Whites in the Uman'-Gaisin region in mid-October [sic], after which Makhno and his units advanced through Aleksandrovsk and captured Pologi and Melitopol".[73] Fighting had indeed broken out between the forces of the Directory and the denikintsy near Uman', but in September, and not in alliance with the makhnovtsy.[74] Kiev newspapers reported inaccurately in early October that Petliura's forces had beaten the insurgents, who 'broke and ran'.[75]

After the engagement at Peregonovka, Makhno's forces turned eastwards again, and divided into three groups.[76] Denikin's headquarters were seriously concerned, but lacked solid intelligence – they did not know whether Makhno's army was in an alliance with Petliura, and they were unclear as to his objectives. Slashchev assigned only one regiment in pursuit.[77] Makhno's main central column consisted of two army corps, a machine-gun regiment and cavalry, and followed the route Dobrovelychkivka-Novo Ukrainka-Vyshnyakivka-Verblyuzhka (at which point Makhno detoured to Pishchanyi Brid to visit his mother-in-law for two days) Petrove-Sofiivka-Chumaky-Khortytsia, and finally Aleksandrovsk.[78] The left hand column, to the north, consisted of infantry regiments, and moved via Novoarkhanhel's'k-Velyka Vyska-Elisavetgrad-Adzhamka-Nova Praha-Novyi Starodub-Kam'yanka and finally to Ekaterinoslav. The southernmost, right hand column moved through Pishchanyi Brid-Sofiivka-Bobrynets-Dolynska-Kryvyi Rih-Apostolove-Nikopol'.[79] The march met some challenges: the northern column, commanded by Kalashnikov, became involved in clashes with the Whites near Elisavetgrad and – ignoring orders – occupied Krivoi Rog. Nevertheless, within ten days the makhnovtsy had won control of most of southern Ukraine, advancing as far south-east as Mariupol'.

The detachments diverged from each other by as much as 30–55 kilometres.[80] The central column slowed down and may have rested when Makhno visited his mother-in-law in Pischanyi Brid.[81] Volin claims that tachanki with sprung suspension could cover between 60–70 kilometres a day, and if needed even 90 to 100 kilometres a day.[82] Viktor Belash says the army covered 350 versty

(373 kilometres) from Uman' in seven days, a rate of advance of 53 kilometres a day. Arshinov suggests that the day after the battle Makhno was already over 95 kilometres away from Peregonovka, with the main body of his army about 50 kilometres behind him – rapid movement for tired troops immediately after combat, even if mounted or moving in *tachanki*. On 28 September, again according to Arshinov, the different columns captured Dolinskaia (220 km. from Peregonovka), Krivoi Rog (265 km.), and Nikopol' (370 km.); on 29 September they took the Kichkas bridge (465 km.) and occupied Aleksandrovsk. In his memoirs Denikin states that Makhno only reached Guliaipole, 590 kilometres from Uman', on 7 October, having covered the distance using *tachanki* to move the infantry.[83] This would have represented an average rate of march of 50–55 kilometres a day for 10 or 11 days.

Independent sources throw some light on this question of the rate of advance. John Hodgson, a British army officer who served with Denikin in 1919, says that Makhno only reached Aleksandrovsk in the first week in October, when he blew up the railway bridge and cut the telegraph wires: this confirms Denikin's account.[84] The differences may be attributable to varied calculations of the distances involved. Using the folded sketch map in the original edition of Arshinov's book, which is drawn to a scale of 66.66 *versty* to the inch, the distance *as the crow flies* from Uman' to Guliaipole is 445 *versty* or approximately 475 kilometres. Using modern maps, the direct distance can be calculated as 480 kilometres.[85] But the distance by road was longer, around 570 kilometres. For the *makhnovtsy* to have arrived in Guliaipole sometime between 7 and 11 October, would have required a rate of advance of between 40 to 50 kilometres a day, in *tachanki*. Was this feasible? Perhaps: conventional military wisdom has it that on level terrain, at cavalry pace, following trails or roadways, and in good weather conditions, mounted troops on fit horses can cover between 50 and 80 kilometres a day, riding for ten hours a day with rest breaks. Horses pulling vehicles such as *tachanki* can cover about half that distance per day – between 25 to 40 kilometres. These speeds are sustainable for perhaps four days at a time without changing horses. We know from contemporary sources that fresh horses were indeed requisitioned: '... the *makhnovtsy* have caused a lot of trouble ... they go extremely fast, *capturing horses and wagons* ...'[86] Nevertheless, the story is that the *makhnovtsy* – who were not fresh troops, but men exhausted by an earlier two-month retreat, the last part over rough terrain in hot weather, followed by a brutal action against a resolute enemy – sustained this pace for perhaps as long as two weeks.

An alternative interpretation, supported to some extent by contemporary documentation, is that this was not *exclusively* a forced march by an army, although that did take place, but simultaneously the spread of generalised peasant insurrection. Even at the time, the view was expressed in local newspapers that the situation behind the lines was like a tinderbox, only in need

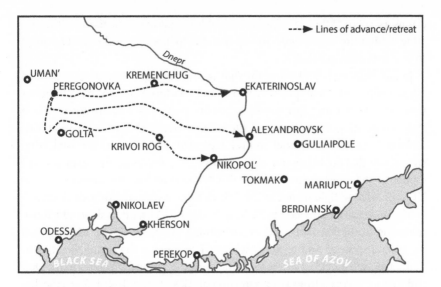

Map 5.2   The Advance Eastwards by the *Makhnovtsy*, late 1919

This is a detailed mapping of the three-pronged advance eastwards after Peregonovka back into Makhno's main area of influence, cutting the White supply lines to the north. The advance was accompanied by widespread peasant uprisings. (Cartographer: Jenny Sandler)

of a spark to detonate.[87] The Whites anxiously issued stern warnings that if any villages gave shelter to rebels, or 'facilitated the provision of food', then 'such a treacherous village' would be 'mercilessly punished'.[88] Additionally, the columns gradually broke up into smaller units with specific missions, confusing enemy intelligence even further.[89] Belash paused from time to time to raise autonomous units in different places, as was common practice among the partisans:[90] for example, peasant groups in western Ukraine hid weapons in caves and ravines in readiness for an uprising.[91] Trotsky warned in December 1919 that 'partisan detachments in Ukraine easily arise and disappear, being dissolved into the mass of the armed peasant population'.[92] Denikin described the spread of the insurrection across southeastern Ukraine as having been *like wildfire*, and estimated that the insurgent army grew significantly, to a number somewhere between 10,000 and 40,000 men by the middle of October. He mentions the existence of semi-autonomous groups which often operated independently.[93] The apparently rapid growth in numbers plus the existence of such semi-independent groups suggest that existing bands may simply have become active after Makhno's breakthrough.[94] There were also cases of whole detachments deserting to join Makhno.[95] Litvinov argues along similar lines, quoting White and Red estimates of the number of *makhnovtsy* that range from 15,000 through 40–50 thousand to as many as 100,000 effectives (Belash

claims 250,000).[96] But, says Litvinov, 'Makhno had many partisan units operating behind the White lines' and he was able to 'knock together regular units
from partisan formations'.[97]

In any case, by late October the *makhnovtsy*, in one shape or another, had
taken control of Melitopol', Berdiansk and Mariupol' – only 95 kilometres
from Denikin's campaign headquarters in Taganrog. The insurgents were
also approaching Sinel'nikov and threatening Denikin's artillery base at Volnovakh.[98] As their territorial control expanded, Makhno and the leadership
were aware that the behaviour of the insurgents in newly-occupied areas – and
especially the cities – was 'a matter of life and death' for the movement. The
VRS appealed to fighters not to rob, kill, or behave violently towards citizens.[99]

The *makhnovtsy* crossed the Kichkas Bridge in Aleksandrovsk on 5 October,
returning to the left-bank and overwhelming White garrisons. Makhno had
no general strategy, and repeated what he had done in the spring, heading to
Berdiansk, and blocking access to Crimea and Odessa by the Whites in the Don
and Kuban.[100] Apart from the occupation of Aleksandrovsk and Ekaterinoslav,
which changed hands several times, Makhno's hardest blow against the *denikintsy* at this time was the recapture of Berdiansk and the probably accidental
destruction of the Varshavskii Armoury, with 20 million rounds of ammunition and 60,000 artillery shells destined for Kiev, Kursk and Orel'.[101] The British
had warned Denikin that Berdiansk was vulnerable, but he had taken no steps
either to secure or to move the munitions, claiming he had no railway wagons
available.[102]

Berdiansk was well-defended by 2,000 troops, including a detachment of
Kuban Cossacks, with access to the sea for reinforcements and supplies.[103]
However, the local White Guards had carried out mass executions of workers
and peasants suspected of Red sympathies, and were consequently deeply
unpopular.[104] Makhno's forces surrounded the city at dawn on 8 October.[105]
From outside the city, according to one eyewitness account, Makhno mobilised a group of local fishermen, who captured some White artillery and
bombarded the town. Scenes of confusion followed, with fleeing Whites and
bourgeois citizens crowding onto steamships – insurgent artillery fire sank two
of these vessels.[106] Then, during the battle for the city, the Varshavskii Armoury
suddenly blew up:

> ... the earth suddenly trembled, buildings swayed, windows shattered ... A
> massive explosion followed by an even bigger one ... The explosions buried
> the White Guards who remained on the promontory, and for a long time
> afterwards the waves washed their torn bodies up onto the shore.[107]

Despite the destruction, the *makhnovtsy*'s haul of captured materiel was impres-
sive: 2,000 shells, 26 British and Russian guns, 3 million rounds of ammunition,

50 machine-guns, 30 lorries and five cars, two motorcycles, five armoured cars, 50,000 pounds of grain, 3,000 uniforms.[108]

There was also a working aeroplane.

The *makhnovtsy* never managed to exploit their limited opportunities for air warfare, although they had captured seven combat aircraft in Ekaterinoslav in late December 1918. In March 1919 they again captured five Farman-HF.30 aircraft in Berdiansk. This model, designed in 1915, had been used mainly by the Imperial Russian Air Service but was slow – the propeller was at the back – and was used mainly for reconnaissance. As a Red Army Brigade Commander, Makhno requested mechanics and spare parts as well as pilots, and soon afterwards one of the aeroplanes took part in Makhno's capture of Mariupol' on 28–9 March, dropping some bombs and carrying out scouting missions. A couple of days later Makhno flew from Berdiansk to Guliaipole in just over two hours.[109] The *makhnovtsy* subsequently captured aircraft on other occasions – for example in August 1920 in Khar'kov – but they never flew them, lacking both aviation fuel and trained pilots.[110]

For several days the *makhnovtsy* struggled to establish full control of Berdiansk, combing the streets looking for Whites and shooting any that they captured, as well as looting shops and stores.[111] The White defenders finally broke and ran in the afternoon on 12 October, attempting to evacuate in boats to waiting steamships. Most of them were cut down by machine-gun fire from the harbour walls.[112] Several days of chaos followed. The *makhnovtsy* reportedly demolished the prison and gave the bricks away to peasants for use on their smallholdings – imprisonment was considered unnecessary, and robbery was a capital offence. Grain stores were also distributed: wagons loaded with booty and armaments streamed out of the city. The *makhnovtsy* hunted down any White officers who were in hiding, paying street boys 100 rubles per head for betraying them.[113] Eventually the executions stopped, and about four days after the fall of the city, according to an eyewitness, Makhno himself arrived in Berdiansk.[114]

The loss of the Berdiansk armoury was a factor in halting the White advance northwards,[115] but the loss of a single armoury and even the extended lines of communication resulting from the rapid advances do not explain the speed and ferocity with which the insurrection spread behind Denikin's front-line. Denikin had lost the political battle for the hearts and minds of the people of the borderlands, a battle he never really saw as necessary. In an atmosphere of political improvisation, Makhno's victory at Peregonovka was a contributory factor to Denikin's defeat, but not necessarily the decisive one. His return to the left-bank sparked an insurrection, but the insurrection was prepared by Denikin's policies, driven by his narrow class interests. Perhaps the need to remove fighting divisions and Cossack brigades from the front to combat the insurgency tipped the balance in the Orel' salient, but that was a military and not an ideological decision.[116] In any event, between October and the end of the year the main White offensive collapsed. Conditions in Ekaterinoslav province, and most especially in Aleksandrovsk region, were as confused politically as they were militarily. The Whites, stunned by the Red Army's successful adoption of cavalry tactics from September onwards, were pushed back in disorderly retreat across terrain in which they commanded little support.[117] Local Bolshevik structures behind the frontline adopted conspiratorial, underground methods to counteract anarchist influence – and in case the Whites returned. The presence of the unruly anarchist bands made underground work difficult. One party worker in Berdiansk complained that the *makhnovtsy* were robbing people and beating up party sympathisers. The Berdiansk party chairperson was saved from death only when a Communist commander intervened, and permission for meetings was often refused, despite an anarchist commitment to free political activity.[118]

G. L. Levko – secretary of the Party provincial committee in Ekaterinoslav – wrote several reports in January and February 1920 which describe vividly just how dangerous it could be to have a known political affiliation.[119] On his way to Khar'kov via Kursk, Levko noted that the mood among the White Guards varied from 'apprehensive' to 'downcast'.[120] In Khar'kov he discovered why: Makhno was operating in the southern part of the area around Ekaterinoslav with a strong force of between 10,000 and 15,000 men. He had captured several towns, including Nikopol', Pologi and Aleksandrovsk, where he stayed for four weeks, using it as his headquarters. By the time Levko managed to reach Ekaterinoslav, Makhno had occupied it (Ekaterinoslav changed hands several times during the autumn of 1919).[121] The insurgents took the city late in October, and the Whites then promptly dug in nearby, on the left-bank. They shelled the city from armoured trains on a daily basis, until they were able to retake it at the end of November.[122] After the initial rampage from Peregonovka, Makhno's forces were being pushed westwards again during this period, while the main front moved south, although Denikin's claim that the whole left bank was cleared of partisans by 23 November is probably an exaggeration.[123] In addition, there is some evidence to indicate that the *makhnovtsy* may have been operating further north and west than was their custom during October and November. One contemporary report puts them in Sumy, northwest of Khar'kov, and all over Poltava in early November.[124] Another document reports breakthroughs in Znamenka and around Kherson, while a third account describes communist concern about the spread of insurgency on the right bank generally.[125]

According to Levko, the communist underground continued their work while Makhno was in Aleksandrovsk. The local committee managed to maintain contact with party cells within the units of the insurgent army, although it is unclear whether these had been formed by means of infiltration of party members or through conversion of former anarchists. While it was obviously in Levko's interests to exaggerate local successes in infiltrating insurgent ranks, anarchist sources confirm that this was indeed a constant problem.[126] In a later report, Levko claimed that 'a whole group of experienced comrades' was added to the existing cells during the period of Makhno's occupation of Ekaterinoslav.[127] But the departure of the Makhno army left the small Bolshevik group in an extremely vulnerable position if the Whites were to return, and they followed their unknowing and unwilling protectors in Ekaterinoslav.

Ekaterinoslav had a population of around 1.9 million people, of whom nearly 70 percent were Ukrainians, with a large Russian-speaking minority as well as both Germans and Jews. The population was youthful: nearly 750,000 of the city's inhabitants were less than 15 years old.[128] The party's organisation in Ekaterinoslav was even weaker than that in Aleksandrovsk – the provincial committee had no contact with the suburbs, to say nothing of the countryside. Southern districts such as Melitopol', Mariupol' and Berdiansk were only in touch with the Aleksandrovsk structures.[129] Given the vulnerability of the Ekaterinoslav structures, Levko set up an underground committee of three people, linked to a network of party members whose affiliation was publicly unknown. This conspiratorial structure was to operate if the Whites came back to the city.

The anarchists tried to work with other groups. In Aleksandrovsk they held a meeting that resolved to ask the trade union council to call a local conference on the immediate tasks for social and economic construction. But the council, dominated by Right SRs and Mensheviks, replied that the meeting had not been properly mandated and so the resolution had no force. For the *makhnovtsy*, this amounted to sabotage.[130] The council also turned down an anarchist proposal to distribute 15,000 *pudy* of wheat to the poor.[131] The anarchists then published an article attacking the atitude of the trade unionists in *Put' k Svobode*, headlined 'Pozor' [Shame].[132]

Makhnovshchina was unusual among the peasant rebellions of the *atamanshchina* in its conscious allocation of resources to the production of newspapers and other documents such as proclamations.[133] The movement produced eleven newspaper titles altogether, putting out 50 issues of the most important one, *Put' k Svobode* [The Road to Freedom] between May 1919 and November 1920.[134] The first newspapers associated with the movement were the *Izvestiia* of the Guliaipole VRS, and *Guliaipol'skii Nabat*, which appeared in March 1919, just after the second congress of the movement in February. Both were published in Russian and were edited by the anarchists of the Nabat Confederation in Khar'kov, a group with ambitions to coordinate all anarchist activity in Ukraine.[135] Makhno, whose relations with Nabat were sometimes strained, was dissatisfied with this arrangement, which his movement was supporting financially, and established *Put' k Svobode* under the editorship of Petr Arshinov. The newspaper was published variously in Aleksandrovsk, Ekaterinoslav and Guliaipole, constrained by the changing military situation. Movement newspapers were published in Ukrainian late in 1919 – *Shliakh do Voli* (Ekaterinoslav) and *Anarkhist-Povstanets'* (published in Poltava); the reason that more publications were not produced in Ukrainian was 'not because of any anti-Ukrainian language policy, but because of the lack of Ukrainian-language proofreaders, editors and, most importantly, Ukrainian fonts'.[136]

Makhno's relationship to concepts of freedom of expression was often conflicted. Viktor Belash recounts that he wanted to have the editorial board of the Ekaterinoslav newspaper *Zvezda* arrested for publishing articles that he did not like. He became enraged when he read an article on the ideology of the Makhno movement by a certain Goronev, and wanted to order the *Kontrradvezka* to shoot the unfortunate author. He was eventually dissuaded.[137]

The production of these newspapers was organised in difficult circumstances. In November and December 1919

> ... the editorial offices ... occupied a whole house at no.97 Katerynyns'kyi Prospekt ... *Put' k Svobode*, the most authoritative publication, was on the ground floor ... the editorial offices of *Shliakh do Voli* were on the second floor. *Borot'by* was on the third floor ... the editors personally received the authors between 11.00 and 13.00 every day except holidays and weekends ... authors usually submitted their articles under pseudonyms ...[138]

The newspapers were distributed by young activists, and were sold at different prices to different social categories, to individuals and to groups. Readers were asked not to throw the papers away, but to pass them around. They were pasted onto walls at train stations, using thick glue so that they could not easily be torn down – and with warnings against doing so.[139]

In October 1919, the *makhnovtsy* called a regional congress of peasants and workers in Aleksandrovsk, which was attended by 180 peasant delegates and 20 workers. The congress agenda included both military and political questions, but even with regard to technical questions on the future of the Insurgent Army, the anarchist principle of not imposing authority onto the proceedings was followed. Volin chaired the sessions, and says that he tried to limit his role to steering the congress, following the agenda and recognising speakers.[140]

The *makhnovtsy* did not allow any sort of electoral campaign to take place before the congress, prohibited party representation, and only presented an agenda which delegates were free to change. Volin recounts a visit before the congress from a Left SR, Lubim, who expressed reservations about this procedure, especially as it would allow 'counter-revolutionaries' to be elected as delegates. Lubim intervened during the opening session, calling for the chair to exercise its functions more decisively. He was shouted down. The congress decided, among other things, that all males below 48 years of age would 'voluntarily' serve in the Insurgent Army, and that the Army would be fed by 'free gifts' of food from the peasantry.[141] The congress organised a 'freelance medical service' for wounded or sick insurgents, and appointed a commission of enquiry into the activities of Makhno's security service, which was accused of various excesses, including arbitrary arrests, executions, and torture. The structure and behaviour of the insurgent security services are poorly documented, but abuses of power did take place. Volin admits that a kind of 'warrior clique' formed itself around the *bat'ko* and that brutalities were committed.[142] A secondary source names the Zadov brothers as the commanders of security operations.[143] There may even have been two services, the *razvedka* and the *Kommissia Protivmakhnoskikh Del*.[144]

* * *

The insurgents persecuted those whom they saw as their class enemies, especially the *zolotopogonniki* or former Tsarist officers. In one incident around October, witnessed by a Bolshevik agent, a train from Aleksandrovsk to Ekaterinoslav was stopped by a detachment of *makhnovtsy* armed with machine-guns. Six officers who were on board were summarily shot, after being told that they were to receive a reward of 'ten thousand [rubles] for the *pomeshchik*'s land'. The insurgents then rode the train for a while before dramatically stopping it in the open steppe and disappearing into the night.[145] Despite such brutalities, in this period neither the Bolshevik underground nor the beleaguered Whites could plausibly deny the broad appeal of *makhnovshchina*. 'Makhno's advance', wrote an anonymous journalist in November, was 'more than a simple military operation. It was, at the same time a broad popular movement', that had succeeded in capturing the support of the working masses.[146] In the opinion of Sergei Shchetinin, who as governor of Ekaterinoslav organised his own security police, the struggle was therefore 'not against Makhno, but against the peasantry of the province as a whole'.[147]

The *makhnovtsy* apparently tried seriously in Ekaterinoslav and Aleksandrovsk to emphasise to the inhabitants that they were neither a new occupying power, nor a party, but rather a guarantee of the absence of both. At the same time, efforts were made by the Bolshevik underground in Ekaterinoslav to ensure continued trade union support, especially during intervals of White rule. After Makhno's arrival in October, the unions reverted to a semi-legal status and became much more passive, only to resume militant action again in the period between Makhno's final expulsion at the end of November and the arrival of the Red Army on 30 December.[148] Political work in Ekaterinoslav – under artillery bombardment – was more difficult than in Aleksandrovsk. The *makhnovtsy* held a couple of general conferences at which they urged ideas of self-management and workers' control – one outcome was that railway workers elected a committee to draw up time-tables and control the fare structure.[149]

During the insurgent occupation, the Bolsheviks began to publish a daily paper, *Zvezda* (The Star) which launched a campaign against anarchism as an ideology, and incited workers to take action against the *makhnovtsy* in preparation for the imminent arrival of the Red Army from the north.[150] Makhno, while waging a fierce anti-Bolshevik war of words, remained true to his principles and took no action against the local party organisation.[151]

The *makhnovtsy* permitted Right and Left SRs as well as the Bolsheviks to publish newspapers, and even published a proclamation on socialist freedom of the press and of association:

1. All socialist political parties, organisations and tendencies have the right to propagate their ideas, theories, views and opinions freely, both in speech and in writing. No restriction of socialist freedom of speech or of the press will be permitted, and no persecution may take place in this respect.

Observation: Military communiqués may not be printed unless they are supplied by the editors of *Put' k Svobode* ...[152]

According to Levko, a campaign of infiltration into the insurgent ranks was given 'special attention' in Ekaterinoslav. The objective was to lower morale and to identify units which might be smoothly integrated into the Red Army later on.[153] Desertion was a constant feature in all armies, with some fighters having changed sides as often as three or four times, so this tactic made sense.[154] Infiltrated Bolsheviks were ordered to stay with the *makhnovtsy*, because the Red Army was close by.[155] The Bolsheviks even succeeded in subverting an insurgent brigade commander, Polonskii, who was eventually arrested with seven others on charges of conspiring to poison Makhno.[156] They were all condemned to death by firing squad. Despite a combination of appeals for mercy, propaganda and threats from the Bolsheviks, the *makhnovtsy* refused to release the condemned men, but the issue became academic when the retreating White Guards suddenly pushed Makhno out of the city again in late November.[157] In what was now becoming almost a routine, the major part of the city's quasi-legal Bolshevik organisation left with him.

By mid-December the Bolshevik underground had got itself organised, had received funding, and was organising revolutionary committees in nearby districts. On 29 December the Ekaterinoslav military revolutionary committee formally took power. Red divisions occupied local railway stations. On 30 December the Red Army returned to Ekaterinoslav and legal political structures accompanied the communist troops as they entered the city.[158]

6

Red versus White, Red versus Green: The Bolsheviks Assert Control

In the winter of 1919–20 the prospects for the anarchist project in Ukraine were dim: the moment seemed to have passed. By January 1920 Denikin had been defeated, although the White threat had not yet been completely eliminated. The year 1920 was to be a time of famine, of deadly epidemics, of drought and widespread destructive wildfires,[1] a year of brutal Red terror and of anarchist counter-terror, an 'implacable struggle' by the *makhnovtsy* against the Bolshevik policy of war communism.[2] Revolutionary fought revolutionary. It was the year in which the first generation of the Soviet military elite matured into leadership – Egorov, Tukhachevskii, Budenny, Voroshilov and others.[3] It was the year of the 'final battle of the peasants fighting for their rights'.[4]

In the chaotic last months of 1919, the Bolsheviks had been engaged in fierce political struggles in Ukrainian cities. Rival communist groupings with nationalist inclinations were to be neutralised, absorbed or liquidated. The word '*makhnovtsy*' was thrown around – by Trotsky among others – as a catchall form of abuse for anti-Bolsheviks or even Bolshevik dissenters.[5] At the ninth Congress of the Russian Communist Party (Bolsheviks) or RKP(b), Lenin attacked the 'democratic centralists' who wanted a collective administration rather than using bourgeois experts. 'I know very well that Comrade Osinskii and the others *do not share the views of Makhno*' said Lenin sarcastically, suggesting the opposite. Their dissension would, in any case, he implied, lend comfort to Makhno.[6]

In the last few days of 1919, the beaten Whites extricated themselves from the threat of complete annihilation by the advancing Red Army – at least partly as a result of poor decisions by the Bolsheviks.[7] The White commander General Iakov Slashchev was engaged with Makhno's forces near Ekaterinoslav in conditions of 'thick mud and almost completely impassable country roads'.[8] Slashchev – nicknamed 'the hangman'[9] and described by Wrangel as 'a slave to drink and drugs' and 'a man in the throes of mental sickness'[10] – decided not to attempt to defend northern Tauride against the Reds, but to push Makhno back to the Kichkas bridge and then to evacuate the White infantry behind a cavalry screen from Ekaterinoslav to Nikolaev, and then by ship to Sevastopol'. In the ensuing battle for the bridge over the Dnepr, Makhno's forces were badly mauled and withdrew, losing five artillery pieces. The Whites then executed their own withdrawal from Ekaterinoslav without more fighting. Slashchev subsequently made a stand at Perekop, at the entrance to Crimea, and prevented a Red occupation for the winter. If the Reds had thrown their full weight behind the attack, the whole Wrangel episode might have been avoided.[11]

Up to January 1920 the new Red strategy of splitting their offensive forces into two mobile groups, which had been adopted at the end of October, had been successful. But there was a new factor in the balance of forces – the appearance in the rear of Denikin's forces of fighters from the Revolutionary Insurgent Army, which, as we have seen, had captured Berdiansk, Mariupol' and Nikolaev. They blocked access to Odessa and to the White Guard artillery base at Volnovakha (near Donetsk), cutting the White's supply lines. Most of all however, they cut the vital supply of ammunition to the advancing Whites.[12] They also tied down a significant number of White troops, perhaps as many as 20,000. This had certainly assisted, directly or indirectly, Budenny's cavalry victory at Voronezh on 24 October, and had continued to pay off handsomely. The demoralised Whites, chopping and changing their commanders, were pushed back over 650 kilometres. Nevertheless, the Bolsheviks were unable to secure a complete victory, and the fighting was prolonged for another year. The Whites succeeded in hanging on to Crimea, defending it against superior numbers of Red troops and securing a base where they could regroup and from which they could launch new campaigns.

Denikin had few doubts that the Bolsheviks' inability to remain on good terms with Makhno's Insurgent Army was a major factor in saving the Whites. In January 1920, he wrote later, 'Makhno drove a wedge within the disposition of the 14th Soviet Army, and by harassing it until October [1920] prevented the Bolsheviks' offensive against Crimea'.[13] Second, in a scrambled evacuation, the Whites were able to move some of the remnants of the shattered Volunteer Army, as well as various Cossack units, by sea to Crimea. The Bolsheviks, with no sea power in the south, were helpless to prevent it.

At the beginning of the year, despite the acrimonious break between the Bolsheviks and the *makhnovtsy* which had taken place the previous summer, relations between the two sides in the field were amicable, continuing the kind of informal if grudging cooperation that had sometimes developed behind White lines in late 1919. Around New Year, the Red 45th Infantry, which was advancing against Denikin's demoralised forces, occupied Ekaterinoslav and Aleksandrovsk. According to one version, the Reds disarmed the *makhnovtsy* in both Aleksandrovsk and Nikopol', but another account claims that the returning Red Army contacted the *makhnovtsy* in Aleksandrovsk earlier, in December 1919, and joint meetings were held.[14]

But this brief rapprochement between the two armies did not last long.[15] Early in January the headquarters of the 14th Red Army under Voroshilov sent Makhno a formal order instructing him to proceed with his entire army to take up positions on the Polish front.[16] This was a provocation, an obvious 'political manoeuvre':[17] in Litvinov's words 'from the viewpoint of military strategy, the order was so meaningless that it immediately provoked a protest, not only from the rebels, but even from some thoughtful Soviet commanders'.[18] The Bolsheviks were trying to separate the partisans from their political base by sending them to a front where they would have no political influence. They would either break up as a coherent force, or end up integrated into the regular formations of the Red Army.[19] The *makhnovtsy* refused the order: the Insurgent Army would stay in Ukraine where it belonged.[20] There was no point in moving to the Polish Front, and anyway, typhus had decimated their ranks.

This was not a mere excuse. Lice-borne typhus played a major role in the civil war, claiming between two and three million lives between 1918 and 1922.[21] The Russian epidemic was 'unprecedented in the history of the disease', and official records alone reported seven million cases in the country as a whole. Unofficial contemporary estimates put the total as high as 15 to 25 million cases.[22] There is no data specifically for Ukraine for the two years 1918 and 1919, and information even for the later period is 'very incomplete', but there is no doubt that it was hard hit.[23] Lenin believed the three 'simple problems' facing his government were bread, fuel and the louse: typhus might even be the 'calamity that will prevent our tackling any sort of socialist development'.[24] This was not to over-dramatise: 'either the louse will defeat socialism, or socialism will defeat the louse'.[25]

The 'body louse' (Russian *platianaia vash*' or clothing louse) was spread by unwashed soldiers and refugees in crowded conditions; there were shortages of soap and disinfectants, and immune systems were weakened by hunger.[26] Soldiers' clothes crawled with lice: when uniforms were deloused, the dead insects on the floor of the disinfecting rooms looked like gray sand.[27] Death sometimes seemed only a single louse bite away.[28] The disease advanced and retreated

> ... with the 'regular' Red and White forces, the irregular units of various Ukrainian 'governments', the anarchist bands of Nestor Makhno, and waves of refugees. The White retreat during the winter of 1919–20 was hampered by the tens of thousands of typhus sufferers who overwhelmed makeshift hospitals ...[29]

The louse came close to destroying the Makhno insurgency altogether. The *makhnovtsy* often wore their hair long, put together bits and pieces of whatever uniforms they came across, and were poorly nourished: they were highly susceptible to typhus and other diseases, often passing infections to the peasants and getting them back again. It was in the common interest to nurse them, regardless of political sympathy.[30] They lacked medical equipment and soap. The typhus epidemic in October-November 1919 reduced their numbers by half and was a key reason for the abandonment of Ekaterinoslav to Slashchev at the end of November 1919.[31] By January 1920 the situation had not improved: the headquarters staff were all sick, including Makhno himself.[32] He was comatose for several days and was hidden in peasant houses in and around Guliaipole while the Bolsheviks conducted a house-to-house search for him. Through luck and the 'fanatical devotion' of his followers, he survived both the illness and the manhunt: Golovanov, mixing his metaphors, writes dramatically that he was 'dragged from behind the curtains and thrown back onto the stage, back into the arena like a dying gladiator'.[33]

At the same time that they sent off their refusal to move to the Polish front, the headquarters of the Revolutionary Insurgent Army (makhnovists), or RPA(m), published an appeal addressed directly to the rank and file of the Red Army, asking for their solidarity in the face of provocation.[34] The Bolsheviks did not waste any time in reacting to Makhno's expected refusal to obey their orders. On the 9th, the All-Ukrainian Revolutionary Committee in Khar'kov, chaired by Petrovskii, issued a decree declaring the *makhnovtsy*, 'as deserters and traitors' who had refused to 'take up arms against the Poles, and declared war against our liberation army' to be outlaws.[35] Even before the publication of the decree, Estonian and Latvian regiments moved to disarm the *makhnovtsy*.[36] Soon afterwards the Nabat federation in Khar'kov declared Makhno unfit as a leader and disassociated themselves from his movement.[37]

The emphasis on Makhno's role in the defeat of Denikin in newspaper articles and the spread of anarchist and nationalist ideas were a source of worry for some Bolsheviks. Sergo Ordzhonikidze pointed out that 'Makhno is not the driver of the uprising; the masses as a whole are in revolt against Denikin and for Soviet power' he wrote.[38] One report from Krivoi Rog said that although the mood of the peasantry was hard to evaluate, their attitude towards the *makhnovshchina* was negative.[39] Another report said that party work was difficult, and the *makhnovtsy* were carrying on a 'furious' propaganda campaign, while the Bolsheviks lacked party workers, literature or funds to counteract it.[40] Some of the insurgent propaganda has survived: one declaration lists eleven points, repealing all the legislation passed by Denikin's administration, as well as any Communist legislation that might be objected to by 'the working people': Land is to be transferred to the peasants, and factories and mines to the workers; there are to be 'free Soviets' and the Cheka is to be abolished. The document guarantees freedom of speech, the press, assembly, union activity 'and the like'. It declares that the workers and peasants must not allow any 'counter-revolutionary demonstrations by the bourgeoisie or the officers', and that anybody

convicted of banditry 'will be summarily shot'. The declaration states that '...
the exchange of goods and the products of labour will be free. This activity will
not be assumed by organisations of workers and peasants for the present ...
the exchange of the products of labour should occur mainly between working
people'.[41]

In its turn, the Bolshevik propaganda machine attacked the insurgents,
accusing them of actually causing the defeats of the summer of 1919, of wanting
to set up their own state, of propagating anarchy,[42] of executing commissars
and of refusing to go to the Polish front. Thousand of Red Army soldiers had
fallen in battle against the 'gangs of the gold-epaulets'[43] mainly because of
the instability created behind the lines 'by a gang of bandits ... organising a
kingdom in Guliaipole ... [which] became a separate state'. The makhnovtsy
were 'self-seeking marauders' but in the end all the 'honest partisans will come
over to our side'.[44]

There followed 'eight months of the most savage fighting in which the makhnovtsy were ever engaged'.[45] But unlike the campaigns of 1919, this was not a
war of large set battles. It was a fluid semi-guerrilla drive in which the Bolsheviks by and large retained the initiative, and kept the makhnovtsy – many fewer
than at the end of 1919 – pushed back onto the defensive. In this respect it was
a precursor to the type of fighting that took place in 1921, ending in final defeat
for Makhno. The Bolsheviks' two key objectives were to eliminate Makhno's
forces militarily, and to neutralise peasant support for the partizanshchina. This
was a war of movement, with territory frequently changing hands. Guliaipole
was captured and then lost several times.[46] The makhnovtsy could not mount
full-scale conventional offensives, and were restricted to harassing the Red
forces, or picking off units which had become isolated.

Nonetheless, the makhnovtsy fought on: Golovanov romantically explains
that 'it is impossible to tell a tree that resistance is useless, that it will be cut
down, sawn up and made into a coffin' and just as that tree is nonetheless fated
by its nature to resist the axe and the saw, so was Makhno destined to fight
on.[47] But without recourse to metaphor, the truth for most of the year was more
prosaic. Both sides employed terror. Trotsky was preoccupied with the danger
that anarchist ideas represented for Red Army discipline, and his order no. 180
of 11 December 1919 ordered 'merciless punishment' against partisans and any
of their supporters.[48] The Cheka would move into a newly occupied village and
kill any makhnovtsy that they found. Communists would be placed in positions
of power, and a militia would be set up. But such positions were insecure: the
grain requisition policies of war communism had created resentment among
the peasantry, and when the makhnovtsy appeared again they would reverse
the process, shooting the Bolshevik functionaries in their turn.[49] Soviet
accounts describe an anarchist terror aimed at the destruction of 'the police,
the Cheka, and the grain requisition detachments' as well as the Komsomol and

the Committees of Poor Peasants (*komnezamy*).[50] On orders from Makhno, Kuz'menko and Lev Zadov, communists, security officers, industrial workers, heads of state farms and collective farm chairmen were executed. No quarter was given, and 'mountains of chopped corpses appeared' – one Soviet source claims that as many as 1,000 workers were killed in a nine-month period.[51] Belash writes that the 'Black Terror' – which justified almost every killing – was brutal, random and 'motiveless': 'anyone who served with Denikin as an officer, gendarme, prison guard, counterintelligence agent, provocateur, [or who had a] direct relation to punitive or investigative institutions was shot'.[52] In addition, 'desertion, physical violence against a woman or against civilians accompanied either by beatings or killing, obvious treason, forgery, [and] use of an official position for personal financial gain' were all punishable by death.[53]

To what extent was this brutality 'an integral part of *ataman* leadership – a mode of behaviour resulting from a way of living that can be called a "culture of violence"'?[54] Modern social theory has addressed the question in various ways, making the important point that violence can be seen as a constant feature of human society with communicable meanings, not only transmitted from per-petrators to victims, but also to witnesses, whether or not they are willing.[55] As the civil war progressed, it became in fact a veritable

> ... school of violence, provid[ing] the space, or 'spaces' where violent acts could be exercised and observed ... it created a cast of perpetrators, who had no difficulties committing atrocities, and a much larger contingent of spec-tators, who did not shy away ... the war had discredited the state ... people began to accustom themselves to the idea of acting independently, without expecting official sanction ...[56]

In this context of increased brutality and natural disaster, Makhno's semi-guer-rilla campaigns of 1920 and 1921 both differed from the fighting of mid-1919, and the 1920 campaign was different in one important respect from the engagements of 1921: in 1920, as in 1919, Bolshevik attention was still divided among various active enemies of the Soviet state. At the beginning of the year several imminent threats – apart from the Whites – promised to create diffi-culties for the Soviet government when winter was over. Petliura had not yet been completely neutralised, and in what has been described as 'one of the most sordid pages'[57] of Ukrainian history had fled to Warsaw at the end of 1919 and promised the Poles to cede Galicia west of the Zbruch River as well as Volynia, in exchange for support in driving the Bolsheviks out of Ukraine. Some nation-alist partisan activity continued between the Zbruch and the Dnepr under the leadership of Omelianovych-Pavlenko and Iurko Tiutiunnyk.[58] At the same time, Poland was becoming increasingly hostile: in the spring of 1920, Józef Pił-sudski, the Polish head of state, decided to attempt to incite a Ukrainian revolt and to re-establish Poland's eighteenth-century eastern frontiers, undefined in the Treaty of Versailles.

By mid-April Makhno's relations with the Bolsheviks had deteriorated to the point that his forces were actively harassing Bolshevik troop movements to the Polish Front. Obviously, the Bolshevik command took this kind of action seriously, and it was remembered with bitterness in the months to come.[59] In any event, in the spring of 1920 Makhno's forces were weak and isolated in a hostile environment: at the time, wild speculation about possible alliances was widespread. In mid-April, for example, Red intelligence reported that Petliurist bands in the rear of the 14th Red Army were considering an alliance either with Makhno, or with the Whites in the Tauride.[60]

Thanks to the publication in 2006 of Danilov and Shanin's documentary history, a body of published primary documentation is now available on the activities of *makhnovshchina* in the period after it was declared outlawed, until the renewed alliance with the Red Army in November. This includes 150 pages of varied materials on, for example, the short period of 'strategic retreat' at the beginning of January, propaganda and other types of material produced by the RPA(M) itself, documents from the Cheka on the activities of the *makhnovtsy* and the struggle against them, and some other materials from Wrangel's Whites.[61] In addition, Viktor Belash devotes two chapters of more than 100 pages to the events between February and November 1920.[62]

One particular document that has been the source of controversy since the 1920s is the so-called 'diary of Makhno's wife', a handwritten notebook with the (Russian) annotation on the cover '*Dnevnik zheny Makhno*'.[63] The document, written in Ukrainian[64] and supposedly captured by the Red Army, covers the period from February to March, and has been known of since the 1920s[65] – in 1927, for example, Kubanin quoted from it in support of the idea that representatives of the 'hated administration of the city' such as policemen and customs officials were special targets for peasant violence.[66] Arshinov dismisses the whole text as counterfeit on the grounds that Makhno's wife, Galina Kuz'menko, was never captured by the Bolsheviks.[67] The entries document the casual brutality of the *makhnovtsy*, while incidentally providing a rare woman's perspective on issues such as the conduct of the campaign, Makhno's frequent drunkenness and the frontier justice meted out to grain requisition officials.

The document raises two questions: is it genuine, and if so, less importantly, who wrote it? Sergei Semanov, who began writing about Makhno in the 1960s, reported that he wrote to Kuz'menko, then an elderly woman in exile in Kazakhstan, asking her directly. She responded that

Nestor really wanted the history of the movement … to be recorded. At headquarters there was a high-school student, whose special task was to keep a diary … I also kept a diary, I borrowed a notebook from Fany Gaenko, she was a young woman, Lev Zadov's lover ... the first page of the notebook was in her handwriting ... I wrote the entire notebook. Once Fany and I were driving along a road in a wagon ... Red cavalrymen appeared ... A suitcase with our things was on another wagon, they took it, and there was a diary. Then an article appeared in some Soviet newspaper about the diary of Feodora Gaenko, Makhno's wife. Arshinov angrily denied it, *but in fact, I did keep a diary.*[68]

Some commentators sympathetic to *makhnovshchina* continue to deny the authenticity of the document, arguing that Kuz'menko, in replying to Semanov, was trying to avoid 'complicating the lives of herself and her daughter with stories that denied the official historiography'. In fact, this line of analysis continues, the diary was 'fabricated within the walls of the All-Ukrainian Cheka, and in a terrible hurry, and consequently the forgery turned out to be very crude'.[69] At least partly, the objection seems to be that the diary shows the *makhnovtsy* in a bad light rather than focussing on Bolshevik misdeeds. A couple of extracts give the flavour:

25 February ... Moved to Maior'ske. Three grain requisition agents were caught. They were shot ...
7 March ... the Bat'ko had begun to drink ... he and his lieutenant Karetnik got completely drunk ... he cursed indecently in the street. He yelled like crazy, cursing in front of small children and women. Finally, he mounted his horse and rode off to Guliaipole. On the way, he almost fell into the mud. Karetnik began to play the fool in his own way – he went to the machine guns and started firing them ...[70]

If the text is genuine, the debate over authorship fades into insignificance: the extracts do not depend on the author's intimate relationship with Nestor Makhno for authenticity or interest. Even if Gaenko had been a rank-and-file member of *makhnovshchina*, or a mere camp follower, her comments would still ring true. In fact, she was more than merely Zadov's lover. Belash, calling her 'not a woman, but a kind of executioner' describes an incident in which she shot to death a group of prisoners belonging to an enemy detachment that had killed her father shortly before.[71] Both Faenko and Kuz'menko were committed eye-witnesses: this type of source can in any event, 'only answer questions of a certain type – about emotional perceptions and immediate reactions to events, about expectations, and the details of life'.[72] The author was writing a contextual account of 'events taking place around her' and therein lies its value.[73]

The debate around Gaenko also raises the issue of Makhno's sexual mores. Volin was censorious:

[a] failing of Makhno and of many of his close associates was their attitude towards women. These men, especially when intoxicated, could not refrain from behaviour that was improper – disgusting would often be the correct adjective – amounting almost to orgies in which certain women were obliged to participate.[74]

It seems quite probable that Makhno had other women companions who might well have stayed with him for relatively prolonged periods: whether he was personally 'debauched' is another question. For example, in May 1919, according to one story, the *makhnovtsy* found a stash of short pornographic or erotic films, made by the French studio Pathé,[75] in a cinema in Berdiansk.[76] Both Makhno and Shchus' watched some of these films with other *makhnovtsy*, and subsequently visited a nearby house of prostitution.[77] It seems likely, however, that in this kind of behaviour the *makhnovtsy* were neither better nor worse than the soldiers of other armies.

In the meantime, the Whites in Crimea were trying to reorganise. They had been driven from Odessa, which fell to the Red Army on 7 February, and Novorossisk, which fell on 27 March. At the beginning of April, obsessed with 'conspiracies', which he believed were being hatched against him, Denikin concluded that he would have to give up his command if the White cause were to survive. After a Council of War, held on 3 April, had expressed its preference, Denikin resigned as commander-in-chief and appointed as his successor a man whom he had effectively cashiered a few weeks earlier, the aristocratic Baron Petr Nikolaevich Wrangel.[78] The new commander passed his first two months re-forming his army, securing the defences of the narrow entrance to Crimea and establishing civil order. Wrangel and his advisors realised that he had to win the active loyalty of at least part of the civilian population over which he ruled if he was to succeed in his military aims. He introduced a semblance of civilian government, established a professional police force and even set about undertaking limited agrarian reform to win over the peasantry. His methods have been described, in a widely quoted phrase, as 'leftist policies by rightist hands'.[79]

Wrangel believed he could not defeat the Soviet government, but that he could keep 'the honour of the Russian flag' unstained.[80] The war between the Bolsheviks and Poland now gave him an opportunity to launch a limited offensive beyond Crimea, while the Bolsheviks' attention was concentrated elsewhere. This was good for morale, and gave the Whites access to the northern Tauride, a grain-producing area bordered on the south by the Black and Azov seas, and to the northwest by the lower reaches of the Dnepr, below Aleksandrovsk. It was not only food that was running short, moreover, but also such essentials as ammunition, clothing and fuel. On 6 June, against British advice, Wrangel moved into the northern Tauride and made sea-borne landings on the Azov coast. By the end of the month, the northern Tauride was entirely in White hands, and Wrangel had captured 11,000 Red soldiers, dozens of artillery pieces, hundreds of machine-guns and even two armoured cars.[81] But he had lost British support and needed new allies.

It was in this context that Wrangel wrote – in his order no. 3130 of 13 May from Sevastopol' – that in order to achieve the 'sacred purpose' of destroying communism, the 'main enemy of Holy Russia', his commanders should be prepared to cooperate with Makhno's insurgents or with the Ukrainian nationalists.[82] This comment functioned as the seed for subsequent claims of actual cooperation, constituting what amounted to a fully-fledged disinformation campaign. Contemporary sources from the summer of 1920 are full of confused reports about Makhno's relations with Wrangel and there is extensive documentation alleging that a formal alliance had been contracted.[83] In this period Makhno was harassing the Bolshevik rear and destroying supplies and administrative structures, but there is no doubt that the sudden descent of the Whites onto the plains of the northern Tauride placed him in a vulnerable position. Nevertheless, an alliance with Wrangel, even if informal, would have constituted an act of extraordinarily cynical opportunism on his part.[84]

Even so, the existence of an alliance was widely believed. On 10 July a UNR reconnaissance dispatch claimed that a large Makhnovite levy was operating in Poltava province, and cooperating with Wrangel's forces.[85] In early August the *Times* of London reported that Wrangel had reached an agreement with Makhno, whom it described as 'the real master' of the country immediately to the east and the south-east of Ekaterinoslav.[86] Two weeks later the same newspaper belatedly reported Wrangel's order to assist anti-Bolshevik forces, adding that Makhno had done the same, which the reporter interpreted as a *de facto* alliance.[87] In September the Prague-based Russian newspaper *Volia Rossii* quoted an overtly anti-Semitic and certainly fraudulent 'order' from Makhno that read:

> Russians! Save Russia and beat the Jews! I come to the aid of my brother Wrangel, whose army is truly Russian, and not Jewish.[88]

The article claimed that it was only Makhno's assistance that had enabled Wrangel to retain a foothold in Crimea, and that France was supporting a collection of '*condottieri*, adventurers, thieves and reactionaries' in Ukraine in an attempt to 'transform Russia into Mexico'.[89] Overall, Wrangel actively sought to spread rumours that he had forged an alliance with Makhno, especially in the chancelleries of the West, on which he depended for support and supplies.[90] On 14 August one of his representatives in Paris stated baldly that there was an agreement between Makhno and Wrangel to coordinate operations from the north down to Aleksandrovsk, and even credited the insurgents with the defeat of a Red cavalry offensive near Aleksandrovsk.[91]

The *makhnovtsy* were having none of this, and responded fiercely to what they regarded as a 'vicious slander' in a declaration addressed to the workers and peasants in Wrangel's army, addressed directly as comrades. An alliance with the enemies of the working people, the *makhnovtsy* declared, was an impossibility. As a vanguard revolutionary movement, their commitment was to fight against all forms of counter-revolution. They had fought the Austrians, they had fought against Denikin and they would continue to fight Wrangel, who stood only for 'hunger and cold, death and enslavement, gallows and prisons, mass executions of workers and peasants, mountains of corpses, a sea of blood and tears'.[92] The declaration ended with an appeal to the troops to abandon the Whites and to join the insurgent army for the coming decisive battle against 'power and capital'.[93] Soon afterwards – around 20 October – when the Starobel'sk agreement had been concluded between the Bolsheviks and Makhno, the People's Commissariat for War admitted that there had never been an alliance:

... the French press has written a great deal about a union between Wrangel and Makhno. The Soviet press also published from time to time documents which testified to a formal alliance ... Now this information has turned out to be untrue. Undoubtedly Makhno rendered real assistance to this Polish gentleman, Wrangel, inasmuch as they fought the Red Army simultaneously. But there was no formal alliance between them. All the documents that mention a formal alliance are forgeries of Wrangel's ... Wrangel really did attempt to contact the *makhnovtsy* and sent two representatives to Makhno's headquarters for talks ... not only did the *makhnovtsy* not join up with Wrangel, but they publicly hanged his representatives ... '[94]

The 1920 campaign was a *guerrilla* in nature, a war without major manoeuvres or pitched battles. The period is – perhaps as a consequence – rich in anecdotes such as those concerning Makhno's attitude towards money, the arts, and education. A UNR reconnaissance unit, for instance, reported in July 1920 that Makhno had issued banknotes to the value of 1,000 *karbovanets*,[95] and a newspaper article in October carried a version of the story, which was later repeated in secondary sources.[96] The American journalist and historian W. H. Chamberlin, for instance, wrote over twenty years later that Makhno had not only issued his own currency, but that the notes bore an ironical anarchist warning that nobody would be prosecuted for forging them.[97] In fact, the story is not inherently improbable, given that there was often a shortage of legally-issued coins and notes, and all sorts of odd local solutions were improvised – there were over 350 different issues of currency 'by cooperatives, enterprises, trading firms, clubs, shops, cafés, canteens, and restaurants' in the remote corners of the collapsing Empire.[98] What have survived are some examples of banknotes issued by other authorities, overstamped with Makhno's slogans.[99]

The movement paid serious attention to its revolutionary symbolism and iconography, mixing black and red flags and – in the spring of 1919 while part of the Red Army – using an artist, A. A. Briantsev, to prepare slogans in gold lettering on dark red banners. Some of the anarchist black flags were made of velvet.[100] Despite some evidence that the movement demonstrated contradictory iconoclastic and philistine tendencies, as mentioned earlier, its newspapers did publish poetry, and it is claimed that there was a theatre section, divided into units specialising in musical, dramatic, operatic and satirical performances.[101] Antonov-Ovseenko's report to Rakovskii in early May 1919 stated that

> organisational work in the area is worthy of note: children's communes and schools are being established, and Guliaipole is an important cultural centre, with … three secondary schools … up to ten hospitals for the wounded and a workshop organised to repair guns …[102]

There was also a brass band, and accomplished harmonica and accordion players – although Viktor Belash admits that some of the performers were not much good. Women took part in these activities, as well as in education.[103] The educational efforts of the insurgents were led by Galina Kuz'menko, who had graduated as a primary school teacher from the Dobrovelichkovskii Women Teachers Seminary in 1916, having studied Russian and Old Church Slavonic, mathematics, geography, calligraphy and practical pedagogy, among other subjects.[104] The school was not an unqualified success, with one violent incident during a kind of play military training resulting in the death of an unfortunate twelve-year-old boy.[105]

Another perspective on *makhnovshchina* in 1920 is provided by the writings of the Russian-American anarchists Emma Goldman and Alexander Berkman, both of whom were in the country at the time. Goldman and Berkman had been stripped of citizenship and deported from the United States on shaky legal grounds for opposing compulsory military service. Both had been born in Russia, but had moved to North America as adolescents. Neither of them harboured misgivings about the nature of the Bolshevik regime, and Goldman, in a dramatic gesture, refused to appeal against her deportation order, saying she preferred to return to revolutionary Russia. They were shocked by the brutality of Bolshevik actions towards political opponents, and disillusionment soon set in.[106] In a conversation with Goldman and Berkman as well as the Russo-Italian Angelica Balabanoff, who had deputised for a time as Ukrainian Commissar for Foreign Affairs, Lenin himself denied that the Soviet government jailed anarchists for their beliefs. The Bolsheviks were, he said, only suppressing bandits and followers of Makhno.[107] But a little later, in Khar'kov prison, the two visitors were shown an old peasant woman, allegedly a Makhnovite, who Goldman describes as a 'stupefied old creature ... half-crazed with the solitary and the fear of execution'.[108]

Goldman and Berkman were intensely interested in anarchist activities, and were soon attracted to *makhnovshchina*. They wanted to meet Makhno and talk to him, but although the possibility was discussed, the encounter never took place.[109] The two Americans did succeed in visiting the ailing Kropotkin at Dmitrov, however, and the old man's wife, Sofia, informed them that Makhno had somehow 'contrived to supply [the Kropotkins] with extra provisions', an extraordinary feat given the distance involved and wartime conditions.[110] By the end of July or in early August Goldman and Berkman had travelled south towards Kiev, where they were handed the official line on Makhno, namely that in 1919 he had mutinied and opened the front to Denikin. Since then he had fought against the Bolsheviks and helped the enemies of the revolution.[111] But in Kiev, Goldman was introduced to a 'young woman in peasant costume' who turned out to be Galina Kuz'menko, Makhno's wife. Kuz'menko told Goldman that the Bolsheviks had put a price on Makhno's head and killed his brother, as well as several members of her own family. Makhno was planning to capture the train which was to carry Goldman and Berkman southwards, so that he could meet them, and he would then escort them back to Soviet territory. He wanted them to refute accusations of anti-Semitism to the world, and to explain *makhnovshchina*'s aims. Goldman, however, could not overcome her scruples about deceiving her hosts, and nothing came of the plan. Instead, she and Kuz'menko spent the night talking about women's rights, birth control and related issues. Goldman subsequently reduced her ties to the Bolsheviks.[112]

Berkman was also busy making contacts with southern anarchists. In August he visited Iosif Gotman at the *Vol'noe Bratstvo* (Free Brotherhood) book shop in Khar'kov. Gotman was better known under his penname, Emigrant, with which he signed articles in *Nabat*, and had also worked as a teacher in Makhnovite camps. Gotman disliked the Bolsheviks: 'I consider Makhno's *povstantsy* movement as a most promising beginning of a great popular movement against the new tyranny', he told Berkman, while another anarchist who was present added that 'there isn't enough left of the Revolution to make a fig-leaf for Bolshevik nakedness'.[113] Gotman believed that *makhnovshchina* represented 'the real spirit of October' and that kulaks were a minority in the movement.[114] While he admitted that there was no freedom of speech for Communists in Makhnovite-controlled areas, there certainly was for Maximalists and Left SRs.[115]

While the Americans travelled around, sporadic guerrilla actions continued. In early May the 9th Cavalry Division engaged Makhno near Aleksandrovsk, but the contact was inconclusive.[116] Throughout late July and early August the military situation remained fluid. Late in July, according to Red reports, Wrangel's forces were active around Aleksandrovsk and Guliaipole, where they held the line of rail Kamyshevatka-Orekhov.[117] But by 4 August Red forces were able to advance without opposition into the villages around Guliaipole. At Tsarekonstantinovka, however, they met stiff White resistance, and were forced to fall back to the east.[118] By mid-September, nonetheless, the Reds were well-established at Guliaipole, which was by that time the headquarters of the 13th Army's 42nd Division.[119] The Division's main tasks, among others, were to defend the Gaichur river valley from south of Chaplino across to Guliaipole.[120] At this time, according to an estimate by a foreign reporter, Makhno's core of effective troops was only about 2,000 men, but he could draw on up to 20 or 30 thousand reserves from the villages.[121]

Through the summer the *makhnovtsy* conducted three long-distance raids on the left bank, covering a distance of 1,500 kilometres, tying the Red Army down and encouraging desertion.[122] Belash says that as many as 45 percent of the insurgents were Red Army deserters at this time.[123] On 24 August, in what was apparently a push eastwards, Makhno occupied Gubinikha, about twelve miles north of Novomoskovska, with a force of 3,000 infantry and about 700 cavalrymen. But the Reds were unsure of his intentions, or in which direction he intended to move. An order was issued concentrating the forces of the 2nd Cavalry Army against Makhno, and organising the rear, especially with regard to intelligence gathering.[124] Ferocious fighting followed. In one engagement at Kocherezhki village, on the night of 25–6 August, two Makhno infantry regiments with 30 machine-guns, and with another three regiments in reserve, were pushed back eastwards by the 115th Red Cavalry Regiment under A. A. Derevenskii. The *makhnovtsy* sustained heavy losses, with over 200 fighters taken prisoner; Derevenskii was later awarded the Order of the Red Banner.[125]

The game of alliances continued. In late August, the Petliurists remained unsure of Makhno's intentions in the absence of reliable information about the composition of his forces, the seat of his administration and the basis of his military operations. The only source of intelligence was via Wrangel, already in the business of disinformation. The Petliurists were also uneasy about what one document termed Wrangel's 'relatively unclear political views on Ukrainian matters' although they were willing to talk to him about military cooperation. In the military sphere, the objective was to avoid 'regrettable conflicts' between the two sides, which would 'only serve to benefit the Bolsheviks'.[126] The Petliurists estimated the size of Wrangel's forces at 35,000 men, believing that *makhnovshchina* was larger.[127] The Petliurists were also overly optimistic about the hold that Ukrainian nationalist ideas had on Red Army men, reporting for example that some of Budenny's cavalrymen had made Ukrainian flags, presumably in preparation for some sort of nationalist demonstration.[128] In the summer of 1920 reports surfaced of Makhno's forces operating against river-boats and even from aircraft. On 1 August, for example, the *makhnovtsy* machine-gunned the steamer *Nadezhda* on the Dnepr River, and then boarded the vessel and robbed officers and passengers. The Jewish passengers were taken away into the forest, and the boat was burned.[129] Later in August an unverified account claimed that Makhno's proclamations were being dropped from aircraft and were confusing the peasantry.[130]

On 24 September 1920 Kamenev defined the two main tactical objectives for his southern forces as first, preventing Wrangel from descending on the Kuban again, and second, liquidating *makhnovshchina*. As we shall see, this second objective was achieved in another sense by the beginning of October, through the forging of a real alliance. It was necessary, ordered Kamenev, to pay special attention to consolidating the coastlines of the Sea of Azov and the Black Sea, as well as reinforcing and training Red troops, including garrisons in 'unreliable regions and spots'.[131] Politically the Reds supposed that 'if Wrangel disappears, then Makhno will disappear as well', believing that victory over the Whites and the establishment of a 'solid revolutionary regime' in Ukraine would remove the conditions in which Makhno thrived – an analysis that events showed to be wide of the mark.[132]

Makhnovshchina's ability to sustain guerrilla warfare of the type which took place for months on end in 1920 and 1921 cannot, however, be understood simply in military terms:

> ... the project for a system of free Soviets in its development and opposition to the Bolshevik project of Soviet power is usually presented as the background for the dashing battles and guerrilla raids of the *makhnovtsy*. It should be the other way around.[133]

In such a context, despite the fact that the Red Army's attention was strategically divided in 1920 (as it was not in 1921), the Ukrainian communists' agrarian policy was a determinant factor in 1920. Peasant discontent was widespread, and the policy actually fanned the flames of class warfare among the peasantry. As mentioned earlier, the KP(b)U had passed a decree in April 1919 establishing Committees of Poor Peasants (*kombedy*).[134] In March 1920, the fourth All-Ukrainian Conference of the KP(b)U, meeting in Khar'kov adopted yet another decision in favour of the continued existence of the *kombedy*.[135]

The *kombedy* in Russia had been introduced in mid-1918 with two main objectives, namely to split the peasantry, and to provide a system of informers who could assist in requisitioning grain from the 'rich peasants' (*kulaki* or 'tight-fisted ones'; Ukrainian *kurkul'y*).[136] Food supplies had dropped sharply because of the loss of grain-producing areas, and an overall falling trend in agricultural productivity that predated the revolution. It was assumed that the kulaks, holding over a third of the land and producing half the marketed grain, were withholding surplus, and that the actions of informers would intensify the split – the class division – between rich and poor peasants. But the *kombedy* did not work as planned in Russia, and created serious problems into the bargain. The Bolsheviks expected class hatred to intensify, thus helping the grain requisition detachments by using the animosity of the poor against the rich. But although the *kombedy* spread rapidly to villages in Russia, the number of truly landless peasants had fallen since the redistribution of 1917, and many landless peasants had effectively become middle peasants. Unsurprisingly, many peasants wanted to *become* kulaks – successful farmers – rather than fighting against them.[137] Some scholars believe that the class differentiation of the peasantry was not as developed at this time as the Bolsheviks supposed.[138] Indeed, Teodor Shanin has argued that there is no evidence for the kulak nature of peasant rebellions, which were rather 'general peasant revolt[s] against extensive taxation and poor supplies'.[139] In December 1918 the All-Russian Central Executive Committee (VTsIK) decreed disbandment of the committees.

The Ukrainian Bolsheviks believed, as Carr indicates, that the capitalist and large-scale character of agriculture in Ukraine meant that their country was particularly ready for socialism. The corollary was a perception that the kulaks were also relatively more powerful than they were in Russia. The *kombedy* thus lasted longest in Ukraine, continuing until 1923, well into the NEP period, because peasant capitalist relations in agriculture were most developed there.[140] The land expropriations had destroyed large-scale agriculture and thus denied the Bolsheviks the crops (such as cotton) that they needed to sustain industrial development.[141] In Ukraine, seen as both a grain-surplus area and as a territory of counter-revolution, the *komnezamy* may have continued to facilitate access by poorer peasants to implements and draught animals.[142] Additionally, the *komnezamy* may have survived in Ukraine because of Bolshevik political weakness. Unlike the rural soviets (*rady*), they were Bolshevik-controlled. They were used to police the unruly Ukrainian villages, and most especially the rural intelligentsia (teachers, agronomists and others) – and by the end of the period their membership was no longer largely poor peasant.[143] Indeed, 'they were composed largely of "lumpen-proletariat" elements from the city, charged with performing police functions'.[144]

In June and July 1920 Wrangel was in a weak position. He had to hold on to the northern Tauride to secure food supplies for his forces in Crimea. His only international support by this time came from the French.[145] His army consisted of 25,000 infantry and 6,000 cavalry, to defend a 500-kilometre front.[146] It was essential that his forces secure this front before the full weight of the Red Army, with an estimated 350,000 men available if they were needed, and no longer occupied with the Poles, was turned to crush the Whites. Wrangel's territory was flanked on the left by the river Dnepr, upstream as far as the Kichkas pass at Aleksandrovsk, which was easy to defend. His right flank stretched from Aleksandrovsk down to Berdiansk on the Sea of Azov coast, and was much more vulnerable. In an attempt to pre-empt pressure on this right flank, Wrangel began to push north-eastwards in early September, along the coast towards Mariupol' and Taganrog, threatening to overrun Makhno's heartland around Guliaipole. In the weeks that followed, the Whites succeeded in capturing several urban centres: Aleksandrovsk, Melitopol', Mariupol' and Nikopol' and the key railway junction at Sinel'nikovo, to the east of Ekaterinoslav.

The successful White advance into Makhno's territory was clearly a major threat to the insurgents, who were now faced for the second time with the possibility of finding themselves in a war on two fronts against two superior enemies. According to anarchist sources, Makhno's VRS was the first to propose a cease-fire and an alliance to the Red Army, and in fact did so twice, in July and then again in August, but the Bolsheviks did not reply to these overtures.[147] By the end of September, much of Makhno's home territory around Guliaipole was effectively in Wrangel's hands. Makhno had been doing little more than raiding the transport systems and food depots in the rear. Even Russian anarchists seem to have realised that the Makhno insurgency was in a difficult situation. The anarchist newspaper *Nabat* wrote in a contemporary editorial:

> Anarchism, which always leaned upon the mass movement of the workers, has to support the Makhno movement with all its power; it has to join this movement and close ranks with it. Hence, we must also become a part of the leading organ of this movement, the army, and try to organize with the help of the latter the movement as a whole.[148]

This was not a period when anarchists had much cause for optimism: indeed, Kropotkin gloomily told Volin at Dmitrov in November 1920 that this 'typical unsuccessful revolution' could well end in 'profound reaction'.[149] But there would be one more roll of the dice before the year was out.

The Last Act: Alliance at Starobel'sk, Wrangel's Defeat, and Betrayal at Perekop

By late 1920 the possibility of an 'all-left coalition' on a large scale had disappeared, and political identities had 'crystallised' and hardened into inflexible positioning.[1] Makhno's fourth and last alliance with the Bolsheviks was a final attempt to forge such a coalition politically, within the broad framework of *atamanshchina*, the movements of local chieftains. Soviet historians later argued that it was Makhno's precarious military and political situation that forced him to negotiate another alliance with the Red Army.[2] However, this was as much a political moment as a military one, and despite the importance of properly understanding the military history of the Makhno movement, the details of the fourth agreement show the extent to which it is an error to classify Makhno as merely a daring partisan leader with anarchist ideas. The movement he led was not fundamentally a military movement at all. Azarov argues that the armistice between the Bolsheviks and the *makhnovtsy* in late September, and the political provisions of the formal agreement signed a few days later, on 2 October, constituted a lost opportunity. If it had been possible to implement the political provisions, the Starobel'sk agreement might have constituted 'a turning point ... [in] the development of constructive anarchism, as well as the transformation of the political systems of Ukraine and Russia.'[3] Makhno had no intention of renouncing his territorial claims for military advantage, or of abandoning the concept of an 'Autonomous Republic of Free Soviets'.[4] However, a combination of short-sightedness, mistrust, resentment and eventually betrayal by the various actors, in the horrendous conditions of late 1920, combined to deliver precisely the outcome that Makhno wished to avoid.[5]

On 27 September, the 'hugely talented' Bolshevik military theorist Mikhail Frunze arrived in Khar'kov to take over operations against Wrangel.[6] Frunze had been successful in other theatres, and was personally courageous.[7] 'Our task,' he decided immediately, 'is not the occupation of territory, but the destruction of the living forces of the enemy.'[8] From Wrangel's point of view, it made sense to engage the Red Army on the steppe of the northern Tauride for as long as possible. The terrain favoured his experienced cavalry in a war of manoeuvre, and he would be able to delay a retreat southward to ensure supplies for winter. Given the disparity in numbers in favour of the Reds, this was a high-risk strategy, unless the line of retreat to Crimea could be secured. Frunze, commanding the 4th, 6th and 13th Red Armies as well as the 2nd Cavalry Army, had two choices. He could either accept Wrangel's challenge to fight on the steppe while trying to cut off his retreat in an encirclement campaign; or he could simply push him back with the Red Army's superior numbers to his defensive lines and besiege Crimea.

As late as August, the Bolsheviks were confident that they needed no allies. They outnumbered the Whites by a significant margin: 26,000 infantry and 4,000 cavalry, with tanks, armoured trains and aircraft, against Wrangel's 15,000 infantry and 10,000 cavalry. It was only in cavalry that Wrangel held an advantage.[9] Makhno's forces, 12,000 strong, consisted mainly of his widely admired cavalry.[10] If Frunze was to trap Wrangel, the Reds needed to deploy such mobile troops. In late September, Kamenev ordered Budenny's and Voroshilov's 1st Cavalry Army back from the Polish Front, but it had been in heavy fighting in August and took several weeks to arrive in southern Ukraine. Anxious to avoid another lengthy winter campaign, Frunze opted for the first choice.[11] Makhno's forces were occupying an area 'where [the Bolsheviks] had no troops at all'[12] and within 48 hours of taking command Frunze was working to neutralise *makhnovshchina* as an anti-Bolshevik force.[13]

Negotiations between the Bolsheviks and the *makhnovtsy* began in late September, and quickly moved forward.[14] In a telephone conversation between the two sides on 29 September, Makhno's representative, Dmitri Popov, started to deliver a political speech about revolutionary purity (mentioning the *makhnovtsy's* hanging of two emissaries from Wrangel). The Bolshevik, Mantsev, responded impatiently

> ... you did not answer my ... questions. Everything that you say has been said several times, but we understood from your telegram today that you seriously wanted to [meet] and that your situation is unbearable ... if we are mistaken in the interpretation of your telegram, [then] there is no ground for further conversations ...[15]

A delegation came to the camp at Starobel'sk, in western Khar'kov province, where Makhno's headquarters had been established. The details of the agreement which was eventually concluded were then finalised. In the telephone conversation already mentioned, Mantsev had told Popov that partisan command structures would remain in place; hostile action would cease immediately; and anarchist prisoners (including Volin in Moscow) would be released.[16] The Bolshevik delegation was not authorised to ratify the accord, however, and it was sent back to Khar'kov for approval. A delegation of three *makhnovtsy* accompanied the document.[17] On 29 September – the same day – Frunze told Kamenev that 'a final answer from Makhno must be received by midday today, but there's nothing from him yet'.[18]

Published KP(b)U Politburo minutes explain what Frunze was referring to. On the same day as his call, 29 September, it was resolved to nominate a representative to Makhno, to order the underground Bolshevik structures to assist *makhnovshchina* and to strengthen insurgent discipline. There was to be no integration of the insurgents into the Red Army's structures, and cooperation was to be limited to operational contacts. As Mantsev told Popov, the Bolsheviks consented 'not to object in principle' to the release of anarchist prisoners.[19] Trotsky remained suspicious: in a telegram to Frunze on 1 October, he asked for reassurances that Makhno would not just take his supplies and then turn against the Red Army again.[20]

On 4 October Frunze and Bela Kun sent a secret message to the headquarters of the 6th and 13th Armies, and to the 2nd Cavalry Army, among others, reporting that Makhno's VRS had asked for a ceasefire on 30 September (after the Politburo meeting). Frunze added that he had issued an order on 2 October halting operations against the *makhnovtsy* in return for recognition of Soviet power and submission to the command of the Front. Makhno was to join the struggle against Wrangel.[21] Clarification was needed for this about-turn. The Ukrainian Central Committee wrote to the Ekaterinoslav provincial committee representing the Starobel'sk agreement as a *purely military* affair, with the objective of moving Makhno's forces to Wrangel's rear. The blocking of contact between Red units and *makhnovtsy* remained in place, the letter stated, even though the *makhnovtsy*, except for criminals, were to be amnestied.[22] The Central Committee had already decided on 29 September that news of the Starobel'sk agreement was not to be published until after Makhno's forces were in action in Wrangel's rear.[23] The *makhnovtsy* refused to implement the agreement until it was published, but the Bolsheviks only partially released the text, leaving one clause out altogether.[24]

The agreement consisted of two sections, a military accord and, importantly, a political one. The Bolsheviks published the military part first, considering it to be the most important.[25] As agreed on the telephone, this allowed the *makhnovtsy* to retain their internal command structure, while accepting subordination to the Red Army. It also laid down restrictions on the acceptance of Red deserters into insurgent ranks and extended Red Army welfare provisions to the families of partisans. When the Ukrainian Council of People's Commissars minuted its approval of both sections on 31 October, it added that the decree on assistance to soldiers' families should be publicised among the insurgents.[26] The Bolsheviks may have believed that the extension of welfare provisions would have the effect of locking the Insurgent Army into the agreement as far as other provisions were concerned: in exchange for the partisans fighting for the Reds, the Reds fed the partisans' families.[27]

The political agreement required concessions on both sides.[28] Azarov, posing the question of whether the agreement should be deemed a victory or a defeat for the *makhnovtsy*, comments that for modern anarchists, accustomed to an 'uncompromising denial of the state' the political provisions might look like a defeat, but they nevertheless represented an opportunity, made possible by legalisation, to shift from an unwinnable armed struggle to a *political struggle within the Soviet state*.[29] This idea had been discussed as early as February, at a meeting in Nikolaev, when the commander Ivan Dolzhenko argued that the *makhnovtsy* should hand over their weapons to the 'museum of the revolution' and organise 'a few free communes ... under Soviet conditions'.[30]

Ukrainian Bolsheviks were more accepting of aspects of anarchist thinking than their Russian counterparts. This was partly a consequence of their political weakness and their 'extreme heterogeneity'.[31] The party dismissed as utopianism the idea of denying state power during the revolutionary process, adding

> ... if we understand anarchism as a struggle against bureaucratic centralism, as the development of initiatives by the working masses, as the desire of the masses themselves to encourage a conscious participation in socialist creativity, we see no harm ...[32]

In this context, the agreement included three main political points. Anarchist prisoners were to be released immediately; *makhnovshchina* was to enjoy freedom of expression and the press, including access to printing houses; and, most importantly, the *makhnovtsy* were to have the right to participate in the December elections to the Ukrainian Congress of Soviets. The *makhnovtsy* attempted unsuccessfully to get the Reds to agree to a fourth clause, arguing that since a basic principle of their movement was the struggle for self-management by workers, they had to insist that:

> ... in the region where Makhno's army is operating, the population of workers and peasants will create its own institutions of economic and political self-management; these institutions will be autonomous and joined in federation, by means of agreements, with the government organs of the Soviet republic.[33]

This paragraph became a source of conflict. The Bolsheviks told the insurgents that they would have to refer the proposal to Moscow for approval; but the subject was quietly dropped.[34] Regardless, the Starobel'sk agreement – even in its restricted form – must be seen as

... truly an unprecedented agreement ... nobody, no single party, no single movement had been able to extract more from the Bolsheviks than the *makhnovtsy* ... the Rebel Army maintained complete internal independence and its principles of organisation; mobilisation ... in the liberated areas was permitted; the families of the *makhnovtsy* enjoyed the same benefits as Red Army families ...[35]

Later – when they no longer needed the *makhnovtsy* as a cavalry force[36] – the Bolsheviks moved to negate the concessions and even now continued to launch verbal assaults despite the guarantee that 'all forms of persecution' would cease.

Trotsky was not the only Bolshevik who was worried about Makhno's reliability. In a speech on 3 November, Lenin grouped Makhno with Iudenich, Kolchak and Petliura as 'remnants of the Kerensky gang, the SRs and the social democrats', merely different kinds of counter-revolutionary.[37] But on 9 October he reassured a meeting in Moscow that the Bolsheviks could only gain from the alliance. Makhno was 'hedged around with guarantees', and his men, having experienced Wrangel's policies once, were not keen to repeat the ordeal. This was an important point: by acting as he did in Guliaipole and its environs, Wrangel had helped mobilise support for Makhno. Ignoring the rights of the peasantry was the same mistake that Denikin and Kolchak had made.[38] Trotsky returned to the subject in a text published on 10 October, in which he acknowledged that Makhno had 'offered his services' but asked rhetorically whether such an alliance was permissible as well as dangerous. Ukraine lagged behind Russia in political development, and the German invasion followed by repeated regime changes had created confusion, exploited by the kulaks who 'united the village' against the advanced proletariat.[39] The *makhnovtsy*, Trotsky continued, must clear their ranks of kulaks and bandits and become familiar with 'the work of the Soviet government'. In any case, he concluded, the strength of the partisans should not be exaggerated: they were 'only a very small detachment'.[40]

In October the *makhnovtsy* were called upon to play an active part in Frunze's ultimately unsuccessful attempt to encircle Wrangel before winter came and before he could pull back into the Crimean Peninsula. By the 15th of the month Frunze had decided to move the insurgents to the eastern flank and on 21 October the *makhnovtsy* were ordered to advance, by a forced march at night, to the east of the Whites, in the direction of Iantsevo-Sofievka, where they were to cut off an armoured train and strike at Wrangel's rear.[41] On 22 October Makhno helped to capture over 4,000 prisoners from a White division retreating towards Aleksandrovsk, which was recaptured.[42] This success did not satisfy Frunze, who believed that the *makhnovtsy* were not reacting quickly enough. A few days later the Bolshevik command exhorted them to continue to carry out orders energetically, and to move in the direction of Orekhov-B.

Tokmak-Melitopol', raiding transport links, communications and railways. They were to reach the Crimean isthmus no later than 29 October.[43]

On 26 October Frunze ordered a general advance, and notified Lenin that their chances of completing the encirclement and capturing the isthmus were not good. He was unable to get his troops moving fast enough, and displayed 'an almost complete failure in the coordination of arms' (i.e. cavalry and artillery with the infantry), reacting quite slowly to events on the ground: 'his rapid reactions, when they occurred, were almost always tactical and not strategic', and he missed opportunities to eliminate the Wrangel threat because of this.[44] Lenin was dissatisfied. 'I am outraged by your optimistic tone, when you go on to report that there is only one chance in a hundred ...'[45] he thundered. But not even Lenin was able to get the Red forces moving. On 28 October, a full two days after the order had been issued, Frunze's army group moved into action. The group was deployed along a gently curved front, with the 6th Army and the two Cavalry Armies facing Wrangel's left flank across the Dnepr, and the 4th and 13th Armies opposite his more exposed right flank, from Aleksandrovsk down to the Sea of Azov.

Meanwhile Makhno stormed enemy entrenchments and captured 200 prisoners and four artillery pieces – but his rate of advance was too slow for the impatient Frunze, who was under pressure from Moscow and saw his chances of encircling Wrangel slipping away. Makhno's forces passed to the west of Tokmak only on the morning of 29 October.[46] The next day, units of the 13th Red Army occupied Melitopol', and two days later entered Akimova, capturing 'immense prizes', in what Red dispatches described as a 'swift blow'. By the beginning of November, thanks to Bolshevik sluggishness, Wrangel had executed an 'active retirement' from the Northern Tauride past the 1st Cavalry Army and other Red forces, and was ensconced behind the Perekop-Chongar defensive lines, across the series of narrow isthmuses and peninsulas which either connect or almost connect the body of the Crimea to the Ukrainian mainland.[47]

The main westward approach to Crimea, the isthmus of Perekop, was between eight and eleven kilometres across, protected by the Turkish Wall, an ancient military earthwork with a deep ditch in front of it on the northern side. From the bottom of the ditch to the top of the rampart was 20 metres, a steep 45-degree slope. Wrangel had set up forward defensive lines a few kilometres in front of the rampart. His last line of defence was the Iushun' line, just under 20 kilometres to the south, strategically located in an area dotted with small inland lakes, at a point where the Perekop isthmus widened out into the Crimean peninsula proper.[48] To the east of Perekop, three long and narrow spits of land jut out into the Sivash Sea. The first of these, which sticks out from the side of the Perekop isthmus south of the Turkish Wall, is the Lithuanian Peninsula, which reaches northwards to within five kilometres of the Ukrainian mainland.

Fifty kilometres to the east, the Chongar Peninsula reaches southwards from the mainland to within a few hundred metres of Crimea. The Whites destroyed two bridges across this stretch of water when they retreated from the Northern Tauride.

The most important of the land connections was the longest and narrowest of all, the Arabat Spit, which runs parallel to the eastern coast of the Crimea proper, and connects the Kerch Peninsula almost to the mainland. It was possible to cross from the Arabat Spit into Crimea behind the defensive lines prepared by Wrangel, and this had been done in earlier battles in the area, but the presence of unopposed White naval forces in the Sea of Azov made it a suicidal manoeuvre.[49] Since he was unable to outflank the White positions along the Arabat Spit, Frunze was compelled to launch frontal assaults on the prepared defensive positions of Perekop and Chongar.[50]

For the assault, the *makhnovtsy* were deployed with six other divisions and a brigade as part of the 4th Red Army, opposite Chongar. Makhno's strength is given in an apparently authoritative table from Frunze's office as being 4,000 infantry, 1,000 cavalry and 6,000 'other troops', with 13,600 support personnel, 250 machine-guns and 12 artillery pieces.[51] However, they were ill-equipped for a cold weather campaign: on 2 November Belash sent a telegram to Frunze asking for greatcoats, boots and underwear, as well as rifles, ammunition and hand-grenades. The list included saddles for the cavalry.[52] On 5 November, Frunze ordered the *makhnovtsy* to move before the 8th to a line Vladimirovka–Stroganovka–Malyi Kugaran, in order to be ready to attack the Perekop positions from the rear at the same time as the main Red forces launched a frontal attack.[53]

Unfortunately, although some units of the 6th Red Army succeeded in wading across the Sivash to the Lithuanian Peninsula early on the morning of 8 November in unusual weather conditions, they were quickly spotted by the Whites: 'our advancing units can be seen and fired on by long-range artillery at a distance of 8–10 kilometres', reported one commander.[54] Nevertheless, the Bolshevik forces established a beach-head on the peninsula. But Frunze was still unable to coordinate his forces – no artillery barrage was laid down on the Perekop fortifications, shrouded by fog, and no infantry attack was attempted.[55] It was only during the early afternoon of 8 November that he managed to get a frontal assault on the Perekop fortifications under way. At high cost to the Reds, the Whites managed to beat back a series of infantry charges throughout the afternoon and on into the night.[56]

Meanwhile, the weather had changed, and the waters were rising at the fords which the 6th Army units had used to cross over to the Lithuanian Peninsula. Frunze ordered another vigorous attack on the Perekop fortifications, set men to work to keep the fords open, and ordered two cavalry divisions and the Insurgent Army across the Sivash to reinforce the 6th Army beach-head. The cavalry commanded by Marchenko crossed first, on the morning of the 9th, followed by a machine-gun regiment under Foma Kozhin. Makhno crossed at 4:00 a.m. in fog.[57] The crossing was made under fire with many casualties, including Kozhin himself.[58] In the meantime, Frunze's repeated battering of the Turkish Wall had at last paid off, and early that same morning Wrangel pulled his main defensive force back to the Iushun' line to avoid being outflanked by the 6th Army and the *makhnovtsy*.[59]

The fighting was not yet over, although White commanders believed that the battle was already lost.[60] Wrangel had managed to withdraw his troops down the Perekop Peninsula without heavy losses, was still in possession of a defensible line at Iushun', and was advanced in his preparations for a full evacuation if necessary. Frunze still had the upper hand, with superiority in numbers, now including cavalry. He was on the offensive; the partisans were harassing Wrangel's rear; Wrangel knew that he did not have to make a stand; and Wrangel had lost international support.[61]

The battle for the Iushun' line was fiercely contested. While it raged, Frunze was starting to apply pressure in Chongar, and two rifle regiments won the Order of the Red Banner for their persistence, which resulted in the over-running of two White regiments and the fall of the small Crimean town of Tiup-Dzhankoi on 11 November.[62] By this time Wrangel had already decided for evacuation, and on the same day, 11 November, ignoring a demand from Frunze that he surrender, he issued a general proclamation to the people of Russia:

> … I now order the evacuation and embarkation at the Crimean ports of all those who are following the Russian army on its road to Calvary; that is to say, the families of the soldiers, the officials of the Civil Administration and their families, and anyone else who would be in danger if they fell into the hands of the enemy … May God grant us strength to endure this period of Russian misery …[63]

The evacuation was carried out without major panic, and by 14 November Sevastopol' was empty of Whites. On the 13th or 14th *makhnovtsy* troops under Semen Karetnik[64] occupied Simferopol'.[65] The operation was repeated at a series of coastal cities, until on 16 November the last White ship steamed away from Kerch. The evacuation removed 145,693 people in 126 ships from what was now Soviet soil.[66]

It is difficult to evaluate the importance of the role of the *makhnovtsy* in the defeat of Wrangel.[67] In the Soviet period, their participation was rarely mentioned, and when it was acknowledged it was often 'minimised or distorted'.[68] Litvinov claims that the Makhno forces played a 'glorious' role[69] and Jacobs says that 'without Makhno's actions at Perekop the war might well have gone into the winter campaign which Lenin feared'.[70] Frunze began to disparage the

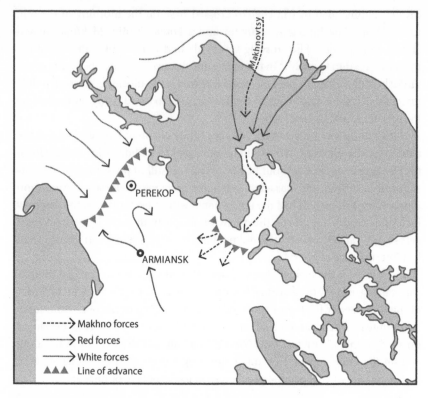

Map 7.1   The Battle against Wrangel, Perekop, Crimea, 1920

The *makhnovtsy* played a role in the definitive defeat of the Whites under Wrangel, but as soon as their military usefulness expired, the Bolsheviks attempted to neutralise them. (Cartographer: Jenny Sandler).

makhnovtsy almost immediately. On 13 November, in reply to a question from Kamenev about the behaviour of the insurgents, Frunze remarked that 'in the most recent engagements the insurgents played their part indifferently. They avoided in an obvious way missions which entailed the risk of serious losses'.[71] A few days later he accused Makhno of only sending 'an insignificant bunch of his followers' to the front against Wrangel.[72]

The Bolsheviks now began to put into action their plans, approved by Lenin, to liquidate the *makhnovtsy*. They were finalised at a meeting – attended by Trotsky – of the Central Committee of the KP(b)U in Khar'kov on 14 November.[73] The process was to be much the same as it had been on earlier occasions – 'a sudden strike at the commanders and staff at the top of the army, and then arrests and a wave of slanders'.[74] The same day, the insurgents sent a telegram to the headquarters of the Southern Front protesting the 'illegal harassment and arrests' of Makhno's supporters in the villages 'in the name of the struggle against banditry'.[75] They had good reasons for concern. The next day Frunze warned his commanders that he was preparing plans 'to clear the territory of Ukraine from bandit gangs as soon as possible'[76] and on the 17th he issued the first of a series of orders intended to liquidate the anarchists. Order 00106 abolished the Southern Front and transferred units to other commands. Makhno's insurgent army was passed over to the command of the 4th Red Army, which meant that the *makhnovtsy*, together with the 9th Infantry Division, were to move to the Caucasus. The actual order was buried in a long text dealing with various Southern Front matters.[77]

The next order, 00149, was issued on 23 November and was addressed specifically to Makhno, repeating the instructions and expanding on them. Since Wrangel had been defeated, the order argued (completely ignoring the provisions of the Starobel'sk accord) that, 'the task of the Insurgent Army is completed ... There is no longer any reason for [it] to continue to exist'. All insurgent units in Crimea were to be incorporated into the 4th Army; units at Guliaipole were to be dissolved and the soldiers sent to the reserve; and the insurgent VRS was to explain to its soldiers why the steps were necessary.[78]

Makhno's counter-intelligence was alerted by Red troop movements. Some Cheka agents were captured and they confirmed that preparations were underway to attack the *makhnovtsy*.[79] Frunze reported to Lenin that the 'liquidation of the remnants of the partisans' would begin within 48 hours,[80] and on the 24th issued order 00155 telling his subordinates to get ready 'at any moment' to crush the kulak-anarchists 'boldly, decisively and mercilessly'.[81] The order accuses 'various groups, calling themselves *makhnovtsy*' of robbery and the killing of Red Army soldiers, and adds that 'front-line units of the Insurgent Army refused on 20 November 1920 to obey the Front's combat order to move to the Caucasus'. It concludes with several paragraphs of invective, concluding that 'all bandit gangs must be destroyed and all weapons seized'.[82]

The Bolsheviks accused Makhno of refusing to obey orders, but it is possible that they were never in fact received.[83] The published copy of order 00106 is marked 'Secret' and is addressed, 'To all, besides the Commander of the 4th. To the Commanders of the 4th, 6th, 1st and 2nd Cavalry. Copy to Commander-in-Chief'. Arshinov says that Makhno was recovering from a leg wound and 'did not concern himself at all with paperwork' which was handled by subordinates. According to Arshinov, accusations were circulating on the *makhnovtsy* side that Bolshevik spies had been captured and a plot to assassinate Makhno uncovered 'which must have taken at least ten or 15 days' to prepare. The Bolsheviks, for their part, accused the *makhnovtsy* of distributing copies of the unofficial 4th political clause of the Starobel'sk agreement as part of a call for a general insurrection.[84]

The Bolsheviks moved decisively against *makhnovshchina* on 26 November but failed to close the net completely. At 3:00 a.m. Makhno's delegation in Khar'kov was arrested, along with large numbers of anarchists all over Ukraine.

At 5:00 a.m., Bolshevik forces began an artillery bombardment of insurgent positions in Guliaipole; simultaneously units in Crimea were attacked, and insurgent staff members, including Semen Karetnik, were arrested in Mariupol' and summarily shot.[85] Arshinov insists that the orders were not received by either the headquarters in Guliaipole or the *makhnovtsy* delegation in Khar'kov. The order dated 23 November, he says, was published for the first time in the Khar'kov newspaper *Kommunist* for 15 December.[86]

On 26 November order 00131 accused Makhno of mobilising against the Red Army and of launching hostilities around Guliaipole. The order declared that 'Makhno and all his units' were to be considered enemies of the Soviet Republic and the revolution. The *makhnovtsy* were to be disarmed, and if they resisted, were to be 'annihilated'. The whole territory of the Ukrainian SSR', the order concluded, was to be 'cleansed'.[87] But the attempt to liquidate the Makhno movement at one blow had failed, and clearing it out of Ukrainian territory was to prove a more difficult task than Frunze had anticipated.

There is some evidence to indicate that the Bolsheviks had decided to liquidate the anarchist-Makhno menace even before the end of the campaign against Wrangel. According to one eye-witness, a former Chekist, when the *makhnovtsy* entered Sevastopol' with the victorious Red Army, they raised the cry 'Our Crimea and everything in it!' – beginning an orgy of plunder, murder and rape.[88] Additionally, the last clause of the Starobel'sk political agreement would have allowed these same disruptive *makhnovtsy* to participate in elections to the Soviets in the Ukraine, and to the 5th All-Ukrainian Congress of Soviets in December.

Evidence of Bolshevik bad faith is widely cited by anarchist sources. The *makhnovtsy* found undated leaflets on Red Army prisoners proclaiming, 'Death to *makhnovshchina*!' The captives said that they had been distributed as early as 15 and 16 November, immediately after it had become clear that Wrangel had been defeated.[89] Even more convincing, however, is the series of sweeps which took place at this time against anarchists and their organisations. The Cheka moved against the Khar'kov-based Nabat federation, arresting many prominent figures, including Volin, and sending them to Moscow, where Grigorii Maksimov, Kh. Z. Iarchuk and others were also imprisoned.[90] Arrests were also made in Elisavetgrad, and in Khar'kov the *Vol'noe Bratstvo* bookshop was raided.[91] Some of the more courageous anarchists tried to raise their voices in protest, but in vain.[92]

There is controversy about deadlines and whether documents were delivered or even read. Nevertheless, there is no doubt that the Bolsheviks betrayed their allies in late November 1920. The accusations levied against the *makhnovtsy* were relatively trivial, and the order to disband was a violation of the Starobel'sk agreement. Frunze was playing out a 'comedy', in which 'the essence of the issue [was that] not one of the ... orders *was officially handed to the makhnovtsy*' thus enabling him to claim that 'Makhno openly opposed the Soviet government and the Red Army'[93] as a justification for the attack. Litvinov, in a lengthy denunciation, comments scathingly that the confusion was deliberate:

> ... at first glance, this [narrative] ... looks quite convincing, especially since its basis is not just someone's speculation, *but official orders from the commander of the Southern Front* ... However, if one thinks about these orders more deeply and ... considers them in connection with other official documents, then an unattractive picture of the *conscious falsification of historical facts* emerges ... Frunze had no right to unilaterally demand from Makhno the fulfilment of his orders ... Frunze was deliberately lying when he asserted that his order of 23 November was brought to the attention of Makhno ...[94]

The story of the Starobel'sk negotiations is nonetheless puzzling given the prior history of mistrust and bad faith between the protagonists, and the delicacy of the political and military circumstances at the end of 1920. Golovanov puts the question bluntly: 'why did Makhno, knowing Bolshevik methods of political struggle, believe that the alliance was serious?'[95]

The failure of the Red Army to eliminate *makhnovshchina* in November, set the scene for what Chop and Lyman dramatically call 'brutal combat' (*zhorstokii bytvi*) between two 'great generals'.[96] The *makhnovtsy* and the other rural revolts of this period were, however, finally beaten by a combination of overwhelming, concentrated military force, appropriate tactics, famine and arguably above all by the introduction – in Russia in early 1921 and in Ukraine in the autumn – of the New Economic Policy (NEP). From the peasants' viewpoint, the NEP meant principally the disappearance of the hated grain requisition detachments of the 'war communism' period and hence the removal of one of their main grievances against the Bolsheviks.[97]

Peasant complaints were centred on the question of food policy. Under war communism, the Bolsheviks had been brutally demanding. *Prodrazverstka* (the forced requisitioning of grain) cleaned out peasant storehouses to feed the industrial working class, causing bitter resentment. A limited attempt in 1919 to collectivise peasant production in *kommuny* was implemented in authoritarian style and threatened to kill off any idea of independent land-ownership. It was a failure, as was the policy of *ogosudarstvlenie* (governmentalisation) which would have imposed sowing plans on peasant households.[98] War communism had attempted to organise state production and distribution along communist lines and had fostered the illusion that socialist transformation was a real short-term possibility. Consequent labour obligations, grain requisitioning and attempts at collectivisation all combined with the disruptive impact of the war to fuel peasant discontent until revolts 'erupted like a chain of volcanoes'.[99]

The impact of the NEP was gradual. The situation in eastern Ukraine remained 'chaotic and uncontrolled' well into 1922, and sporadic violence – including by groups described as *makhnovtsy* – continued in the Ukrainian countryside until as late as 1926.[100] The NEP represented both the nemesis of *makhnovshchina* – and perhaps of the *atamanshchina* in general – and ironically, its victory. It was its nemesis because a generalised peasant insurrection became unsustainable, not only because of exhaustion and war weariness, but also because important causes of its discontent were disappearing. Makhno retained enough passive peasant support to keep fighting until August 1921, but the peasantry was no longer prepared to take up arms in defence of village democracy. On the other hand, the NEP was in some sense Makhno's 'victory' because

> ... together with the Kronshtadt [sic] mutiny and a series of workers' revolts, [peasant wars] forced the Bolshevik leadership in March 1921 to abandon the unpopular policies of war communism in favour of free trade under the NEP. Having defeated the White Army ... the Bolshevik government surrendered before its own peasantry.[101]

Other historians have argued that the movement actually increased its support in this final period, dismissing the idea that Makhno fought on only to survive. On the contrary,

> ... *the power of the Bolsheviks 'hung in the balance'*. Peasant uprisings swept the whole country, the workers of Petrograd went on strike, and Kronstadt rebelled. And all demanded the abandonment of the policy of ... 'war communism' and its elimination together with the one-party dictatorship ... after the Kronstadt uprising, the Bolsheviks made serious concessions to the peasantry ... to preserve their monopoly on power. The process of introducing the NEP stretched out over the spring-summer of 1921 ... in 1921 *there was still a chance of overthrowing the Bolshevik regime*.[102]

Winter was closing in, and Makhno needed to regroup, survive the winter and prepare for fighting in the spring. With most of his staff lost, individual initiative was priceless. The *makhnovtsy* cavalry commander, Marchenko, with about 200 men, managed to break through an encirclement by the 4th Red Army at Perekop, to meet up with Makhno and the rest of the Insurgent Army on 7 December at Kermenchik, in Mariupol' district, near the Sea of Azov. Makhno had broken out of encirclement at Guliaipole with between 150 and 200 fighters, and had been roaming the nearby countryside on a recruitment drive, which increased the size of his forces to 2,500 troops, of whom 1,500 were mounted.[103] On 1 December the *makhnovtsy* – three regiments of cavalry and two of infantry – were in action against units of the 1st Cavalry Army around Timoshevka, where Makhno was reportedly 'conducting a violent offensive along the whole sector with a continuous line of machine-guns', while trying to push through to the north-east.[104]

This engagement ended badly for the insurgents: by the afternoon, according to Red Army dispatches, the infantry regiments had been destroyed and the cavalry badly mauled, with many horses and *tachanki* captured. The survivors fled, pursued by Red cavalry.[105] Despite this setback, Makhno returned to attack Guliaipole on 3 December, expelling the Red Army's 42nd Division, and taking, it was claimed, nearly 6,000 prisoners, of whom 2,000 became recruits in their turn and the others were sent home.[106] A few days later, Makhno attacked again near Andreevka, and again took many prisoners. On 17 December, Frunze reported to Lenin and Trotsky that Makhno had broken through a triple encirclement three days earlier, and was now moving northwards with a large force and eight field-guns.[107] Within the space of a few days the *makhnovtsy* also fought actions at Komar', Tsarekonstantinovka and Berdiansk.[108] During the raid on Berdiansk on 12 December, under Makhno's personal command, the *makhnovtsy* allegedly killed 83 communists.[109]

The move towards the Sea of Azov and the raid on Berdiansk were motivated by a desire to link up with Udovychenko and to capture more horses. The idea was to shift away from Guliaipole, where there was a concentration of Red Army forces that left little room for manoeuvre.[110] Berdiansk was a trap, heavily fortified and with the sea to the south, but Makhno understood the approaches to the city:[111] what was required was to fall into the trap, show himself to the enemy, create the expectation of unanticipated victory and then slip out from the trap at the last moment.[112]

After the failure of the attempt to eliminate *makhnovshchina* by a swift surprise attack, the Red command fell back on a broad strategy of encirclement by large numbers.[113] Makhno switched to guerrilla tactics, relying for his advantage on rapid movement by horse and *tachanka*, on his own intimate knowledge of the terrain and on the tacit sympathy of the local population.[114] To keep his forces mobile, Makhno left the wounded behind in villages and hid arms and ammunition for later recovery.[115] By the middle of December, he had managed to rock the ill-prepared Red forces back on their heels, had acquired enough recruits from among his captives to double the size of his army and had accumulated quantities of arms, ammunition and equipment.[116] The threat that he posed to the pacification of the region was of grave concern to the Bolsheviks. They increased the effort which they were devoting to the campaign of encirclement, but to little avail. On 16 December Makhno's army was attacked by a large Red force at Federovka, to the south of Guliaipole, but after a long engagement lasting from 2 o'clock in the morning until 4 o'clock in the afternoon, he again broke through Bolshevik lines.[117] In this battle, Makhno lost all eight of his field-guns and much of his captured equipment. Three days later, on 17 December, Frunze reported to Lenin and Trotsky that Makhno had escaped with a handful of cavalry who were now being pursued. His infantry was dispersed.[118]

The Bolsheviks realised quite early on that this campaign could not be won by military means alone. But they were at a loss to discover what an appropriate politico-military strategy would look like. Frunze dispatched Antonov-Saratovskii, the People's Commissar for Internal Affairs in the Ukraine, to the *makhnovtsy* areas with 450 political workers. Their instructions were to strengthen the apparatus of Soviet power and to liquidate banditry – in other words to put political pressure on the civilian population to stop supporting Makhno.[119]

Insurgent prisoners were in a 'mood of extreme fatigue and demoralisation', wrote Frunze, and 'all that remains ... is to secure the position'.[120] The lack of enthusiasm among the troops on both sides for yet another winter campaign in the snow and icy mud of the Ukrainian steppe was evidenced by the frequency of desertion. Frunze's reference to the fatigue and demoralisation of the *makhnovtsy* rings true; but it applied with equal force to his own soldiers.[121] One of the most famous of these desertions happened in January 1921, when the commander of the 1st Brigade of Budenny's 4th Cavalry Division, Maslak (or Maslakov), deserted to Makhno, along with his whole unit. By March 1921 Maslak was commanding Makhno's operations in the Don and the Kuban.[122]

Such desertions encouraged the illusion among the partisans that a few victories would be enough to compel a Bolshevik withdrawal from Ukraine. However, the gradual closing of the net around the insurgent army and the large numbers deployed against them forced them to face reality. The Bolsheviks could not afford to let Ukraine go its own way, because Russia depended on it for food supply. If *makhnovshchina* was to avoid annihilation, an organised retreat was going to be necessary. They took a collective decision to allow Makhno complete tactical freedom regarding the direction of retreat.[123]

The Cheka took punitive measures against those suspected of being sympathisers with *makhnovshchina*.[124] These aimed to destroy Makhno's informal intelligence network among the local peasants.[125] In the conditions of flux which prevailed at the time, men, women and children, beggars, army deserters and orphans were used to maintain a constant stream of information to the *makhnovtsy* staff concerning Bolshevik movements and troop strengths.[126] They were the classic intelligence resources of people's war.[127]

The Red Army commander Robert Eideman – who wrote several texts on the civil war – developed an idiosyncratic line of analysis in which he argued that mobile partisan groups in left-bank Ukraine were unconnected to a 'passive' underground network that he believed existed mainly on the right bank. However, the 'active' *makhnovtsy* relied heavily on the reserve, not only for fighters, but also for such services as food supplies, medical services and logistics. Eideman's ignorance on this score, Litvinov concluded

> ... was so striking that even after a whole year he was completely convinced that the guerrillas of the underground and the raiding insurgents not only did not have a permanent internal connection, but that they were even geographically separate.[128]

Much Ukrainian terrain is unsuitable for guerrilla warfare. The countryside consists of a flat open plain, the steppe, without scattered towns and few natural hiding places. Military movements can be seen for kilometres. Only in the extreme north is there a belt of forests and swamps suitable for guerrillas to hide in.[129] It was a simple matter, with so many troops, for the Bolsheviks to bar the insurgents from access to roads and railway lines, and to slow their movement by forcing them onto the open steppe. The *makhnovtsy* were compelled to abandon heavy equipment, such as field-guns, so as to remain as mobile. Large military formations were restructured into manoeuvrable cavalry units of 150 to 200 riders.[130] They avoided pitched battles, ranging far outside their zone of influence, and even outside Ukraine – insurgent units raided as far afield as the Volga, the Kuban and the Don.[131] There were other changes: the *makhnovtsy* had lost many of their experienced commanders and discipline suffered. The insurgents started to kill communist prisoners unless they came over to their side, and to consider Chinese, Estonian, Latvian and Hungarian Red Army soldiers as mercenaries, not entitled to be treated as prisoners-of-war.[132] Peasant support began to waver, with supplies of fodder for the horses becoming more difficult to obtain.[133]

In the meantime, the Red Army, unaccustomed to this kind of fighting, faced the usual difficulties of large military formations when they are suddenly confronted by a different set of circumstances or by a different type of enemy. As the Reds blundered about, they developed a set of tactics – hardly a strategy – which, if not guaranteed to produce immediate results, did at least keep the insurgents on the run. These included continuous pursuit, the use of fast-reaction units with armoured cars, the denial of access to the home base and a hearts-and-minds campaign at village level.[134]

By early February the deployment of all these resources had had little effect and Lenin was warning Sklianskii 'one more time' that a result was expected. Makhno had escaped yet again, although faced by superior forces under strict orders. What, demanded Lenin, were the cavalry, armoured trains and cars, aircraft and other military hardware being used for? Grain and fuel were being lost, he added, while the Red Army was 'a million strong'.[135]

By the spring of 1921, the Bolsheviks were preparing to adapt to new economic conditions. The set of policies that constituted 'war communism' were replaced by the New Economic Policy (NEP), which in broad terms 'attempted to use commodity relations as the basis for constructing an alliance with the poor and middle peasantry, as a strategy for the construction of socialism'.[136] The NEP was a response to the domestic economic and political crisis of 1921:

> [t]he country as a whole was cold, hungry, disease-ridden, exhausted and embittered; and this was true as regards the majority of the industrial workers and a good many of the rank-and-file Communists.[137]

The most important plank in this policy platform was the tax-in-kind, introduced in Russia in March and described by Lenin as marking 'a transition ... to a regular socialist exchange of products'.[138] Grain requisitioning was replaced by the tax in an attempt to win peasant support. After the government had taken 25 per cent of the crop, the peasants could dispose of the remainder as they pleased. Significantly, the tax was to be less than what had been taken by requisitioning; it was to be progressive; responsibility for payment was individual, not collective; and the amount was to be fixed before the spring sowing.[139]

But things were not so simple. On 2 March Vladimirov, the Ukrainian Commissar for Food Supply, reported to Moscow that working conditions were 'such as to wreck all plans'. Makhno had completely destroyed the food supply system in both Aleksandrovsk and Berdiansk, and had massacred food supply workers there.[140] He was now doing the same around Kherson. He had crossed the Dnepr from Dneprovsk *uezd*, and had killed the district supply commissar as well as 42 workers from the Greater Aleksandrovsk food supply committee. From the Ukrainian point of view, continuing to supply the Donbass and the Red Army was an 'almost insoluble problem'. Food requisitioning in the Ukraine had altogether cost the lives of 1,700 workers.[141] Vladimirov was uneasy about the imminent change-over from grain requisitioning to the tax-in-kind, which he described as 'dangerous'. He argued that the peasants would contest the official crop assessments, acceptance of which was the basis for paying the tax and permitting the barter of the remaining crops.[142] Despite these and other objections, the tax-in-kind was promulgated on 15 March 1921.[143] Lenin commented to Trotsky that 'the Ukrainian communists are wrong. The conclusion is not against the tax, but for stronger measures for the total annihilation of Makhno'.[144] Nevertheless, the introduction of the NEP in Ukraine was delayed by six months. While Vladimirov was complaining about the change of policy, the unit led by the deserter Maslak, which despite the need for mobility still possessed two field-guns, was moving north-eastwards towards the undefended town of Tsaritsyn, where 500,000 *pudy* (about 9,000 tons) of grain, the only reserves for Astrakhan', were stored.[145]

The Bolsheviks were also counting on the war weariness of the Ukrainian peasants to help them liquidate *makhnovshchina*. Different approaches were tried. The 5th All-Ukrainian Congress of Soviets offered an amnesty to all 'bandits' who voluntarily turned themselves over to the authorities by 15 April, and later on the VTsIK extended the deadline. In April *Plamia Truda* reported some surrenders under the terms of this amnesty, including one allegedly involving 63 former insurgents in Guliaipole. On 1 June the same newspaper reported that some *makhnovtsy* insurgents had surrendered at Zmiev *uezd*, in Khar'kov, and had been given land.[146]

By March 1921, Makhno's situation had become desperate. His army was split up into marauding groups which carried out sabotage actions as they tried to survive by plundering military warehouses, or by battening onto the weary peasantry.[147] Makhno could only ride with difficulty because of a wounded foot, but saddled up to lead the insurgents in the now almost daily engagements, often fought with sabres, which the *makhnovtsy* grimly dubbed *rubki* ('choppings' or 'hackings').[148] He was wounded several times, in the stomach, leg and neck, and on each occasion was rescued by *tachanka*.[149] On 16 March, for example, after a pursuit which lasted 13 hours and covered about 180 kilometres, Makhno only managed to slip through the net thanks to a rear-guard action by a unit of Lewis machine-gunners, who all perished.[150]

The summer of 1921 was hot and dry, and Ukraine suffered from severe drought. Harvests failed in Ekaterinoslav, Tauride, parts of Kherson and Poltava, as well as on the Don. The Volga provinces were already suffering from famine conditions, and Ukraine was expected to step into the gap and send food to Petrograd and to Moscow. But Ukraine was also starving, although the fact was not mentioned in the Soviet press at the time.[151] In such conditions, even passive peasant support began to wither and dry up, and Makhno was forced to range wider and wider to find food. According to Frunze, who may well have wished to explain away his own failure to eliminate *partizanshchina*, he was operating in no less than fifteen *raiony* of Ukraine, with up to 15,000 well-armed cavalrymen.[152] Makhno claimed that his forces were in action in Ekaterinoslav, the Tauride, parts of Khar'kov and Poltava, the Don region, towards Kuban, and below Tsaritsyn and Saratov, and that he had led a raid across the Volga.[153] Certainly *makhnovtsy* units were active in Poltava, to the northwest and far from *makhnovshchina*'s traditional base of support, at the end of July and the beginning of August, although they were being pushed steadily north-westwards.[154] On one occasion Makhno reportedly clashed with a 1st Cavalry Army unit under the personal command of Semen Budenny, whom he described in a letter, quoted by Arshinov, as a 'disgraceful coward', although in later years he expressed respect for him as a worthy adversary.[155]

By July it was clear that time was running out, and that Makhno was fighting a rear-guard action. For whatever reasons, he failed to rethink his strategy, and although the movement expanded the areas in which it was active, it was unable to deliver any decisive blows. The partisan detachments that emerged in

Poltava and Chernigov regions had only weak links to Makhno and his ideas, although they revolted under his slogans. At the same time, the Bolsheviks began to adopt brutal scorched earth tactics, destroying entire villages suspected of supporting Makhno. The ranks of *makhnovshchina* began to melt away.[156]

Thousands of his troops surrendered to the Bolsheviks. At an open meeting in July, attended by about 1,000 partisans, Makhno argued for a retreat to Polish Galicia, while Viktor Belash expressed his willingness to go to Turkey to fight for Mustafa Kemal. The army began to disintegrate into small groups.[157] Newspaper reports published as far away as the United States announced, only a little prematurely, that Makhno had been 'hopelessly beaten' and that several of his commanders had surrendered.[158]

Meanwhile, the political campaign to equate *makhnovshchina* with straightforward banditry was gathering force.[159] At the first congress of the Profintern, the Russians took a tough position in the face of criticism from foreign delegates, some of whom had syndicalist sympathies. At one session of the Presidium, two Soviet representatives, Rykov and Tseperovich, declared 'in the name of the Russian delegation' that the 'important persons' who were complaining about Makhno's ill-treatment must themselves be involved with his gang. Indeed, they went on, some of them had known counter-revolutionary connections, for example with people at Kronstadt.[160]

At the last session, speaking in the name of the Central Committee, Bukharin created uproar among the foreign anarcho-syndicalist delegates by first reducing Russian anarchism to *makhnovshchina*, and then by reducing *makhnovshchina* to banditry.[161] His speech presents a detailed defence of Bolshevik policy towards *makhnovshchina* in this final period:

> As is known to all comrades, a few of those present here have an interest in the problems of the Russian anarchists ... our Russian anarchism appears to be a modern phenomenon of a different order than anarchism in Western Europe and America ... our pure-Russian anarchism is not based on the proletariat, but on some other social categories. The principal trend in Russian anarchism does not appear as a social product of the working class but ... in reality appears as the product of a certain stratum of our peasantry.
>
> [...] The majority of our people are peasants; moreover, a stratum of especially rich peasants is concentrated in some parts of our huge country, in geographical terms. First among these areas, we have Ukraine. And in this very same Ukraine, it seems that we have the motherland of our authentic Russian anarchism. And not by accident, but necessarily, we see that our Russian anarchism finds its real embodiment, especially clearly, in the partisan gangs of the notorious Makhno ... It is also clear that this form of anarchism finds itself precisely in sympathy with the kulak peasantry.

When we, representing proletarian power, go to the villages, and above all to the rich villages, we must take from these rich peasants, mainly in the form of bread, in order to give to the hungry workers. Up to now we could only use the requisitioning method. At present we obtain bread by means of a tax-in-kind, in other words, we steal grain from the rich peasants and make it work in the interests of the working class. ... the White generals also stole bread from the peasants. When the Reds come, now the peasants are against the Reds; but when the Whites come, now the peasants are against the Whites.

On this soil, an anarchist ideology has grown up. In outward appearance it is a specifically Russian anarchism. Insofar as it is directed against the Whites, it is for us communists ... but when it is directed against the economy of the proletariat, it plays the part of the rich peasant vandals against the proletariat ...

If the evaluation which I have made of this movement is correct, then this anarchist revolution must be seen under absolutely objective conditions as a counter-revolution.[162]

This was the line that was to permeate Soviet historiography of *makhnovsh-china* for the next seventy years.

8

The Bitter Politics of the Long Exile: Romania, Poland, Germany, and France, 1921–34

The four years of anarchist revolt in eastern Ukraine ended, in T. S. Eliot's often-quoted line, 'not with a bang but a whimper'. There was no dramatic last stand against overwhelming odds, no capture of the ringleaders and no-show trial. Instead, by the first few months of 1921, Makhno's once large and well-organised army of tens of thousands had been reduced to a few hundred tattered and exhausted fugitives, hunted and harried westwards towards the Romanian and Polish borders with Ukraine. With the defeat of Wrangel in late 1920, the final Bolshevik victory in the war of 'Red versus White' had been secured; the elimination of *makhnovshchina* a few months later was to mark the end of the war of 'Red versus Green', as well as the definitive loss of any opportunity for a different revolutionary outcome.[1] The Makhno insurgency would never again represent a genuine military threat to Bolshevik dominance in Ukraine, although an anarchist underground persisted in clandestine conditions through the 1920s and 1930s, and some small-scale guerrilla activity even continued into the mid-1920s.[2] But the anarchist moment had passed, defeated by a more ruthless and better organised opponent, and Makhno was to pass the rest of his life in a long and desperate exile in countries both embarrassed and frightened by his presence. Other émigré groupings tried at all costs to suppress the story of the role of the Makhno movement in the revolution, or to distort the narrative of events.[3] Makhno was isolated by his ignorance of languages other than his native Russian, and ended his life engaging in sharp but despairing polemics with his former comrades (and others), fuelled by lingering resentments over political errors and tactical mistakes.[4]

The insurgents were no longer the effective, centrally-structured military force that they had been in earlier periods. A report compiled from Soviet intelligence sources in June 1921 was scathing, describing the command structure as little more than 'a lifeless and unsuccessful attempt to imitate the organisation of military units'. The commanders' roles were 'vague and muddled' and titles such as chief of staff or adjutant were 'honorary' rather than indicating the competence of a leader able to exercise command. Some of the commanders were illiterate.[5] However accurate this Soviet assessment might have been, the insurgents had to some extent adapted to the new reality by breaking up into 'a multitude of independent detachments and small groups' relying on their existing intelligence networks to keep channels of communication open.[6] Indeed, by 1921 even the once-hated German colonists were providing the insurgents with information about the Red Army movements.[7]

By early summer 1921, while his supporters and detractors argued in Moscow, Makhno's situation had become unsustainable. In mid-August, a small group of cavalry managed to fight their way to the banks of the Dnestr, the border with Romania, where Makhno sought refuge.[8] He needed fresh horses, and the men were exhausted; even the wheels of the *tachanki* lacked lubrication.[9] Taking the fresh horses provoked a hostile reaction from local villagers, who attacked the insurgents while they were sleeping without having posted guards: in the mêlée Makhno was wounded in the legs, and the insurgents lost 30 men taken prisoner, and another 20 wounded.[10] The trap was closing. After several hopeless encounters with Red cavalry units, on the 22nd Makhno was wounded again, this time in the face, and had to be moved in a *tachanka*. Finally, on 28 August, Makhno and a few companions crossed the Dnestr River into Romania, in conditions of secrecy.[11] The *bat'ko* was unconscious because of his injuries.[12] He was never to set foot in Ukraine again.[13] Other fighters managed to flee Ukrainian territory by other routes to neighbouring countries, in small groups or individually, but many remained.[14]

Crossing the Dnestr, Makhno and his companions entered the territory of Bessarabia, part of the Kingdom of Romania.[15] It may have been that Makhno and his commanders had hoped to cross a frontier further north, into the Polish Galician borderlands, where they might have been able to agitate among the Ukrainians in the rural population, but that route was closed to them; nonetheless, even in Bessarabia Makhno hoped to be able to recruit fighters.[16] The Red Army commanders were embarrassed by their inability to deal with Makhno:[17] Frunze, who had taken charge of anti-Makhno operations in June,[18] was frustrated by the escape of 'the Makhno gang' after a pursuit of hundreds of kilometres over a period of months, especially after the defeat of Wrangel. He visited the border area to confirm that his enemy was out of reach.[19]

The crossing itself was not easy, since the Romanian border guards opened fire on the group, and only admitted them after they claimed to be Ukrainian Cossacks, and not Bolsheviks.[20] Another version claims that a small group disguised in Red Army uniforms and led by the intelligence chief Lev Zadov tricked and disarmed the guards, allowing the group to cross unhindered.[21] Soon after their application for political asylum was rejected, the insurgents were disarmed, and quantities of gold and paper money were confiscated.[22]

The main group numbered between 78 and 120 people.[23] The Romanian authorities loaded them onto trucks and moved them to Raşcov, then to Bălţi and eventually to an internment camp in Braşov.[24] Together with a couple of aides, Makhno and Kuz'menko were allowed to move to Bucharest (possibly for medical treatment),[25] while the rest of the group remained in internment.[26] Officially, however, the Romanians denied any knowledge of Makhno's whereabouts.[27] Makhno's entry into Romania provoked problems between the Romanian and Soviet governments, already on poor terms over the Bessarabian issue and frontier incidents provoked by Petliurists and White Guards.[28] Although Bessarabian towns were full of anti-Soviet refugees and were well-disposed towards the Romanian annexation, the Moldovan-speaking peasantry was restless.[29]

Border crossings by armed groups were a source of tension. The Soviet governments of Russia and Ukraine constantly complained about the presence on Romanian soil of representatives of the Petliura 'government', asserting that Romania, including Bessarabia and Bukovina, was being used as a base for espionage and 'for assaults by brigands against Ukraine'.[30] The Romanians believed they too had grounds for protest. On 26 August the Foreign Minister, Take-Ionesco, complained to Georgii Chicherin (the Commissar for Foreign Affairs of Russia) that 'several people' had tried to cross the Dnestr in boats, but had been turned back. Rifle and machine-gun fire had then been aimed at the Romanians from the Soviet side of the river.[31] Chicherin ignored this protest, and the Soviet governments of Russia and Ukraine set about trying to get Makhno and his comrades extradited. On 17 September Chicherin and Christian Rakovskii, the Chairman of the Council of People's Commissars of Ukraine, sent a note on behalf of Russia and Ukraine to General Alexandru Averescu, demanding that Makhno and the people who crossed the border with him should be handed over. The famous bandit Makhno, it stated

> ... crossed the Bessarabian frontier on 23 August ... with a band of followers, seeking asylum in a territory which is under the de facto control of Rumania [... he] has committed a number of crimes ... including burning and plundering villages, massacring peaceful populations, and extorting their goods by torture ... the Russian and Ukrainian governments address a formal request ... to hand over as common criminals the afore-mentioned brigand chief and his followers.[32]

The Romanian reply, sent ten days later on 27 September, was a lesson in the niceties of diplomatic discourse. General Averescu refused to accept the message. He pointed out that according to standard practice, an extradition request had to be made by the *judicial authorities* of the requesting country, after an order for arrest had been made. The accused persons had to be properly identified. There was no death penalty in the Kingdom of Romania, so a formal assurance was required that the accused would not be sentenced to death.[33]

When the request satisfied all these norms, Averescu added, even though there was no extradition treaty between the three countries, his government would consider it on its merits.[34]

Chicherin replied to Take-Ionesco at length on 22 October, complaining that Averescu's note did not even confirm that Makhno was in Romania. Nevertheless, 'as soon as the necessary materials have been assembled, and put into the legal format which you request, we will send you the result'.[35] He attacked the conduct of the Romanian government over the question of Bessarabia, in which the basic argument was that a government which failed to respect international norms on territorial matters was ill-placed to deliver lectures on the international law of extradition to others. He concluded by affirming that for his government the Makhno case was a security issue: 'it is beyond doubt that if the bandit Makhno and his accomplices were to be tried in a Bessarabian court they would be condemned to death'.[36] The Soviet government hoped that after the formalities were satisfied, the Romanians would 'consider it a duty to satisfy such an elementary and just request'.[37]

Take-Ionesco replied on 29 October that he was unable to confirm Makhno's presence in Romania because he did not know who had been interned. He promised to investigate; meanwhile he awaited the promised supporting documentation. As for the Bessarabian and other issues, Take-Ionesco replied 'you know very well that I cannot discuss [these matters] with you' as they concerned the domestic affairs of Romania.[38]

Chicherin promised on 11 November to furnish documentary and even photographic evidence in support of the judicial claims of the Russian and Ukrainian governments for Makhno's extradition. He welcomed the Romanian government's declaration that it followed a policy of 'peaceful good-neighbourliness'. Finally, he claimed he had documentary evidence and depositions from prisoners that Makhno was preparing attacks on Ukraine in cooperation with the Petliurists. The area chosen for these operations was to be Odessa.[39] While this exchange dragged on, with the Romanian government continuing to deny knowledge of his whereabouts, Makhno remained in Bucharest, talking to the Petliurists in the first of several attempts to rally support for his return to Ukraine.[40] Makhno claimed, although the Petliurists doubted it, that he had intended to cross into Poland near the Zbruch river with a detachment of well-armed cavalry, to join up with Petliurist headquarters, but one of his men was captured and the route was betrayed. The Petliurist witness to the conversations complains about the evasiveness and vagueness of his interlocutors, who were 'extremely cautious, failing to speak frankly' about their intentions.[41]

The *makhnovtsy* asserted that the local population supported them 'in every way possible', but the Petliurists, noting that the detachment had been compelled to fight its way out of Ukraine without even resting for a single night, assessed this as triumphalism. Makhno was impatient, not wanting to wait for some future uprising of anti-Soviet forces in which his movement might play a subsidiary role. He organised a 'centre' for subversive activity, infiltrating seven saboteurs into Ukraine in early 1922, and another 15 in the spring.[42] The Bolsheviks, with no other enemies to deal with, were in a much better position to annihilate *makhnovshchina* than ever before.[43] Makhno's tactics had been effective when he was able to take advantage of two large armies fighting each other, working in the rear and attacking their flanks, wrote the author of the Petliurist report. But now those circumstances no longer obtained, and even the fact of '[the *makhnovtsy's*] wish to reach an understanding with us ... truly shows that they have been beaten'.[44]

Makhno agreed to conditions for closer cooperation: recognition of the UNR government; subordination of his forces to nationalist command; and acceptance of Petliurist political slogans.[45] He was certainly bluffing,[46] well aware that nothing was likely to come of such an accord – the Petliurists, like the Makhno insurgency, were a defeated movement, and much of their analysis of the insurgents' situation applied equally to their own.[47] Nevertheless, the Petliurists were right: Makhno was no longer a player. Recovering from his wounds, he continued to live under police supervision in Romania, while his partisans remained in internment camps. Despite the gloomy political prospects, Makhno had not given up. He called on his supporters to begin acquiring weapons: Ivan Lepetchenko in Ploieşti stole a revolver and brought it to Bucharest, while Makhno himself also acquired a weapon.[48] This was feeble stuff: even an attempt to cross into Poland undetected was betrayed, and a list of potential contacts was confiscated.[49]

The Soviet authorities did not limit themselves to judicial methods in trying to neutralise the Makhno threat. They turned unsuccessfully to targeted assassination, sending a group of Cheka operatives to Bălţi under the leadership of Dimitri Medvedev,[50] who had been involved in the struggle against the anarchists in eastern Ukraine during the civil war. Makhno was not there, so the hitmen had to abandon their mission and return home.[51] In early 1922, when the Ukrainian authorities announced amnesty for people who had fought against Soviet power during the conflict, with the exception of key leaders such as Makhno himself, many *makhnovtsy* were mistrustful, not least because of the attempted assassination.[52] In addition, the Romanian foreign minister, Take Ionescu, believed that the resolution of the problem of Makhno was more important for the normalisation of Romanian–Soviet relations than even the Bessarabian question.[53] The situation was obviously becoming increasingly dangerous, and in circumstances that are not entirely clear, on 11 April 1922 Makhno and a small group of supporters left Romania and crossed into Poland.

There are various conflicting narratives about the departure for Poland.[54] According to one of these, based on reports in the Romanian press from early

1922, Makhno and a small group of partisans were arrested in the forests of Buzău county while trying to cross back into Soviet territory, presumably to try to start another uprising. Another story had it that a group of 17 insurgents hijacked a vehicle, possibly a bus, and simply drove it to Poland.[55] It is also possible that the Romanians expelled the group. In any event, on 11 April 1922, Makhno, Kuz'menko and a reduced group of 17 supporters crossed from Romania to Poland and were promptly interned yet again.[56] Not much is known of the fates of the rest of the 70 or so insurgents who had crossed the Dnestr in August 1921. Some found work as agricultural labourers or in sawmills, like Lepetchenko or the two Zadov brothers. The Zadovs were recruited by the Romanian security services in 1924 and infiltrated back into Soviet territory, where they surrendered to the State Political Directorate (*Gosudarstvennoe Politicheskoe Upravlenie* or GPU).[57]

As soon as they crossed the border into Poland, Makhno and the rest of the group were moved to the Strzałkowo refugee camp[58] at Szczypiorno, near Kalisz in the centre of the country, where they remained for six months.[59] Makhno later remarked that when he crossed the border into Poland he was 'counting on the hospitality of a brotherly Slavic country'.[60] He was to be disappointed. While he and his supporters launched a campaign to be allowed to leave Poland for either Czechoslovakia or Germany, the Soviet government again demanded their extradition,[61] and opened trials of captured *makhnovtsy*: Viktor Belash and other general staff were put on trial in Khar'kov.[62] Some were accused *in absentia*; on 19 May 1922 Makhno was convicted of several robberies on Ukrainian territory.[63]

There was no extradition treaty between Ukraine and Poland,[64] and the Polish government refused to hand him over to the Soviets, ostensibly because they did not consider him to be a criminal.[65] In reply, the Ukrainians accused the Poles of 'purely formal thinking' adding that they could not accept a refusal to extradite Makhno. He was a criminal who had been proven to be guilty of 'many robberies, murders, rapes and other crimes' that would be punishable 'regardless of the political system of the state' – and in fact the Polish authorities themselves were proposing a 'judicial investigation'.[66] But the Poles were unmoved, and refused to deny Makhno the status of a political asylum-seeker, or to treat him as merely a common criminal. They saw the matter as a domestic one.[67]

While this diplomatic manoeuvring was going on, naturally enough the Polish authorities kept a close eye on the dangerous revolutionaries, and came to the conclusion that they were plotting with the Bolsheviks in Russia to foment a separatist uprising in eastern Galicia in order to reclaim it as Soviet territory. Galicia had long been seen by Tsarist officials as 'a Russian land, populated … by Russian people'[68] and this was consequently a sensitive issue for the Poles, whose country had only been reconstituted as an independent state in 1918, especially since Galicia included a large Ukrainian-speaking ethnic minority.[69] In October, Makhno, together with Iakov Domashchenko and Ivan Khmara,[70] was transferred to Mokotów prison in Warsaw: an internal police memorandum at the time warned nervously that 'it is advisable to take precautions when escorting the above persons'.[71] Makhno, Kuz'menko, Domashcheno and Khmara were subsequently arraigned for treason under article 102 of the Polish criminal code, an offence that carried a sentence of ten to fifteen years in prison.[72] Meanwhile, on 30 October 1922, Kuz'menko gave birth to a baby girl.[73]

The months that followed were marked by multiple clandestine meetings and the hatching of plots and counter-plots. Makhno was at a disadvantage in that his only source of intelligence was word-of-mouth gossip from fellow inmates who were able to talk to the Polish guards; he was under constant surveillance.[74] The Soviets attempted a complex plan to tempt Makhno and his comrades into an anti-Polish conspiracy, creating grounds for a stronger extradition claim. An intelligence officer from the internment camp reported on 30 July that the only thing the *makhnovtsy* wanted was 'to escape from the camp, return to Ukraine and continue to conduct guerrilla warfare'. When Kuz'menko returned from Warsaw, they began to consider joining up with the Bolsheviks. They were plotting to flee to Czechoslovakia to join Petrushevych.[75]

In July, Kuz'menko obtained permission to travel to Warsaw, and Makhno took advantage of the opportunity to contact the representatives of Soviet Ukraine.[76] She discussed plans for Makhno to foster separatist uprisings in eastern Galicia.[77] The Soviet representatives promised that her husband would receive the assistance he needed, but in reality they were setting a trap – there was no genuine intention to cooperate with an enemy who had so recently been involved in armed struggle against Soviet power.[78] It is possible that Kuz'menko, nevertheless, trusted her interlocutors. She asked for money and told them that the *makhnovtsy* were isolated in the camp from other Ukrainians (supporters of Petliura), that they had lost much of their fighting spirit and that they were dissatisfied.[79] On 22 July Kuz'menko signed a statement requesting a visa to visit Khar'kov, and asking that the Nabat anarchists and the left SRs who had fought with Makhno should be released from Soviet prisons and allowed to return to their homes, that persecution should cease, that Makhno's supporters should enjoy freedom of the press, movement and expression, and that they should be allowed to participate in soviets and congresses. In return, the *makhnovtsy* would lay down their arms and negotiate a 'long-term relationship' with the Soviet authorities in Ukraine.[80] But there was no possibility of such an agreement, and the mission subsequently received instructions from Kiev not to promise anything, to maintain 'an absolutely passive line' and to take into account the weakness of the group.[81]

Makhno was still interested in a possible move to Czechoslovakia: on 28 July he wrote to the Polish authorities asking for permission to leave with 16 of his supporters. His situation in Poland, he stated, made for 'an impossible existence'.[82] The camp administration reported that seven of Makhno's men had escaped from internment in late July and early August, intending 'to go to the Soviet mission in Warsaw, and to return to Soviet Russia ... Ataman Makhno is negotiating with the Soviet mission in Warsaw about conditions for return ...'[83]

There is much unverified information about this period of Makhno's life, with rumour and disinformation in the form of press reports, government memoranda and correspondence between the various participants. The defector Grigorii Besedovskii states in his memoirs, published in 1930, that a meeting was held in 1922 outside Vienna, between Ukraine, Poland, Germany and Czechoslovakia, where the diplomats toyed with the idea of making some use of Galician infantry 'and also of the famous Makhno, who had already offered his services'.[84] The idea was eventually dropped.

Whatever the plot, real or imaginary, Makhno went on trial on 27 November 1923 in Warsaw, accused of having actually attempted to foment such a Galician revolt in 1922, and of having offered his services to Russia if another Polish–Soviet war should break out.[85] The trial was presided over by Justice Grzybowski sitting with two assessors, judges Rykaczewski and Jasiński,[86] and received extensive coverage in Polish newspapers such as *Gazeta Warszawska*, *Robotnik* and *Kurier Poranny*, with some of the reports transcribing verbatim the actual exchanges between the lawyers, judges and witnesses.[87] Alongside Makhno in the dock as co-defendants were Kuz'menko, Khmara and Domashchenko. Contemporary press reports described Makhno as short and slim, wearing a black coat and boots, clean-shaven with his long hair combed back, and with a 'sly smile'. He seemed confident, and referred to himself in the third person. Kuz'menko was modestly dressed and wearing spectacles; Khmara was tall, blond, and broad-shouldered, while Domashchenko was 'not very intelligent'.[88] The prosecution's case, involving encrypted correspondence, clandestine visits to Warsaw and stacks of banknotes, nevertheless relied heavily on testimony by a Polish *agent provocateur* as well as 'inconclusive' handwriting analysis.[89] One of the liaison officials, Adolf Krasnowolski, was an ethnic Pole, who had lived in Guliaipole and even went to school there; he had been passing information about the negotiations back to Polish intelligence.[90]

The indictment accused Makhno and his comrades of having established contact with Soviet diplomats in Warsaw, 'by means of the fugitives from the [internment] camp and his mistress, Kuz'menko', in order to plan the 'provocation of an armed uprising in Eastern Galicia and the separation of the district from the Republic of Poland'. A note had even been sent to Moscow about the idea.[91] The defence announced that they would be calling 32 witnesses, and using five court interpreters. In a lengthy speech in Russian on the opening day,

Makhno presented himself as a political activist, 'a defender of the Ukrainian people and a sympathiser of Poland, at the same time a fierce enemy of the Bolsheviks, incapable of engaging in any dealings with them, especially regarding actions that would harm Poland'.[92] Indeed, the insurgents had actively assisted Poland in 1920, when Soviet cavalry threatened Warsaw, by harassing Budenny's 1st Cavalry Army as it crossed Ukrainian territory.[93]

The trial lasted five days, beginning at 10 o'clock each morning in a courthouse on Miodowa Street in Warsaw's old town.[94] It was a sensational event, the trial of a man who, in the popular imagination, was a 'blood-soaked legend': popular opinion, encouraged by unfavourable press coverage, was hostile to the defendants. Headlines in the popular newspapers – 'The Perpetrators of Bloody Slaughter in Ukraine', 'Makhno and His Gang in Court' – did nothing to calm the atmosphere. There was little doubt that the four accused would be convicted, and Makhno himself predicted a sentence of eight years. Anarchist organisations in other countries protested the whole proceeding, believing that the Russians and the Poles had somehow come to an agreement either to kill Makhno, or to hand him over to the Soviets.[95]

Much of the trial was given over to lurid accounts of robbery and banditry, rape and mutilation, charges which Makhno denied forcefully. He testified in court, maintaining a calm and dignified demeanour and declaring his expectation that a brotherly Slavic nation would treat him fairly.[96] The only moment of drama occurred during an exchange about the execution of Ataman Grigor'ev. This had been ordered in July 1919, said Makhno, because Grigor'ev and his group had carried out a pogrom in Elisavetgrad in which 2,000 Jews had been killed. The presiding judge then asked 'Did the accused himself shoot him?' to which Makhno responded indignantly, raising his voice 'for the first and only time in the court proceedings', that, no, he did not need to do so because he had 'people who unhesitatingly carried out every order'.[97] The judges did not take long to hand down a verdict. On 31 November, 'in an atmosphere of considerable interest and excitement'[98] and to widespread surprise, it was announced that the defendants were all acquitted.[99] This verdict 'caused a sensation in the courtroom', with supporters rushing to shake the hands of the accused and to ask for autographs.[100] Makhno was clearly astonished, while Kuz'menko, grasping the railing around the dock, could only repeat 'What? What?' over and over again. Both Khmara and Domashchenko reacted with joy and excitement.[101]

The acquittal did not mean that Makhno's travails were over. Rumours – possibly of Soviet origin – began to circulate suggesting that the accused had been released because they had reached agreement with the Polish military to launch a new insurrection in Ukraine. If true, this would have meant that their surprise at the verdict had been feigned. Whatever the case, Makhno and his comrades were all released on 3 December, and issued with residence permits

– Makhno and Kuz'menko for Toruń, Khmara for Poznań and Domaszenko for Bydgoszcz.[102]

Makhno and his family, reportedly accompanied by Lepetchenko and Ivan Khmara, moved to Toruń within a few weeks, arriving there at the end of December 1923. They were put up in a hotel to begin with, but later moved into an apartment. Life was difficult, and the rent that they had to pay for accommodation was expensive. Makhno and some comrades tried to establish themselves as shoemakers in a nearby street,[103] but both the Polish police and military intelligence kept the anarchists under close surveillance. The Poles were working on the assumption that sooner or later Makhno would attempt to escape and return home in order to foment rebellion, and in the uncertainty following the death of Lenin on 21 January 1924, the authorities were understandably nervous at the prospect.[104] Makhno was repeatedly summoned for interrogation (certainly with the objective of intimidating him) and his correspondence was censored. A police report noted that the surveillance did indeed have a distressing effect on Makhno, who 'knew he was being watched' and was constantly dodging into doorways and around street corners.[105]

Soon after his arrival in Toruń, in early January 1924, Makhno returned to Warsaw, ostensibly to settle some personal matters, but was arrested when he arrived there.[106] While he was away, Kuz'menko was busy informing the authorities about their contacts with anarchist groups in the United States and in Germany, as well as revealing such details as how they had managed to smuggle messages to each other when they were in prison.[107] In March, Makhno returned again to Warsaw, in order to ask for permission for himself and his family to attend an anarchist congress in Berlin.[108] The sticking point was that Makhno declared his desire to return to Poland, but the Polish authorities were only too glad of an opportunity to see the back of him.[109] However, Makhno was denied a visa to travel to Germany and, possibly as a consequence, some German anarchists sent a comrade to visit him in Poland. She was arrested on arrival after subversive literature was found in her bags, put on trial, and sentenced to hard labour.[110] It seems that Makhno's relationship with Kuz'menko had deteriorated under the strain of such events, with frequent quarrels, during which he accused her of having an affair with Khmara. The Russian historian Golovanov writes of her that

There was no peace in her, but there was unremitting passion and an explosive personality – just the woman needed for the years of struggle. When the war ended, her relationship with Makhno went bad, and, although she bore him a daughter, the family fell apart. They split up and reunited; she had affairs ... in public [Makhno's] wife was often harsh with him, and it seemed ... that she had never loved him, and ended up with him only because she was flattered to be the wife of the most powerful chieftain in Ukraine. He, oddly enough, was a faithful husband ... even though at the height of his fame he could have taken any lover.[111]

Together with these domestic difficulties, Makhno's inability to obtain permission to travel, the political pressures he was under and the police intimidation together seem to have had a serious effect on his morale, and on 14 April he unsuccessfully attempted suicide by cutting his throat; however, his life was saved by local emergency medical services and he was hospitalised.[112] A short time after he was released, he was arrested again in May, but this time for being drunk and disorderly rather than for political reasons.[113] It seems that it was around this time that he took the definite decision to leave Poland: the Polish authorities agreed to give him permission to depart, but denied him the right to return.[114]

Makhno's intentions are not entirely clear at this point, and the sequence of events is murky. We know that from Poland he travelled to Danzig, which at that time enjoyed the ambiguous status of a 'Free City', officially neither German nor Polish,[115] arriving there on 2 July 1924.[116] The family settled in the satellite town of Zoppot (*Polish* Sopot), where they were constantly harassed by Soviet 'trade representatives' who offered them a chance to return to what was by now the Soviet Union.[117] According to one narrative, on arrival in Danzig Makhno was diagnosed with tuberculosis and hospitalised against his will under communicable disease regulations.[118] He managed to escape, and then seems to have become foolishly involved in a Soviet plot to take him, ostensibly, to Berlin, where Petr Arshinov and Volin were living, as well as other anarchist comrades such as Berkman. This turned out to be a trap, and Makhno was lucky to escape, returning to Danzig,[119] where he was then promptly arrested again, on charges related to the killings of German Mennonites in Taurida and Ekaterinoslav during the war, as well as problems with his undocumented status. While in jail he again attempted suicide, and was again saved and hospitalised. A group of anarchist supporters then organised his escape and flight to Germany, which involved Makhno remaining in hiding for 40 days waiting for a false passport and the embezzlement by Volin of some funds sent from the United States by a supporter.[120] Details of the escape to Berlin remain unclear to this day: it is not even clear whether he travelled overland or by sea.[121]

The stay in Berlin seems to have been brief, not least because of Makhno's fears that the German authorities would return him to the Soviet Union. He was, however, supported by the anarchist Black Cross network and was able to meet such figures as Rudolf Rocker and Ugo Fedeli, with whom he had frequent discussions.[122] The next step, the move to Paris, was by all accounts much better organised, and Makhno was able to transit through Belgium and arrive safely in Paris on 14 April 1925.[123] Compared to his brief stays in Romania (seven months), Poland (just over two years), Danzig (five months), and Germany (four months), Makhno was to spend the remaining ten years of his life in France, living in relative obscurity but in a city that had become a magnet for Russian and Ukrainian exiles of all political stripes.

He found manual work for brief periods (reportedly working intermittently as a turner in a Renault car factory, a carpenter, a painter and a shoemaker[124]), but devoted his real energies to engaging in political activities, including producing polemical writings and struggling to complete his memoirs. Petr Arshinov had become the editor of the journal *Delo Truda*, and Makhno regularly submitted

> ... confused articles which Arshinov found unacceptable, and was obliged to revise and correct, thus incurring Makhno's wrath. If they were published, it was more from respect for the author's name than because of their own quality.[125]

Makhno was irritated by criticism from people whom he considered armchair theoreticians, people who had never held a gun or ridden a horse, had never fought for their beliefs and had more respect for Volin and Arshinov than they did for him. Additionally, he was upset by the controversies around his name and reputation which accompanied the publication of Joseph Kessel's novel *Makhno et sa juive*,[126] which accused him of anti-Semitism, as well as by the sensational trial that followed the assassination of Symon Petliura in Paris by the Jewish anarchist Scholem Schwartzbard on 25 May 1926. Schwarzbard was acquitted by the French courts, which controversially accepted his defence that he was avenging the victims of pogroms committed by Petliura's forces during the war.[127] Of course, political engagement of whatever kind did not pay the rent, and the family came to depend on the generosity of comrades, most especially the Spanish anarchist groups.[128] Both Makhno and Kuz'menko relied on odd jobs and artisanal production to make a little money. Finally, in 1927, the couple divorced and Kuz'menko moved outside Paris where she became close to a pro-Soviet Ukrainian exile organisation, and repeatedly but unsuccessfully applied for permission to return to the Soviet Union.[129]

In the meantime, Makhno still enjoyed a certain status in anarchist circles, and closely followed events in Spain, where anarchists were influential. He campaigned for various causes such as the liberation of anarchists who had been jailed in the Soviet Union, as well as for Sacco and Vanzetti, two anarchists executed in 1927 in the United States.[130] He also maintained contact with Polish anarchist comrades.[131] He appears to have made at least some effort to socialise outside anarchist circles. In 1928, for example, he is reported to have briefly attended a Soviet Russian soirée held in a Masonic lodge in rue Cadet in Paris. The journalist Nikulin, who exchanged a few words with him at the event, described him as having a pronounced limp and a deep scar across his face, as well as an unmistakably Russian appearance: 'he was dressed as Russians dress when they are abroad'. After a while he left with a companion, 'smiling in embarrassment'.[132]

Nevertheless, by far the most significant aspect historically of Makhno's ten years in Paris was his participation in the emergence and subsequent controversy around the Organisational Platform, a topic that still provokes heated debate in anarchist circles to the present day.[133]

As early as 1922 some among the Russian anarchists in exile had come reluctantly to the conclusion that their cause was lost in Russia and Ukraine for the foreseeable future: Russian anarchism had been 'an astounding failure'.[134] In Ukraine, as in the larger Soviet Union, most of the movement's members were either dead, silenced, or exiled; their newspapers and periodicals had been closed down, their clubs dissolved or forced into hiding; the remnants of their only organised military force, Makhno's peasant army, had been driven out of Soviet territory, and despite all the plotting already described, had little immediate chance of reigniting the 'black flame'.[135] They could not, in Golovanov's words, 'return to history'.[136] Nonetheless, Makhno and his comrades, including the intellectuals, were in general unprepared to recognise defeat, and move on to the rest of their lives. Many of them were, as revolutionaries, unwelcome in their countries of exile, and were ill-equipped to earn a living in a foreign society. So, they clustered together, sought out fellow anarchists in their new countries, founded newspapers and journals and began to conduct a raucous, rancorous and detailed post-mortem on exactly where things had gone wrong.[137]

Anarchist theory posits that the success of revolution depends on a transformation of social values, most especially respect for authority – in other words, the spread of ideas. However, different tendencies within anarchism propose different solutions to the problem of how to spread such new ideas and attitudes. Some believe in spontaneous and informal networks, others in the key role of revolutionary trade unions, still others in the need, at least temporarily, for some kind of anarchist political organisation.[138] The question for the exiled *makhnovtsy*, as well as the Nabat anarchists, was why had they lost their opportunity in eastern Ukraine? Why had the workers and peasants not adopted anarchist ideas in a more lasting way? How had the Bolsheviks managed to defeat a volunteer partisan army with conscripted forces?[139] Was the fault with them, the anarchists, or were the objective social, political and economic conditions simply not ready?

It was inevitable that the personal and the political should have become inextricably entangled in the debates around these questions. Makhno's relations with both Arshinov and Volin – who were not themselves the best of friends – were volatile and difficult. Although Makhno managed to maintain more-or-less cordial relations with Arshinov until the latter's decision to return to Russia in 1933, the falling-out with Volin was rapid. Using fugitive source material, Skirda devotes several pages to a critique of Volin's behaviour in exile: Volin 'switches back and forth between eulogy and the most acerbic criticism' in these writings.[140] Such hostility, argues Skirda, derived 'from the run-ins they had had as emigrés, both personally ... and theoretically'.[141] Since Makhno never succeeded in learning any French, Volin had effectively become the local spokesperson of the movement. His anecdotes and explanations were expressed with such animation that

> ... for those who were ignorant of the background and ... did not know that Volin had only taken part in the movement for a mere six months, it was conceivable that Makhno had been a remarkable military chief, but improbable that he had been the spiritual guide of the movement.[142]

Makhno's dislike of Volin's ineffectiveness went back to the days of the revolution. According to one account, he had once upbraided Volin for not having his own opinions on practical matters, for being spineless, for failing to stand up for himself.[143] To the contempt he had formerly held for Volin, Makhno now added jealousy and frustrated irritation.[144] It was in this context of such tense *personal* relationships that the *political* controversy around Petr Arshinov's anarchist 'organisational platform' emerged.

The exiled Russian anarchists had clustered into three main tendencies, some anarcho-syndicalists (Maksimov and others) who believed that the creation of unions to run social and economic affairs was the main task; a group formed around the concrete experience of the Makhno insurgency, the *Gruppa Russkikh Anarkhistov za Granitsei* (GRAZ); and a Federation of Communist Anarchists based in North America, which was strongly opposed to any kind of formal organisation.[145] Among these groupings in the early 1920s there was considerable disagreement about a real issue, namely actual cooperation by anarchists within the Soviet regime, and it was in this context that the Organisational Platform emerged.

The earliest exchanges focused on the role of a handful of militants who had worked inside the Soviet government's structures, hoping at least to spread some anarchist ideas, despite the systematic destruction of independent anarchism in Russia and Ukraine after 1921.[146] These 'Soviet anarchists' or 'anarchist-Bolsheviks' were men and women who claimed that they could reconcile personal anarchist convictions with service under the communists. The two most prominent and controversial of these were the Ukrainian German Sandomirskii[147] and Iuda Grossman, sometimes known as Grossman-Roshchin.[148] Other anarchists who held positions under the communist government included Victor Serge, Bill Shatov, Aba Gordin, Daniil Novomirskii and even

Volin, who in 1918 worked briefly in the Department of Education in Khar'kov and Voronezh.[149]

Sandomirskii played a key role. He made various attempts to convince anarchists abroad that the interests of the revolution were best served by supporting the Bolshevik regime. He paid an official visit to Italy in April 1922, was interviewed by Errico Malatesta, and engaged in published debates with Malatesta and others.[150] In May, the anarchist journal *Umanità Nova* published a series of articles by Malatesta attacking Sandomirskii's positions on political as well as tactical grounds.[151] He disputed the idea that a Bolshevik government must be defended, because any regime that replaced it would represent a move to the right. Anarchists should not be called upon to choose between two evils: they had refused to do so during the Great War. There followed an exchange of letters to the editor between Sandomirskii and Malatesta, raising issues that soon sparked a wider debate in Italian, French and Russian periodicals. Volin was particularly incensed: he accused Sandomirskii of having supported Kerensky in February 1917 and of 'vacillation' after October 1917. Perhaps Sandomirskii had been sent to Italy to disarm left criticism of the Bolsheviks? Sandomirskii had claimed that anarchism lacked mass support; Volin pointed to the Makhno insurgency as evidence to the contrary. Dismissing Sandomirskii's claim to be any kind of anarchist at all, Volin told him and the others of his kind to 'leave anarchism in peace'.[152]

Things now became both more heated and more personal. The French journal *Le Libertaire* refused to publish a letter from Sandomirskii, and wrote that as an anarchist he could not hold a government position.[153] Volin then accused Sandomirskii of having shown bias when acting as a translator for the Soviets during negotiations for Makhno's extradition from Romania, and added that he believed that Grossman-Roshchin had been a Soviet agent, as long ago as April 1919.[154] This was incendiary stuff; reputations were at stake in the enclosed universe of the Russian and Ukrainian exiles. Attempts to calm things down were unsuccessful, and the idea of a commission to investigate matters was rejected out of hand as positions hardened.

In mid-1923, Volin published an article in *Anarkhicheskii Vestnik* arguing for a distinction to be made between 'anarchist-communists', who wanted to get rid of political authority in all its forms, and 'anarchist-bolsheviks', who were 'renegades' subverting genuinely revolutionary anarchist thinking. They had to be opposed at all costs.[155] The same issue of the journal carried a text by Petr Arshinov which perhaps pointed the way forward to the thinking of the Platform. Arshinov identified two key factors that had led to 'anarchist-Bolshevism'; the defeat of the 1905 revolution, and the role of Lenin. Three measures taken by the Bolsheviks under Lenin's leadership should, in principle, have been unacceptable to anarchists: the Brest-Litovsk treaty with Germany in 1918; the long-drawn-out repression of the Makhno insurgency;

and the crushing of the Kronstadt revolt in 1921. To defend such things was to help the Bolsheviks fend off criticism from the left, and to weaken the anarchist movement as a whole.[156]

The 'Organisational Platform of the General Union of Anarchists (Draft)' – to give it its full title – was dated 20 June 1926, and was published as a proposal (*proekt*), prepared by GRAZ together with the General Union of Anarchists.[157] The four-page introduction was signed by Arshinov. The document consisted of three sections, labelled 'general', 'constructive' and 'organisational'. The first section was further divided into chapters on class struggle, the necessity for violent social revolution, anarchism and anarchist-communism, the 'denial of democracy', the 'denial of government and authority' and the role of the masses and the anarchists in the struggle and the revolution. The 'constructive' section consisted of economic and other proposals for the 'first period of the social revolution', especially such sectors as manufacturing, food, land and defence. The final – and most controversial – section dealt with ways of organising anarchists politically. The platform contained three central planks: the theoretical unity of all individual and organisational members of the union; tactical unity, to avoid contradictory actions by individuals; and finally, collective responsibility. It must be admitted that the document was not particularly well-written, and indeed, 'many of its formulations are contradictory or lend themselves to misinterpretation.[158]

The publication in 1926 provoked an uproar, but in fact the idea of anarchist organisation along the lines proposed was not entirely new: 'the *Platform* and "Platformism" were not a break with the anarchist tradition but a fairly orthodox *restatement* of well-established views' going all the way back to Bakunin.[159] At a congress in Amsterdam in 1907, for example, the idea had been raised in a debate between syndicalists and anarchist-communists. Emma Goldman had laid down a firm pre-condition: anarchist organisation had to be based on 'absolute respect for *all* individual initiatives and should not hamper their free play and development'.[160]

Despite, or perhaps because of its long-lasting controversial reputation, the Platform merits careful reading to establish what it in fact argues.[161] Its starting point is a definition of anarchism as 'the idea of the complete negation of the social system based on classes and the State, and of the replacement of this by a free, stateless society of self-governing workers'.[162] In order to achieve this goal, a General Union was to be established for preparatory and educational work among the workers and peasants. The Platform recognised that revolutionary consciousness would not emerge of its own accord from such a union, and a battle of ideas would have to be waged, especially in the unions, because it was this that

... united 'workers on a basis of production, revolutionary syndicalism, like all groups based on professions, has no determining theory', and 'always reflects the ideologies of diverse political groupings notably of those who work most intensely in its ranks'. Consequently, the 'tasks of anarchists in the ranks of the [union] movement consist of developing libertarian theory, and pointing it in a libertarian direction, in order to transform it into an active arm of the social revolution'.[163]

The union was not to be established with the idea of seizing power itself: but spontaneous and informal methods would not lead to a free society, as experience showed. Years earlier Bakunin himself, the authors asserted, had never opposed the concept of organisation. In fact, his ideas and activities 'give us every right to view him as an active advocate of precisely such a mode of organisation [as this]'.[164]

Many anarchists were not prepared to subordinate local autonomy for tactical and ideological unity. Volin responded in a manifesto published early in 1927, accusing Arshinov of wanting to set up an anarchist party, of having bureaucratic and centralist inclinations, and of 'flirting with Bolshevik dogma'.[165] There was no need for a union because

... the first step towards the true unification of our movement, through its serious organisation, must consist of ideological work – far-reaching, amicable, in solidarity and brotherhood – applied to a series of our most important problems: a common attempt to arrive at their clear and clean solution.[166]

Much of this debate was conducted in French: French comrades criticised the Platform on the grounds of its attempt to generalise the experience of the Russian revolution: concrete conditions in France were different.[167] *Le Libertaire* published an exchange between Malatesta and Makhno. Aleksandr Berkman accused Makhno of having a 'militarist temperament' and of being under Arshinov's influence. As for Arshinov himself, added Berkman '... his entire psychology is Bolshevik ... his nature is absolutely arbitrary and tyrannical, dominating'.[168]

The bitter and vehement nature of the controversy over the Platform, so closely associated with the names of Makhno and Arshinov, took its personal toll. For many anti-organisationists, their positions were pre-defined, and their minds were closed to any form of persuasion: some even

... rejected in principle the view that an organisation should have shared political positions, a common strategy, a clearly structured federation, make binding decisions, or direct its press to promote particular stances ... every individual, local group and current should be free to act as it saw fit, as this was efficient, fostered unity, and did not violate the rights of dissenting minorities.[169]

In some circles, these entrenched positions can be found even today. In the 1930s, for Makhno, isolated in a country whose language he did not know, unemployed and unemployable, in poor health, without access to proper medical care, separated from Kuz'menko, the controversy made his time in exile difficult. In 1933, his friend, teacher and comrade Petr Arshinov decided to return to the Soviet Union, where he was arrested and shot four years later, in 1937. This was a severe blow for Makhno – and indeed for the ideas of the Platform, which they had both had spent time and energy defending. Makhno spent his last years living in a single room in Vincennes, a densely-populated eastern suburb of Paris: his tuberculosis was getting worse and his old leg wound continued to cause problems; he was also malnourished, although a local washerwoman cooked for him.[170] Around March 1934, after a harsh winter, according to Kuz'menko, his health worsened and she, with some other old comrades, moved him to the Hôpital Tenon, which specialised in respiratory medicine. Kuz'menko visited him regularly, with some Russian and French anarchist comrades.[171] He had two operations but continued to weaken. Kuz'menko described his last day:

> My husband was in bed, looking pale, with his eyes half closed and swollen hands, separated from other patients by a big screen. There were several comrades who were allowed to be there, even though it was late. I kissed his cheek. He opened his eyes and turned to his daughter and said to her 'Be healthy and happy, my daughter'. Then he closed his eyes and said 'My friends, excuse me, I'm very tired, I want to sleep'.

The visitors went home, but when they returned the next day[172] they found an empty bed, and were told that Makhno had died during the night, at the age of 45.[173] His remains were cremated and the ashes deposited in Père Lachaise cemetery in the 20th arrondissement of Paris.

Much of the narrative of Makhno's last years is informed by a text written by Ida Mett (1901–73), also known as Ida Lazarévitch-Gilman, a Russian-born syndicalist who was close to the group of exiled Russian anarchists in the 1920s. Her short memoir, first circulated in February 1948 and written in French,[174] portrays Makhno in a positive light (he was a doting father; he drank rarely; and so on), while portraying Kuz'menko and Volin as opportunists. Mett says that Kuz'menko was a snob – she believed she was destined for better things in life – that the scar on Makhno's face was the result of her attempt to kill him while they were in Poland, and that she and Volin stole Makhno's diary while he was dying. Mett also states that after Makhno died, Kuz'menko married Volin, and – falsely – that during the German occupation of France she married a German officer and was killed in a bombing raid in Berlin.[175]

Kuz'menko and Olena remained in France until war broke out. The rest of their lives we know only in outline. Olena graduated from secondary school in 1939 and began working as an apprentice in a textile factory: in 1941 she was sent to undertake forced labour in Berlin, and Kuz'menko also ended up there – a more probable explanation than her having married a Nazi.[176] At the end of the war, they were arrested by the Soviet security forces and sent to Kiev. Olena was sentenced to five years for the catch-all offence of 'anti-Soviet activities' although it was clear she had only the vaguest idea of Makhno's activities.[177] She was sent to Taraz, in the Jambyl region of southern Kazakhstan, near the Tian-Shan mountains.[178] Kuz'menko was sentenced to an eight-year term, which she served in Mordovia, in the Volga region.[179] After Stalin's death in 1953, Kuz'menko was granted permission to join her daughter in Taraz. She found a job in a cotton factory, and spent the rest of her life in Jambyl, never receiving formal political rehabilitation. Kuz'menko died on 23 March 1978. OIena graduated from the local Hydro-Melioration Institute, and worked there until she died in 1993.[180] In Guliaipole, Makhno's surviving relatives and the descendants of people who had known him continued to be harassed by the Soviet authorities well into the 1970s and 1980s.[181]

9

Why Anarchism? Why Ukraine? Contextualising *Makhnovshchina*

The Russian revolution of 1917 was not just 'Russian', nor was it a single event: it is better understood rather as a 'kaleidoscopic process ... a complex pattern of overlapping revolutions ... [with] distinctive dynamics of their own'.[1] It took place at a moment when 'inter-imperial rivalries' were leading to the collapse of the great European multi-national and multi-ethnic state formations.[2] For the Russian Empire, the revolution changed relations among nationalities most dramatically 'in the triangle of imperial Russian national identity' within which the dominant axis subsumed Ukraine into Russia.[3] In this context, as we have seen, *makhnovshchina* sought, not so much to break Ukraine away from imperial rule as to deconstruct the entire state-based national paradigm, and build local socio-economic relations from the bottom up on anarchist principles.

Far from being a coup d'état, the revolution and its immediate aftermath can fairly be described as 'an explosion of democracy and activity from below'.[4] Democracy may, after all, manifest itself 'within the most diverse political constitutional forms' apart from the ballot box and the elected legislature.[5] The civil war that followed what Alexander Rabinowitch has pointedly termed the '*coming* to power'[6] of Lenin's Bolsheviks was made up of a series of interlinked conflicts that had already started before the revolution of 1917 took place, and which continued until at least 1926, in a prolonged struggle to resolve the question of whether the communist regime could survive.[7] The revolution was not so much a dramatic rupture with the past as the logical consequence of processes of modernisation in the Russian Empire that had begun decades before. The peasants, *muzhiki* (to use the mildly derogatory Russian term), the 'half-savage, stupid, heavy people of the Russian village'[8] in Maxim Gorky's dismissive characterisation, famously compared to potatoes in a sack by Karl Marx,[9] turned out on closer inspection not to constitute an unproblematic collectivity, and to have agency in unexpected forms, for example in their complex and nuanced relations with the state judiciary, whether Tsarist or revolutionary, or in their high levels of participation in electoral processes of different kinds.[10]

The processes of liberation at work in the revolution were not necessarily 'nationalist' in character, and independence from foreign rule was not necessarily seen in terms of reproducing the structures of the state at regional level. The dominant discourse of 'Great Russia' and its correlative 'Little Russia' was used historically – and not entirely unsuccessfully – as a device to frame Ukrainian identity as a subset of a hypothetical larger Russian nation. This attitude has not disappeared even today – the widely-reported but unconfirmed remark by Putin to George Bush that 'You have to understand, Ukraine is not even a state' resonates *even if never spoken*.[11] But the 'liberation' that the *makhnovtsy* sought in left-bank Ukraine did not require the construction of a national state in place of a Russian Imperial one: it was primarily about radical socio-political transformation, and so the question of Ukrainian national identity is largely irrelevant to understanding *makhnovshchina*. Indeed, it is possible to see the Russian revolution and the First World War from which Makhno emerged as the start of a process of European liberatory *decolonisation*, within the borders of a great land empire.[12] This applies to the European territories – such as Ukraine – as much as to Asian ones with their predominantly Muslim populations.[13]

It is now widely accepted that the revolution – in the widest spatial and temporal sense of the term – can be best understood in this context 'of a multi-ethnic empire desperately seeking to compete with three other empires'.[14] Even within Russia proper, it is clear that 'each province has its own story, with local concerns, conditions and interests dominating the ways that the revolution was received and understood'.[15] Struggles around local identity were further complicated by fierce class resentments, with aggrieved peasants pitched against contemptuous landlords and angry workers against the self-satisfied bourgeoisie. In Russia – as in Europe generally – the arrogant wealthy believed that to be rich was to be virtuous, and that to be poor was somehow to deserve your plight.[16] Writing of the period before 1914, George Orwell commented that the vulgarity of wealth was especially intense at that time: '... the goodness of money was as unmistakable as the goodness of health or beauty, and ... was mixed up in people's minds with the idea of actual moral virtue' – a comment that could be applied to pre-1914 Russia as much as to England.[17] A key difference, however, was that in the Russian Empire the war eventually created a social category of *frontoviki*, armed soldiers who returned to the villages 'fed up with a political system *and a social order* that treated them like animals and cannon fodder'.[18] The extreme violence of the civil war was fuelled by such resentments.

The 'regional turn' in the historiography of the revolution and civil war in Russia has not only focussed on social class and geography, but also on concepts of rupture and continuity. Indeed, some have contended that even '1917 is the wrong departure point for a full analysis of the social, cultural, political, and economic development of the Bolshevik project' and their opposition.[19] The revolution was played out over a longer timeframe, and not only in the urban settings of Moscow and St. Petersburg, but in small towns and rural spaces, in provinces and territories all over the empire, in differing social, linguistic and economic contexts, in each one of which specific local processes were working themselves out.[20]

The general view of the timeline of the revolutionary narrative has thereby expanded to include the processes of modernisation that were interrupted by the outbreak of the First World War. Thus, general histories of the revolution published in English since the early 1990s tend to cover the last years of the empire as an integral part of the historical narrative: for example, Richard Pipes starts his first volume in 1899 and ends his second in 1924;[21] Orlando Figes goes back even further, to 1891.[22] More recently, Laura Engelstein's history begins with the outbreak of war in 1914;[23] Jonathan Smele presents his argument in the very title of his book on the civil war, covering ten years from 1916 to 1926.[24] The idea that the revolution represented the culmination of a process with its roots in the early twentieth century has been accompanied by a realisation that the process did not end with the 'ten days that shook the world' and that even the First World War did not come to a tidy end on 11 November 1918 – it rather 'failed to end' until it petered out in the mid-1920s.[25]

This is in broad terms the framework for the account of the rural anarchist uprising in Ukraine led by Nestor Makhno that is the subject of this book. Since the collapse of the Soviet Union in 1991 and the variegated opening up of archives to researchers, there have been significant shifts in the way historians understand the revolution. Russian and foreign scholars are now free to collaborate in ways that were impossible in Soviet times. But it is important to note that the quantity of Western research on the revolution and civil war has diminished in comparison with the last decades of the Cold War, when political considerations tended to underpin the funding of various manifestations of 'area studies'.[26] In addition, as S. A. Smith has pointed out, the broad sympathy of the left for the ideals of the revolution and for more generous concepts of its democratic character has largely disappeared and been replaced by the project of 'demonstrating the inevitability of a minority revolution leading to totalitarian dictatorship'.[27]

The revolutionary-military movement that Makhno led has been viewed from various angles over the past century. Seen from the traditional perspective of a general history of the 'Russian revolution' it is usually regarded as an interesting provincial peasant rebellion which, at one particular moment in mid-1919, had a significant impact on the general course of events, meriting a couple of pages or a footnote to the main narrative.[28] Nevertheless, even today the revolt provokes passionate political (as opposed to historical) polemics among defenders and detractors, many of whom continue to self-identify as anarchists, Trotskyites, Ukrainian nationalists and so forth.[29] From one perspective, there is a discourse of Bolshevik treachery and betrayal; from another, accusations of kulak banditry.[30]

This last characterisation has been remarkably persistent over seventy years of triumphalist Soviet historiography: *makhnovshchina* was a kulak-gangster counter-revolutionary movement, struggling for the defeat of Soviet power. Before mid-1919, there was some limited public recognition by the Bolsheviks of the contribution that the *makhnovtsy* had made and could potentially continue to make in defence of the revolution.[31] In the period until April–May 1919, newspaper reports appeared from time to time praising the *makhnovtsy* for their courage in the struggle against the Whites, as we have seen. However, this changed with the defeat of the so-called 'Military Opposition' at the 8th Congress of the Party in late March, which resulted in the effective 'fusion of the party and the Red Army'[32] and the beginning of a fierce propaganda campaign in which the insurgents were consistently characterised as treasonous counter-revolutionaries. By the end of 1919, the dominant political discourse was centred on the urgent need to liquidate the bandit gangs – *partizanshchina*, including the movements of Antonov, Grigor'ev and others, as well as Makhno.[33] This pattern of polemical attacks was repeated in late 1920, after the defeat of Wrangel, when Makhno and his supporters were again characterised as enemies of the socialist state. In this way, even while the civil war was still raging, the pattern was set for what was to become the standard view of *makhnovshchina* in Soviet historiography for the next seventy years. In what Danilov and Shanin term the 'mass consciousness of Russians and citizens of the former USSR'[34] the popular image of Makhno was one of a thuggish leader – cruel, a drunkard, a womaniser – in charge of an anti-Semitic 'anarcho-kulak gang' which looted, raped and murdered at will. This picture was consistently and successfully maintained throughout the Soviet period, despite evidence to the contrary printed in some of the more comprehensive Soviet collections of documentation dealing with the civil war period.[35] It is worth noting that, despite criticism of the tendentious nature of the selection of documents in these Soviet-period collections to support a particular broad meta-narrative, the publication of the fourth volume of *Direktivy komandovaniia frontov Krasnoi Armii* in 1978 – for example – was greeted enthusiastically by Alec Nove as a 'gold mine' containing 'a remarkable amount of new information', and including mentions of 'un-rehabilitated leaders' such as Trotsky.[36]

Publications on Makhno and *makhnovshchina* – some at least consisting of more than polemic – began to appear in the Soviet Union soon after the end of the civil war. These works included not only monographs, but also periodical articles in such journals as *Armiia i Revoliutsiia* by military analysts seeking to understand the tactical and strategic lessons of the war; they invariably took the bandit nature of the Makhno rebellion as a given, and mostly focussed on operations in the period 1920–21.[37] Authors included such figures as the former Red Army commander Roberts Eidemanis (1895–1937), a Latvian better known by his Russian name as Robert Eideman. Eideman had developed an eccentric theory according to which the military formations of the *makhnovtsy*, and the clandestine village networks that supported them, were independent phenomena.[38] One or two monographs and articles were published outside this pattern, such as the book by the reformed *makhnovets* Isaac Teper (Ilia Gordev),[39] and the unreliable memoir by the former White Guard officer Gerasimenko.[40]

Of greater importance, both because of its comprehensiveness and its author's frankness, is the four-volume memoir, with maps, photographs and facsimiles, by the commander of the Southern Front, Vladimir Antonov-Ovseenko. Antonov was a Ukrainian who commanded the army in Ukraine in 1917, and again in 1918–19, and his memoirs include descriptions of Makhno's participation in the Red Army during the period of the 1919 alliance.[41]

The work of the 'Agrarian Marxist' M. Kubanin, published in 1927, was based on archival research as well as on memoirs and newspaper reports. Kubanin adheres formally to the line that *makhnovshchina* was fundamentally a kulak movement but presents a detailed sociology of its area of operation as well as details of military organisation and tactics. Kubanin argues that opposition to war communism was the driving force behind *makhnovshchina*, and that the movement drew support from all strata of the peasantry, not just kulaks.[42] Kubanin asks why left-bank Ukraine was the region in which the phenomenon of insurgency arose most strongly, and argues that it was precisely because of the developed and commercialised agricultural economy in the region. Middle peasants in fact constituted a majority. What these peasants wanted above all was access to the land that was 'locked up' in the grand estates and what they resisted most fiercely were requisitioning policies, regardless of whose policies they were. Kubanin also emphasises the strongly 'Russian' linguistic and cultural characteristics of the Makhno region. Kubanin was an active member of the Agrarian Marxist group led by L. N. Kritsman, and he investigated the tendency of peasant households to split up as capitalist relations developed in the countryside.[43] His book, together with a similarly semi-heterodox work by V. V. Rudnev,[44] fell rapidly into disfavour at the end of the 1920s and had little or no impact on the Soviet historiography of the civil war from the 1930s through to the 1960s.

The first academic text on the subject of Makhno to be published in the post-war period, breaking decades of silence, appeared in 1966 in the journal *Voprosy Istorii*.[45] The author, Sergei Semanov, had contacted Galina Kuz'menko, Makhno's widow, then living in exile in Kazakhstan, and exchanged some letters with her. Nevertheless, his line of analysis conformed to the general line of Soviet historiography at the time, condemning *makhnovshchina* for adventurism and for fighting against Soviet power. The text was reprinted in at least two revised pamphlet editions in the early 1990s,[46] and Semanov also published two longer monographs in the early 2000s.[47] His work has been criticised as highly repetitive and for containing multiple uncorrected factual errors:[48] in any event, Semanov seems to have been in some limited sense a pioneer.

Vladimir Litvinov, who was born in 1930 and died in the late 1980s, was *sui generis* in the sense that his work on anarchist thought in Russia was considered unorthodox and hence impossible to publish in Soviet conditions and was therefore only available via *samizdat*. He thoroughly researched *makhnovshchina*, travelling to Guliaipole several times in the 1970s to interview participants, tracking down some of Makhno's relatives and reading memoir manuscripts.[49] However, his book manuscript was rejected without even being read and his work was only published abroad, most notably in the form of a detailed study of the 'fourth alliance' between Makhno and the Bolsheviks in 1920, which appeared posthumously, in Russian, in the prestigious *International Review of Social History*.[50]

In the late 1980s, in the period of '*perestroika* and *glasnost*', some Russian and Ukrainian historians and sociologists began to take advantage of the more liberal approach to publication of heterodox viewpoints, questioning and deconstructing the general condemnation of Makhno as simply a counter-revolutionary gangster. The new approach included in some cases an explicit recognition of anarchist ideology as something to be taken seriously. An example was the publication in the authoritative *Literaturnaia Gazeta* (which despite its title, covered socio-political as well as literary and cultural topics), of a piece on Makhno by the journalist Vasilii Golovanov,[51] an event considered so startling at the time that it was even reported by the US-funded anti-communist broadcaster Radio Liberty.[52] Golovanov describes Makhno ironically as a 'werewolf' in the title of his article, and argues that the detailed history of the movement is less important than the way it illustrates how utopian democratic ideas – such as anarchist ideology – rapidly and inevitably degenerate into cruel dictatorship. In adopting this perspective, Golovanov foreshadows what was to become a key element in 'Western' post-Soviet historiography in the twenty-first century, which sees

> ... the revolution as the initiation of a cycle of violence that led inexorably to the horrors of Stalinism ... rather than as a flawed attempt to create a better world. They are more likely to see the mass mobilization as [more] motivated by irrationalism and aggression than by outrage at injustice or a yearning to be free.[53]

In the 1990s, in post-Soviet Russia and Ukraine, the pendulum began to some extent to swing in the other direction. The principle interpretative line in the broadly sympathetic Russian historiography of the post-Soviet period has argued that *makhnovshchina* was a comprehensible rebellion of the left-bank peasantry against the predations of war communism, an argument that had

in fact been put forward by Kubanin as early as 1927. In support of revision-
ist interpretations such as this, two ground-breaking and important Ukrainian
documentary collections appeared at this time, the first edited by Vladyslav
Verstiuk and published in Kiev,[54] the second edited institutionally by the
Gosudarstvennyi Arkhiv (*state archive*) of Dnepropetrovsk oblast (formerly
Ekaterinoslav) and including new primary materials.[55]

Alongside these two documentary collections, a wave of new texts began to
appear in Russia and in Ukraine in this period. A noticeable trend was to treat
the historical figure of Makhno in quasi-heroic terms, as a kind of Ukrainian
Robin Hood. As Danilov and Shanin note, Makhno is frequently characterised
as a

> ... 'Stenka Razin of the twentieth century', a 'Shamil' of the steppes', and so on
> ... in several works, researchers focus their main attention on ... the person
> of N. I. Makhno ... Often, a simplified image of a peasant leader is formed,
> a kind of chieftain of the latter-day Cossacks ... as a result, the conclusion is
> that *makhnovshchina* was 'meaningless and merciless' ...[56]

Among the generation of scholars researching *makhnovshchina* who emerged
in this period, the names of Golovanov,[57] Aleksandr Shubin,[58] Timoshchuk
(whose focus is on military aspects),[59] Verstiuk[60] and Volkovinskii (Ukrainian
spelling: Volkovyns'kyi)[61] come to mind. Of these writers, Golovanov is the
most given to speculation and reflection, and Verstiuk is the most emphatic in
recognising Makhno as a genuine revolutionary. Timoshchuk's book is explic-
itly a study of the organisation and combat activities of *makhnovshchina* from
September 1917 to August 1921, and draws on extensive archival research.

Aleksandr Shubin, despite the fact that his later books include quantities of
repeated passages taken verbatim from his earlier publications, was the first
Russian scholar to suggest that both Makhno and his followers were directly
motivated by anarchist ideology itself, and that it is impossible to understand
the history of *makhnovshchina* without taking this into account. In his study
of the peasantry in Khar'kov province between 1914 and 1921 Baker rejects
the importance of ideology, arguing that 'uprisings were provoked primarily
by communist policies' and that the insurgencies were generally 'non-political'
and 'motivated by ... local interests'.[62] Shubin's further argument that Makhno's
support was actually growing in 1921 after the break engineered by Frunze in
November 1920, and that there was still a chance of overthrowing the communists is much less convincing.[63]

In 1993 Aleksandr Belash, the son of Viktor Belash, who had been Makhno's
chief of staff, published the book *Dorogi Nestora Makhno*, based on a manuscript in three exercise books written by his father in the early 1920s while
a prisoner of the Cheka. Although the book makes no pretence to scientific

objectivity, it includes multiple transcriptions of primary documentation inter-
woven into the biographical narrative of the elder Belash, and thus remains
one of the richest printed sources available for the study of *makhnovshchina*. A
digitised version in PDF format is easily available online, however passages and
even whole pages are missing, and additionally the pagination is not the same
as the printed book.[64] Similarly indispensable among modern publications is
the extraordinary collection of 456 primary documents – orders, telegrams,
memoirs, intelligence reports, minutes of meetings – assembled with great care
by Teodor Shanin and the late Viktor Danilov.[65]

Most recently, the two Ukrainian historians Volodomyr Chop and his collaborator Ihor Lyman have published two valuable monographs on, respectively,
Makhno's four 'visits' to the city of Berdiansk, and on the Azov operation in
1920 that led to the final break between the *makhnovtsy* and the Bolsheviks.[66]
Azarov's book[67] on the implications of the Starobel'sk agreement is an explic-
itly political rather than military study, and takes the organisational and social
claims of *makhnovshchina* seriously, filling a major gap in the literature, which
tends to have a predominantly biographical orientation.[68]

What was it, then, about the specific conditions in Ukraine during the revolution and civil war that allowed anarchist ideas, an ideology of liberation from
both Russia *and from the state*, to flourish to the extent that they did? Why
anarchism, and why in Ukraine? Firstly, the country is among the most fertile
grain-growing areas in the world and at the end of the nineteenth and beginning of the twentieth centuries it was a crucially important agricultural zone
within the Russian Empire. Immediately before the revolution there were about
36 million hectares under cultivation in Ukraine, constituting just over 40 per
cent of the total planted area of the empire.[69] On a world scale, in the early
twentieth century, Ukraine produced 43 per cent of the world's barley, 20 per
cent of its wheat, and 10 per cent of its corn.[70] In Ekaterinoslav province alone,
in 1913, of nearly 1,800 metric tonnes of wheat produced, 860 tonnes or nearly
half were exported.[71] In 1912 the region's agro-businesses accounted for 21 per
cent of the empire's income, but Ukraine only received in return 12 per cent
of central expenditure, contributing 306 million more rubles to the exchequer
than it got back.[72] In 1914 more than half Russia's exports consisted of cereals
and other foodstuffs – one-third of the wheat imports of Western Europe came
from the Russian Empire, and nearly 90 per cent of the empire's wheat exports
came from the Ukraine. Although wheat was the empire's major export commodity, it was not Ukraine's top cash crop. On the right bank, Polish, Russian
and Jewish sugar barons prospered from large-scale sugar-beet production
from the 1840s onwards, while on the left-bank tobacco accounted for over half
of imperial production. Ukraine was also a major source of distilled alcohol.[73]
Although the empire exported substantial quantities of cash crops, raw mate-

rials and semi-manufactures, it was heavily dependent on chemical, metal and machinery imports.[74]

The government actively encouraged grain exports. The state bank granted credits, and calculated rail-freight rates for long-distance haulage of grain to Europe on special favourable scales. In Ukraine, the system depended in part on the existence of large numbers of poor peasants, who flooded the market with cheap wheat surpluses in return for cash with which to pay off back-taxes and debts incurred for seed. Between 1894 and 1914 production of wheat (the export grain) rose by 75 per cent; production of rye (the grain of domestic consumption) increased hardly at all.[75] The Russian Minister of Finance summed up this policy with the words 'We may go hungry, but we will export'.[76]

The physical geography and agricultural economies of different areas in Ukraine varied. Except in right-bank Ukraine, the fertility of the black earth belt that runs across the region was offset by the aridity of the climate. The spring thaws were rapid, and moisture did not soak into the soil. The sudden rushes of water disappeared as they cut deep ravines and gullies into the earth.[77] Left-bank Ukraine had evolved a tradition of landholding that was not exactly communal, nor yet entirely private.[78] A system had developed in which peasant obligations to landowners were paid in labour (*barshchina*), as opposed to the Russian obligations, which were payable in cash or kind (*obrok*). As the population increased, a system evolved in which each large family unit (*siabr*) received a land allotment, but without accompanying rights to any particular piece. As the family grew and divided it could split the share, sell it to another *siabr*, or even, under certain conditions, to an outsider. This system was hardly redistributional and holdings were not specifically defined in physical or territorial terms, and therefore could not be sold with complete freedom. On the other hand, it did not amount to private property in land either.

Ukrainian farming was more commercial than in the north.[79] Capitalist farming, in the sense of large-scale enterprise employing wage labour, also had a specific regional character in Ukraine. In Great Russia around 77 per cent of agricultural land was held through the commune, but this proportion diminished as one moved southwards and westwards. In 1905, according to a government source, 29 per cent of the land and 23 per cent of households in the Trans-Dnepr region were in communes. On the southern steppe the figures were 94 per cent for land and 98 per cent for households.[80] Nearly two-thirds of the peasant population were *batraki* or *bedniaki*,[81] and 45 per cent of peasant households had no draught animals. Although the poorer peasants owned 57 per cent of the farms in Ukraine, they occupied only 12 per cent of the land. One peasant in six had no land at all. Class differentiation and impoverishment among the Ukrainian peasantry sharpened from the mid-nineteenth century onwards, especially after the emancipation of 1861. The kulaks (in Ukrainian *kurkuli*) made up about 15 per cent of the peasantry, and held on average around 26 to 30 hectares of land. The *seredniaki*[82] were around 30 per cent and the poor peasants (*bedniaki* and *batraki*) a good half of the village population.[83]

In Novorossia (including the commercial farming zones on the right bank) only 14 per cent of total peasant landholdings were communal.[84] Commercial farming was widespread in the Tauride, Kherson and Ekaterinoslav – Makhno's home territories – even in the 1880s.[85] The three provinces were early on recognised as a distinct case. Collectively nicknamed 'the Troika', they were the object of one of the first analytical treatments of *zemstvo* statistics.[86] In these three provinces, two-fifths of the *dvory* ('households') making up about three-tenths of the population, owned one-eighth of the crop area. Another 40 per cent, the households of the middle peasants, supported themselves on their land. The kulaks (one-fifth of the households; three-tenths of the population) owned approximately half the total crop area. Their farming heavily favoured commercial crops. Over half of their harvested grain was surplus and provided them with steady incomes of between 574 and 1,500 rubles per year.[87] Just as a few hands controlled a high proportion of alienable land, so they controlled allotment land, livestock and implements. The rural bourgeoisie (20 per cent of the *dvory*) owned 93 per cent of mowing machines. The natural consequence of this concentration of land and capital was that the agricultural technology of commercial farming was the most advanced. Productivity per unit of expenditure was correspondingly higher, ensuring the continuing dominance of this type of production.[88]

The growth of commercial farming and of industrialisation in the cities resulted in increasing numbers of younger sons leaving the land for longer and longer periods. This exodus deprived the *dvor* of labour, and therefore, under the system of reallocation, eventually of land. The rate of emigration was a clear reflection of the level of land hunger and of dissatisfaction with the system. Between 1896 and 1906 over 1.6 million Ukrainians left for the Far East, and by 1914 there were 2 million Ukrainians resident there, mainly around the Amur basin.[89] The reforms implemented in 1906 by the Tsarist minister and landowner Stolypin went further than any previous administrative measures in attempting to dismantle the commune and to create and strengthen a peasant bourgeoisie – a capitalist class in the countryside.[90] Stolypin decreed that land of non-reallocating communes (defined as those that had not conducted a general partition for at least 24 years) passed into the ownership of the peasants who held it, unless they did so through rental. The peasants in those communes that still practised reallocation could have their land allotment under the system transferred to them, at any time, as private property. Such a provision clearly and deliberately favoured those who had more land than the average at the time of separation. Stolypin's so-called 'wager on the strong' aimed to establish a stable system of commercial agriculture. Unfortunately, the commune, even at its most degenerate, still protected those peasants who needed its stability because they lacked the capital to set themselves up in commercial enterprise.

It is difficult to calculate accurately the number of households that left the communes because of *stolypinshchina*. It seems likely that the figure for the whole empire over a ten-year period was about 4 million households, of which perhaps half were in Ukraine.[91] The peasants seized the opportunities offered by Stolypin's measure with enthusiasm in right-bank Ukraine, where rural capitalism was already highly developed. Something like half the communal land passed into private ownership. In the southern steppe (including Ekaterinoslav, the Tauride and Kherson) average holdings in 1906–8 were 8.9 hectares. It seems likely that the development of the money economy with an expanding market provided good conditions for such rationalisation. If repartition had continued with a growing population, holdings could only have decreased in size; commercialisation reversed the trend.[92] Nonetheless, even after Stolypin's reform, fully one-third of Ukrainian households farmed less than one hectare: 90 per cent of grain production was wheat. This emphasis on one crop, the economic inefficiency of the mass of tiny holdings, and an agricultural technology in the family sector that had been unchanged in its essentials since the days of Peter the Great, bore disastrous results. In the southern steppes a rotation system that only left one-fifth or one quarter of the soil fallow contributed to this inefficiency. The unbalanced relationship between pasture, arable land and hay land created problems. The shortage of pasture in turn caused a shortage of manure fertiliser. The amount of manure used per hectare was about 10 per cent of contemporary levels in eastern Germany. The attraction of commercial wheat growing for export was the direct cause of this situation; by 1917 nearly 75 per cent of farmland was arable.[93] Such advances as peasant farming could provide were the result of harder work, not of improved techniques. The wooden plough, sowing by hand and reaping with scythe and sickle remained. In the first three-quarters of the nineteenth century the yield-to-seed ratio had improved by only 6 per cent.[94] Even into the twentieth century the average grain yield in Russia itself was only one-quarter of that in Denmark, France or Germany.[95] Nevertheless, average yields in Ukraine were consistently higher than they were in Great Russia. Between 1907 and 1917 the average yield per hectare in Ukraine was higher than in Russia in wheat, rye, barley and oats, and markedly higher even for potatoes.[96]

Ekaterinoslav province, the centre of *makhnovshchina*, can be grouped with Kherson and the Tauride as an area of rapid growth in commercial farming. Between 1860 and 1913 the three provinces experienced an increase of over 100 per cent in the area under cultivation.[97] The new land increasingly fell into fewer hands. By 1905 the average landlord's holdings were over 800 hectares, compared to a figure of between 200 and 600 hectares for the central provinces of great Russia. The population was also far less homogeneous than elsewhere in Ukraine, comprising Ukrainians, Russians and Jews, and also Bulgars, Greeks, Tatars, Germans and others.[98] The pattern of agriculture was also different from that of northern Ukraine – for example, in Kiev province, which followed the rye-growing pattern of Great Russia. The warmer 'Troika' was an area of spring wheat and barley.[99]

This was a part of the Russian Empire where the poor peasants' lot was extremely hard. The commune was disappearing, the kulaks were increasing their wealth, and the *bedniaki* could only produce smaller and smaller harvests.[100] The increasing poverty of the peasants contrasted sharply with the potential fertility of the black-soil regions and with the enrichment of the few kulaks and *pomeshchiki* (landowners).[101] It was not surprising that the peasants of Ukraine and especially the Troika had a history of violent rebellion, robbing and burning estates and cutting down the landlords' forests.[102] Such revolts joined together a mixture of the landless, the poor and 'criminals', protesting against the loss of the protection provided by the *mir*[103] and the growing power of agrarian capitalists.[104]

After the Decree on Land in 1917, the amount of land under peasant control increased sharply. In Ukraine the increase was from 56 to 96 per cent of the total.[105] The mechanism to which the peasantry turned for controlling the distribution of this reclaimed land was, not surprisingly, the commune. The anarchists of the Makhno movement interpreted the use of this mechanism as a demonstration that the peasantry was in sympathy with their ideas about social organisation. The revival of the *form* of the *mir* could not, however, re-establish in Ukraine the economic basis for its vitality. The conditions for communal organisation no longer existed, and could not re-emerge. The position of Ukraine in relation to Russia was, like the position of Russia in relation to Western Europe, essentially that of a subordinate colony to an imperialist centre. Lenin himself commented in the April 1917 introduction to his *Imperializm, kak noveishii etap kapitalizma* that he had originally used Japan as an example when discussing annexation, to evade the censorship. However,

> the careful reader will easily substitute Russia for Japan, and Finland, Poland, Courland, the Ukraine, Khiva, Bokhara, Estonia or other regions peopled by non-Great Russians, for Korea.[106]

The typical characteristic of the epoch of monopoly capitalism is the export of capital itself to the territories of the periphery.[107] This was also true of the Russian Empire. In the two decades from 1894 until the outbreak of the World War, Russia's capital imports averaged 200 million rubles a year.[108]

The great mining and metallurgical region of southern Russia, the Donets River Basin (or *Donbass*), lies to the north and north-east of the Troika, partially enclosing it. It borders Ekaterinoslav in the west, Khar'kov in the north,

Lugansk in the east and Taganrog and Rostov in the south. With major reserves of peat, soft coal, anthracite, oil, iron and manganese, it was an early area of concentration for Russian and foreign capital. By 1914 half the capital invested in the coal industry of the *Donbass* came from abroad, and about 80 per cent of capital in the mining, metallurgical and oil industries. British, French and German capital was dominant, with investments totalling over two billion gold rubles for the whole empire.[109] Only one blast furnace in the pre-revolutionary *Donbass* was completely Russian-owned.[110]

By the end of the nineteenth century the *Donbass* was already an area of major industrial importance. The dense concentration of industry and its rapid growth are often disruptive elements even in the most stable of societies. Russian and Ukrainian rural areas, however, were in a state of some unrest. The rate of development in the *Donbass* had been rapid. Coal production grew at an average of 13 per cent per annum between 1870 and 1900.[111]

After the turn of the century the importance of the *Donbass* to the economic well-being of the empire continued to increase. In 1913, on the eve of the World War, 67 per cent of pig-iron smelting, 57 per cent of iron and steel production and 71 per cent of coal production in the empire took place in what one Soviet economic historian has called the 'progressive south'.[112] Factories were larger and output per worker was generally higher in the *Donbass* than elsewhere in the empire. The concentration of labour was a characteristic of Russian industry – in 1912, 53 per cent of Russian workers worked in factories with over 500 hands, a higher concentration of labour than in either Germany or the United States.[113] The tendency continued in the Troika. In 1912, 17 per cent of Ukrainian mines and metallurgical companies were in the three provinces, employing over half the workers in those industries.[114] The pattern varied in different sectors, however. In foodstuffs the Troika accounted for 13 per cent of the businesses, only 3 per cent of the workers, and 11 per cent of the production.[115] Many skilled workers were Russians, Bulgars or Greeks; in 1897 there were even 370 English in Ekaterinoslav province.[116] Only 22 per cent of the labour force in the coalmines was Ukrainian, and only 20 per cent in the metallurgical industry.

The rapid development and concentration of industry in the south made Ekaterinoslav a natural strike centre and a base for both legal and illegal Bolshevik activities. The great mass of unskilled factory workers was willing to listen to the Bolshevik argument that revolution was the only way to improve their conditions. The Ekaterinoslav mines lost nearly 250,000 working days altogether between June 1914 and February 1917, in 107 strikes by over 55,000 men. The metalworkers of the province were involved in 52 strikes, mostly economic, with the loss of over 500,000 working days.[117] The metalworkers were the nucleus of the radical labour movement, the most politically conscious and the best organised. After 1912 they participated in 84 per cent of political strikes.[118] Their union looked to the west, and even sent to Germany for material on the organisation of trade union activities.[119] Petr Arshinov, Makhno's prison tutor and later his apologist, had been a metalworker in his early days as a Bolshevik.

Between 1905 and 1916, the rate of increase in the number of strikes in Ekaterinoslav was noticeably slower than in St. Petersburg, so it is important not to overestimate the radicalism of the south in comparison with the north.[120] Only about one-twelfth of the workers was organised. In the elections to the Second Duma they supported Mensheviks and Socialist Revolutionaries at least as enthusiastically as they supported Bolsheviks. Ekaterinoslav was nonetheless an important centre for Bolshevik activity and acted as a kind of detonator for the surrounding area. During the years immediately before the revolution the Party operated illegal presses and distribution centres for its literature, organised party centres and committees, and held two conferences.[121]

The impact of the First World War on the industry and agriculture of the Russian Empire was direct and disastrous. Between August 1914 and the middle of 1917 about 14 million men were mobilised, most of them peasants. Between one-third and one-half of rural households were left with no male labour. The Tsarist government adopted a policy of diverting all possible industrial production into war channels. The metal shortage became so severe that even the village smithies ran out. Falling import earnings could not compensate for production losses in farm machinery. The government mobilised horses without any thought for the needs of agriculture. In the first eighteen months of war the peasantry lost 26 million head of cattle to requisition or enemy occupation. Food grain harvests dropped by 21 per cent and fodder harvests by 48 per cent between 1914 and 1917. The importation of fertiliser came to a halt.[122]

The peasantry lost interest in selling the little surplus grain that existed, as inflation robbed the paper rouble of most of its value. Even in 1915, when there were no exports of food, the drop in production and marketing was greater than the savings in non-exported foodstuffs. The cities and even the army felt the shortages. The government bought nearly all the commercially available grain at fixed prices and, just before the February revolution, was preparing to enforce compulsory purchase measures enacted in December 1916.[123]

The civil war was even more disruptive, for it was fought entirely *within* the territory of the former empire. Its effects could not be avoided. One American commentator wrote that to find parallel conditions of urban and economic decay it was necessary to go back to the final days of the Thirty Years War.[124] In 1916 there were 65 blast furnaces operating in Ukraine; by 1920 there was only one.[125] This explains why Ukraine, which had produced 3 million tons of pig iron in 1913, could produce only 15,000 tons in 1920. The production of essential raw materials also fell off sharply, iron ore from nearly 6.5 million tons in 1913 to zero in 1920, and coal from 24.6 million tons to 4.5 million. Steel production fell from 2.4 million tons to 48,000 in the same period.[126]

The spectacular collapse of the industry and agriculture of Ukraine during the civil war was a central factor in the rise of *makhnovshchina*. In normal or near-normal circumstances the peasantry could react to excessive outside pressure in two ways, short of emigrating. By increasing their output and competing in the marketplace, a minority of the better-off peasants could win some degree of economic independence. The kulaks made exactly this kind of step up the social ladder, emerging in a time of religious decline and weak central government. Any peasant willing to ignore social obligations, and who could avoid taxes, might commit his entire surplus to the market and strengthen his position in a money economy. The alternative was to withdraw into self-sufficiency and to market no surplus at all. To curtail consumption to retain individual autonomy was a precarious business. The Bolsheviks found that many peasants were willing to try any strategy, rather than hand over grain to yet another central government. This was especially true after they had received land:

> The peasantry reasoned thus: it was Soviet power that gave land to the peasants [...] it was the Bolsheviks that did it. But the power that carried out the grain requisitioning did not give all the landowners' land back to the peasants: it built *sovkhozy*, it built communes – it is a commune power, not Bolshevik but Communist [...] we are for the Bolsheviks, but against the Communists.[127]

The peasants who supposed that there must be two separate parties of 'Bolsheviks' and 'Communists' were using a particular logic, consistent with their aim of seizing the land. The course of events in Ukraine after the October revolution – the invasion by the Central Powers, the fight against Denikin and Wrangel, the Polish War and the struggles of the various nationalist groups against outside forces – prevented the peasants from following for long even the strategy of withdrawal from the market. The land seizures after 1917 – the 'Black Repartition' – gave the *bedniak* more land, but they did not usually provide him with the tools or the draught animals he needed to work it. Later, as the Bolshevik campaign against the kulaks began to take effect, the landless labourers lost even their chance of employment on the farms of the rich peasants.

The revolution and the civil war were great levellers, and during the period after 1917 the *mir* spontaneously revived. Twelve million peasants in uniform had been politicised by their experiences in the war against Germany. As they poured back to the countryside, they began to channel their fellow peasants back into the communes, cutting short the growth of rural capitalism. The commune was the only mechanism available to the peasantry through which they could redistribute the land that they had seized. Land seizures in the Russian Empire increased a hundredfold between March and July 1917. Thirty per cent of individual peasant land holdings were taken and pooled in the *mir*.[128]

At least two sets of circumstances intersected in the region of left-bank Ukraine around Guliaipole and Ekaterinoslav at a time when the authority of the Russian Imperial regime was crumbling under the twin pressures of the long-term and unresolved contradictions of modernisation and then the war. The characteristics of this 'very heterogeneous'[129] part of Ukraine were highly distinctive, and a significant part of the population was ready to welcome and support a new system of power relations that would rest on 'a network of mass organisations … unions, factory committees, farm labourers' committees, and popular gatherings'.[130]

*   *   *

At the very beginning of this book, I quote the first-century-Roman orator Quintilian (Marcus Fabius Quintilianus) to the effect that history is written to recount what happened, not to prove a point. Quintilian is, of course, only partly correct; history is always written with a purpose. But a significant proportion of the writing on *makhnovshchina* has been produced, unfortunately, *precisely* to prove a political point – that the *makhnovtsy* were a gang of counter-revolutionary cut-throats led by a drunken anti-Semitic thug, or that they were actually true Ukrainian patriots fighting to throw off the Russian yoke, or that the Bolsheviks were all cynical opportunists willing to betray their allies at the drop of a hat. Virtue, in these admittedly exaggerated characterisations, is to be found entirely on one side, and not at all on the others.

Such reductive and simplified narratives are, however, ultimately unconvincing. It was certainly the case that some *makhnovtsy* were guilty of atrocities – such as the massacre of the Mennonites at Eichenfeld – and that Makhno was a ruthless military commander who also got drunk, watched erotic movies and fell off his horse. Nevertheless, tens of thousands of Ukrainian peasants and workers supported his attempts to realise anarchist ideas, and fought in his army. It seems likely that part of the attraction of *makhnovshchina* was the attempt to throw off Russian domination, but not to replace it with a Ukrainian state run by the local bourgeoisie; rather, the peasantry wanted agency in the direct management of local affairs. Similarly, it is true that the Bolsheviks under Frunze turned on the *makhnovtsy* after Wrangel's defeat in 1920, in what must be called a betrayal. But the events that led up to the earlier split between the insurgents and the Red Army in mid-1919 are much harder to categorise. Opinion among the Bolsheviks was in fact divided as to the revolutionary character of the movement, with Antonov-Ovseenko and Kamenev among its defenders.

As we have seen, *makhnovshchina* was eventually defeated by a more ruthless, more efficient and perhaps more realistic enemy with control of the levers of economic power, despite its popular support and the favourable short-term conditions on the left-bank under war communism. In the end, Makhno's vision proved perhaps to be both utopian and unrealisable – but, as Oscar Wilde wrote in 1891, a few years after Makhno's birth and decades before the events described here, 'a map of the world that does not include Utopia is not worth even glancing at'.[131]

Epilogue
The Reframing of Makhno for the Twenty-First Century

In early 2019, the website of the small town of Guliaipole in left-bank Ukraine published a wide-ranging interview with the head of the local administration under the headline: 'Interview with Oleksandr Ishchenko about the hospital, the reburial of the ashes of Nestor Makhno, and the road to Polohi'.[1] In the middle of the interview, Ishchenko revealed that the city council of Guliaipole and the district administration of Zaporizhzhia *raion*[2] had been preparing the necessary documentation to request the return of the ashes of Nestor Makhno from the Père Lachaise cemetery in Paris to the town of his birth, to be displayed in a local museum. After all, Ishchenko proudly declared, Nestor Makhno was a 'world class historical personality', and in order to attract tourists his administration was already preparing various projects along the routes travelled by Makhno's Revolutionary Insurgent Army one hundred years earlier. 'Makhno', he concluded, 'is our brand'.[3]

Thus, with the passage of time, one of the most controversial revolutionary leaders to emerge during the complex matrix of early twentieth century events that made up the Russian revolution has been appropriated and domesticated – reframed – for commercial purposes by precisely the kind of capitalist forces that he struggled against so fiercely during his lifetime. Makhno's consistent and foundational political position was rooted in his conviction that democratic practices belonged at the local level, and that peasants accustomed to collective decision-making in the rural commune were perfectly capable of organising their own lives, a conviction that he attempted to put into practice in the brief periods when he was not waging mobile guerrilla campaigns. Consequently, Makhno is especially revered in anarchist and libertarian circles today as a relatively rare example of mass anarchism in action: that is to say, a movement built on an upsurge of popular rebellion from below, rather than relying on 'propaganda by the deed', isolated violent terrorist attacks carried out in the hope of provoking insurrection.[4]

Nevertheless, the unhappy truth is that after the collapse of the Soviet Union and the independence of Ukraine in August 1991, both the Ukrainian state and a wide gamut of political forces, including neo-Nazis and fascists, have been searching their own history for 'national heroes'. Even such flawed figures as Skoropadskii, Petliura and the Nazi collaborator Stepan Bandera have been brought into service. When he was asked to explain why 'the ideological materials used for the construction of Ukrainian nationalism' were all so reactionary, and why there had been so few attempts to draw on populist or left traditions, the Ukrainian intellectual Volodymyr Ishchenko (no relation to the mayor) responded that

> ... Ukrainian nationalism now mostly has ... right-wing connotations ...
> But when it emerged in the late nineteenth century, Ukrainian national-
> ism was predominantly a leftist, even socialist movement ... the right has
> worked to reinterpret figures such as Makhno along nationalist lines – not as
> an anarchist, but as another Ukrainian who fought against communism. In
> their eyes communism was a Russian imposition ...[5]

Makhno fits the bill precisely because he fought against 'foreign interventions' – by the Germans and Austro-Hungarians as well as by the Russian Bolsheviks. This is adequate only if it is possible to place his inconvenient anarchist ideology to one side: and when this is done, to appropriate Makhno's name and image in order 'to promote an aggressive form of ultra-nationalism'.[6] It is therefore unsurprising to find that Makhno's face appears on commemorative coins and banknotes, that a kitsch golden statue of him has been erected, and that the state flag of Ukraine flutters over public events marking his various anniversaries.

Mayor Oleksandr Ishchenko's project in Gulaipole is only one in a long series of attempts to appropriate the historical personality of Makhno and his movement to a justificatory Ukrainian nationalist meta-narrative. In December 1998, for instance, the State University in Zaporizhzhia (formerly Aleksandrovsk) organised a conference to celebrate the 110th anniversary of Makhno's birth, which was to take place alongside a popular celebration of Makhno and what he stood for, in the centre of the town. The event was attended by scholars as well as by anarcho-syndicalists and 'anarcho-greens', reportedly under the bizarrely inappropriate slogan 'Makhno is our Tsar, Makhno is our God'.[7] On top of this, at the public celebration the blue-and-yellow state flag of Ukraine was flying over the crowd in front of the Palace of Culture, and a Cossack delegation dressed in 'Petlyura and Gaidamac uniforms' with 'golden shoulder straps' appeared – thus, in the words of one outraged attendee, surfacing after so many years 'to smear, foul and debase the memory of Makhno-the-anarchist'. The speeches 'spelled out Nestor Makhno's merits as fighter for the independence of the State of Ukraine *with not a single word about his role as anarchist and revolutionary*'.[8] Fifteen years later, another attempt to mark an anniversary, this time in Guliaipole itself 125 years after Makhno's birth, was described as 'muted'.[9]

Some sources claim that Makhno's name is still well known in popular culture in Ukraine as a symbol representing

> ... the notion of being able to rise up against any government and overthrow authority. In this sense, Makhno reinforces tough and sturdy myths about the Ukrainian character' Unfortunately, however, many Ukrainians have 'no deep understanding' of the anarchist's political movement. ... Ukraine's leftist history has been largely forgotten ...[10]

Meanwhile, actual anarchists in Ukraine are subjected to harassment by the forces of the ultra-right that are, at the same time, attempting cynically to appropriate the name of Nestor Makhno for twenty-first-century purposes.[11] Whatever the lessons that the career of Nestor Makhno and the story of *makhnovshchina* may have for Ukraine, for the left, or indeed for the world, they are submerged when the historical character of his revolutionary struggle for local autonomy and against the power of the state is ignored – regardless of his ideology's utopianism, its realism or its potential impact. Nevertheless, despite all the attempts at appropriation, we can note – in Casey Michel's words – that '*bat'ko*'s legacy limps on', and that the true nature of his movement is not completely forgotten.[12]

Notes

CHAPTER 1   THE DEEP ROOTS OF RURAL DISCONTENT: GULIAIPOLE, 1905–17

1. Some sources say 1889, but Iurii Gaev cites a church register with the date 26 October/8 November 1888 (*Fakti i Komentarii* [13 November 1998]). Valerii Volkovinskii says that Makhno never knew his correct date of birth (*Makhno i ego krakh* [Moscow: Izdat. VZPI, 1991], p. 11); see also Aleksandr Shubin, *Makhno i ego vremia: o velikoi revoliutsii i grazhdanskoi voine, 1917-1922 gg., v Rossii i na Ukraine* (Moscow: Knizhnyi Dom Librokom, 2014), p. 9. The date may have been falsified to avoid military service. For the 1889 date, see e.g. Makhno ('Zapiski', *Anarkhicheskii vestnik* no. 1 [1923], pp. 16–17); Halina Kuz'menko ('Vidpovid' na stattiu Pomer Makhno v Novii Pori vid 9-ho serpnia 1934 roku, hor. Detroita, Mich'. *Probuzhdenie* no. 50–51 [1934], p. 17); and Petr Arshinov (*Istoriia makhnovskogo dvizheniia* [Berlin: Gruppy Russkikh Anarkhistov v Germanii, 1923], p. 49). Soviet sources sometimes gave 1884: e.g. N. V. Gerasimenko, 'Makhno', *Istorik i sovremennik* vol. 3 (1922), p. 151 and S. N. Semanov, 'Makhnovschchina i ee krakh', *Voprosy istorii* no. 9 (1966), p. 38n.
2. For example testimony by Iosif Solov'ev to Denikin's commission on Bolshevik atrocities in August 1919 includes details of Makhno's family background – Viktor Danilov and Teodor Shanin (eds), *Nestor Makhno: krest'ianskoe dvizheniia na Ukraine, 1918-1921. dokumenty e materialy* (Moscow: Rossiiskaia Politicheskaia Entsiklopediia, 2006), p. 191 ff.
3. E.g., Vasilii Golovanov says Gerasimenko's work (cited above, fn.1) 'belongs to the realm of historical mythology and does not contain a grain of truth' and argues that 'we can [therefore] only read carefully what Makhno himself wrote about his family and his early years' (*Nestor Makhno* [Moscow: Molodaia Gvardiia, 2013], pp. 23–4).
4. Of Makhno's four brothers, Emel'ian was shot by the Austrians in 1918, and Policarp, Savelii and Grigorii were all killed during the civil war (O. A. Simonova, 'Obraz Nestora Makhno v vospominaniiakh A. A. Saksaganskoi: vpechatlenie pisatel'nitsy, slukhi, svidetel'stva ochebidtsev', *Rossiia v Soovermennyi Mir* no. 4 [2018], p. 217).
5. Anatol' Hak (pseud.), *Vid Huliai-Polia do N'iu-Iorku: spohadi* (Neu Ulm: the author 1973), p. 24n.
6. Makhno, *Miatezhnaia iunost', 1888-1917* (Paris: Hromada, 2006), p. 11; Makhno, 'Zapiski', pp. 16–17. The actual family name was Mikhnenko; Makhno is an abbreviated form (Shubin, *Makhno i ego vremia*, p. 9). In exile in the 1920s Makhno reverted to Mikhnenko: see also Ida Mett, 'Souvenirs sur Nestor Makhno', ([Paris], 1948), p. 1; Volin, 'Nestor Makhno', *Delo Truda* no. 82 (1934), p. 4.
7. Hak, *Vid Huliai-Polia do N'iu-Iorku*, p. 28.
8. In 1898 the population was 7,196; it had doubled to 16,000 by 1913 (Aleksandr Timoshchuk, *Anarkho-kommunisticheskie formirovaniia N. Makhno, sentiabr' 1918-avgust 1921* [Simferopol': Tavriia, 1996], p. 16).

9. See, e.g. David Macey, 'The Peasant Commune and the Stolypin Reforms: Peasant Attitudes, 1906-14', in: Roger Bartlett (ed.), *Land Commune and Peasant Community in Russia: Communal Forms in Imperial and Early Soviet Society* (London: Palgrave Macmillan, 1990), pp. 219–36.
10. Timoshchuk, *Anarkho-kommunisticheskie formirovaniia N. Makhno*, pp. 16–17.
11. Hak, *Vid Huliai–Polia do N'iu-Iorku*, p. 21. Victor Peters, *Nestor Makhno* (Winnipeg, [1970]), pp. 16–18. Litvinov describes Peter's book as a 'libellous little pamphlet' (Vladimir Litvinov, 'O chetvertom (oktiabr' 1920 g.) voenno-politicheskom soglashenii mezhdu Revoliutsionno-Povstancheskoi Armiei (Makhnovtsev) i kommunisticheskim pravitel'stvom RSFSR', *International Review of Social History* vol. 32, no. 3 (1987), p. 317.
12. In 1897 the population mix in Aleksandrovsk district was 82.5 per cent Ukrainians, 6.9 per cent Russians, 5.1 per cent Jews and 5.2 per cent Germans. M. Kordouba, *Le territoire et la population de l'Ukraine* (Berne: R. Suter, 1919), pp. 94–5.
13. Testimony of Zuichenko, reported in A. V. Belash and V. F. Belash, *Dorogi Nestora Makhno: istoricheskoe povestvovanie* (Kiev: Proza, 1993), p. 13.
14. Makhno, 'Zapiski', pp. 17–18; Kuz'menko, 'Vidpovid' na stattiu Pomer Makhno', p. 17; Hak, *Vid Huliai-Polia do N'iu-Iorku*, p. 28.
15. Peter Lyashchenko, *History of the National Economy of Russia* (New York: Macmillan, 1970), p. 693.
16. Makhno, 'Mon autobiographie, [no. 2]', *Le Libertaire* (26 March 1926), p. 2; see also Arshinov, *Istoriia makhnovskogo dvizheniia*, p. 49.
17. Shubin, *Makhno i ego vremia*, pp. 10–11.
18. Makhno, *The Russian Revolution in Ukraine, March 1917-April 1918* (Edmonton: Black Cat Press, 2009), p. 48.
19. Golovanov denies this (*Nestor Makhno*, p. 23).
20. Gerasimenko, 'Makhno', p. 151. Republished in the USSR as *Bat'ko Makhno: memuary belogvardeitsa* (Moscow, 1928), and in Poland in instalments by Iu. Petrovych, 'Makhno: istoriia odnoho povstanskoho vatashka, na osnovi Istorika i Sovremennika', *Nedilia* vol. 8, nos. 40–46 (1935). Cf. Arshinov, *Istoriia makhnovskogo dvizheniia*, p. 7.
21. Hak, *Vid Huliai-Polia do N'iu-Iorku*, p. 28.
22. Aleksei Chubenko, 'Dnevnik' in: Danilov and Shanin (eds), *Nestor Makhno*, p. 731; see also Makhno, 'Mon autobiographie', *Le Libertaire* (2 April 1926), p. 3; Makhno, 'Zapiski', p. 18; Arshinov, *Istoriia makhnovskogo dvizheniia*, p. 49.
23. These ideas were developed by Petr Kropotkin. See his *La conquête du pain* (Paris: P.-V. Stock, 1892), *Fields, Factories and Workshops* (London: Hutchinson, 1899), and *Mutual Aid* (London: Heinemann, 1902).
24. Thomas Fedor, *Patterns of Urban Growth in the Russian Empire During the Nineteenth Century* (Chicago: University of Chicago Dept. of Geography, 1975), pp. 138–9.
25. Fedor, *Patterns of Urban Growth in the Russian Empire*, p. 187.
26. Shanin, *The Roots of Otherness: Russia's Turn of Century. Vol.1: Russia as a Developing Society* (London: Macmillan, 1985), p. 66.
27. Shanin, *The Roots of Otherness: Russia's Turn of Century. Vol.1*, p. 66.
28. Esther Kingston-Mann, *Lenin and the Problem of Marxist Peasant Revolution* (New York: Oxford University Press, 1983), p. 20; see also Shanin, *The Roots of Otherness: Russia's Turn of Century. Vol.1*, pp. 72–81.
29. Kingston-Mann, *Lenin and the Problem of Marxist Peasant Revolution*, p. 23.
30. Shanin, *The Roots of Otherness: Russia's Turn of Century*, vol. 1, p. 73.

31. Mark Baker, *Peasants, Power and Place: Revolution in the Villages of Kharkiv Province, 1914-1921* (Cambridge, Mass.: Harvard University Press, 2016), p. 35.

32. Male labour migration can be estimated from the number of internal passports issued by the authorities to *otkhodniki*. Over 135,000 were issued in Ekaterinoslav province in 1902; the number fell in later years. See Jeffrey Burds, *Peasant Dreams and Market Politics: Labor Migration and the Russian Village, 1861-1905* (Pittsburgh: University of Pittsburgh Press, 1998), p. 22, table 1.2, using data drawn from L. E. Mints, *Otkhod krest'ianskogo naseleniia na zarabotki v SSSR* (Moscow; Voprosy Truda, 1925), pp. 16–18.

33. Aaron B. Retish, *Russia's Peasants in Revolution and Civil War: Citizenship, Identity and the Creation of the Soviet State, 1914-1922* (Cambridge: Cambridge University Press, 2008), pp. 4–5.

34. Jane Burbank, *Russian Peasants Go to Court; Legal Culture in the Countryside, 1905-1917* (Bloomington: Indiana University Press, 2004) argues that peasants made sophisticated use of available legal remedies.

35. Some women 'carved out a position for themselves within this patriarchal system' (Retish, *Russia's Peasants in Revolution and Civil War*, p. 5); the anarchist Marusia Nikiforova was one.

36. Teodor Shanin estimates 6,000 activists for the anarchists and the SR maximalists together in this period (*The Roots of Otherness: Russia's Turn of Century. Vol.2: Russia, 1905-1907: Revolution as a Moment of Truth* [London: Macmillan, 1986], p. 39).

37. G. Novopolin, 'Makhno i guliai-pol'skaia gruppa anarkhistov, po ofitsial'nym dannym', *Katorga i ssylka* no. 34 (1927), p. 71. An extract is printed in Vladyslav Verstiuk (ed.), *Nestor Ivanovich Makhno: vospominaniia, materialy i dokumenty* (Kiev: Dzvin, 1991), pp. 131–7. cf. Hak, *Vid Huliai-Polia do N'iu-Iorku*, p. 25.

38. Novopolin, 'Makhno i guliai-pol'skaia gruppa anarkhistov', p. 75.

39. Novopolin, 'Makhno i guliai-pol'skaia gruppa anarkhistov', p. 71.

40. Hak, *Vid Huliai-Polia do N'iu-Iorku*, p. 29.

41. Mett, 'Souvenirs sur Nestor Makhno', p. 1.

42. Chubenko, 'Dnevnik', p. 731.

43. Before the reform of 1/14 February 1918, Russia used the Julian calendar, 13 days behind the Gregorian calendar used in Western Europe. I follow the convention of indicating both dates.

44. Novopolin, 'Makhno i guliai-pol'skaia gruppa anarkhistov', p. 72.

45. Novopolin, 'Makhno i guliai-pol'skaia gruppa anarkhistov', p. 72.

46. Makhno, *The Russian Revolution in Ukraine*, p. 47.

47. Makhno, 'Zapiski', p. 18.

48. Novopolin, 'Makhno i guliai-pol'skaia gruppa anarkhistov', p. 72.

49. Novopolin, 'Makhno i guliai-pol'skaia gruppa anarkhistov', p. 73.

50. Novopolin, 'Makhno i guliai-pol'skaia gruppa anarkhistov', pp. 72–3.

51. See the police report of 24 February 1908 in Gosudartsvennyi Arkhiv Dneprope-trovskoi Oblasti, *N. Makhno i makhnovskoe dvizhenie: iz istorii povstancheskogo dvizheniia v Ekaterinoslavskoi gubernii. Sbornik dokumentov i materialov* (Dnepro-petrovsk: AO DAES, 1993), p. 6. I am grateful to Sean Patterson for making this rare source available.

52. Makhno, 'Zapiski', p. 18.

53. Chubenko says that Al'tgauzen was a Menshevik who subsequently betrayed Makhno ('Dnevnik', p. 731).

54. Hak says that Makhno did not kill the policeman as some writers have claimed, and that he was not even present at this meeting (*Vid Huliai-Polia do N'iu-Iorku*, p. 29).

55. Administrative exile – away from the towns – was used in the late empire to deal with political offenders, avoiding judicial processes in the courts, which were 'unpredictable, complicated, and time-consuming'. See Jonathan Daly, 'Political crime in late imperial Russia', *Journal of Modern History* vol. 74, no. 1 (2002), p. 79.

56. Novopolin, 'Makhno i guliai-pol'skaia gruppa anarkhistov', p. 74.

57. There were 17 members in the group, including Antoni, Semeniuta, Makhno and Levadnyi. Thirteen were residents of Guliaipole. They were all peasants except Al'tgauzen, who was bourgeois (*meshchanin*). There were several fringe members including a young woman, Mariia Martynova. Not all those brought to trial were core members. Novopolin, 'Makhno i guliai-pol'skaia gruppa anarkhistov', p. 71, p. 74.

58. Novopolin, 'Makhno i guliai-pol'skaia gruppa anarkhistov', p. 74.

59. Novopolin, 'Makhno i guliai-pol'skaia gruppa anarkhistov', p. 71; Makhno, 'Zapiski', p. 18. Chubenko confirms that Al'tgauzen betrayed Makhno to save himself ('Dnevnik', p. 731).

60. Novopolin, 'Makhno i guliai-pol'skaia gruppa anarkhistov', p. 75.

61. Novopolin, 'Makhno i guliai-pol'skaia gruppa anarkhistov', p. 75.

62. Novopolin, 'Makhno i guliai-pol'skaia gruppa anarkhistov', p. 76; Makhno, 'Zapiski', p. 18.

63. Novopolin, 'Makhno i guliai-pol'skaia gruppa anarkhistov', pp. 75-6.

64. Novopolin, 'Makhno i guliai-pol'skaia gruppa anarkhistov', p. 76.

65. Chubenko mentions the killing of Karachentsev but dates it *before* Makhno's arrest ('Dnevnik', p. 731).

66. Hak, *Vid Huliai-Polia do N'iu-Iorku*, pp. 30-31.

67. Hak says that Levadnyi escaped and died of exposure in a blizzard (*Vid Huliai-Polia do N'iu-Iorku*, p. 29).

68. Makhno, 'Mon autobiographie', *Le Libertaire* (23 April 1926), p. 3.

69. Novopolin, 'Makhno i guliai-pol'skaia gruppa anarkhistov', p. 77; Kuz'menko, 'Vidpovid' na stattiu Pomer Makhno', p. 17.

70. This supports the 1889 birth date (see above, note 1). Mett, 'Souvenirs sur Nestor Makhno', p. 1; Kuz'menko, 'Vidpovid' na stattiu Pomer Makhno', p. 17; Makhno, 'Zapiski', p. 18. However, Arshinov dates the trial in 1908 (*Istoriia makhnovskogo dvizheniia*, pp. 49-50).

71. Golovanov, *Nestor Makhno*, p. 42.

72. Novopolin, 'Makhno i guliai-pol'skaia gruppa anarkhistov', p. 77. Makhno, 'Zapiski', p. 18, and Kuz'menko, 'Vidpovid' na stattiu Pomer Makhno', p. 17, both say life imprisonment. See also Arshinov, *Istoriia makhnovskogo dvizheniia*, p. 50; and I. Teper, *Makhno: ot edinogo anarkhizma k stopam rumynskogo korolia* (Kiev: Molodoi Rabochii, 1924), p. 22.

73. Paul Avrich, *The Anarchists in the Russian Revolution* (London: Thames and Hudson, 1973), p. 209.

74. Arshinov, *Dva pobega: iz vospominanii anarkhista 1906-9 gg.* (Paris: Izdat. Delo Truda, 1929), passim; Arshinov, *Istoriia makhnovskogo dvizheniia*, pp. 12-15.

75. Arshinov, *Istoriia makhnovskogo dvizheniia*, pp. 12-15.

76. Makhno, 'Zapiski', p. 18.

77. Makhno, *Miatezhnaia iunost*', p. 52; 'Mon autobiographie,' *Le Libertaire* (9 July 1926), p. 3.

78. Makhno, *Miatezhnaia iunost*', p. 52.

79. Arshinov, *Istoriia makhnovskogo dvizheniia*,p. 50; Z. Iu. Arbatov, 'Bat'ko Makhno', *Vozrozhdenie* no. 29 (1953), p. 114.

80. Makhno, *Miatezhnaia iunost'*, p. 52–3; Makhno, 'Zapiski', p. 18.

81. Makhno, *The Russian Revolution in Ukraine*, p. 89.

82. Arshinov, *Istoriia makhnovskogo dvizheniia*,p. 153; see also H. Limbach, *Ukrainische Schreckenstage: Erinnerungen eines Schweizers* (Bern: Francke, 1919), p. 78.

83. Makhno, *Miatezhnaia iunost'*, p. 59; Makhno, 'Mon autobiographie, no. 18', *Le libertaire* (13 August 1926), p. 3.

84. Mett, 'Souvenirs sur Nestor Makhno', p. 2.

85. R. P. Browder and Alexander Kerensky (eds), *The Russian Provisional Government 1917: Documents* (Stanford: Stanford University Press, 1961), vol. 1, pp. 196–7.

86. Makhno vividly describes the events leading to his release in his *Miatezhnaia iunost'*, pp. 64–5.

87. The description is taken from Golovanov, *Nestor Makhno*, pp. 41–2.

88. Belash and Belash, *Dorogi Nestora Makhno*, p. 19.

89. Makhno, *Miatezhnaia iunost'*, pp. 66–7; P. Arshinov, *Istoriia makhnovskogo dvizheniia*, p. 50.

90. Aleksandr Shubin argues that 'in that moment, his prison past was a source of authority' (*Makhno i makhnovskoe dvizhenie* [Moscow: Izdat MIK, 1998], p. 35). Belash says that he was shown 'honour and trust' (Belash and Belash, *Dorogi Nestora Makhno*, p. 19).

91. Respectively documents no. 1, no. 2, no. 4, and no. 5, dated between 19 May and 1 June 1917, in Danilov and Shanin (eds), *Nestor Makhno*, pp. 37–9.

92. Golovanov, *Nestor Makhno*, p. 54.

93. Belash says he constantly interfered in 'all the little things', and caused scandals (Belash and Belash, *Dorogi Nestora Makhno*, p. 20).

94. Golovanov, *Nestor Makhno*, pp. 42–4, quoting an interview with the writer Lev Nikulin.

95. Timoshchuk points to the absence of studies on the period from September 1917 to April 1918 (*Anarkho-kommunisticheskie formirovaniia N. Makhno*, pp. 10–11).

96. Belash and Belash, *Dorogi Nestora Makhno*, p. 19.

97. Golovanov, *Nestor Makhno*, p. 42. Belash and Belash describe her as 'beautiful' (*Dorogi Nestora Makhno*, p. 21).

98. Valerii Volkovinskii speculates that this hardened Makhno: 'in his eyes the lives of others … were worthless' (*Makhno i ego krakh* [Moscow: Izdat VZPI, 1991], p. 31, quoting an archival source).

99. Mykhailo Hrushevs'kyi (1866–1934), academic historian and politician.

100. Serhii Plokhy, *Lost Kingdom: A History of Russian Nationalism from Ivan the Great to Vladimir Putin* (London: Penguin, 2018), pp. 194–5.

101. Plokhy, *Lost Kingdom*, p. 195.

102. Makhno, *The Russian Revolution in Ukraine*, p. 35.

103. Makhno, *The Russian Revolution in Ukraine*, p. 31.

104. *Biulleten' osvedomitel'nogo biuro anarkhistov Rossii* (15 December 1917), pp. 4–5; according to this source the group had eight active members at the end of 1917. However, Belash, quoting Nazarii Zuichenko, claims that over eleven years membership had grown to 80 (Belash and Belash, *Dorogi Nestora Makhno*, p. 19).

105. Belash and Belash, *Dorogi Nestora Makhno*, p. 19.

106. Makhno, *The Russian Revolution in Ukraine*, pp. 37–8.

107. Makhno, *The Russian Revolution in Ukraine*, pp. 52–3.

108. Makhno, *The Russian Revolution in Ukraine*, pp. 37–8.

109. The Socialist Revolutionaries were a major agrarian socialist political party that was split into 'left' or pro-Bolshevik, and 'right' or anti-Bolshevik factions.
110. Makhno, *The Russian Revolution in Ukraine*, p. 39.
111. Makhno, *The Russian Revolution in Ukraine*, p. 43.
112. Makhno, *The Russian Revolution in Ukraine*, p. 44.
113. Makhno, *The Russian Revolution in Ukraine*, p. 44. Timoshchuk dates this in August (*Anarkho-kommunisticheskie formirovaniia N. Makhno*, p. 17).
114. Makhno, *The Russian Revolution in Ukraine*, pp. 47–50.
115. Leon Trotsky, *The History of the Russian Revolution* (London: Pluto Press, 1977), p. 1065.
116. For a description of the way in which events in Petrograd impacted on the provinces, see Roger Pethybridge, *The Spread of the Russian Revolution: Essays on 1917* (London: Macmillan, 1972), pp. 176–214.
117. Held in Kiev, 19–21 (6–8 old style) April 1917.
118. J. S. Reshetar, *The Ukrainian Revolution, 1917-1920: A Study in Nationalism* (Princeton: Princeton University Press, 1952), pp. 50–51.
119. *Katsap*, pl. *katsapy* (Ukrainian), a derogatory nickname for a Russian (Makhno, *The Russian Revolution in Ukraine*, p. 79).
120. Aleksandr Shubin, *Anarkhiia mat' poriadka: mezhdu krasnymi i belymi* (Moscow: Iada, Eksmo, 2005), p. 63.
121. Shubin, *Anarkhiia mat' poriadka*, pp. 63–7.
122. Makhno, *The Russian Revolution in Ukraine*, p. 65.
123. Makhno, *The Russian Revolution in Ukraine*, pp. 65–70.
124. Makhno, *The Russian Revolution in Ukraine*, pp. 84–92.
125. Makhno, *The Russian Revolution in Ukraine*, p. 97.
126. Kornilov was killed in 1918. See Alexander Rabinowitch, *The Bolsheviks Come to Power: The Revolution of 1917 in Petrograd*, new edn. (London: Pluto Press, 2017), pp. 129–52.
127. Arshinov, *Istoriia makhnovskogo dvizheniia*, p. 51; confirmation that the landlords were permitted to keep a share is contained in a letter from a Mennonite émigré to Victor Peters, quoted in his *Nestor Makhno* (Winnipeg: Echo Books, 1970), p. 32.
128. Makhno, 'Le grande octobre en Ukraine', *Autogestion et socialisme* nos. 18–19 (1972), p. 245.
129. Makhno, *The Russian Revolution in Ukraine*, p. 100; M. Kubanin, *Makhnovshchina: krest'ianskoe dvizhenie v stepnoi Ukrainev gody grazhdanskoi voiny* (Leningrad: Izdat. Priboi, [1927]), pp. 31–2. Peters, *Nestor Makhno*, pp. 32–4, quotes unpublished émigré accounts of this period.
130. The term is Rabinowitch's, from the title of his book (*The Bolsheviks Come to Power*).
131. Makhno, 'Le grande octobre', p. 246.
132. Makhno, *The Russian Revolution in Ukraine*, p. 130.
133. *Velikaia oktiabr'skaia sotsialisticheskaia revoliutsiia na Ukraine* (Kiev: Gospolitizdat UkSSR, 1957), vol. 1, p. 621; vol. 2, p. 115.
134. Iu. Mahalevs'kyi, 'Bat'ko Makhno', *Kalendar-Al'manakh Dnipro*, vol. 7 (1929) p. 67.
135. Belash and Belash, *Dorogi Nestora Makhno*, p. 21.
136. Belash and Belash, *Dorogi Nestora Makhno*, p. 22.
137. Belash and Belash, *Dorogi Nestora Makhno*, p. 22.
138. This Russian word, made up of Makhno's name with the suffix *–shchina*, is not entirely accurately translated simply as 'the Makhno movement', since it can

have derogatory overtones. Arshinov, the former participant and apologist for the movement, preferred the neutral expression *makhnovskoe dvizhenie* (see his *Istoriia makhnovskogo dvizheniia*).

139. Timoshchuk, *Anarkho-kommunisticheskie formirovaniia N. Makhno*, p. 19.
140. Makhno, *The Russian Revolution in Ukraine*, p. 137.
141. Makhno, *The Russian Revolution in Ukraine*, pp. 149–62.
142. Timoshchuk, *Anarkho-kommunisticheskie formirovaniia N. Makhno*, pp. 19–20.
143. Timoshchuk, *Anarkho-kommunisticheskie formirovaniia N. Makhno*, pp. 19–20.
144. Makhno later described this action as Jesuitical – 'making promises and failing to honour them' (Makhno, *The Russian Revolution in Ukraine*, p. 172).
145. Makhno, *The Russian Revolution in Ukraine*, pp. 174–84.
146. Makhno, *The Russian Revolution in Ukraine*, pp. 198–209.
147. Makhno, *The Russian Revolution in Ukraine*, p. 214.
148. Makhno, *The Russian Revolution in Ukraine*, p. 213.
149. Francisco Ferrer Guardia (1859–1909) founded the *Escuela Moderna* in Barcelona in 1901, offending the Catholic Church. In 1909 he was executed by firing squad.
150. Makhno, *The Russian Revolution in Ukraine*, pp. 212–20.
151. Makhno, *The Russian Revolution in Ukraine*, p. 214.
152. Volkovinskii, *Makhno i ego krakh*, p. 31.
153. M. Luther, 'The Birth of the Soviet Ukraine', (Ph. D. dissertation, Columbia University, 1962), pp. 55–92; see also Luther's introduction to Serhii Mazlakh and Vasyl' Shakhrai, *On the Current Situation in the Ukraine* (Ann Arbor: University of Michigan Press, 1970), pp. v–xxx.

CHAPTER 2   THE TURNING POINT: ORGANISING RESISTANCE TO THE GERMAN INVASION, 1918

1. Aleksandr Shubin, *Makhno i ego vremia: o velikoi revoliutsii i grazhdanskoi voine, 1917-1922 gg., v Rossii i na Ukraine* (Moscow: Knizhnyi Dom Librokom, 2014), p. 80.
2. Serhii Plokhy, *The Gates of Europe: A History of Ukraine* (London: Penguin, 2015), p. 200. The Germans recognised Ukrainian independence in January 1918, ceding territory to the new republic.
3. Peter Lieb and Wolfram Dornik, 'Military Operations', in: Wolfram Dornik *et al.*, *The Emergence of Ukraine: Self-Determination, Occupation, and War in Ukraine, 1917-1922* (Edmonton: Canadian Institute of Ukrainian Studies Press, 2015), pp. 155–201.
4. Lieb and Dornik, 'Military Operations', p. 155.
5. The exact date is disputed. See Georgiy Kasianov, 'Ukraine between revolution, independence and foreign domination', in: Dornik *et al.*, *The Emergence of Ukraine*, p. 80.
6. Austrian troops remained in Ekaterinoslav until November 1918. Oleh Fedyshyn, *Germany's Drive to the East and the Ukrainian Revolution* (New Brunswick: Rutgers University Press, 1971), p. 103.
7. Fedyshyn, *Germany's Drive to the East*, pp. 103–4.
8. See Borislav Chernev, *Twilight of Empire: The Brest-Litovsk Conference and the Remaking of East-Central Europe, 1917–1918* (Toronto: University of Toronto Press, 2017).
9. Two-thirds of iron ore reserves, and nearly 90 per cent of its coal were handed over, as Russia became 'the first vanquished state of the Great War'. The loss of

territory amounted to 1.6 sq.km. (Robert Gerwarth, *The Vanquished; Why the First World War Failed to End, 1917-1923* [London: Penguin, 2017], pp. 39–40). Ukraine had provided 39 per cent of Russia's grain exports, 80 per cent of sugar exports, 65 per cent of coal production and 65 per cent of iron output, and was the economic 'artery' of the Empire (Gustav Streseman to the Reichstag, 20 February 1918, quoted in R. H. Lutz, *The Fall of the German Empire* (Stanford, 1932), vol.1, p. 813).

10. M. Luther, 'The Birth of Soviet Ukraine', (Ph.D. dissertation, Columbia University, 1962), pp. 177–8.

11. As late as 17 March the Ukrainian Bolshevik fractions used the 2nd All-Ukrainian Congress of Soviets to argue out their differences on the invasion, on relations with Soviet Russia and other issues (Luther, 'The Birth of Soviet Ukraine', pp. 189–92). Texts of the resolutions are given in the documentary collection *Velikaia oktiabr'skaia sotsialisticheskaia revoliutsiia na Ukraine, fevral' 1917-aprel' 1918: sbornik dokumentov e materialov* (Kiev: Gosizdat. Politicheskoi Literatury USSR, 1957), vol. 3, pp. 323–5.

12. Mark Baker, *Peasants, Power and Place: Revolution in the Villages of Kharkiv Province, 1914-1921* (Cambridge, Mass.: Harvard University Press, 2016), p. 91.

13. German intelligence report in James Bunyan (ed.), *Intervention, Civil War and Communism in Russia* (Baltimore: Johns Hopkins Press, 1936), pp. 4–5.

14. F. Fischer, *Germany's Aims in the First World War* (London, 1967), p. 534. However, Baker says Red Guard resistance in Khar'kov province was 'formidable' (*Peasants, Power and Place*, p. 92). The 'Red Guards' consisted of under-equipped volunteers and some sailors, with no centralised command structure, lax discipline, and minimal training. Their poor showing led to acceptance of Trotsky's policy of using former Tsarist officers to build a professional Red Army. See David Footman, *Civil War in Russia* (London: Faber, 1961), pp. 135–41).

15. '... power had diffused to the localities' very quickly (Baker, *Peasants, Power and place*, p. 93).

16. Baker, *Peasants, Power and Place*, pp. 92–3.

17. Baker, *Peasants, Power and Place*, p. 93.

18. Vasilii Golovanov, *Nestor Makhno* (Moscow: Molodaia Gvardiia, 2013), p. 56. On the 'procurements system' see Wolfram Dornik and Peter Lieb 'Economic Utilization', in: Dornik et al., *The Emergence of Ukraine*, pp. 248–64.

19. Lutz, *The Fall of the German Empire*, vol. 1, pp. 816–17.

20. Ihor Kamenetsky, 'Hrushevskyi and the Central *Rada*: internal politics and foreign interventions', in: Taras Hunczak (ed.), *The Ukraine, 1917-1921: A Study in Revolution* (Cambridge, Mass.: Harvard University Press, 1977), p. 55.

21. H. Tintrup, *Krieg in der Ukraine* (Essen, 1938), pp. 66–7 and 71.

22. Hans Limbach, *Ukrainisches Schreckenstage: Erinnerungen eines Schweizers* (Berlin: Francke, 1919), pp. 77–8.

23. Limbach, *Ukrainisches Schreckenstage*, pp. 75–6.

24. Declaration of the *Iuzhnaia Assotsiatsiia Anarkhistov*, in Viktor Danilov and Teodor Shanin (eds), *Nestor Makhno: krest'ianskoe dvizheniia na Ukraine, 1918-1921. Dokumenty i materialy* (Moscow: Rossiiskaia Politicheskaia Entsiklopediia, 2006), pp. 45–6.

25. Nestor Makhno, *The Russian Revolution in Ukraine, March 1917-April 1918* (Edmonton: Black Cat Press, 2009), p. 141 and 221. The Russian original was published as *Russkaia revoliutsiia na Ukraine, mart 1917-aprel' 1918 g.* (Paris: Biblioteka Makhnovtsev, 1929), and has been reprinted e.g. by Vladimir Cherkasov-Georgievskii in his *Nestor Makhno: azbuka anarkhista* (Moscow: Prozaik, 2013), pp. 22–173. The full text is also available online: royallib.com/

read/mahno_nestor/russkaya_revolyutsiya_na_ukraine.html, accessed 28 February 2020. I do not have a copy of the original Paris edition, and cite the English translation here instead.

26. Makhno, *The Russian Revolution in Ukraine*, p. 238.

27. Followers of Makhno. I use the Russian term throughout this book as an alternative to the clumsy English 'Makhnovites' or 'Makhnovists'.

28. Makhno, *The Russian Revolution in Ukraine*, pp. 239–40, 243; the unreliable N. V. Gerasimenko, 'Makhno', *Istorik i Sovremennik*, vol. 3 (1922), pp. 154–61 gives earlier dates throughout 1918.

29. Makhno, *The Russian Revolution in Ukraine*, p. 244.

30. Makhno, *The Russian Revolution in Ukraine*, p. 228.

31. Makhno, *The Russian Revolution in Ukraine*, p. 232.

32. Makhno, *The Russian Revolution in Ukraine*, p. 245; Golovanov, *Nestor Makhno*, p. 56. Golovanov mistakenly calls Egorov 'Pavel'.

33. Belash noticed his tendency to interfere in minor matters (A. V. Belash and V. F. Belash, *Dorogi Nestora Makhno: istoricheskoe povestvovanie* [Kiev: Proza, 1993], p. 20).

34. Makhno, *The Russian Revolution in Ukraine*, p. 245.

35. Sometimes called Veretel'nik or Veretennikov. See Petr Arshinov, *Istoriia makhnovskogo dvizheniia, 1918-1921* (Berlin: Gruppy Russkikh Anarkhistov v Germanii, 1923), p. 221; and the important Soviet-period documentary collection *Grazhdanskaia voina na Ukraine, 1918-1920: sbornik dokumentov i materialov* (Kiev: Izdat. Naukova Dumka, 1967), vol. 1, pt. 2, p. 362.

36. Makhno, *The Russian Revolution in Ukraine*, pp. 245–6.

37. Makhno, *The Russian Revolution in Ukraine*, p. 248.

38. Makhno 'suffered a tantrum' at the news (Golovanov, *Nestor Makhno*, p. 56); Makhno, *The Russian Revolution in Ukraine*, p. 250. The 'haidamaky' were originally Cossack bands in the eighteenth century.

39. Mariia Grigor'evna Nikiforova (1885–1919), known as 'Marusia' or 'Maruska' was an anarchist leader who pushed Makhno towards more radical positions (Palij, *The Anarchism of Nestor Makhno*, pp. 73–4). She was captured and executed by the Bolsheviks in Crimea in September 1919. See V. D. Ermakov, 'Marusia: portret anarkhisti', *Sotsiologicheskie Issledovanie* no. 3 (1991), pp. 91–95; D. V. Drobyshevskii, 'Zhenshchiny v makhnovskom dvizhenii', *Novyi Istoricheskii Vestnik* no. 15 (2006), pp. 154–9; Mila Cotlenko, *Maria Nikiforova, la révolution sans attendre: l'épopée d'une anarchiste à travers l'Ukraine,1885-1919* (Paris: Mutines Séditions, 2014); and Malcolm Archibald, *Atamansha: The Life of Maria Nikiforova* (Tacoma, Washington: Lunaria Press, 2014).

40. Cotlenko and Archibald comment on Nikiforova's influence over Makhno from mid-1917 onwards (Cotlenko, *Maria Nikiforova*, p. 6; and Archibald, *Atamansha*, p. 1). Born in Aleksandrovsk in 1885, she left home as an adolescent and joined an anarchist cell, participating in insurrectionist actions between 1905 and 1907. Like Makhno, she was captured, sentenced to death, but subsequently reprieved as a minor and sent to serve a 20-year sentence in Siberia. She fled to the United States via Japan and was later active in western Europe, graduating from a military academy in France and serving briefly in the French army (Archibald, *Atamansha*, pp. 3–4). She returned to Ukraine in 1917, proving too radical even for Makhno (Drobyshevskii, 'Zhenshchiny v makhnovskom dvizhenii', p. 156).

41. Makhno, *The Russian Revolution in Ukraine*, p. 250.

42. Makhno, *The Russian Revolution in Ukraine*, pp. 249–51; Makhno, *Pod udarami kontr-revoliutsii, aprel'-iiun' 1918 g.* (Paris: Izdat. Komiteta N. Makhno, 1936), p. 11.

43. Communication by the German ambassador, quoted by Belash and Belash, *Dorogi Nestora Makhno*, p. 10.

44. Bunyan, *Intervention, Civil War and Communism in Russia*, pp. 7–8.

45. See Taras Hunczak, 'The Ukraine under *Hetman* Pavlo Skoropadskyi', in Hunczak (ed.), *The Ukraine, 1917-1921*, pp. 61–81; Reshetar, *The Ukrainian Revolution*, pp. 145–6; Michael Palij, *The Anarchism of Nestor Makhno, 1918-1921: An Aspect of the Ukrainian Revolution* (Seattle: University of Washington Press), p. 33.

46. Bunyan, *Intervention, Civil War and Communism in Russia*, p. 6; Fischer, *Germany's aims*, p. 540.

47. Erich Ludendorff, *Meine Kriegserrinerungen, 1914-1918* (Berlin: Mittler und Sohn, 1919), p. 502.

48. Fischer, *Germany's aims*, p. 541.

49. Ermakov, 'Marusia', p. 92; Danilov and Teodor Shanin (eds), *Nestor Makhno*, pp. 46–8 and 850n.

50. Makhno, *Pod udarami kontr-revoliutsii*, pp. 16–17; Makhno, 'Pechal'nye stranitsy russkoi revoliutsii', *Rassvet* vol. 16 (29 January–18 February 1932), p. 6.

51. Paul Avrich, *The Russian Anarchists* (Princeton: Princeton University Press, 1967), pp. 184–5; Bunyan and Fisher, *Bolshevik Revolution*, p. 584.

52. *Marx, Engels, Lenin: Anarchism and Anarcho-syndicalism* (Moscow: Progress Publishers, 1972), pp. 287–8.

53. Makhno, *Pod udarami kontr-revoliutsii*, p. 19.

54. David Footman, *Civil war in Russia* (London: Faber and Faber, 1961), p. 251.

55. Makhno, *Pod udarami kontr-revoliutsii*, pp. 20–22.

56. Makhno, *Pod udarami kontr-revoliutsii*, pp. 26–32.

57. Makhno, *Pod udarami kontr-revoliutsii*, pp. 32–5.

58. Makhno, *Pod udarami kontr-revoliutsii*, pp. 66–71.

59. Makhno, *Pod udarami kontr-revoliutsii*, pp. 47–61. On revolutionary events in Saratov, see Donald Raleigh, *Experiencing Russia's Civil War: Politics, Society and Revolutionary Culture in Saratov, 1917-1922* (Princeton: Princeton University Press, 2002).

60. Makhno, *Pod udarami kontr-revoliutsii*, p. 72. VTsIK stands for Vserossiiskii (later Vsesoiuznyi) Tsentral'nyi Ispolnitel'nyi Komitet or All-Russian (All-Union) Central Executive Committee.

61. In 1921 Saratov suffered an 'explosion of discontent' involving strikes and peasant unrest in response to the 'militarisation of labour' by the Bolsheviks (Raleigh, *Experiencing Russia's civil war*, pp. 407–8).

62. Astrakhan remained in Bolshevik hands from January 1918 until the end of the Civil War.

63. The poem, 'Prizyv', (The Call), was reprinted in *Probuzhdenie* no. 50/51 (1934), p. 16. Makhno's return to Guliaipole had been reported in the *Biulleten' osvedomitel'nogo biuro anarkhistov Rossii* (15 December 1917), pp. 4–5, using the nickname. See libcom.org/library/summons-makhno, accessed 28 February 2020 for an English translation.

64. Makhno, *Pod udarami kontr-revoliutsii*, pp. 80–86. From Astrakhan to Nizhnii Novgorod took five days. Roger Pethybridge, *The Spread of the Russian Revolution* (London: Macmillan, 1972), p. 3.

65. Tambov was the home of the Antonov peasant rebellion: see Erik Landis, *Bandits and Partisans: The Antonov movement in the Russian civil war* (Pittsburgh: University of Pittsburgh Press, 2008).

66. Makhno, *Pod udarami kontr-revoliutsii*, pp. 86–92.

67. One of the assassins, Nikolai Andreev, subsequently died in action fighting 'alongside Makhno'. Victor Serge, *Year One of the Russian Revolution* (London: Bookmarks and Pluto Press, 1992), p. 411; Chamberlin, *The Russian Revolution*, pp. 52–3.

68. E. H. Carr, *The Bolshevik Revolution, 1917-1923* (Harmondsworth: Penguin, 1966), vol. 1, p. 175.

69. Makhno, *Pod udarami kontr-revoliutsii*, p. 93. Makhno had a difficult time finding accommodation and affordable food in Moscow.

70. Makhno, *Pod udarami kontr-revoliutsii*, pp. 115–16.

71. For a detailed analysis of Kropotkin's thought, see Caroline Cahm, *Kropotkin and the Rise of Revolutionary Anarchism* (Cambridge: Cambridge University Press, 1989).

72. Makhno, *The Russian Revolution in Ukraine*, pp. 84–5.

73. Emma. Goldman, *Living my Life* (New York: Dover, 1970), vol. 2, p. 769; Alexander Berkman, *The Bolshevik Myth: Diary, 1920-1922* (London: Hutchinson, 1925), p. 75.

74. Makhno, *Pod udarami kontr-revoliutsii*, pp. 107–8.

75. Makhno, *Pod udarami kontr-revoliutsii*, pp. 119–35. In English, the account of the meeting is available as *My Visit to the Kremlin* (Edmonton: Black Cat Press, 1993). See also *Under the Blows of the Counter-revolution* (Edmonton: Black Cat Press, 2009), pp. 129–45.

76. See G. N. Golikov and others (compilers) *Vladimir Il'ich Lenin: biograficheskii khronika* (Moscow: Sov. Entsiklopediia, 1970–82; 12 vols.): there is no mention of a meeting with Makhno. Arshinov, who was in Moscow, describes Makhno's visit but is silent about an encounter with Lenin (*Istoriia makhnovskogo dvizheniia*, p. 52).

77. L. Fischer, *Life of Lenin* (London, 1965), p. 363.

78. Aleksandr Shubin, *Anarkhiia mat' poriadka: mezhdu krasnymi i belymi. Nestor Makhno kak zerkalo Rossiiskoi revoliutsii* (Moscow: Iauza, Eksmo, 2005), p. 112. The same comment appears in Shubin's later book with the additional cautionary remark that 'the memoirs ... are not always accurate' (*Makhno i ego vremia*, p. 90).

79. For instance, Makhno claims to have heard a speech by Voroshilov in Tsaritsyn in May 1918 but Voroshilov only arrived there in June (Shubin, *Makhno i ego vremia*, p. 85).

80. Presumably by Volin (*My visit to the Kremlin*, pp. 5–6).

81. Iakov Sverdlov (1885–1919) was the chairperson of VTsIK and a close colleague of Lenin's; he died of an illness, probably influenza, in March 1919.

82. Shubin, *Anarkhiia mat' poriadka*, p. 79, emphasis added.

83. Trotsky confirms this: 'Lenin and I seriously considered at one time allotting certain territories to the Anarchists, naturally with the consent of the local population, and letting them carry on their experiment of a stateless social order there' (*Stalin: An Appraisal of the Man and His Influence* [London: Hollis and Carter, 1947], p. 337). See also Victor Serge, *Memoirs of a Revolutionary, 1901-1941* (London; Oxford University Press, 1963, p. 119).

84. Makhno was unaware that an armistice between Soviet Russia and the Ukraine had been concluded on 14 June 1918 (Makhno, *Pod udarami kontr-revoliutsii*, pp. 126–35 and 140; Arshinov, *Istoriia makhnovskogo dvizheniia*, p. 52).

85. Makhno, *Pod udarami kontr-revoliutsii*, p. 149; Arshinov, *Istoriia makhnovskogo dvizheniia*, p. 52.

86. Baker, *Peasants, Power and Place*, p. 101, citing Malyk and Vynnychenko as examples.

87. Baker, *Peasants, Power and Place*, p. 104.

88. Bunyan, *Intervention, Civil War and Communism in Russia*, p. 27.

89. The 2nd All-Ukrainian Congress of Peasants passed anti-Hetman and anti-German resolutions, 8–10 May 1918. Pavlo Khrystiuk (ed.), *Zamitky i materialy do istorii ukrains'koi revoliutsii* (Vienna: Ukraïns'kyii sotsiologichnyi instytut, 1921–22), vol. 3, p. 15.

90. Bunyan, *Intervention, Civil War and Communism in Russia*, pp. 22–3. Andrew Lamis has argued in a review article that Ukrainian nationalism was both patriotic *and* reformist, and that the anti-German uprising was nationalist in character ('Some Observations on the Ukrainian National Movement and the Ukrainian Revolution, 1917-1921', *Harvard Ukrainian Studies* vol. 2, no. 4 [1978], pp. 526–27).

91. Frank Epp, 'Mennonites in the Soviet Union', in R. H. Marshall (ed.), *Aspects of Religion in the Soviet Union, 1917-1967* (Chicago, 1971), p. 290.

92. E.g. *Der Bote* (Saskatoon) (28 December 1965), p. 9; Diederich Navall, A *Russian Dance of Death: Revolution and Civil War in the Ukraine* (Winnipeg: Hyperion Press, 1977), *passim*; J. G. Rempel, *Mein Heimatdorf Nieder Chortitza* (Rosthern, Saskatoon: the author, [1958]), p. 65.

93. Sean Patterson, 'The Eichenfeld Massacre: Recontextualizing Mennonite and Makhnovist Narratives', *Journal of Mennonite Studies* vol. 32 (March 2017), p. 169. Articles by Aleksandr Beznosov on aspects of the Mennonite engagement with the Makhno movement, in Russian and based on archival research and interviews are available on the website *Entsiklopediia Nemtsev Rossii* at https://tinyurl.com/y3tvkrl2, accessed 28 February 2020. I am grateful to Patterson for allowing me access to the manuscript of his book *Makhno and Memory: Anarchist and Mennonite Narratives of Ukraine's Civil War, 1917-1921* (Winnipeg: University of Manitoba Press, 2020), in which he draws attention to Beznosov's work.

94. *Novaia Zhizn* (3 July 1918) quoted by Bunyan, *Intervention, Civil War and Communism in Russia*, p. 23.

95. Makhno, *Pod udarami kontr-revoliutsii*, p. 155.

96. Arshinov, *Istoriia makhnovskogo dvizheniia*, p. 52.

97. Makhno, *Ukrainskaia revoliutsiia, iiul'-dekabr' 1918 g.* (Paris: Izdat Komiteta N. Makhno, 1937), pp. 7–8.

98. Makhno, *Ukrainskaia revoliutsiia*, pp. 9–10.

99. Danilov and Shanin include two Hetmanate documents from August and one from October, and some Soviet army materials on martial law (docs. nos. 19–21 in Danilov and Shanin (eds), *Nestor Makhno*, pp. 48–51).

100. Makhno, *Ukrainskaia revoliutsiia*, pp. 25–7.

101. Makhno, *Ukrainskaia revoliutsiia*, p. 32.

102. Z. A. B. Zeman (ed.), *Germany and the Revolution in Russia, 1915-1918: Documents from the Archives of the German Foreign Ministry* (London: Oxford University Press, 1958), p. 135.

103. Fedyshyn, *Germany's Drive to the East*, p. 254 ff.

104. Bundesarchiv, Kl. Erwerbungen, Restnachlass von Dr. Rohrbach 1869–1956, Bd.2, Bach to Rohrbach.

105. Makhno, *Ukrainskaia revoliutsiia*, pp. 35–6; Gerasimenko dates the earliest attacks in March, and alleges that Makhno made 118 raids between April and June – possibly meaning August and September ('Makhno', pp. 158–61). Arshinov, *Istoriia makhnovskogo dvizheniia*, p. 53, glides over these early problems of recruitment and organisation.

106. Aleksandr Timoshchuk, *Anarkho-kommunisticheskie formirovaniia N. Makhno, sentiabr' 1918-avgust 1921* (Simferopol': Tavriia, 1996), pp. 22–3.

107. The Confederation held its first conference in Kursk in November 1918. The delegates were enthusiastic about political opportunities in Ukraine, and recognised Makhno's bands as the best means of defending the revolution. They passed a resolution recommending that 'Nabat' should form its own partisan bands, to operate independently of other forces (*Pervaia konferentsiia anarkhistskikh organizatsii Ukrainy 'Nabat'* [Buenos Aires: Izdat. Rabochaia Gruppa v Resp. Argentinie, 1922], pp. 13–27).

108. Avrich, *The Russian Anarchists*, pp. 204–5. Gerasimenko is probably referring to these arrivals when he describes Nabat members joining Makhno in June 1918 ('Makhno', p. 159).

109. Makhno, *Ukrainskaia revoliutsiia*, pp. 37–8.

110. Makhno, *Ukrainskaia revoliutsiia*, pp. 39–49.

111. Makhno, *Ukrainskaia revoliutsiia*, pp. 50–63.

112. Makhno, *Ukrainskaia revoliutsiia*, pp. 64–70; Makhno, 'Zapiski', *Anarkhicheskii vestnik* no. 2 (1923), p. 32.

113. Makhno, *Ukrainskaia revoliutsiia*, pp. 64–70, pp. 70–71; Arshinov, *Istoriia makhnovskogo dvizheniia*, p. 225.; Victor Peters, *Nestor Makhno: The Life of an Anarchist* (Winnipeg: Echo Books, 1970), p. 10.

114. Makhno, *Ukrainskaia revoliutsiia*, pp. 73–4. Other large detachments, including those of the partisans Kurilenko, from Berdiansk, and Petrenko-Platonov, from Grishino, joined forces with Makhno at this time (Arshinov, *Istoriia makhnovskogo dvizheniia*, p. 56).

115. Peters, *Nestor Makhno*, p. 41. This chimed perfectly with the ideas which underlay the *chernyi peredel* or 'black repartition' in 1917.

116. This was also the Nabat assessment (*Pervaia konferentsiia anarkhistskikh organizatsii Ukrainy 'Nabat'*, pp. 13–27).

117. Makhno, *Ukrainskaia revoliutsiia*, p. 82; Arshinov, *Istoriia makhnovskogo dvizheniia*, p. 57.

118. 'Makhno's memory of the defeat of two Hungarian companies and 80 Warta seems to be fictional' (Timoshchuk, *Anarkho-kommunisticheskie formirovaniia N. Makhno*, pp. 23–4).

119. Makhno, *Ukrainskaia revoliutsiia*, p. 84; Arshinov, *Istoriia makhnovskogo dvizheniia*, p. 58; Shubin, *Makhno i ego vremia*, p. 95. *Bat'ko* is Ukrainian for father, and was attributed to other Ukrainian *atamany*.

120. Golovanov, *Nestor Makhno*, p. 82.

121. In an engagement with the Austrians at Temirovka, nearly half the *makhnovtsy* in a detachment of 350 men were killed (Makhno, *Ukrainskaia revoliutsiia*, pp. 129–36). Timoshchuk comments that Makhno recovered 'only after the evacuation of the Austro-Hungarian troops' (*Anarkho-kommunisticheskie formirovaniia N. Makhno*, p. 24.

122. Gerasimenko, 'Makhno', p. 160.

123. Arshinov, *Istoriia makhnovskogo dvizheniia*, p. 58; Makhno, *Ukrainskaia revoliutsiia*, p. 96.

124. V. N. Volkovinskii, *Makhno e ego krakh* (Moscow: Izdat. VZPI, 1991), p. 49.

125. Makhno, *Ukrainskaia revoliutsiia*, pp. 136–7; Arshinov, *Istoriia makhnovskogo dvizheniia*, p. 81.

126. Makhno, *Ukrainskaia revoliutsiia*, pp. 138, 163.

127. Makhno, *Ukrainskaia revoliutsiia*, pp. 142–3.

128. Michael Palij argues that Makhno was possibly jealous of professional soldiers (*The Anarchism of Nestor Makhno, 1918-1921: An Aspect of the Ukrainian Revolution* [Seattle: University of Washington Press], p. 108). Ida Mett on the other hand

recalled Makhno expressing admiration for the military skills of Budenny and Voroshilov ('Souvenirs sur Nestor Makhno' [Paris, 1948], p. 6).

129. Timoshchuk, *Anarkho-kommunisticheskie formirovaniia N. Makhno*, p. 25.

130. N. Sukhogorskaia, 'The Personal Side of Nestor Makhno', translated by Will Firth. Available at https://www.theyliewedie.org/ressources/biblio/en/Collective_-_The_Personal_Side_of_Nestor_Makhno.html, accessed 14 July 2019. The memoir was originally published in Odessa in a volume titled *Kandal'nyi zbon*, and later extracted in V. F. Verstiuk (ed.), *Nestor Ivanovich Makhno: vospominaniia, materialy i dokumenty* (Kiev: Dzvin, 1991), pp. 102–6.

131. Sukhogorskaia, 'The Personal Side of Nestor Makhno'; Volodymyr Chop and Ihor Lyman, *Vol'nyi Berdiansk: misto v period anarkhists'koho sotsial'noho eksperimentu, 1918-1921 rr.* (Zaporizhzhia: RA Tandem-U, 2007), pp. 14–15.

132. The news reached Guliaipole on 20 November; Makhno was away at the time (*Ukrainskaia revoliutsiia*, p. 153).

133. Makhno, *Ukrainskaia revoliutsiia*, p. 154.

134. Makhno, *Ukrainskaia revoliutsiia*, pp. 154–5, 172.

135. Makhno, *Ukrainskaia revoliutsiia*, pp. 172–73.

136. Khrystiuk (ed.), *Zamitky i materialy do istorii ukrains'koi revoliutsii*, vol. 4, p. 15 et seq.

137. The progressive tone of the Directory's programme was largely the result of Vynnychenko's influence.

138. Timoshchuk, *Anarkho-kommunisticheskie formirovaniia N. Makhno*, pp. 26–7.

139. Timoshchuk, *Anarkho-kommunisticheskie formirovaniia N. Makhno*, p. 27.

140. The Red militias had been consolidated into a single command structure in September.

141. Antonov had commanded Red forces in Ukraine in late 1917, but Trotsky believed that he was 'naturally an impulsive optimist, far more apt at improvisation than calculation' (*The History of the Russian Revolution* [London: Pluto Press, 1977], p. 1144).

142. Antonov-Ovseenko, *Zapiski o grazhdanskoi voine*, p. 30. The subsequent bitter row poisoned relations between Antonov and Vatsetis for more than a year.

143. Vladimir A. Antonov-Ovseenko, *Zapiski o grazhdanskoi voine, 1917-1918* (Moscow: Vysshii Voennyi Redaktsionnyi Sovet, 1924–33), vol. 3, p. 13.

144. Antonov-Ovseenko, *Zapiski o grazhdanskoi voine*, pp. 17–18.

145. *Zvezda* (4 December 1918) quoted in the Soviet-period documentary collection *Grazhdanskaia voina na Ukraine, 1918-1920: sbornik dokumentov i materialov* (Kiev: Izdat. Naukova Dumka, 1967), vol. 1, book 1, p. 476.

146. Arshinov, *Istoriia makhnovskogo dvizheniia*, pp. 81–2; Volin, *La révolution inconnue, 1917-1921: documentation inédite sur la révolution russe* (Paris: Les Amis de Voline, 1947), p. 540.

147. Arshinov, *Istoriia makhnovskogo dvizheniia*, p. 82.

148. Timoshchuk comments that Soviet historiography largely obscured the important role of the *makhnovtsy* in supporting the establishment of communist power in left-bank Ukraine in late 1918 (*Anarkho-kommunisticheskie formirovaniia N. Makhno*, p. 25).

149. Dmitrii Lebed', *Itogi i uroki trekh let anarkho-makhnovshchiny* (Khar'kov: Vseukrainskoe gosudarstvennoe izdatel´stvo, 1921), p. 13.

150. Arshinov, *Istoriia makhnovskogo dvizheniia*, p. 82; *Izvestia Khar'kovskogo Soveta Rabochikh Deputatov* (3 January 1919) quoted in *Grazhdanskaia voina na Ukraine*, vol. 1, book 1, p. 537; M. Kubanin, *Makhnovshchina: krest'ianskoe dvizhenie v stepnoi Ukraine v gody grazhdanskoi voiny* (Leningrad: Izdat. Priboi, [1926]), p. 41.

151. This was approved by the Central Committee of the KP(b)U. Arshinov, *Istoriia makhnovskogo dvizheniia*, p. 82; Kubanin, *Makhnovshchina*, pp. 40–41.

152. Golovanov dismisses one story of Makhno in a wedding dress arriving at a ball held by the landowner Mirgorodskii and then carrying out a massacre, as 'apparently false' (*Nestor Makhno*, p. 80).

153. Palij writes that this particular trick was repeated successfully in October 1919, when the *makhnovtsy* again captured Ekaterinoslav (*The Anarchism of Nestor Makhno*, p. 199).

154. *Izvestiia Khar'kovskogo Soveta Rabochikh Deputatov* (3 January 1919) quoted in *Grazhdanskaia voina na Ukraine*, vol.1, book 1, p. 537; Lebed', *Itogi i uroki trekh let anarkho-makhnovshchiny*, p. 13; Kubanin, *Makhnovshchina*, p. 43.

155. Arshinov, *Istoriia makhnovskogo dvizheniia*, p. 83; Kubanin, *Makhnovshchina*, pp. 41–3; *Grazhdanskaia voina na Ukraine*, vol.1, book 1, p. 537.

156. Danilov and Teodor Shanin (eds), *Nestor Makhno*, p. 9, 14.

157. Z. Iu. Arbatov, 'Ekaterinoslav 1917-1922 gg', *Arkhiv Russkoi Revoliutsii*, vol. 12 (1923), pp. 85–6, quoted in an analysis of vandalising *mentalités* at this time by Richard Stites, who characterises this type of destruction as both symbolic and iconoclastic ('Iconoclastic Currents in the Russian Revolution: Destroying and Preserving the past', in Abbott. Gleason, Peter Kenez and Richard Stites (eds), *Bolshevik Culture: Experiment and Order in the Russian Revolution* [Bloomington: Indiana University Press, 1985], p. 5).

158. Arshinov, *Istoriia makhnovskogo dvizheniia*, p. 83.

159. Belash and Belash, *Dorogi Nestora Makhno*, p. 32.

160. Volin, *La révolution inconnue*, p. 544. Belash claims that a pamphlet by Apollon Karelin (1863–1926) was especially popular and quotes from it at length (Belash and Belash, *Dorogi Nestora Makhno*, p. 58–61).

161. Arshinov, *Istoriia makhnovskogo dvizheniia*, pp. 85–6.

162. Volin, *La révolution inconnue*, p. 543.

163. Volin, *La révolution inconnue*, p. 543; Arshinov, *Istoriia makhnovskogo dvizheniia*, p. 176.

164. Volin, *La révolution inconnue*, p. 543; Arshinov, *Istoriia makhnovskogo dvizheniia*, p. 80.

165. G. Igrenev, 'Ekaterinoslavskaia vospominaniia', *Arkhiv russkoi revoliutsii* vol.3 (1921), p. 240.

CHAPTER 3   BRIGADE COMMANDER AND PARTISAN: MAKHNO'S CAMPAIGNS AGAINST DENIKIN, JANUARY–MAY 1919

1. Aleksei Chubenko described December 1918 in his diary as 'terribly cold' – Viktor Danilov and Teodor Shanin (eds), *Nestor Makhno: krest'ianskoe dvizheniia na Ukraine, 1918-1921. Dokumenty i materialy* (Moscow: Rossiiskaia Politicheskaia Entsiklopediia, 2006), p. 738.

2. The Russian response was that these were Ukrainian partisans, not Red Army regulars (Vasilii Golovanov, *Nestor Makhno* [Moscow: Molodaia Gvardiia, 2013], p. 100). See also A. V. Belash and V. F. Belash, *Dorogi Nestora Makhno: istoricheskoe povestvovanie* (Kiev: Proza, 1993), p. 62.

3. Golovanov, *Nestor Makhno*, p. 100.

4. Cabinet paper p. 112, Cab.29/2, 'Report of a visit to the headquarters of the Volunteer Army in South Russia by Major-General F. C. Poole', (January 1919), quoted in Richard Ullman, *Britain and the Russian civil war, November 1918-February 1920* (Princeton: Princeton University Press, 1968), p. 49.

5. Petr Arshinov, *Istoriia makhnovskogo dvizheniia, 1918-1921* (Berlin: Gruppy Russkikh Anarkhistov v Germanii, 1923), p. 91; Volin, *La révolution inconnue, 1917-1921: documentation inédite sur la révolution russe* (Paris: Les Amis de Voline, 1947), p. 549.

6. Antonov had already ordered Dybenko to contact Makhno and carry out reconnaissance – Danilov and Shanin (eds), *Nestor Makhno*, document no. 29, p. 61, and Vladimir A. Antonov-Ovseenko, *Zapiski o grazhdanskoi voine, 1917-1918* (Moscow: Vysshii Voennyi Redaktsionnyi Sovet, 1924–33), vol. 3, p. 107.

7. In February 1919 the insurgents received 9,000 rifles, 20 machine guns, some artillery, ammunition, and funds from their new allies (V. A. Savchenko, *Makhno* [Kharkiv: Folio, 2003], p. 83).

8. Fedor T. Fomin, *Zapiski starogo Chekista* (Moscow: Gospolitizdat., 1962) pp. 73–4; see also the documentary collection *Grazhdanskaia voina na Ukraine, 1918-1920: sbornik dokumentov i materialov* (Kiev: Izdat. Naukova Dumka, 1967), vol. 1, book 2, p. 81. Golovanov points out that, although the troop strength was probably constant at around 5,000 men, in a peasant insurgency 'there was rotation: some left [for home], and others took their place, therefore … more than five thousand were involved' (*Nestor Makhno*, pp. 101–2).

9. *Grazhdanskaia voina na Ukraine*, vol. 1, book 2, p. 136: compare Arshinov's claim that there were 20,000 volunteers in Makhno's army at the time of the congress (*Istoriia makhnovskogo dvizheniia*, p. 87).

10. Aleksandr Shubin, *Makhno i makhnovskoe dvizhenie* (Moscow: Izdat. MIK, 1998), p. 71.

11. Fomin, *Zapiski starogo Chekista*, pp. 74–5.

12. Belash and Belash, *Dorogi Nestora Makhno*, p. 65, point out that Bolshevik doctrine was to boycott other parties politically, and only communists could be members of an RVS.

13. Even in Berdiansk, as early as the end of March, heated arguments took place between Makhno and a commissar named Petrov over who exactly was authorised to do what. See Volodymyr Chop and Ihor Lyman, *Vol'nyi Berdiansk: misto v period anarkhists'koho sotsial'noho eksperimentu, 1918-1921 rr.* (Zaporizhzhia: RA Tandem-U, 2007), pp. 89–90.

14. *Grazhdanskaia voina na Ukraine*, vol. 1, book 2, documents nos. 137, 274, 290 (March–April 1919); M. Kubanin, *Makhnovshchina: krest'ianskoe dvizhenie v stepnoi Ukrainev gody grazhdanskoi voiny* (Leningrad: Izdat. Priboi, [1926]), p. 48.

15. Danilov and Shanin (eds), *Nestor Makhno*, document no. 37, pp. 66–7 ; Volin, *La révolution inconnue*, p. 550.

16. Volin, *La révolution inconnue*, pp. 544–5.

17. Shubin, *Makhno i makhnovskoe dvizhenie*, p. 60. Aleksei Chubenko gives an account of Shchus's brutality at this time in his diary (Danilov and Shanin (eds), *Nestor Makhno*, pp. 740–41).

18. Shubin says that it is hard to see such actions as 'spontaneous' in an anarchist sense (*Makhno i makhnovskoe dvizhenie*, p. 59). He admits that in January 1919 Makhno and his lieutenants 'engaged in brutal killings', but later claims that subsequently such actions ended for a long period (p. 69).

19. 'We [*makhnovtsy*] were simple souls', lamented Belash later (*Dorogi Nestora Makhno*, p. 66).

20. Grigor'ev is the Russian transcription: he is also referred to as Hryhoriiv.

21. Laura Engelstein, *Russia in Flames* (New York: Oxford University Press, 2018), p. 453.

22. Engelstein (*Russia in Flames*, p. 453) remarks dryly that he 'allowed his politics to wander'.

23. For a survey of the historiography on Grigor'ev, see V. S. Horak, 'Hrihor'ievs'kyi povstans'kyi rukh, serpen' 1918-serpen' 1919 rr.: pytannia istoriohrafii', *Ukrains'kyi Istorychnyi Zhurnal* no. 2 (2013), pp. 154–77.

24. However, it seems that Makhno's general staff structure was dissolved and replaced with military specialists during the process of integration. See Chop and Lyman, *Vol'nyi Berdiansk*, p. 88.

25. Arshinov, *Istoriia makhnovskogo dvizheniia*, pp. 93–5; Volin, *La révolution inconnue*, pp. 551–2.

26. The anarchist former sailor Mikhail Uralov argued with Makhno that mass mobilisation was a bad idea, and an all-volunteer army would be more effective (Chop and Lyman, *Vol'nyi Berdiansk*, p. 81). Nevertheless, there is evidence of compulsory induction into the ranks of the partisans. See, for example, the unpublished memoirs of Ivan Topolye (pseud.), quoted in Victor Peters, *Nestor Makhno* (Winnipeg: Echo Books, [1970]), pp. 45–7; and I. Savin, 'Boevye dni', in M. Afonin and A. Iurtsev, *Na fronte i na fronte: sbornik vospominanii* (Moscow: Moskovskii Rabochii, 1927), pp. 17–25; and the mobilisation order of 24 January printed by Danilov and Shanin, *Nestor Makhno*, doc. 31, p. 62.

27. Volin, *La révolution inconnue*, p. 553.

28. The unquestioning carrying out of orders, however, is scarcely an anarchist practice. Strzałkowski, *Ataman Machno*, pp. 52–7, quoted by Michał Przyborowski and Darius Wierzchoś, *Nestor Machno w Polsce* (Poznań: Oficyna Brastwa Trojka, 2012), p. 196.

29. The *Latyshkie Strelki* were formed during the First World War, and went over to the Bolsheviks in May 1917. See G. Swain, 'The Disillusioning of the Revolution's Praetorian Guard: The Latvian Riflemen, summer-autumn 1918', *Europe-Asia Studies* vol. 51, no. 4 (1999), pp. 667–86.

30. See for example, the leaflet *K molodym liudiam*, (June 1920), published by L. J. van Rossum (ed.), 'Proclamations of the Machno movement, 1920', *International Review of Social History*, vol. 13, no. 2 (1968), pp. 263–4.

31. Trotsky, *My life* (Harmondsworth: Penguin, 1975), pp. 454–5.

32. Trotsky, *Stalin: An Appraisal of the Man and his Influence* (London: Hollis and Carter, 1947) pp. 275–8; Chapter 36 'The Military Opposition' in his *My Life: An Attempt at an Autobiography* (Harmondsworth: Penguin, 1975); cf. his *Kak vooruzhalas revoliutsiia na voennoi rabote* (Moscow: Vysshii Voennyi Redak. Sovet, 1923–25) for the contemporary military writings. See also Isaac Deutscher, *The Prophet Armed: Trotsky 1879-1921* (London: Oxford University Press, 1970), p. 405 ff., especially the 'Note on Trotsky's military writings', pp. 477–85.

33. Political report no. 1, 5 March 1919, in *Grazhdanskaia voina na Ukraine*, vol. 1, book 2, p. 192.

34. The minutes were published in *Russkaia mysl'* nos. 1–2 (1921), pp. 226–31; see also Danilov and Shanin (eds), *Nestor Makhno*, pp. 70–91.

35. Danilov and Shanin (eds), *Nestor Makhno*, p. 70.

36. Danilov and Shanin (eds), *Nestor Makhno*, p. 73.

37. Shubin, *Makhno i makhnovskoe dvizhenie*, pp. 59–60.

38. Arshinov, *Istoriia makhnovskogo dvizheniia*, p. 87; Volin, *La révolution inconnue*, pp. 545–6; Danilov and Shanin (eds), *Nestor Makhno*, pp. 70–91.

39. Shubin, *Makhno i makhnovskoe dvizhenie*, pp. 67–8.

40. Arshinov, *Istoriia makhnovskogo dvizheniia*, pp. 86–9; Volin, *La révolution inconnue*, pp. 545–6; *Put' k svobode* no. 2 (24 May 1919), p. 1.

41. Shubin says that Soviet Ukraine, by comparison, had only 46,000 armed fighters (*Makhno i makhnovskoe dvizhenie*, p. 67).

42. *Grazhdanskaia voina na Ukraine*, vol. 1, book 2, p. 150.
43. Shubin, *Makhno i makhnovskoe dvizhenie*, p. 72.
44. *Grazhdanskaia voina na Ukraine*, vol. 1, book 2, p. 100.
45. *Grazhdanskaia voina na Ukraine*, vol. 1, book 2, pp. 148–9.
46. *Grazhdanskaia voina na Ukraine*, vol. 1, book 2, p. 126, 161.
47. *Grazhdanskaia voina na Ukraine*, vol. 1, book 2, p. 204.
48. Chop and Lyman, *Vol'nyi Berdiansk*, pp. 26–7.
49. Chop and Lyman, *Vol'nyi Berdiansk*, p. 28.
50. Telegram from Dybenko's headquarters to the Revvoensovet, in Danilov and Shanin (eds), *Nestor Makhno*. pp. 65–6.
51. Chop and Lyman, who point out (*Vol'nyi Berdiansk*, p. 29) that Viktor Belash praised Makhno's 'ingenuity and courage' (see Belash and Belash, *Dorogi Nestora Makhno*, p. 67).
52. Chop and Lyman, *Vol'nyi Berdiansk*, p. 29.
53. *Grazhdanskaia voina na Ukraine*, vol. 1, book 2, p. 220, 222.
54. *Grazhdanskaia voina na Ukraine*, vol. 1, book 2, p. 232.
55. *Grazhdanskaia voina na Ukraine*, vol. 1, book 2, p. 224.
56. Quoted in Chop and Lyman, *Vol'nyi Berdiansk*, p. 30. 'Our forces' consisted substantially at this time of Dybenko's troops plus Makhno's and Grigor'ev's groups. Grigor'ev joined in mid-February.
57. N. Sukhogorskaia, 'The Personal Side of Nestor Makhno', translated by Will Firth. Available at www.theyliewedie.org/ressources/biblio/en/Collective_-_The_Personal_Side_of_Nestor_Makhno.html, accessed 14 July 2019.
58. Chop and Lyman provide some details taken from a local almanac published in 1915: Berdiansk was a middling port, through which about 25 million *pudy* of wheat per year were exported. There were banks, libraries, hotels, vineyards, piped water and electicity – and some foreign consular representation (*Vol'nyi Berdiansk*, pp. 8–9, and 53–5).
59. Golovanov, *Nestor Makhno* (Moscow: Molodaia Gvardiia, 2013), p. 107.
60. Chop and Lyman *Vol'nyi Berdiansk*, dispute three 'myths' in the Soviet historiography of the fall of Berdiansk. These are that the local soviet made heroic sacrifices; that there was a communist-led uprising against the White Guards on 11–12 March; and that communist women played a leading role in liberating the town (p. 31). They also point to 'considerable confusion' in the sources about the correct date (p. 37).
61. For a discussion of the role of extreme violence as an integral part of the mode of leadership of the *atamany*, and especially in the case of Makhno, see Felix Schnell, 'Tear them apart ... and be done with it! The ataman-leadership of Nestor Makhno as a culture of violence', *Ab Imperio*, vol. 3 (2008), pp. 195–221.
62. Chop and Lyman, *Vol'nyi Berdiansk*, pp. 38–9.
63. Savchenko, *Makhno*, p. 92 says that a total of ten White officers were shot. Golovanov, *Nestor Makhno*, p. 108, also says that the brutality described by Soviet sources was 'the product of their over-zealous imaginations'.
64. Anatol Skachko was Commander of the Khar'kov group (the 2nd Division and other units joined to it) and hence subordinate to Antonov while outranking Dybenko (*Grazhdanskaia voina na Ukraine*, vol. 1, book 2, p. 238, 240).
65. *Grazhdanskaia voina na Ukraine*, vol. 1, book 2, p. 259.
66. For a collection of translated primary documents on the war in Rostov, taken from a local archive, see Brian Murphy, *Rostov in the Russian Civil War, 1917-1920: The Key to Victory* (Abingdon: Routledge, 2005).

67. Jan Meyer (ed.), *The Trotsky Papers* (The Hague: Mouton, 1964–71), vol. 1, pp. 374–5.

68. Arthur Adams comments on this arrangement: 'This was a reasonable decision, since Makhno had for some time been engaged against White forces around Mariupol and was therefore the anchor of the whole western flank of the Southern Front'. *Bolsheviks in the Ukraine: The Second Campaign, 1918-1919* (New Haven, Conn.: Yale University Press, 1963), p. 247.

69. Antonov-Ovseenko, *Zapiski o grazhdanskoi voine*, vol. 3. p. 246; vol. 4, pp. 98–101.

70. Belash and Belash, *Dorogi Nestora Makhno*, pp. 107–8.

71. *Pravda* (3 April 1919); *Izvestiia* (6 April 1919).

72. *Grazhdanskaia voina na Ukraine*, vol. 1, book 2, pp. 296–7.

73. *Kievshchina v gody grazhdanskoi voiny i inostrannoi voenoi interventsii, 1918-1920 gg.: sbornik dokumentov e materialov* (Kiev: Gospolitizdat USSR, 1962), pp. 201–2; compare the original decree, in K. Chernenko and M. Smirtiukov (eds), *Resheniia partii i pravitel'stva po khoziaistvennym voprosam* (Moscow: Izd-vo Polit. Literatury, 1967), vol. 1, pp. 91–4. The experiment was renewed in 1920.

74. Belash comments that this was an attempt to 'destroy the unity of the peasantry' (*Dorogi Nestora Makhno*, p 63).

75. Kubanin, *Makhnovshchina*, pp. 59–60.

76. *Kievshchina v gody grazhdanskoi voiny*, pp. 201–2.

77. The *komnezamy* continued to function until 1933. See James Mace, 'The *komitety nezamozhnykh selyan* and the Structure of Soviet Rule in the Ukrainian Countryside, 1920-1933', *Soviet Studies* vol. 35, no. 4 (1983), pp. 487–503.

78. Quoted by E. H. Carr, *The Bolshevik Revolution, 1917-1923* (Harmondsworth: Penguin, 1966), vol. 1, p. 163n.

79. *Vos'moi Vserossiiskii S'ezd Sovetov Rabochikh, Krest'ianskikh, Krasnoarmeiskikh i Kazach'ikh Deputatov: stenograficheskii otchet* (Moscow, 1921), p. 202.

80. Fomin, *Zapiski starogo Chekista*, p. 75.

81. Minutes of the second regional congress, in Danilov and Shanin (eds), *Nestor Makhno*, p. 77, also in Belash and Belash, *Dorogi Nestora Makhno*, p. 77.

82. *Grazhdanskaia voina na Ukraine*, vol. 1, book 2, pp. 340–41.

83. *Grazhdanskaia voina na Ukraine*, vol. 1, book 2, p. 362; Arshinov, *Istoriia makhnovskogo dvizheniia*, p. 221–2; Volin, *La révolution inconnue*, p. 665.

84. *Grazhdanskaia voina na Ukraine*, vol. 1, book 2, p. 374.

85. E.g. document 86 in Danilov and Shanin (eds), *Nestor Makhno*, p. 144.

86. Antonov-Ovseenko, *Zapiski o grazhdanskoi voine*, vol. 4, pp. 195–6.

87. The Nabat Confederation was forcibly dissolved by the Bolsheviks in mid-1919, driving many of its members into the ranks of the *makhnovtsy*.

88. Volin (spelling varies: Wolin, Voline), pseudonym of Vsevolod Mikhailovich Ekhembaum (1882–1945), a prominent anarcho-syndicalist, writer, speaker, member of the Nabat secretariat, who played a leading role in the Makhno movement from August to December 1919. See Danilov and Shanin (eds), *Nestor Makhno*, p. 889.

89. Golovanov, *Nestor Makhno*, pp. 135–6.

90. *Rezoliutsii Pervogo S'ezda Konfederatsii Anarkhistskikh Organizatsii Ukrainy 'Nabat'* (Buenos Aires: Rabochei izdatel'skoi gruppy v resp. Argentine, 1923), p. 18. See also Belash and Belash, *Dorogi Nestora Makhno*, p. 128.

91. Quoted by Belash and Belash, *Dorogi Nestora Makhno*, p. 127.

92. Antonov-Ovseenko, *Zapiski o grazhdanskoi voine*, vol. 4, p. 51 ff.

93. The congress resolution is printed by Danilov and Shanin (eds), *Nestor Makhno*, document no. 63, pp. 111–12.

94. A. V. Likholat, *Pod leninskim znamenem druzhby narodov: edinstvo deistvii tru-diashchikhsia Ukrainy i Rossii v bor'be za pobedy i ukreplenie Sovetskoe vlasti* (Moscow: Izdat. Nauka, 1970), p. 356; *Put' k svobode* no. 2 (24 May 1919), p. 1.
95. Arshinov, *Istoriia makhnovskogo dvizheniia*, p. 98.
96. For the complete text, see Arshinov, *Istoriia makhnovskogo dvizheniia*, pp. 98-103.
97. Arshinov, *Istoriia makhnovskogo dvizheniia*, p. 101.
98. Arshinov, *Istoriia makhnovskogo dvizheniia*, p. 101.
99. See Dybenko's order of 9 April (*Grazhdanskaia voina na Ukraine*, vol. 1, book 2, p. 317).
100. His troops were 'notorious' for looting and carrying out pogroms (Orlando Figes, *A People's Tragedy: The Russian Revolution, 1891-1924* [London: Jonathan Cape, 1996], p. 666). See also Shkuro's memoir *Grazhdanskaia voina v Rossii: zapiski belogo partizana* (Moscow: Izdat. ACT, 2004), which is available online at militera. lib.ru/memo/russian/shkuro_ag/index.html.
101. H. N. H. Williamson, *Farewell to the Don; The Russian Revolution in the Journals of Brigadier H.N.H. Williamson* (New York: J. Day, 1971), pp. 68-9; Antonov-Ovseenko, *Zapiski o grazhdanskoi voine*, vol. 4, p. 51 ff. Another study calls him 'scarcely more than a glorified bandit' (W. Bruce Lincoln, *Red Victory: A History of the Russian Civil War* [New York: Simon and Schuster, 1989], p. 216).
102. *Grazhdanskaia voina na Ukraine*, vol. 1, book 2, pp. 376-7.
103. Meyer (ed.), *The Trotsky Papers*, vol. 1, pp. 374-5.
104. *Grazhdanskaia voina na Ukraine*, vol. 1, book 2, p. 328.
105. *Grazhdanskaia voina na Ukraine*, vol. 1, book 2, p. 328. At this time Dybenko was attempting to capture Sevastopol'. Dybenko's campaign in the Crimea was undertaken in isolation from the major hostilities of the Ukrainian front, removing troops that were needed there.
106. Antonov-Ovseenko, *Zapiski o grazhdanskoi voine*, vol. 4, p. 129.
107. Yaroslavsky, *History of Anarchism in Russia* (New York: International Publishers, 1937), p. 64.
108. By June about 170,000 tons (10.5 million pud) had been collected but not sent (*Istoriia KP(b)U v materiialakh i dokumentakh [khrestomatiia] 1917-1920 rr.*, 2nd ed. [Kiev, 1934], p. 457); although the total harvest in 1919 was 9.7 million tons, the food agencies had demanded only 2.3 million tons to be delivered, 700,000 tons by March. According to Stalin, only 32,000 tons were finally collected, because of Makhno's manhunt against food officials (Speech to the 4th Conference of the KP(b)U, in his *Collected works* [Moscow: Foreign Languages Publishing House, 1952-55], vol. 4, p. 311). For a nuanced case study of how the different food procurement campaigns of 1918 and 1919 actually worked in some provinces, see Orlando Figes, *Peasant Russia, Civil War: The Volga Countryside in Revolution, 1917-1921* (Oxford: Clarendon Press, 1989), pp. 248-73.
109. Meyer, *The Trotsky Papers*, vol. 1, pp. 374-5.
110. Antonov-Ovseenko, *Zapiski o grazhdanskoi voine*, vol. 4, p. 56; *Grazhdanskaia voina na Ukraine*, vol. 1, book 2, p. xxvi.
111. *Grazhdanskaia voina na Ukraine*, vol. 1, book 2, p. xxvii and p. 350.
112. Antonov-Ovseenko, *Zapiski o grazhdanskoi voine*, vol. 4, pp. 56-7.
113. V. I. Lenin, *Polnoe sobranie sochinenii*, 5th ed. (Moscow: Izdat. Politicheskoi Literatury, 1958-1965), vol. 50, pp. 282-3. Lenin was right, since Dybenko ran the risk of being cut off from the main forces to the north.
114. Meyer (ed.), *The Trotsky Papers*, vol. 1, pp. 368-9.
115. Trotsky, *Kak vooruzhalas revoliutsiia*, vol. 2, book 1, p. 238; Meyer (ed.), *The Trotsky Papers*, vol. 1, pp. 370-71.
116. Lenin, *Polnoe sobranie sochinenii*, vol. 50, p. 286.

117. In April 1919 there were 93 uprisings, only four of which were in Ekaterinoslav and eight in Kherson (Shlikhter, 'Bor'ba za khleb na Ukraine v 1919 g'. *Litopys revoliutsii* no. 2 [1928], p. 106, quoted by Adams, *Bolsheviks in the Ukraine*, p. 233).

118. 'We've made a mistake, and a big one', Antonov to Skachko, 20 April 1919 (*Grazhdanskaia voina na Ukraine*, vol. 1, book 2, p. 356; Antonov-Ovseenko, *Zapiski o grazhdanskoi voine*, vol. 4, p. 64).

119. Meyer (ed.), *The Trotsky Papers*, vol. 1, pp. 390–93.

120. Antonov-Ovseenko, *Zapiski o grazhdanskoi voine*, vol. 3, p. 223.

121. Antonov-Ovseenko, *Zapiski o grazhdanskoi voine*, vol. 4, pp. 72–3.

122. Antonov-Ovseenko, *Zapiski o grazhdanskoi voine*, vol. 4, pp. 81–2.

123. Antonov-Ovseenko, *Zapiski o grazhdanskoi voine*, vol. 4, pp. 83–4.

124. Antonov-Ovseenko, *Zapiski o grazhdanskoi voine*, vol. 4, pp. 110.

125. Shubin, *Makhno i makhnovskoe dvizhenie*, p. 61.

126. Antonov-Ovseenko, *Zapiski o grazhdanskoi voine*, vol. 4, p. 113. See also Golovanov, *Nestor Makhno*, p. 134.

127. Antonov-Ovseenko, *Zapiski o grazhdanskoi voine*, vol. 4, p. 111; in fact, Dybenko had already ordered 250,000 cartridges to be sent for these weapons (*Grazhdanskaia voina na Ukraine*, vol. 1, book 2, p. 368).

128. *Grazhdanskaia voina na Ukraine*, vol. 1, book 2, pp. 368–9.

129. V. S., 'Ekspeditsiia L. B. Kameneva dlia prodvizheniia prodgruzov k Moskve v 1919 g'. *Proletarskaia revoliutsiia* no. 6 (1925), p. 138.

CHAPTER 4   BETRAYAL IN THE HEAT OF BATTLE? THE RED–BLACK ALLIANCE FALLS APART, MAY–SEPTEMBER 1919

1. Korine Amacher, 'Lev Kamenev chez Nestor Makhno (Gouliaï-Polié, mai 1919: un récit en quatre temps', *Quaestio Rossica* vol. 5 no. 3 (2017), pp. 738–56.

2. On Shapiro's career, see Amacher, 'Lev Kamenev chez Nestor Makhno', pp. 742–3.

3. Amacher, 'Lev Kamenev chez Nestor Makhno', p. 746.

4. V. S., 'Ekspeditsiia L. B. Kameneva dlia prodvizheniia prodgruzov k Moskve v 1919 g.' *Proletarskaia revoliutsiia* no. 6 (1925), pp. 189–90; the letter is also reprinted in Viktor Danilov and Teodor Shanin (eds), *Nestor Makhno: krest'ianskoe dvizheniia na Ukraine, 1918-1921. dokumenty e materialy* (Moscow: Rossiiskaia Politicheskaia Entsiklopediia, 2006), pp. 136–7. See also the extract in A. V. Belash and V. F. Belash, *Dorogi Nestora Makhno: istoricheskoe povestvovanie* (Kiev: Proza, 1993), pp. 176–8.

5. V. S., 'Ekspeditsiia L. B. Kameneva,' pp. 189–90.

6. V. S., 'Ekspeditsiia L. B. Kameneva,' pp. 189–90.

7. Belash and Belash, *Dorogi Nestora Makhno*, p. 175.

8. Danilov and Shanin (eds), *Nestor Makhno*, pp. 130–31.

9. V. S., 'Ekspeditsiia L. B. Kameneva,' pp. 137–38; Petr Arshinov, *Istoriia makhnovskogo dvizheniia, 1918-1921* (Berlin: Gruppy Russkikh Anarkhistov v Germanii, 1923), p. 104.

10. Petr Arshinov, *Istoriia makhnovskogo dvizheniia*, p. 105.

11. Arshinov, *Istoriia makhnovskogo dvizheniia*, p. 105. Golovanov agrees, writing that 'Kamenev was wary of Makhno and the tone of his conversation with Makhno was suspicious' – see *Nestor Makhno* (Moscow: Molodaia Gvardiia, 2013), p. 119. But Amacher refers to a later text by Sokolin, published in 1949, where he describes an 'enthusiastic clamour' after the speeches, followed by songs and dancing ('Lev Kamenev chez Nestor Makhno', p. 748).

12. V. S., 'Ekspeditsiia L. B. Kameneva,' p. 144.

13. Podvoiskii, as *narkomvoen* of Ukraine, overrode all priorities, and interfered with the work of central government departments in his efforts to keep his armies supplied (V. S., 'Ekspeditsiia L. B. Kameneva', p. 125, 131–2, 144).

14. *Grazhdanskaia voina na Ukraine, 1918-1920: sbornik dokumentov i materialov* (Kiev: Izdat. Naukova Dumka, 1967), vol. 2, p. 8.

15. V. I. Lenin, *Polnoe sobranie sochinenii*, 5th edn. (Moscow: Izdat. Politicheskoi Literatury, 19581965), vol. 50, p. 302–3.

16. Telegram to Kamenev, in Lenin, *Polnoe sobranie sochinenii*,vol. 50, p. 307; *Grazhdanskaia voina na Ukraine*, vol. 2, p. 16; Lenin, *Voennaia perepiska 19171920 gg* (Moscow: Voennoe Izdat. Min. Oborony Soiuza SSR, 1956), p. 117.

17. Lenin, *Polnoe sobranie sochinenii*, vol. 38, p. 356.

18. Lenin, *Polnoe sobranie sochinenii*, vol. 38, p. 378; Jan Meyer (ed.), *The Trotsky papers* (The Hague: Mouton, 1964–1971), vol. 1, p. 406407; *Grazhdanskaia voina na Ukraine*, vol. 2, p. 18.

19. The TsIk was at this time the top state power in Ukraine between sessions of the Congress of Soviets.

20. Belash and Belash, *Dorogi Nestora Makhno*, p. 171.

21. Belash and Belash, quoting V. P. Zatonskii (*Dorogi Nestora Makhno*, p. 171).

22. This was true elsewhere. For a typology of peasant revolts along the Volga in 1920 and 1921, see Orlando Figes, *Peasant Russia, civil war: the Volga countryside in revolution, 1917-1921* (Oxford: Clarendon Press, 1989), pp. 321–53.

23. Laura Engelstein, *Russia in Flames: War, Revolution, Civil War, 1914-1921* (New York: Oxford University Press, 2018), p. 453.

24. *Kommunist* (8 May 1919), quoted by A. V. Likholat, *Pod leninskim znamenem druzhby narodov: edinstvo deistvii trudiashchikhsia Ukrainy i Rossii v bor'be za pobedy i ukreplenie Sovetskoe vlasti* (Moscow: Izdat. Nauka, 1970), p. 357.

25. Vladimir Antonov-Ovseenko, *Zapiski o grazhdanskoi voine* (Moscow: Vysshii Voennyi Redak. Sovet, 1924–33), vol. 4, pp. 203–8.

26. Antonov-Ovseenko, *Zapiski o grazhdanskoi voine*, vol. 4, p. 207.

27. Arshinov, *Istoriia makhnovskogo dvizheniia*, p. 107.

28. Arshinov, *Istoriia makhnovskogo dvizheniia*, pp. 108–9.

29. Text in Arshinov, *Istoriia makhnovskogo dvizheniia*, p. 109.

30. Arshinov, *Istoriia makhnovskogo dvizheniia*, p. 110. Arthur Adams, followed by Palij, argues that Makhno was jealous of Grigor'ev, as a professional soldier, and feared that absorption. (Adams, *Bolsheviks in the Ukraine: The Second Campaign, 1918-1919* [New Haven, Conn.: Yale University Press, 1963], p. 326; Michael Palij, *The Anarchism of Nestor Makhno, 1918-1921: An Aspect of the Ukrainian Revolution* [Seattle: University of Washington Press, 1976], p. 173).

31. Arshinov, *Istoriia makhnovskogo dvizheniia*, p. 112; Antonov-Ovseenko, *Zapiski o grazhdanskoi voine*, vol. 4, p. 254; cf. S. Dubrovskii, 'Grigor'evshchina', *Voina i Revoliutsiia* no. 4 (1928), p. 97.

32. Arshinov, *Istoriia makhnovskogo dvizheniia*, pp. 112–15; longer version in *Put' k svobode* (4 June 1919), pp. 3–4.

33. Arshinov, *Istoriia makhnovskogo dvizheniia*, p. 114.

34. Nonetheless, 'as long as the Whites remained in the field, the peasants were reluctant to challenge the Soviet regime' (Figes, *Peasant Russia, Civil War*, p. 29).

35. J. H. Hertz, *A Decade of Woe and Hope* (London: H. Milford, 1923), p. 11. See also E. Heifetz, *The Slaughter of the Jews in the Ukraine in 1919* (New York: Thomas Seltzer, 1921); Tcherikower, *Di ukrainer pogromen in yor 1919* (New York: YIVO Institute for Jewish Research, 1965).

36. Arshinov, *Istoriia makhnovskogo dvizheniia*, p. 132.

37. *Grazhdanskaia voina na Ukraine*, vol. 2, p. 786.

38. *Grazhdanskaia voina na Ukraine*, vol. 2, pp. 70–71.

39. *Grazhdanskaia voina na Ukraine*, vol. 2, p. 786; A. I. Denikin, *Ocherki russkoi smuty* (Paris: J. Povolozky, 1921–24), vol. 5, p. 104. Arshinov claims the break-through occurred on Makhno's left flank, i.e. in the Red Army's sector (*Istoriia makhnovskogo dvizheniia*, p. 124).

40. Meyer (ed.), *The Trotsky Papers*, vol. 1, document 221.

41. Meyer (ed.), *The Trotsky Papers*, vol. 1, pp. 460–63.

42. Stalin, *Collected Works* (Moscow: Foreign Languages Publishing House, 1952–55), vol. 4, pp. 269–70.

43. Meyer (ed.), *The Trotsky Papers*, vol. 1, pp. 468–9.

44. A. Berkman, *The Bolshevik Myth* (London: Hutcchinson, 1925), p. 189; Arshinov, *Istoriia makhnovskogo dvizheniia*, p. 124; Volin, *La révolution inconnue, 1917-1921: documentation inédite sur la révolution russe* (Paris: Les Amis de Voline, 1947), p. 562.

45. Meyer (ed.), *The Trotsky Papers*, vol. 1, pp. 458–9.

46. *Grazhdanskaia voina na Ukraine*, vol. 2, pp. 78–9.

47. *Grazhdanskaia voina na Ukraine*, vol. 2, pp. 91–2; Meyer (ed.), *The Trotsky Papers*, vol. 1, pp. 476–9.

48. Meyer (ed.), *The Trotsky Papers*, vol. 1, pp. 486–7.

49. Meyer (ed.), *The Trotsky Papers*, vol. 1, pp. 484–93 details the proposal.

50. Meyer (ed.), *The Trotsky Papers*, vol. 1, pp. 486–7.

51. The moment required the putting aside of political differences for the sake of a united front against Denikin, and Trotsky chose not to do so (*Dorogi Nestora Makhno*, p. 278).

52. Aleksandr Shubin, *Makhno i makhnovskoe dvizhenie* (Moscow: Izdat. MIK, 1998), p. 72.

53. Arshinov, *Istoriia makhnovskogo dvizheniia*, pp. 115–17.

54. Belash and Belash, *Dorogi Nestora Makhno*, p. 280.

55. As late as 30 May Dybenko was hauling supplies captured from Grigor'ev to Crimea (Meyer (ed.), *The Trotsky Papers*, vol. 1, pp. 490, 493).

56. Danilov and Shanin (eds), *Nestor Makhno*, pp. 157–8.

57. Danilov and Shanin (eds), *Nestor Makhno*, pp. 158–9; Antonov-Ovseenko, *Zapiski o grazhdanskoi voine*, vol. 4, pp. 307308; S. N. Semanov, 'Makhnovsh-china i ee krakh,' *Voprosy istorii* no. 9 (1966), pp. 4546. Cf. *Grazhdanskaia voina na Ukraine*, vol. 2, p. 786n; Voroshilov knew of Makhno's resignation by 30 May (Meyer (ed.), *The Trotsky Papers*, vol. 1, pp. 486–7).

58. Arshinov, *Istoriia makhnovskogo dvizheniia*, pp. 117–18.

59. Danilov and Shanin (eds), *Nestor Makhno*, p. 160.

60. *Grazhdanskaia voina na Ukraine*, vol. 2, p. 786n.

61. *Vestnik Narkomvnudel UkSSR* no. 9 (1919), pp. 3–11, quoted in *Grazhdanskaia voina na Ukraine*, vol. 2, p. 117.

62. Danilov and Shanin (eds), *Nestor Makhno*, p. 164; Arshinov, *Istoriia makhnovsk-ogo dvizheniia*, pp. 119–20.

63. Trotsky, *Kak vooruzhalas revoliutsiia na voennoi rabote* (Moscow: Vysshii Voennyi Redak. Sovet, 1923–25), vol. 2, book 1, p. 200; Danilov and Shanin (eds), *Nestor Makhno*, pp. 166–7.

64. Arshinov, *Istoriia makhnovskogo dvizheniia*, p. 125; Meyer (ed.), *The Trotsky Papers*, vol. 1, p. 459n; A. I. Denikin, *The White Army* (London: Jonathan Cape, 1930), p. 272.

65. Danilov and Shanin (eds), *Nestor Makhno*, pp. 169–71. Arshinov dates the letter as 9 June.
66. Semanov, 'Makhnovshchina i ee krakh', p. 45.
67. 'Denikin i general Shkuro protiv burzhuazii!' *Put' k svobode* no. 3 (4 June 1919), pp. 2–3.
68. Danilov and Shanin (eds), *Nestor Makhno*, p. 170; Arshinov, *Istoriia makhnovskogo dvizheniia*, pp. 103–4; Fedor T. Fomin repeats the allegation (*Zapiski starogo Chekista* [Moscow: Gospolitizdat., 1962], p. 76).
69. Danilov and Shanin (eds), *Nestor Makhno*, p. 170.
70. Trotsky, *Kak vooruzhalas' revoliutsii*, vol. 2, book 1, pp. 189–91; Danilov and Shanin (eds), *Nestor Makhno*, p. 162.
71. Arshinov, *Istoriia makhnovskogo dvizheniia*, p. 127; M. Kubanin says Makhno was ordered to hand over command (*Makhnovshchina: krest'ianskoe dvizhenie v stepnoi Ukrainev gody grazhdanskoi voiny* [Leningrad: Izdat. Priboi, 1926], pp. 77–8).
72. Golovanov argues that Trotsky needed a scapegoat for military failures, and as a supporter of 'rigorous party dictatorship', could not tolerate anarchist social experimentation or the special position of the *makhnovtsy* in the Red Army (*Nestor Makhno*, p. 154).
73. Danilov and Shanin (eds), *Nestor Makhno*, p. 5. Antonov's memoirs (*Zapiski o grazhdanskoi voine*) were published in four volumes in Moscow between 1924 and 1933.
74. Danilov and Shanin (eds), *Nestor Makhno*, pp. 129–30.
75. Shubin, *Makhno i makhnovskoe dvizhenie*, p. 74. See also his *Anarkhiia mat' poriadka: mezhdu krasnymi i belymi. Nestor Makhno kak zerkalo Rossiiskoi revoliutsii* (Moscow: Iauza, Eksmo, 2005), p. 174; and *Makhno i ego vremia: o velikoi revoliutsii i grazhdanskoi voine, 1917-1922 gg., v Rossii i na Ukraine* (Moscow: Knizhnyi Dom Librokom, 2014), p. 148.
76. Arshinov, *Istoriia makhnovskogo dvizheniia*, p. 128; Volin, *La révolution inconnue*, p. 543n.
77. *Grazhdanskaia voina na Ukraine*, vol. 2, pp. 131–2.
78. *Grazhdanskaia voina na Ukraine*, vol. 2, pp. 147–8.
79. Antonov-Ovseenko, *Zapiski o grazhdanskoi voine*, vol. 4, pp. 321–5; Meyer (ed.), *The Trotsky Papers*, vol. 1, p. 577.
80. *Nabat* (7 July 1919); G. P. Maximoff (Maksimov), *The Guillotine at Work: Twenty Years of Terror in Russia* (Chicago: Chicago Section of the Alexander Berkman Fund, 1940), pp. 423–5; Volin, *La révolution inconnue*, pp. 666–7.
81. Minute no. 146 of the Collegium of the Ukrainian Cheka, printed in Maximoff, *The Guillotine at Work*, p. 435; cf. Volin, *La révolution inconnue*, p. 574.
82. 'Pravda o Makhno,' *Odesskii Nabat* (16 June 1919), p. 1; *Nabat* (15 July 1919); Maximoff, *The Guillotine at Work*, pp. 431–2.
83. On Kolchak's career, see David Footman, *Civil War in Russia* (London: Faber and Faber, 1961), pp. 211–44; and S. P. Mel'gunov, *Tragediia admirala Kolchaka: iz istorii grazhdanskoi voiny na Volgie, Uraliei v Sibiri* (Belgrade: Russkaia Tipografiia, 1930–31), 3 vols. in 4.
84. There was antagonism between Stalin, Voroshilov and the Tsaritsyn army command on one hand, and Trotsky on the other, over questions of tactics, discipline and strategy. See I. Deutscher, *Stalin: A Political Biography*, rev. edn. (Harmondsworth: Penguin Books, 1966), pp. 203–11.

85. See, e.g. the detailed report by the party functionary S. I. Syrtsov to Lenin and Trotsky, dated 17 June 1919, in Danilov and Shanin (eds), *Nestor Makhno*, pp. 172-7.

86. Syrtsov's report, in Danilov and Shanin (eds), *Nestor Makhno*, p. 172.

87. In the summer the Directory joined forces with the Galician army which had been driven from the territory of the former Western Ukraine by the Poles. In June 1919 the combined army began to advance on Kiev, taking advantage of Bolshevik defeats.

88. W. H. Chamberlin, *The Russian Revolution*, new edn. (New York: Grosset and Dunlap, 1965), vol. 2, pp. 244-5.

89. Denikin, *Ocherki russkoi smuty*, vol. 5, pp. 108-9; English translation in Chamberlin, *The Russian Revolution*, vol. 2, pp. 485-6.

90. See the analysis of the failure to reach Moscow by Evan Mawdsley, *The Russian Civil War* (Boston: Unwin Hyman, 1987), pp. 172-4.

91. By autumn, forces were no longer evenly balanced. Mawdsley estimates the Volunteer Army's combat strength in October-November as 97-99,000, against 127,000 infantry and 21,000 cavalry in the Red Southern and Southeastern Army Groups (*The Russian Civil War*, p. 214).

92. Mawdsley, *The Russian Civil War*, pp. 172-3.

93. Mawdsley, *The Russian Civil War*, p. 207.

94. Mawdsley, *The Russian Civil War*, p. 203.

95. Soviet historians give credit to Stalin personally. See e.g. the *History of the Communist Party of the Soviet Union (Bolsheviks): Short Course* (Moscow: Foreign Languages Publishing House, 1939), p. 238.

96. Mawdsley, *The Russian Civil War*, p. 175; W. Bruce Lincoln, *Red Victory: A History of the Russian Civil War* (New York: Simon and Schuster, 1989), p. 224.

97. Trotsky, *Stalin: An Appraisal of the Man and his Influence* (London: Hollis and Carter, 1947), p. 314.

98. Trotsky, *Stalin: An Appraisal*, p. 314.

99. Opinion varies as to who was right. See Mawdsley, *The Russian Civil War*, pp. 176-7 for a discussion of the issues.

100. *Iz istorii grazhdanskoi voiny v SSSR, 1918-1922: sbornik dokumentov i materialov* (Moscow: Sov. Rossiia, 1960-61), vol. 2, p. 512.

101. Mawdsley, *The Russian Civil War*, p. 175.

102. Revealingly, the Whites used the term 'occupied territory' for the area behind their lines (Lincoln, *Red Victory*, p. 219).

103. Golovanov points to modern reassessments of Denikin as a noble figure dedicated to the restoration of Russia, opposed by a rebellious rabble (*Nestor Makhno*, p. 189 ff.).

104. Denikin, *Ocherki russkoi smuty*, vol. 5, p. 134. See also Golovanov's gloss on this idea (*Nestor Makhno*, p. 192).

105. Golovanov, *Nestor Makhno*, p. 194.

106. Richard Pipes, *Russia Under the Bolshevik regime, 1919-1924* (London: Fontana Press, 1995), p. 81.

107. Denikin was in his late forties at this time – see Lincoln, *Red Victory*, pp. 205-9.

108. The garrisons were weak; Denikin wrote later that Makhno's forces could defeat them 'easily' (*Ocherki russkoi smuty*, vol. 5, p. 234).

109. Imperial officers were often corrupt. W. Bruce Lincoln makes much of the depravity of the Volunteer Army (Lincoln, *Red Victory*, p. 218 ff).

110. Hodgson, *With Denikin's Armies*, p. 181.

111. Uralov's diary was extracted in *Put' k Svobode* no. 3 (4 October 1919), subsequently quoted by Belash and Belash, *Dorogi Nestora Makhno*, p. 309.
112. Father G. Shavel'skii, quoted by Lincoln, *Red Victory*, p. 220.
113. Arshinov, *Istoriia makhnovskogo dvizheniia*, p. 131 (emphasis added).
114. A. Hak [pseud.], *Vid Huliai-Polia do N'iu-Iorku: spohady* (Neu Ulm: Ukrainski Wisti, 1973), p. 104.
115. Arshinov, *Istoriia makhnovskogo dvizheniia*, pp. 130–31.
116. See for example a resolution of the peasants of Kremenchug region, *Kommunist* (18 July 1919), reprinted in *Grazhdanskaia voina na Ukraine*, vol. 2, p. 239.
117. Belash and Belash, *Dorogi Nestora Makhno*, p. 257. V. Popov says that anarchist agitators were most active in north Tauride and Kherson provinces – 'Dlia etogo nado byt' bol'shevikom,' in P. I. Iakir and Iu. A. Geller (eds), *Komandarm Iakir: vospominaiia druzei i soratnikov* (Moscow: Voenizdat, 1963), pp. 86–7; cf. I. E. Iakir, *Vospominaniia o grazhdanskoi voine* (Moscow, 1957), p. 35 ff.
118. Aleksei Chubenko in Danilov and Shanin (eds), *Nestor Makhno*, p. 753.
119. Arshinov, *Istoriia makhnovskogo dvizheniia*, pp. 132–3.
120. The most widely disseminated version is that of Arshinov (*Istoriia makhnovskogo dvizheniia*, pp. 133–4). M. Kubanin, *Makhnovshchina*, pp. 81–3, prints A. Chubenko's account; see also Makhno, 'Makhnovshchina i antisemitizm,' *Delo truda* no. 30–31 (1927), p. 18.
121. Arshinov, *Istoriia makhnovskogo dvizheniia*, pp. 133–4.
122. Aleksei Chubenko's diary, in Danilov and Shanin (eds), *Nestor Makhno*, p. 764. But see also Belash and Belash, *Dorogi Nestora Makhno*, p. 297). Grigor'ev was buried with military honours (F. Meleshko, 'Nestor Makhno ta ioho anarkhia,' *Litopys chervonoi kalyny* no. 3 (1935), pp. 9–11).
123. Copy of a copy of the resolution from Protocol no. 4 of the Congress, printed in Elias Heifetz, *The Slaughter of the Jews in the Ukraine in 1919*, pp. 71–2. Arshinov (*Istoriia makhnovskogo dvizheniia*, p. 134n) states that the proceedings of the congress were lost as early as 1920, and it is unclear what Heifetz's source for the document is.
124. *Grazhdanskaia voina na Ukraine*, vol. 2, pp. 281–2; S. Barannyk, Kh. Mishkis and H. Slobods'kyi (eds) *Istoriia KP(b)U v materiialikh i dokumentakh*, 2nd edn., Kiev: Partvydav TsK KP(b)U, 1934, pp. 475–6.
125. Arshinov, *Istoriia makhnovskogo dvizheniia*, p. 135; Volin, *La révolution inconnue*, pp. 579–80.
126. Meyer (ed.), *The Trotsky Papers*, vol. 1, pp. 632–6.
127. Mykola Kapustians'kyi, *Pokhid ukraïns'kykh armii na Kyiv-Odesu v 1919 r*, 2nd edn. (Munich: V-vo Khvyl'ovoho, 1946) vol. 2, p. 156.
128. E. Hurwicz claims that between August and September Makhno suffered 8,000 casualties. (*Staatsmänner und Abenteurer: russische Porträts von Witte bis Trotzki* [Leipzig: Hirschfeld, 1925], pp. 268–9).
129. Volin, *La révolution inconnue*, p. 580; Arshinov, *Istoriia makhnovskogo dvizheniia*, p. 135.
130. M. S., 'Makhno ta ioho viis'ko,' *Litopys Chervonoi Kalyny* vol. 7 no. 6 (June 1935), pp. 16–17.
131. Volin claims that there was 'a kind of military clique or camarilla about Makhno [... which] showed contempt towards all those who were outside it' (*La révolution inconnue*, p. 683).
132. M. S., 'Makhno ta ioho viis'ko,' pp. 16–17.

133. Belash and Belash, *Dorogi Nestora Makhno*, p. 302. A *britzka* is a long covered carriage with four wheels pulled by two horses, large enough to be used as a mobile office.

134. Denikin, *Ocherki russkoi smuty*, vol. 5, p. 234.

135. Volin, *La révolution inconnue*, p. 581.

136. *Grazhdanskaia voina na Ukraine*, vol. 2, p. 362.

137. V. I. Aleksandrova et al., (eds), *Moriaki v bor'be za vlast' sovetov na Ukraine, noiabr' 1917-1920 gg.: sbornik dokumentov* (Kiev, 1963), p. 269.

138. Belash and Belash, *Dorogi Nestora Makhno*, p. 301.

139. Volin, *La révolution inconnue*, p. 578. Litvinov says the RPA(M) *in partisan mode* did not have its own medical or supply services and 'the organised local population ... supplied the army with combat personnel, provided it with transport, food and fodder; it also took the sick and wounded into its care' (Vladimir Litvinov, 'O chetvertom [oktiabr' 1920 goda] voenno-politicheskom soglashenii mezhdu Revoliutsionno-Povstancheskoi Armiei [Makhnovtsev] i kommunisticheskim pravitel'skom RSFSR,' *International Review of Social History*, vol. 32, no. 3 [1987], p. 328).

140. Volin, *La révolution inconnue*, pp. 578-9, 582.

141. At the end of August, Makhno's forces consisted of 1,500 infantry, 500 cavalry, with 50 machine guns and four artillery pieces (Belash and Belash, *Dorogi Nestora Makhno*, p. 299).

142. Volin, *La révolution inconnue*, pp. 582-3; Arshinov, *Istoriia makhnovskogo dvizheniia*, pp. 136-7.

143. Belash and Belash, *Dorogi Nestora Makhno*, p. 299.

144. Belash and Belash, *Dorogi Nestora Makhno*, p. 300.

145. KP(b)U report dated 22 September, in Danilov and Shanin (eds), *Nestor Makhno*, pp. 199-201.

146. Belash and Belash, *Dorogi Nestora Makhno*, pp. 297-8.

147. Belash and Belash, *Dorogi Nestora Makhno*, pp. 300-301.

148. Mawdsley, *The Russian Civil War*, pp. 170-71; Lincoln, *Red Victory*, pp. 214-15.

149. For an attempt to rehabilitate Selivachev's reputation, see A. V. Ganin, *Poslednie dni Generala Selivacheva: neizvestnye stranitsy grazhdanskoi voiny na iuge Rossii* (Moscow: Kuchkogo Pole, 2012).

150. Lenin, *Collected works* (Moscow: Progress Publishers, 1960-71), vol. 35, pp. 420-21.

151. The Whites captured Orel' on 14 October, taking 8,000 prisoners and positioning themselves for the final thrust to Tula and the capture of the armaments factory. They were 400 kilometres from Moscow. Mawdsley, *The Russian Civil War*, pp. 195-6; Lincoln, *Red Victory*, pp. 223-4.

152. Belash and Belash, *Dorogi Nestora Makhno*, p. 303.

153. Slashchev (1885-1929) was assassinated years later by a relative of a victim of his pogroms. For a popular account of his career, see O. S. Smyslov, *General Slashchev-Krymskii: pobedy, emigratsiia, vozvrashenie* (Moscow: Veche, 2013) – on Makhno, especially pp. 151-62.

154. Ia. A. Slashchev, 'Materialy po istorii grazhdanskoi voiny v Rossii,' *Voennyi Vestnik* no. 9/10 (1922), pp. 38-9, quoted in Belash and Belash, *Dorogi Nestora Makhno*, p. 304. See also V. F. Verstiuk, *Makhnovshchyna: selians'kyi povstans'kyi rukh na Ukraini, 1918-1921* (Kiev: Naukova Dumka, 1991), pp. 170-71.

155. Denikin commented that 'trust was not absolute,' (*Ocherki russkoi smuty*, vol. 5, p. 234).

156. Belash and Belash, *Dorogi Nestora Makhno*, p. 305.

157. Volin, *La révolution inconnue*, pp. 583-4; Arshinov, *Istoriia makhnovskogo dvizheniia*, p. 137.

158. Zenon Jaworskyj, 'Alliance of the First USS Brigade with N. Makhno in 1919' (Unpublished typescript, 1973) pp. 4-8. Jaworskyj was the emissary from the Galicians to Makhno.

159. A second agreement was concluded on 20 September: the *makhnovtsy* were to receive ammunition and equipment, and 3,000 sick and wounded were to move to nationalist infirmaries. Political agreement was not reached. Belash and Belash, *Dorogi Nestora Makhno*, p. 305.

160. Jaworskyj, 'Alliance of the First USS Brigade with N. Makhno in 1919', pp. 12-19; Arshinov, *Istoriia makhnovskogo dvizheniia*, p. 137; Volin, *La révolution inconnue*, pp. 584-5; cf. Denikin, op.cit., vol. 5, p. 234.

161. 'Kto takoi Petliura?' paraphrased by Arshinov, *Istoriia makhnovskogo dvizheniia*, p. 138; cf. Jaworskyj, 'Alliance of the First USS Brigade with N. Makhno in 1919', p. 16.

162. Arshinov, *Istoriia makhnovskogo dvizheniia*, p. 138.

163. Jaworskyj, 'Alliance of the First USS Brigade with N. Makhno in 1919', pp. 19-20.

164. In Ukrainian, Perehonivka.

CHAPTER 5   THE LONG MARCH WEST AND THE BATTLE AT PEREGONOVKA

1. Petr Arshinov, *Istoriia makhnovskogo dvizheniia, 1918-1921* (Berlin: Gruppy Russkikh Anarkhistov v Germanii, 1923), pp. 136-7.

2. Arshinov, *Istoriia makhnovskogo dvizheniia*, p. 135.

3. For parts of this line of analysis, see Alexandre Skirda, *Nestor Makhno, le cosaque de l'anarchie: la lutte pour les soviets libres en Ukraine, 1917-1921* (Paris: A.S., 1982), p. 169.

4. Viacheslav Azarov, *Starobel'skoe soglashenie* (Odessa: DP Nabat, 2011), p. 57, emphasis added.

5. E.g. 'For the first time in history, the principles of libertarian communism were applied ...' (Daniel Guérin, *Anarchism from Theory to Practice* [New York: Monthly Review, Press, 1970], pp. 98-9); '... one of the few examples of anarchy in action on a large scale in modern history' (Peter Marshall, *Demanding the Impossible: A History of Anarchism* [London: Fontana Press, 1993], p. 473).

6. Erik C. Landis, *Bandits and Partisans: The Antonov Movement in the Russian Civil War* (Pittsburgh: University of Pittsburgh Press, 2008), p. 127.

7. See also on this question Aleksandr Shubin, *Anarkhiia mat' poriadka: mezhdu krasnymi i belymi. Nestor Makhno kak zerkalo Rossiiskoi revoliutsii* (Moscow: Iauza, Eksmo, 2005), pp. 73-120.

8. Vladyslav Verstiuk (ed.), *Nestor Ivanovich Makhno: vospominaniia, materialy i dokumenty* (Kiev: Dzvin, 1991), p. 159, emphasis added.

9. Verstiuk (ed.), *Nestor Ivanovich Makhno*, pp. 156-64 (no archival source indicated); Alexandre Skirda, *Nestor Makhno, le cosaque de l'anarchie*, pp. 439-53 (see Skirda's note on p. 429). The texts differ in content and the paragraph structure varies. The French translation includes sections on supplies, the land question, the labour question, housing, the financial question, the national question, and culture and education that do not appear in Verstiuk's text.

10. Skirda, *Nestor Makhno, le cosaque de l'anarchie*, p. 392, quoting Makhno's letter to Maximov (*Delo Truda*, no.15 [August 1926], pp. 10-12).

11. Verstiuk (ed.), *Nestor Ivanovich Makhno*, pp. 159-60.

12. Verstiuk (ed.), *Nestor Ivanovich Makhno*, p. 160.
13. Verstiuk (ed.), *Nestor Ivanovich Makhno*, pp. 160–61.
14. Aleksandr Shubin, *Makhno i makhnovskoe dvizhenie* (Moscow: Izdat. MIK, 1998), pp. 146–7; see also his *Makhno i ego vremia: o velikoi revoliutsii i grazhdanskoi voine, 1917-1922 gg., v Rossii i na Ukraine* (Moscow: Knizhnyi Dom Librokom, 2014), p. 284.
15. Arshinov, *Istoriia makhnovskogo dvizheniia*, p. 144; Volin, *La révolution inconnue, 1917-1921: documentation inédite sur la révolution russe* (Paris: Les Amis de Voline, 1947), pp. 595–6, emphasis added.
16. Michael Malet, *Nestor Makhno in the Russian Civil War* (London: Macmillan, 1982), p. 192, quoting Pierre Berland, Moscow correspondent of *Le Temps*, in an obituary of Makhno ('Lettre d'URSS: Makhno', [8 August 1934], p. 2).
17. Michael Palij, *The Anarchism of Nestor Makhno, 1918-1921: An Aspect of the Ukrainian Revolution* (Seattle: University of Washington Press), p. 196.
18. Skirda, *Nestor Makhno, le cosaque de l'anarchie*, p. 176.
19. Shubin, *Makhno i makhnovskoe dvizhenie*, pp. 98–9, emphasis added. The same sentence appears in his *Anarkhiia mat' poriadka*, p. 233; and *Makhno i ego vremia*, p. 191.
20. Shubin, *Makhno i ego vremia*, p. 191, quoting Skirda, *Nestor Makhno, le cosaque de l'anarchie*, p. 177.
21. W. H. Chamberlin, *The Russian Revolution, 1917-1921*, new edn. (New York: Grosset and Dunlap, 1965), vol. 2, pp. 234–5.
22. M. A. Kritskii, 'Krasnaia armiia na iuzhnom fronte v 1918-1920 gg', *Arkhiv Russkoi Revoliutsii* no. 18 (1926), p. 269, quoted by Evan Mawdsley, *The Russian Civil War* (Boston: Unwin Hyman, 1987), pp. 212–13.
23. W. Bruce Lincoln, *Red Victory: A History of the Russian Civil War* (New York: Simon and Schuster, 1989), pp. 326–7.
24. Richard Pipes, *Russia Under the Bolshevik Regime, 1919-1924* (London: Fontana Press, 1995), p. 95, emphasis added. There are other examples: '... perhaps the turning point of the Russian Civil War [...] Makhno [...] actually saved the Soviet Republic' (Max Nomad, 'The Epic of Nestor Makhno, the "Bandit" Who Saved Red Moscow', *Modern Monthly* no. 6 [1935], p. 345). Or: '... Peregonovka was one of the decisive battles of the Civil War in the south'. (David Footman, *Civil War in Russia* [London: Faber, 1961], p. 276).
25. *Tul'skii Oruzheinyi Zavod*, founded in 1712. See Orlando Figes, *A People's Tragedy: The Russian Revolution, 1891-1924* (London: Jonathan Cape, 1996), p. 666, emphasis added. Trotsky wrote that the loss of Tula would have been worse than losing Moscow (*My Life: An Attempt at an Autobiography* [Harmondsworth: Penguin, 1975], p. 473).
26. Vladimir Litvinov, 'O chetvertom (oktiabr' 1920 goda) voenno-politicheskom soglashenii mezhdu Revoliutsionno-Povstancheskoi Armiei (Makhnovtsev) i kommunisticheskim pravitel'skom RSFSR', *International Review of Social History* vol. 32, no. 3 (1987), p. 323.
27. Vasilii Golovanov, *Nestor Makhno* (Moscow: Molodaia Gvardiia, 2013), p. 210. Skirda makes the same point (*Nestor Makhno, le cosaque de l'anarchie*, p. 177). Valerii Volkovyns'kyi says White casualties were as high as 12,000 (*Nestor Makhno: lehendy i real'nist'* [Kiev: Perlit Prodakshn, 1994], p. 140).
28. Vasilii Golovanov, *Nestor Makhno* (Moscow: Molodaia Gvardiia, 2013), p. 210, 212.
29. By former battalion commander Colonel Vladimir Al'mendinger, *Simferopol'skii ofitserskii polk, 1918-1920: stranitsa k istorii belogo dvizheniia na iuge Rossii* (Los

Angeles, 1962), pp. 19–24. See also G. Sakovich, 'Proryv Makhno', *Pereklichka* no.116 (1961), pp. 11–14; and ex-Staff Captain Mustafin, 'Proryv Makhno', *Pereklichka*, no. 121 (1961), pp. 10–14.

30. A. I. Denikin, *Ocherki russkoi smuty* (Paris: J. Povolozky, 1921–24), vol. 5, pp. 234–5.

31. Golovanov, *Nestor Makhno*, pp. 210–11; Ia. Slashchev 'Materialy po istorii grazhdanskoi voiny v Rossii: operatsii belykh, Petliury i Makhno na Ukraine', *Voennyi Vestnik*, nos. 9/10 (1922), pp. 38–43; nos. 12/13 (1922), pp. 49–51.

32. *Grazhdanskaia voina na Ukraine, 1918-1920: sbornik dokumentov i materialov* (Kiev: Izdat. Naukova Dumka, 1967), vol. 2, pp. 456–7.

33. M. Kubanin, *Makhnovshchina: krest'ianskoe dvizhenie v stepnoi Ukrainev gody grazhdanskoi voiny* (Leningrad: Izdat. Priboi, [1927]), pp. 85–6.

34. Arshinov (*Istoriia makhnovskogo dvizheniia*, pp. 139–41); Volin, *La révolution inconnue*, pp. 586–9; A. V. Belash and V. F. Belash, *Dorogi Nestora Makhno: istoricheskoe povestvovanie* (Kiev: Proza, 1993), p. 307 ff. Makhno's 'Razgrom Denikintsev',(*Put' k svobode* no. 4 [3 October 1919]), quoted by Kubanin, *Makhnovshchina*, p. 86.

35. Consisting mainly of quotations from Al'mendinger and Slashchev (*Nestor Makhno, le cosaque de l'anarchie*, pp. 169–78).

36. Slashchev, 'Materialy po istorii grazhdanskoi voiny v Rossii', p. 40.

37. Arshinov, *Istoriia makhnovskogo dvizheniia*, p. 136.

38. Verstiuk says that the Whites were ignorant of the terms of the agreement with Petliura. However, the Whites did capture operational documents when one of Makhno's staff officers was killed (V. F. Verstiuk, *Makhnovshchyna: selians'kyi povstans'kyi rukh na Ukraini, 1918-1921* [Kiev: Naukova Dumka, 1991], p. 173).

39. An order dated 23 September warns of 'attempts by the enemy to break through to the east' (Al'mendinger, *Simferopol'skii ofitserskii polk*, p. 19).

40. Makhno claimed at the time that he had faced 'about twelve to fifteen regiments' ('Razgrom Denikintsev', *Put' k Svobode* no.4 [30 October 1919], quoted by Al'mendinger, *Simferopol'skii ofitserskii polk*, p. 23); four of these, apart from the 1st Simferopol', were the 51st Litovskii, the 2nd Labzinskii, the 42nd Don Cossacks, and the 2nd Tamanskii Cossacks (Al'mendinger, *Simferopol'skii ofitserskii polk*, pp. 19–23; Kubanin, *Makhnovshchina*, p. 86).

41. Makhno had 8,000 men; the 1st Simferopol' had 1,475 men on strength, of whom 43 per cent (635 men) were killed or wounded in action between 2 and 27 September (Al'mendinger, *Simferopol'skii ofitserskii polk*, p. 20, 23).

42. Al'mendinger, *Simferopol'skii ofitserskii polk*, pp. 19–20.

43. Mustafin ('Proryv Makhno', p. 12) and Al'mendinger (*Simferopol'skii ofitserskii polk*) include maps.

44. Al'mendinger, *Simferopol'skii ofitserskii polk*, pp. 20–21.

45. Al'mendinger, *Simferopol'skii ofitserskii polk*, pp. 20–21.

46. Al'mendinger, *Simferopol'skii ofitserskii polk*, pp. 20–21.

47. Arshinov, *Istoriia makhnovskogo dvizheniia*, p. 139.

48. Belash and Belash, *Dorogi Nestora Makhno*, p. 308.

49. Belash and Belash, *Dorogi Nestora Makhno*, p. 308.

50. Al'mendinger, *Simferopol'skii ofitserskii polk*, p. 21; cf. Mustafin, Mustafin, 'Proryv Makhno', p. 13.

51. Skirda, *Nestor Makhno, le cosaque de l'anarchie*, is content simply to quote first Arshinov and then Al'mendinger.

52. Arshinov, *Istoriia makhnovskogo dvizheniia*, p. 140.

53. The Whites began to take Makhno seriously only from the end of August (Verstiuk, *Makhnovshchyna*, p. 169).

54. Slashchev, 'Materialy po istorii grazhdanskoi voiny v Rossii', pp. 38–9.

55. Aleksandr Timoshchuk, *Anarkho-kommunisticheskie formirovaniia N. Makhno, sentiabr' 1917-avgust 1921* (Simferopol': Tavriia, 1996), pp. 4–5.

56. O. Brytkov, 'Nestor Makhno iak avtor teorii shvydkoplynnoi viiny' in: *Mizhnarodni Konferentsii 'Ukraina i mir: gumanitarno-tekhnicheskaia elita i sotsial'nyi progress. Sektsiia 2: Aktual'nye problemy istorii Ukrainy* (Khar'kov: Natsional'nyi Tekhnichnyi Universytet, Kharkivs'kyi Politekhnichnyi Instytut, 2013), pp. 94–5. available at: core.ac.uk/display/50570856, accessed 29 February 2020.

57. 'It was a Ukrainian (Makhno) who developed the theory of lightning warfare, in which victory is achieved quickly before an enemy can mobilise' (Brytkov, 'Nestor Makhno iak avtor teorii shvydkoplynnoi viiny', p. 94).

58. The Lewis light machine-gun weighed only 12 kg., and could be operated by two men. The bulkier German-made Maxim machine-gun, which was also reportedly used by the *makhnovtsy*, weighed 15 kg. but could sustain a higher rate of fire.

59. Verstiuk, *Makhnovshchyna*, p. 185.

60. The signal flags were seen by units at the river, but no action was taken (Al'mendinger, *Simferopol'skii ofitserskii polk*, p. 21).

61. Al'mendinger, *Simferopol'skii ofitserskii polk*, pp. 21–2.

62. Arshinov says 'hundreds' perished in the river (*Istoriia makhnovskogo dvizheniia*, p. 141).

63. Al'mendinger, *Simferopol'skii ofitserskii polk*, pp. 22–3.

64. Makhno, 'Razgrom Denikintsev', quoted by Al'mendinger, *Simferopol'skii ofitserskii polk*, p. 23.

65. Makhno, 'Razgrom Denikintsev', quoted by Kubanin, *Makhnovshchina*, p. 86.

66. Belash and Belash, *Dorogi Nestora Makhno*, p. 308, 310. Belash says the prisoners were disarmed and released.

67. Belash and Belash, *Dorogi Nestora Makhno*, p. 310.

68. A. I. Denikin, *The White Army* (London: Jonathan Cape, 1930), pp. 294–5.

69. Volin, *La révolution inconnue*, p. 550.

70. Winston Churchill, *The Aftermath: Being a Sequel to The World Crisis* (London: Macmillan, 1929), p. 225. J. F. N. Bradley claims that 'the British [negotiated] with Makhno themselves … This initiative came to nothing; after much dangerous talking the rapidly deteriorating situation of the Volunteers precluded an agreement' (*Civil War in Russia, 1917-1920* [London: Batsford, 1975], p. 129). There had in fact been contact between a Red Army delegation (including the *makhnovets* Romanov, who spoke English) and the British on a destroyer in Berdiansk in March 1919 (Volodymyr Chop and Ihor Lyman, *Vol'nyi Berdiansk: misto v period anarkhists'koho sotsial'noho eksperimentu, 1918-1921 rr.* [Zaporizhzhia: RA Tandem-U, 2007], pp. 58–61).

71. *Grazhdanskaia voina na Ukraine*, vol.2, p. 384.

72. Petr Wrangel, *The Memoirs of General Wrangel, The Last Commander-in-Chief of the Russian National Army* (London: Williams and Norgate, 1929), p. 101.

73. 12th Army intelligence report for the period 15 September-25 October 1919, quoted in *Grazhdanskaia voina na Ukraine*, vol. 2, p. 457.

74. Belash and Belash, *Dorogi Nestora Makhno*, p. 307.

75. *Grazhdanskaia voina na Ukraine*, vol.2, pp. 488–9.

76. See inter alia Belash and Belash, *Dorogi Nestora Makhno*, p. 310; Palij, *The Anarchism of Nestor Makhno*, p. 196; Skirda, *Nestor Makhno, le cosaque de l'anarchie*, p. 177.

77. Verstiuk, *Makhnovshchyna*, pp. 176–7.

78. Aleksandrovsk is about 460 km. from Peregonovka by road; to have reached the city by the 29th, the insurgents would have had to cover about 150 km. a day for three days (Arshinov, *Istoriia makhnovskogo dvizheniia*, p. 142).

79. These are Ukrainian transcriptions of the place names. Belash and Belash, from whom these routes are taken, spell them in Russian (see *Dorogi Nestora Makhno*, p. 310).

80. In modern times there are three road routes from Uman' to Guliaipole, varying in distance from 345 to 371 miles. (Letter from Iuri Shevchenko, Khar'kov University, to the author, 24 May 1994).

81. Belash and Belash, *Dorogi Nestora Makhno*, pp. 310–14.

82. Volin, *La révolution inconnue*, p. 548.

83. Denikin, *Ocherki russkoi smuty* (Paris–Berlin, 1921–26), vol. 5, p. 234.

84. J. E. Hodgson, *With Denikin's Armies, Being a Description of the Cossack Counter-revolution in South Russia, 1918-1920* (London: Lincoln Williams, 1932), pp. 118–19.

85. According to the Faculty of Geology and Geography at Khar'kov University, the distance is 480 km. as the crow flies (Letter from Iuri Shevchenko, Khar'kov University, to the author, 24 May 1994).

86. Quotation from Verstiuk, *Makhnovshchyna*, p. 178.

87. 'Front i tyl Denikina', *Zvezda* (Ekaterinoslav), 15 November 1919, quoted by Verstiuk, *Makhnovshchyna*, pp. 180–81.

88. Quoted in Verstiuk, *Makhnovshchyna*, p. 178.

89. Verstiuk, *Makhnovshchyna*, p. 177.

90. Ossip Tsebry (Osip Tsebrii), *Memories of a Makhnovist Partisan* (London: Kate Sharpley Library, 1993), p. 16; O. S. Smyslov, *General Slashchev-Krymskii: pobedy, emigratsiia, vozvrashenie* (Moscow: Veche, 2013), p. 154.

91. Tsebry, *Memories of a Makhnovist Partisan*, pp. 9–10.

92. Order no.180, paragraph 7, in Trotsky, *Kak vooruzhalas revoliutsiia na voennoi rabote* (Moscow: Vysshii Voennyi Redak. Sovet, 1923-1925), vol. 2, book 1, p. 310.

93. Makhno recognised that 'detachments' using his name would be operating independently at various times, and encouraged them (Tsebry, *Memories of a Makhnovist Partisan*, p. 16).

94. Belash and Belash, *Dorogi Nestora Makhno*, pp. 310–14. Verstiuk argues that variations in estimates between 20,000 up to 100,000 fighters is evidence of the presence of irregulars, who would join combat units, fight in some engagements, and then go home (*Makhovshchyna*, pp. 186–7).

95. In October '... two officers and three companies of the 2nd Nikolaev Battalion treacherously crossed to the side of Makhno ...' Verstiuk, *Makhnovshchyna*, p. 179.

96. Belash and Belash, *Dorogi Nestora Makhno*, p. 395.

97. Litvinov, 'O chetvertom (oktiabr' 1920 goda) voenno-politicheskom soglashenii', pp. 321–2.

98. Denikin, *Ocherki russkoi smuty*, vol. 5, p. 234.

99. Kubanin, *Makhnovshchina*, pp. 88–9; Chop and Lyman, *Vol'nyi Berdiansk*, p. 177.

100. Chop and Lyman, *Vol'nyi Berdiansk*, p. 178.

101. Belash and Belash, *Dorogi Nestora Makhno*, p. 314.

102. Hodgson comments that he saw a White general's train of 44 coaches at about this time (*With Denikin's Armies*, p. 155).

103. Chop and Lyman, *Vol'nyi Berdiansk*, p. 180; Belash and Belash, *Dorogi Nestora Makhno*, p. 314.

104. Chop and Lyman, *Vol'nyi Berdiansk*, pp. 181–2.
105. Belash and Belash, *Dorogi Nestora Makhno*, p. 314.
106. Chop and Lyman, *Vol'nyi Berdiansk*, p. 186; Belash and Belash, *Dorogi Nestora Makhno*, p. 314.
107. Belash and Belash, *Dorogi Nestora Makhno*, p. 314.
108. Belash and Belash, *Dorogi Nestora Makhno*, p. 314.
109. Arshinov, *Istoriia makhnovskogo dvizheniia*, p. 105.
110. On Makhno and aviation see the article by Vladimir Chop, 'Aviatsiia Makhno', *Ekspeditsiia XXI* no. 10 (2008), available at www.makhno.ru/lit/chop/6.pdf, accessed 8 September 2016; and Chop and Lyman, *Vol'nyi Berdiansk*, p. 97–103, which repeats much the same information.
111. Captured officers were summarily shot (Chop and Lyman, *Vol'nyi Berdiansk*, p. 187).
112. Chop and Lyman, *Vol'nyi Berdiansk*, p. 190.
113. Chop and Lyman, *Vol'nyi Berdiansk*, p. 197.
114. This last detail, suggesting that Makhno was four days behind his vanguard, supports the argument for a spreading insurrection as well as an advancing army. J. Petrovich, 'Makhno: istoriia odnoho povstanskoho vatashka', *Nedilia*, no. 43 (1935), quoted by Peters, *Nestor Makhno*, p. 84.
115. As cited at the beginning of this chapter; see also Alexander Berkman, *The Bolshevik Myth: Diary, 1920-1922* (London: Hutchinson, 1925), p. 194.
116. By the end of October, Denikin had moved two divisions and three Cossack brigades with other units to the rear, 'regardless of the serious situation at the front' (Denikin, *Ocherki russkoi smuty*, vol. 5, pp. 234–35); cf. Hodgson, *With Denikin's Armies*, pp. 119–20. In November he moved another regiment to the rear in the Kiev sector (*Grazhdanskaia voina na Ukraine*, vol. 2, p. 508).
117. Mawdsley argues that it was the Mamontov raid which changed Red opposition to the 'outdated' and 'elitist' concept of the cavalry army into enthusiastic utilisation of it (*The Russian Civil War*, pp. 220–21). Budenny's successes convinced them they were right.
118. *Grazhdanskaia voina na Ukraine*, vol. 2, p. 572.
119. The text of the first report, dated January 1920, was published in *Letopis' Revoliutsii*, no. 4 (1925), pp. 95–8, and reprinted in A. Ia. Pashchenko (ed.), *Grazhdanskaia voina na Ekaterinoslavshchine, fevral' 1918-1920 gg.: dokumenty i materialy* (Dnepropetrovsk: Izd-vo Promin, 1968), pp. 184–8. A summary of a second report survives in a newspaper account dated 23 February 1920, published in *Izvestiia Ekaterinoslavskogo Gubernskogo Revoliutsionnogo Komiteta* no.38 (29 February 1920), and reprinted by Pashchenko, pp. 205–6.
120. Pashchenko (ed.), *Grazhdanskaia voina na Ekaterinoslavshchine*, p. 184.
121. Denikin, *Ocherki russkoi smuty*, vol. 5, p. 235.
122. Volin, *La révolution inconnue*, p. 595 and 621.
123. Denikin, *Ocherki russkoi smuty*, vol. 5, p. 235.
124. *Grazhdanskaia voina na Ukraine*, vol. 2, p. 484.
125. *Grazhdanskaia voina na Ukraine*, vol. 2, pp. 474, 616–17.
126. Arshinov's text is full of complaints about spies and agents provocateurs (*Istoriia makhnovskogo dvizheniia*, passim).
127. Pashchenko (ed.), *Grazhdanskaia voina na Ekaterinoslavshchine*, p. 205.
128. The Central Statistical Board of Ukraine estimate for 1920 was 1,910,000, against V. A. Arnautov's figure of 1,782,500 (in *Golod i deti na Ukraine* [Khar'kov: Redaktsionno-Izdatel'skii Otdel NKP, 1922], quoted by Ivan Herasymovych, *Holod na*

Ukraini [Berlin: Ukr. Slovo, 1922], p. 9). The breakdown of the city's population by nationality and age is also from Herasymovich, p. 12.

129. Pashchenko (ed.), *Grazhdanskaia voina na Ekaterinoslavshchine*, p. 185.
130. Belash and Belash, *Dorogi Nestora Makhno*, pp. 318–19.
131. Belash and Belash, *Dorogi Nestora Makhno*, p. 319.
132. *Put' k Svobode*, no. 7 (12 October 1919), as cited by Belash and Belash, *Dorogi Nestora Makhno*, p. 319.
133. For Aleksandr Timoshchuk, newspapers 'of all orientations' are 'the *most important* sources' of all for the study of *makhnovtsy* formations (*Anarkho-kommunisticheskie formirovaniia N. Makhno, sentiabr' 1918-avgust 1921* [Simferopol': Tavriia, 1996], p. 13, emphasis added.
134. V. N. Chop, 'Gazety makhnovs'koho rukhu', available at www.makhno.ru/lit/chop/6.php, accessed 19 August 2019.
135. Chop, 'Gazety makhnovs'koho rukhu'.
136. Chop, 'Gazety makhnovs'koho rukhu'.
137. Belash and Belash, *Dorogi Nestora Makhno*, p. 354.
138. Chop, 'Gazety makhnovs'koho rukhu'.
139. Chop includes several extracts from *Put' k Svobode* as appendices to his article on the press ('Gazety makhnovs'koho rukhu'). Viktor Danilov and Teodor Shanin reprint issues nos.5 and 11 of *Put' k Svobode*, and no.4 of *Vol'nyi Berdiansk* in their collection *Nestor Makhno: krest'ianskoe dvizheniia na Ukraine, 1918-1921. dokumenty e materialy* (Moscow: Rossiiskaia Politicheskaia Entsiklopediia, 2006), pp. 205–23. Chop and Lyman, *Vol'nyi Berdiansk*, also include newpaper materials in their appendices, pp. 406–80.
140. Volin, *La révolution inconnue*, pp. 603–20.
141. For the texts of the resolutions, see Danilov and Shanin (eds) *Nestor Makhno*, documents nos.145–6, pp. 226–35, and Belash and Belash, *Dorogi Nestora Makhno*, pp. 321–6, quoting various issues of *Put' k Svobode*.
142. Volin, *La révolution inconnue*, p. 683.
143. Yaroslavsky, *History of anarchism in Russia* (New York: International Publishers, 1937), p. 71.
144. The Russian word *razvedka* means intelligence service; the other name translates as Commission of Anti-Makhno Activities (Kubanin, *Makhnovshchina*, pp. 116–17; Footman, *Civil War in Russia*, p. 288). See also Viacheslav Azarov, *Kontrrazvedka* [counter-intelligence]: *The Story of the Makhnovist Intelligence Service* (Edmonton: Black Cat Press, 2009). On White intelligence, see Viktor Bortnevski, *White Intelligence and Counter-intelligence During the Russian Civil War* (Pittsburgh: Center for Russian and East European Studies, 1995).
145. The report adds that 22 officers were shot that day, ten arrested and many others wounded (Pashchenko (ed.), *Grazhdanskaia voina na Ekaterinoslavshchine*, pp. 177–8).
146. Verstiuk, *Makhnovshchyna*, p. 183.
147. Verstiuk, *Makhnovshchyna*, p. 183.
148. A detailed account of local trade union activity in Ekaterinoslav during late 1919, by one Brin, is printed in Pashchenko (ed.), *Grazhdanskaia voina na Ekaterinoslavshchine*, pp. 202–4.
149. Arshinov, *Istoriia makhnovskogo dvizheniia*, pp. 145–6. This incident may have been the origin for Yaroslavsky's contemptuously-told story that Makhno advised the Aleksandrovsk rail workers to get money or food from their passengers: '[…] we don't need the railways, and if you do then get bread from those who want your railway […]' (*History of Anarchism in Russia*, p. 72).

150. Pashchenko (ed.), *Grazhdanskaia voina na Ekaterinoslavshchine*, pp. 177–8.
151. Arshinov, *Istoriia makhnovskogo dvizheniia*, p. 146; Pashchenko (ed.), *Grazhdanskaia voina na Ekaterinoslavshchine*, p. 186.
152. Datelined Ekaterinoslav, 5 November 1919 (Arshinov, *Istoriia makhnovskogo dvizheniia*, pp. 151–2).
153. Levko's reports show that the absorption of *makhnovshchina* into the Red Army remained a constant Bolshevik objective throughout 1919 and 1920 (Pashchenko (ed.), *Grazhdanskaia voina na Ekaterinoslavshchine*, pp. 186, 205).
154. Verstiuk, *Makhnovshchyna*, p. 187.
155. Pashchenko (ed.), *Grazhdanskaia voina na Ekaterinoslavshchine*, p. 205.
156. Pashchenko (ed.), *Grazhdanskaia voina na Ekaterinoslavshchine*, pp. 186–7.
157. Levko's first report concludes with an account of the difficulties faced by the underground organization in converting Soviet rubles into Denikin rubles in order to continue subversive work (Pashchenko (ed.), *Grazhdanskaia voina na Ekaterinoslavshchine*, pp. 187–8).
158. Pashchenko (ed.), *Grazhdanskaia voina na Ekaterinoslavshchine*, p. 206.

CHAPTER 6   RED VERSUS WHITE, RED VERSUS GREEN:
THE BOLSHEVIKS ASSERT CONTROL

1. Vasilii Golovanov, *Nestor Makhno* (Moscow: Molodaia Gvardiia, 2013), p. 283.
2. A. V. Belash and V. F. Belash, *Dorogi Nestora Makhno: istoricheskoe povestvovanie* (Kiev: Proza, 1993), p. 24.
3. Golovanov, *Nestor Makhno*, p. 282.
4. Golovanov, *Nestor Makhno*, p. 298.
5. Referring to the SR-linked Borot'bist (or 'Struggle') group, the UKP(b) (as opposed to the KP[b]U), Trotsky recommended in December that 'implacable retribution' be meted out to the '*makhnovtsy*' in its ranks. Jan Meyer (ed.), *The Trotsky papers* (The Hague: Mouton, 1964–1971), vol. 1, pp. 790–91. The term *makhnovets* is occasionally used in Russian even today as a term of opprobrium, meaning an undisciplined or badly-behaved person.
6. Lenin, *Polnoe sobranie sochinenii*, 5th edn. (Moscow: Izdat. Politicheskoi Literatury, 1958–65), vol. 40, p. 260, emphasis added. See also *Lektsii po istorii KPSS*, issue 2 (Moscow: Izdat. Mysl', 1966), p. 219; *Ocherki istorii KPSS*, 5th edn. (Moscow: Izdat. Politicheskoi Literatury, 1971), p. 206.
7. Litvinov is scathing: 'the final result of Red Army military policy … at the end of 1919 and the beginning of 1920 were as follows: on the internal front, mistakes … led to an increase in Makhno's political influence, and on the external front the Red Army missed the opportunity to defeat the Whites completely in early 1920'. See Vladimir Litvinov, 'O chetvertom (oktiabr' 1920 g.) voenno-politicheskom soglashenii mezhdu Revoliutsionno-Povstancheskoi Armiei (Makhnovtsev) i kommunisticheskim pravitel'stvom RSFSR,' *International Review of Social History*, vol. 32, no. 3 (1987), p. 334.
8. Ia. Slashchev, *Krym v 1920 g.: otryvki iz vospominanii* (Moscow, Leningrad: Gos. Izd-vo, 1923), p. 24.
9. Jonathan Smele, *The 'Russian' Civil Wars, 1916-1925: Ten Years that Shook the World* (New York: Oxford University Press, 2017), p. 53.
10. Quoted by Laura Engelstein, *Russia in Flames: War, Revolution, Civil War, 1914-1921* (New York: Oxford University Press, 2018), p. 551; W. Bruce Lincoln says that Slashchev had 'crossed that fragile boundary that separates eccentricity

from madness' (*Red Victory: A History of the Russian Civil War* [New York: Simon and Schuster, 1989], pp. 436–7).

11. Slashchev, *Krym v 1920 g.*, pp. 24–5; W. H. Chamberlin, *The Russian Revolution, 1917-1921*, new ed. (New York: Grosset and Dunlap, 1965), vol. 2, p. 281.

12. Vladimir Litvinov, 'O chetvertom (oktiabr' 1920 g.) voenno-politicheskom soglashenii', p. 320.

13. A. I. Denikin, *The White Army* (Cambridge: Ian Faulkner, 1992), p. 337 [emphasis added].

14. V. V. Popov, 'Dlia etogo nado byt' bol'shevikom,' in P. I. Iakir and Iu. A. Geller, *Komandarm Iakir: vospominaniia druzei i sovratnikov* (Moscow: Voennoe Izdat. Ministerstva Oborony SSSR, 1963), p. 234; Michael Palij, *The Anarchism of Nestor Makhno, 1918-1921: An Aspect of the Ukrainian Revolution* (Seattle: University of Washington Press), p. 209.

15. Petr Arshinov, *Istoriia makhnovskogo dvizheniia, 1918-1921* (Berlin: Gruppy Russkikh Anarkhistov v Germanii, 1923), p. 157.

16. See document no. 666, dated 8 January, in *Grazhdanskaia voina na Ukraine, 1918-1920: sbornik dokumentov i materialov* (Kiev: Izdat. Naukova Dumka, 1967), vol. 2, p. 635; also, Arshinov, *Istoriia makhnovskogo dvizheniia*, p. 157. Palij comments that 'the author of the order realised that there was no real war between the Poles and the Bolsheviks at that time' (*The Anarchism of Nestor Makhno*, p. 210).

17. Uberovich to Iakir, quoted in Aleksandr Timoshchuk, *Anarkho-kommunistich-eskie formirovaniia N. Makhno, sentiabr' 1917-avgust 1921* (Simferopol': Tavriia, 1996), pp. 98–9.

18. Litvinov, 'O chetvertom (oktiabr' 1920 g.) voenno-politicheskom soglashenii', p. 332.

19. There was no expectation on the Bolshevik side that Makhno would obey the order (Litvinov, 'O chetvertom (oktiabr' 1920 g.) voenno-politicheskom soglash-enii', pp. 332–3). David Footman points out that this tactic was used successfully with 'difficult partisan leaders' in Siberia on other occasions (*Civil war in Russia* [London: Faber and Faber, 1961], p. 291).

20. Arshinov, *Istoriia makhnovskogo dvizheniia*, pp. 157–8.

21. K. David Patterson, 'Typhus and its control in Russia, 1870-1940,' *Medical History* vol. 37 (1993), p. 361.

22. A. Sysin, 'Epidemii v Rossii v 1914-22 godakh,' *Vrachebnaya gazeta* no. 10–11 (1927), pp. 265–9; L. A. Tarassevich, 'Epidemii poslednikh let v Rossii', *Obshchest-vennyi Vrach* no. 1 (1922), pp. 43–50, quoted by Patterson 'Typhus and its control in Russia, 1870-1940,' p. 376.

23. Patterson 'Typhus and its control in Russia, 1870-1940,' p. 376.

24. Lenin reporting to the 8th All-Russian Conference of the Russian Communist Party, *Collected works* (Moscow: Progress Publishers, 1960–1971), vol. 30, p. 185.

25. Lenin at the 7th All-Russian Congress of Soviets, *Collected works*, vol. 30, p. 228.

26. In 1919 urban mortality rose to the 'the astounding rate of 80 per thousand (*owing principally to the typhus epidemic*)' (Daniel Brower, 'The city in danger: the civil war and the Russian urban population,' in Diane Koenker, William Rosenberg and Ronald Grigor Suny [eds], *Party, state and society in the Russian civil war: explorations in social history* [Bloomington: Indiana University Press, 1989], p. 62, emphasis added).

27. *Pravda* (14 March 1920), quoted by Chamberlin, *The Russian revolution*, vol. 2, p. 337.

28. Pitirim Sorokin wrote in his diary: 'today I caught an insect on my body. Is it a typhus louse or not? ... If it is typhus, that means the end of me. I am too weak

to live through the fever'. *Leaves from a Russian Diary* (New York: E. P. Dutton, 1924), p. 234, quoted by Lincoln, *Red Victory*, p. 64.

29. Patterson 'Typhus and its Control in Russia, 1870-1940', p. 374.
30. Victor Peters, *Nestor Makhno* (Winnipeg: Echo Books, 1970), p. 62, quotes an account of insurgents having their hair combed to remove lice, which were then crushed with a fingernail. He quotes an estimate that in one village occupied by the *makhnovtsy* between 11 and 15 percent of the population died of typhus (p. 67).
31. Arshinov, *Istoriia makhnovskogo dvizheniia*, p. 157. Slashchev, however, describes some fierce fighting (*Krym v 1920 g.*, p. 24).
32. Makhno was so ill in January 1920 that he had to appoint Kalishnikov as acting commander of the insurgent army in his place (Volodymyr Chop and Ihor Lyman, *Vol'nyi Berdiansk: misto v period anarkhizms'koho sotsial'noho eksperymentu, 1918-1921 r.* [Zaporizhzhia: RA Tandem-U, 2007], p. 40).
33. Golovanov, *Nestor Makhno*, p. 280; see also Arshinov, *Istoriia makhnovskogo dvizheniia*, p. 159.
34. Arshinov, *Istoriia makhnovskogo dvizheniia*, p. 158.
35. A. Ia. Pashchenko (ed.), *Grazhdanskaia voina na Ekaterinoslavshchine, fevral' 1918-1920 gg.: dokumenty i materialy* (Dnepropetrovsk: Izd-vo Promin, 1968), pp. 210–11; Viktor Danilov and Teodor Shanin (eds), *Nestor Makhno: krest'ianskoe dvizheniia na Ukraine, 1918-1921. dokumenty e materialy* (Moscow: Rossiiskaia Politicheskaia Entsiklopediia, 2006), document no. 193, p. 301; *Grazhdanskaia voina na Ukraine*, doc. 668, vol. 2, pp. 636–7.
36. Timoshchuk, *Anarkho-kommunisticheskie formirovaniia N. Makhno*, p. 99.
37. This step was presumably taken to placate the Bolsheviks (Golovanov, *Nestor Makhno*, p. 314).
38. Ordzhonikidze was working for the RVS of the 14th Army at the time (quoted by L. Nikulin, 'Gibel' makhnovshchiny', *Znamia* no. 3 [1941], p. 181).
39. Pashchenko (ed.), *Grazhdanskaia voina na Ekaterinoslavshchine*, p. 220.
40. Report dated 'not earlier than 25 January' in Pashchenko (ed.), *Grazhdanskaia voina na Ekaterinoslavshchine*, p. 213.
41. L. J. van Rossum (ed.), 'Proclamations of the Machno movement, 1920', *International Review of Social History* vol. 13, no. 2 (1968), p. 254 (capitalisation in the original).
42. The Russian word *bezvlastie* (anarchy) is used instead of the neutral *anarkhizm* (anarchism).
43. *Zolotopogonniki* — slang for officers in the Imperial Russian Army before 1917 and for White Guard officers during the civil war, with reference to the gold braid on their uniforms.
44. Originally published by the Agitprop Soviet of the Ekaterinoslav Military Revolutionary Committee, the Russian text of this document, 'Doloi Makhnovshchinu', (Down with *makhnovshchina*) is printed in Pashchenko (ed.), *Grazhdanskaia voina na Ekaterinoslavshchine*, pp. 217–18. It was also published in the Khar'kov *Izvestiia* in April 1919 (Danilov and Shanin (eds), *Nestor Makhno*, p. 138). See also Gosudartsvennyi Arkhiv Dnepropetrovskoi Oblasti (hereafter GADO), *N. Makhno i makhnovskoe dvizhenie: iz istorii povstancheskogo dvizheniia v Ekaterinoslavskoi gubernii. Sbornik dokumentov i materialov* (Dnepropetrovsk: AO DAES, 1993), pp. 33–4.
45. Footman, *Civil War in Russia*, p. 291.
46. Arshinov, *Istoriia makhnovskogo dvizheniia*, p. 160.
47. Golovanov, *Nestor Makhno*, p. 297.

48. Trotsky, *Kak vooruzhalas revoliutsiia na voennoi rabote* (Moscow: Vysshii Voennyi Redak. Sovet, 1923-25), vol. 2, book 1, pp. 308-10.

49. Arshinov, *Istoriia makhnovskogo dvizheniia*, pp. 160-61.

50. I. Ia. Trifonov, *Klassy i klassovaia bor'ba v SSSR v nachale NEPA (1921-1923 gg.) Chast' 1: Bor'ba s vooruzhennoi kulatskoi kontrrevoliutsiei* (Leningrad: Izdat. Leningradskogo Universiteta, 1964), p. 126.

51. Trifonov, *Klassy i klassovaia bor'ba v SSSR*, pp. 126-7.

52. Belash and Belash, *Dorogi Nestora Makhno*, p. 349.

53. Belash and Belash, *Dorogi Nestora Makhno*, p. 349.

54. Felix Schnell, 'Tear Them Apart and Be Done with it: The Ataman-Leadership of Nestor Makhno as a Culture of Violence', *Ab Imperio*, vol. 3 (2008), p. 195. Schnell's case study is based on an account of the hacking to death with sabres of captured Hetman soldiers in 1918, as recounted in N. V. Gerasimenko's notoriously unreliable text *Bat'ko Makhno* (he cites a 1990 Moscow reprint). Regardless, Schnell's article addresses important theoretical questions about terror and violence as a social phenomenon in the civil war and in general.

55. For 'some conceptual remarks' in the context of *makhnovshchina*, see Schnell, 'Tear them apart and be done with it,' pp. 197-200.

56. Mikhail Akulov, 'War without Fronts: Atamans and Commissars in Ukraine, 1917-1919' (Ph. D. dissertation, Harvard University, 2013), p. 31.

57. John Reshetar, *The Ukrainian Revolution, 1917-1920: A Study in Nationalism* (Princeton: Princeton University Press, 1952), p. 299. Reshetar prints an English translation of the treaty between Petliura and the Poles on 21 April 1920 (pp. 301-2).

58. Reshetar, *The Ukrainian Revolution, 1917-1920*, p. 299.

59. There was skirmishing against the *makhnovtsy* at this time (*Kievshchina v gody grazhdanskoi voiny i inostrannoi voenoi interventsii, 1918-1920 gg.: sbornik dokumentov e materialov* [Kiev: Gospolitizdat USSR, 1962], pp. 397-8).

60. Report dated 13 April 1920, in *Grazhdanskaia voina na Ukraine*, vol. 3, p. 41.

61. Danilov and Shanin (eds), *Nestor Makhno*, docs.203-64, pp. 323-474.

62. See chapter 9, February to September, pp. 381-448, and chapter 10, September to November, pp. 449-93 in Belash and Belash, *Dorogi Nestora Makhno*.

63. Published in Russian as a pamphlet, *40 dnei v Guliai-Pole: dnevnik matushki Galiny, zheny Bat'ki Makhno* (Moscow: Tsentr «Istorik» pri Sovetskoi Assotsiatsii Molodykh Istorikov, 1990). See also Danilov and Shanin (eds), *Nestor Makhno*, doc.454, pp. 828-38.

64. See the Ukrainian text 'Shchodennyk Halyny Kuz'menko,' in *Berezil'* [Khar'kov] no. 3 (1991), pp. 133-43.

65. It was supposedly quoted as early as 1921 – see R. P. Eideman, *Bor'ba s kulatskim vosstaniem i banditizmom* (Khar'kov: Politupr. vsekh vooruzh. sil Ukrainy i Kryma, 1921), quoted by V. N. Litvinov, 'Neraskrytaia taina dnevnika zheny Makhno,' *Obshchina* (Moscow) no. 43 (1990), pp. 6-9, available online at www.makhno.ru/st/98.php, accessed 29 February 2020. I have not seen the Eideman pamphlet.

66. M. Kubanin, *Makhnovshchina: krest'ianskoe dvizhenie v stepnoi Ukraine v gody grazhdanskoi voiny* (Leningrad: Izdat. Priboi, 1927), p. 145. See also Ia. Iakovlev, *Russkii anarkhizm v velikoi russkoi revoliutsii* (Moscow: Gosizdat., 1921), p. 30; and E. Yaroslavsky, *History of Anarchism in Russia* (New York: International Publishers, 1937), pp. 73-4, quoting extracts dating from February and March, but also, improbably, from June, July, August and December 1920.

67. Arshinov, *Istoriia makhnovskogo dvizheniia*, p. 219.

68. Sergei Semanov, *Pod chernym znamenem: zhizn' i smert' Nestora Makhno* (Moscow: Tovarishchestvo Vozrozhlenie, 1990), pp. 44–5, emphasis added (see also his more or less identical publication *Makhno kak on est': dokumental'no-istoricheskaia povest'* (Moscow: Tovarishchestvo Sovetskikh Pisatelei, 1991), part 2, pp. 9–10.

69. Litvinov, 'Neraskrytaia taina dnevnika zheny Makhno.'

70. Danilov and Shanin (eds), *Nestor Makhno*, pp. 829 and 832.

71. Belash and Belash, *Dorogi Nestora Makhno*, p. 299.

72. T. F. Ermolenko and O. M. Morozova, *Pogony i budenovki: grazhdanskaia voina glazami belykh ofitserov i krasnoarmeitsev* (Moscow: Rossiiskii Gumanitarnyi Nauchnyi Fond, 2013), p. 5.

73. Ermolenko and Morozova, *Pogony i budenovki*, p. 6. These authors confirm that keeping a diary was not unusual during the civil war (p. 11).

74. Volin, *La révolution inconnue, 1917-1921: documentation inédite sur la révolution russe* (Paris: Les Amis de Voline, 1947), p. 682.

75. Richard Abel, *The Ciné Goes to town: French Cinema 1896-1914*, rev.ed. (Berkeley: University of California Press, 1998), pp. 117–21. In a footnote, Abel says the earliest pornographic cinemas in France date to 1906 (p. 496, fn.46).

76. Chop and Lyman use the adjective '*pornohrafichnyi*' to describe these films (Chop and Lyman, *Vol'nyi Berdiansk*, p. 131).

77. Chop and Lyman, *Vol'nyi Berdiansk*, pp. 131–35.

78. A Baltic German by ancestry, Wrangel (Russian: *Vrangel'*) was a conservative monarchist, but more realistic and more flexible than Denikin. Trained as a staff officer, he had been a cavalry commander in a Cossack unit; he was bitterly anti-communist, and showed no mercy to his enemies.

79. The White Guard officer V. Obolenskii uses the phrase in a brief discussion of Wrangel's policies in his memoir *Krym pri Vrangele: memuary belogvardeitsa* (Moscow: Gos. Izd-vo, 1928), p. 7.

80. Petr Wrangel, *The Memoirs of General Wrangel: The Last Commander-in-chief of the Russian National Army* (London: Williams and Norgate, 1929), p. 142.

81. Wrangel, *The Memoirs*, p. 254.

82. Danilov and Shanin (eds), *Nestor Makhno*, doc. 229, p. 370; doc.107 in *Grazhdanskaia voina na Ukraine*, vol. 3, pp. 115–16.

83. This was denied by the Bolsheviks after the Starobel'sk agreement in October 1920, but has been repeated ever since, especially in Soviet general histories of the Stalin period: the *History of the Communist Party of the Soviet Union (Bolsheviks): short course* (Moscow: Foreign Languages Publishing House, 1939) says ambiguously that Makhno 'assisted' Wrangel (pp. 242–43); the official *Istoriia Ukrains'koi RSR* (Kiev: Akademiia Nauk USSR, 1953–1958), vol. 2, p. 189, says there was a formal alliance, an assertion that is repeated without correction in the second edition of the same work ([Kiev, 1967], vol. 2, p. 138).

84. This was recognised even in Soviet accounts before the 1930s: e.g. A. Bubnov, S. Kamenev and R. Eidemanis, *Grazhdanskaia voina, 1918-1921 gg.* (Moscow: Izd-vo Voennyi Vestnik, 1928–30), vol. 3, pp. 511–12.

85. Pavlo Shandruk (ed.), *Ukrains'ko-moskovs'ka viina v 1920 r. v dokumentakh* (Warsaw, 1933–), vol. 1, p. 97.

86. *The Times* [London] (3 August 1920), p. 9.

87. *The Times* [London] (20 August 1920), p. 9.

88. Such sentiments are clearly irreconcilable with Makhno's political positions. 'Soiuz Vrangel'-Makhno,' *Volia Rossii* (Prague) (25 September 1920).

89. 'Soiuz Vrangel'-Makhno.'

90. The Bolsheviks knew that this was propaganda. In a telephone conversation in late September with a commander of the *makhnovtsy*, the Bolshevik representative remarks that 'Baron Wrangel is boasting abroad and in the White newspapers in Crimea that Makhno is his ally' (Danilov and Shanin (eds), *Nestor Makhno*, p. 475 quoting a transcript).

91. *Iz istoriia grazhdanskoi voiny v SSSR: sbornik dokumentov i materialov, 1918-1922* (Moscow: Izdat Sovetskaia Rossiia, 1960–61), vol. 3, p. 147. The original source is given as a document from a captured German archive.

92. Document dated 30 October 1920, in GADO, *N. Makhno i makhnovskoe dvizhenie*, document no. 30, pp. 39–40.

93. GADO, *N. Makhno i makhnovskoe dvizhenie*, p. 40.

94. *Kommunist* no. 234 (20 October 1920), reprinted in *Grazhdanskaia voina na Ukraine*, vol. 3, p. 642; see also Leon Trotsky, *Kak vooruzhalas' revoliutsiia na voennoi rabote* (Moscow: Vysshii Voennyi Redak. Sovet, 1923–1925) vol. 2, book 2, p. 214. The piece appeared in other Khar'kov newspapers.

95. Shandruk (ed.), *Ukrains'ko-moskovs'ka viina*, vol. 1, p. 97. The *karbovanets* is a Ukrainian coin.

96. 'Makhnovskie den'gi,' *Krasnyi Boets* no. 209 (22 October 1920), printed in Belash and Belash, *Dorogi Nestora Makhno*, p. 466.

97. W. H. Chamberlin, *The Ukraine: A Submerged Nation* (New York: Macmillan, 1944), p. 50. Alexandre Skirda repeats some similar anecdotes (*Nestor Makhno, le cosaque de l'anarchie: la lutte pour les soviets libres en Ukraine, 1917-1921* [Paris: A.S., 1982], p. 347.

98. Mikhail Khodjakov, *Money of the Russian Revolution* (Newcastle-upon-Tyne: Cambridge Scholars Publishing, 2014), p. xi.

99. Images of such notes are easily found on the Internet, but their authenticity remains unconfirmed. See the two articles: V. Kutilin, 'Eshche o den'gakh Makhno,' available at www.makhno.ru/st/21.php; and Valeryi Stepkin and Eduard Shteinbuk, 'Na tsi groshi ne kupysh i voshi: istorii o tom, kak Nestor Ivanovich Makhno den'gi pechatal,' (24 January 1998), available at www.makhno.ru/st/17.php.

100. Iuryi Kravets, 'Znamena Povstancheskoi Armii N. Makhno, 1918-1921 gg'. *Muzeinyi Visnyk* [Zaporozh'e] no. 7 (2007), available online at www.makhno.ru/st/109.pdf, accessed 29 February 2020. Two of the flags survive in a museum in Ukraine.

101. Belash and Belash, *Dorogi Nestora Makhno*, p. 350.

102. Bullet point no. 10 (Danilov and Shanin (eds), *Nestor Makhno*, p. 129).

103. Belash and Belash, *Dorogi Nestora Makhno*, p. 350.

104. Danilov and Shanin (eds), *Nestor Makhno*, pp. 824–5.

105. Belash and Belash, *Dorogi Nestora Makhno*, p. 351.

106. See e.g. H. J. Goldberg, 'The Anarchists View the Soviet Regime, 1918-1922,' (Ph.D. dissertation, University of Wisconsin, 1973), especially pp. 155–8. For Goldman's reminiscences, see *My Disillusionment in Russia* (New York: Doubleday, Page, 1923); *My Further Disillusionment in Russia* (New York: Doubleday, 1924); and *Living My Life*. Berkman also published an account of this period: *The Bolshevik Myth: Diary 1920-1922* (London: Hutchinson, 1925).

107. Goldman, *Living My Life*, vol. 2, p. 765; Angelica Balabanoff, *My Life as a Rebel*, 3rd edn. (New York: Greenwood Press, 1968), p. 255.

108. Goldman, *Living My Life*, vol. 2, pp. 810–11.

109. Berkman, *The Bolshevik myth*, p. 196.

110. Goldman, *Living My Life*, vol. 2, p. 769.

111. Berkman, *The Bolshevik myth*, p. 177.

112. Goldman, *Living My Life*, vol. 2, pp. 829-31.
113. Berkman, *The Bolshevik Myth*, pp. 184-85.
114. *The Bolshevik Myth*, p. 187.
115. *The Bolshevik Myth*, p. 188. Gotman was killed by the Bolsheviks in the autumn of 1920 while on his way to Starobel'sk, then Makhno's headquarters (A. Gorelik and others, *Goneniia na anarkhizm v sovetskoi Rossii* [Berlin: Izdat. Gruppy russkikh anarkhistov v Germanii, 1922], p. 29).
116. *Grazhdanskaia voina na Ukraine*, vol. 3, p. 92.
117. Report covering the period up to 1 August, in *Grazhdanskaia voina na Ukraine*, vol. 3, p. 329.
118. *Grazhdanskaia voina na Ukraine*, vol. 3, p. 338.
119. *Grazhdanskaia voina na Ukraine*, vol. 3, p. 502.
120. *Grazhdanskaia voina na Ukraine*, vol. 3, p. 531.
121. *The Times* [London] (20 August 1920), p. 9. Again, the distinction between regulars and irregulars is blurred in the estimation of Makhno's troop strength.
122. Danilov and Shanin (eds), *Nestor Makhno*, p. 24.
123. Belash and Belash, *Dorogi Nestora Makhno*, p. 444.
124. *Grazhdanskaia voina na Ukraine*, vol. 3, p. 408.
125. *Grazhdanskaia voina na Ukraine*, vol. 3, pp. 450-51.
126. Letter dated 24 August from the Directory's 'Ministry of Foreign Affairs', in *Grazhdanskaia voina na Ukraine*, vol. 3, pp. 409-10.
127. *Grazhdanskaia voina na Ukraine*, vol. 3, p. 480.
128. *Grazhdanskaia voina na Ukraine*, vol. 3, p. 480.
129. The report, from the commander of the Dnepr Military Flotilla, assumes that the Jews were killed, but provides no evidence for this. The Flotilla later used river patrol-boats against the *makhnovtsy* (*Moriaki v bor'be za vlast' sovetov na Ukraine: noiabr' 1917-1920 gg.* [Kiev: Akademiia Nauk USSR, 1963], p. 385).
130. *Moriaki v bor'be za vlast' sovetov na Ukraine*, p. 501.
131. *Grazhdanskaia voina na Ukraine*, vol. 3, p. 522.
132. *Grazhdanskaia voina na Ukraine*, vol. 3, p. 526.
133. Viacheslav Azarov, *Starobel'skoe soglashenie* (Odessa: DP Nabat, 2011), p. 3, emphasis added.
134. *Komitety Bednoty*, abbreviated to *kombedy* in Russian; *komnezamy* or *komnezamozhi* in Ukrainian. *Nezamozhnik* means 'poor peasant' in Ukrainian.
135. Stalin, *Collected Works* (Moscow: Foreign Languages Publishing House, 1952-55), vol. 4, p. 447; see also *Chetverta Konferentsiia Komunistychnoi Partii (bil'shovykiv) Ukrainy, 17-23 bereznia 1920 r. Stenograma* (Kiev: Vidavnychyi Dim Al'ternatyvi, 2003).
136. The term was originally slang for a rural money-lender.
137. James Mace, 'The *komitety nezamozhnykh selyan* and the structure of Soviet rule in the Ukrainian countryside, 1920-1933,' *Soviet Studies*, vol. 35 no. 4 (1983), p. 488.
138. Charles Bettelheim, *Class Struggles in the USSR. First Period: 1917-1923* (New York: Monthly Review Press, 1976), p. 223. On conceptual difficulties around the idea of 'differentiation, see Heinz-Dietrich Löwe, 'Differentiation in Russian Peasant Society: Causes and Trends, 1880-1905,' in Roger Bartlett (ed.), *Land Commune and Peasant Community in Russia: Communal Forms in Imperial and Early Soviet Society* (London: Palgrave Macmillan, 1990), especially pp. 173-4. See also E. H. Carr, *The Bolshevik revolution, 1917-1923* (Harmondsworth: Penguin, 1966), vol. 2, pp. 161-3.

139. Viktor Aver'ev, *Komitety bednoty* (Moscow: Sel'chozgiz, 1933; 2 vols.), quoted by T. Shanin, *The Awkward Class: Political Sociology of Peasantry in a Developing Society* (Oxford: Oxford University Press, 1972), p. 147.
140. Carr, *The Bolshevik Revolution*, vol. 2, pp. 161–3.
141. G. Littlejohn, *A Sociology of the Soviet Union* (London: Macmillan, 1984), pp. 47–8.
142. Littlejohn, *A Sociology of the Soviet Union* p. 49.
143. Bohdan Krawchenko, *Social Change and National Consciousness in Twentieth Century Ukraine* (London: Palgrave Macmillan, 1985), pp. 65–6.
144. Krawchenko, *Social Change and National Consciousness in Twentieth Century Ukraine*, p. 61.
145. The British would not permit even private support from business. The French discussed aid, but did not in practice provide it (Evan Mawdsley, *The Russian Civil War* [Boston: Unwin Hyman, 1987], p. 267).
146. Richard Luckett, *The White Generals: An Account of the White Movement and the Russian Civil War* (London: Longman, 1971), p. 368. Lincoln puts the cavalry figure much higher at 11,795 (see I. S. Korotkov, *Razgrom Vrangelia* [Moscow: Voen. Izd-vo Ministerstva Oborony SSSR, 1955], p. 206, quoted in *Red victory*, p. 441).
147. Arshinov, *Istoriia makhnovskogo dvizheniia*, p. 171.
148. *Nabat* quoted by G. Maksimov, *The Guillotine at Work: Twenty Years of Terror and Documents* (Chicago: Chicago Section of the Alexander Berkman Fund, 1940), p. 459.
149. George Woodcock and I. Avakumovic, *The Anarchist Prince* [London: Boardman, 1950), p. 428.

CHAPTER 7   THE LAST ACT: ALLIANCE AT STAROBEL'SK,
WRANGEL'S DEFEAT, AND BETRAYAL AT PEREKOP

1. *Atamanshchina* might have been in some ways a 'workable manifestation' of such a left coalition: Mikhail Akulov, 'War Without Fronts: Atamans and Commissars in Ukraine, 1917-1919', (Ph.D. dissertation, Harvard University, 2013), p. 40. Political *blocs* rather than *party* affiliation were often 'more meaningful and more important [than] individual party politics' (Badcock, 'The Russian revolution: broadening understandings of 1917', *History Compass*, vol. 6 no. 1 [2008], p. 246).
2. A. Bubnov, S. Kamenev and R. Eidemanis, *Grazhdanskaia voina, 1918-1921 gg.* (Moscow: Izd-vo Voennyi Vestnik, 1928–30), vol. 3, pp. 511–12. Aleksandr Shubin believes Makhno understood that his presence behind the front was objectively helping the Whites (*Makhno i makhnovskoe dvizhenie* [Moscow: Izdat. MIK, 1998], p. 136).
3. Viacheslav Azarov, *Starobel'skoe soglashenie* (Odessa: DP Nabat, 2011), p. 4.
4. Volodomyr Chop and Ihor Lyman, *Mistsiamy pam'iati povstans'kykh peremoh u Zaporoz'komu krai: Azovs'ka operatsiia Nestora Makhna* (Zaporizhzhia: Berdians'kyi Derzhavynyi Pedahohichnyi Universytet, 2017), p. 10.
5. For a detailed analysis of the Starobel'sk agreement, the negotiations themselves, the important military role played by the anarchists in Wrangel's defeat and the eventual breakdown of the agreement, see Vladimir Litvinov 'O chetverstom (oktiabr' 1920 goda) voenno-politicheskom soglashenii mezhdu Revoliutsionno-Povstancheskoi Armiei (Makhnovtsev) i kommunisticheskim pravitel'stvom RSFSR', *International Review of Social History*, vol. 32 (1987), pp. 315–401.

6. 'One of the great strategists of the early days of the Soviet republic' (Walter Jacobs, *Frunze: The Soviet Clausewitz, 18851925* [The Hague: Martinus Nijhoff, 1969], p. vii); a 'talented officer' (Laura Engelstein, *Russia in Flames: War, Revolution, Civil War, 1914-1921* [New York: Oxford University Press, 2018], p. 558); 'hugely talented' and 'brilliant' (Jonathan Smele, *The 'Russian' Civil Wars, 1916-1926: Ten Years that Shook the World* [New York: Oxford University Press, 2017], p. 114, 118).

7. See, e.g., V. Arkhangel'skii, *Frunze* (Moscow: Izdat. Molodaia Gvardiia, 1970), p. 489.

8. W. Bruce Lincoln, *Red Victory: A History of the Russian Civil War* (New York: Simon and Schuster, 1989), pp. 442–3. The Bolsheviks believed that 'the fight against Makhno was the key to victory over the Whites' and hence effectively 'ignored' Wrangel for several months (Litvinov, 'O chetverstom (oktiabr' 1920 goda) voenno-politicheskom soglashenii', p. 351).

9. Litvinov 'O chetverstom (oktiabr' 1920 goda) voenno-politicheskom soglashenii', p. 352.

10. Litvinov 'O chetverstom (oktiabr' 1920 goda) voenno-politicheskom soglashenii', p. 355. On respect for Makhno's cavalry, see Viktor Danilov and Teodor Shanin (eds), *Nestor Makhno: krest'ianskoe dvizheniia na Ukraine, 1918-1921. dokumenty e materialy* (Moscow: Rossiiskaia Politicheskaia Entsiklopediia, 2006), p. 200.

11. For an analysis of this campaign see Walter Jacobs, *Frunze: The Soviet Clausewitz, 1885-1925* (The Hague: Martinus Nijhoff, 1969), pp. 209–26.

12. M. V. Frunze, *Sobranie sochinenii* (Moscow: Gosizdat, 1926–1929), vol. 1, p. 271.

13. Litvinov describes the Bolsheviks 'rushing about the steppes' pursuing the *makhnovtsy* 'as if in a fever' but eventually recognising the need to cooperate (Litvinov 'O chetverstom (oktiabr' 1920 goda) voenno-politicheskom soglashenii', p. 151).

14. Makhno was ill, and handed over responsibility for the negotiation to Belash (A. V. Belash and V. F. Belash, *Dorogi Nestora Makhno: istoricheskoe povestvovanie* [Kiev: Proza, 1993], p. 449).

15. Danilov and Shanin (eds), *Nestor Makhno*, p. 476. See also Azarov, *Starobel'skoe soglashenie*, p. 4.

16. Danilov and Shanin (eds), *Nestor Makhno*, pp. 478–9.

17. Arshinov, *Istoriia makhnovskogo dvizheniia*, p. 171.

18. *Grazhdanskaia voina na Ukraine, 1918-1920: sbornik dokumentov i materialov* (Kiev: Izdat. Naukova Dumka, 1967), vol. 3, p. 550.

19. Politburo of the Central Committee of the KP(b)U, minutes, 29 September 1920, in *Grazhdanskaia voina na Ukraine*, vol. 3, pp. 549–50.

20. Danilov and Shanin (eds), *Nestor Makhno*, p. 483.

21. *Grazhdanskaia voina na Ukraine*, vol. 3, p. 580.

22. *Grazhdanskaia voina na Ukraine*, vol. 3, p. 637.

23. *Grazhdanskaia voina na Ukraine*, vol. 3, p. 550. See also Belash and Belash, *Dorogi Nestora Makhno*, pp. 481–2.

24. Arshinov, *Istoriia makhnovskogo dvizheniia*, p. 174.

25. Arshinov, *Istoriia makhnovskogo dvizheniia*, p. 174.

26. *Grazhdanskaia voina na Ukraine*, vol. 3, p. 680.

27. Danilov and Shanin (eds), *Nestor Makhno*, p. 485–6. The introductory paragraph states that the insurgent army had 'decided to end the armed struggle with the Soviet government, establishing a military-political agreement with it in order to decisively defeat the domestic and world counter-revolution'. See also Arshinov, *Istoriia makhnovskogo dvizheniia*, p. 172–3; *Grazhdanskaia voina na Ukraine*,

vol. 3, pp. 571-2, reprinted from Isaak Teper, *Makhno: ot 'edinogo anarkhizm' k stopam rumynskogo korolia* (Kiev: Molodoi Rabochii, 1924), pp. 117-19.

28. The negotiations were difficult (Azarov, *Starobel'skoe soglashenie*, p. 140).

29. Azarov, *Starobel'skoe soglashenie*, pp. 5-6 and p. 140.

30. Azarov, *Starobel'skoe soglashenie*, p. 6. This would have brought *makhnovshchina* close to alignment with the so-called 'Soviet Anarchists' who recognised the Bolshevik state as a transitional stage.

31. Azarov, *Starobel'skoe soglashenie*, p. 158.

32. Article in *Kommunist* no. 5 (15 November 1920), p. 99, printed in Belash and Belash, *Dorogi Nestora Makhno*, p. 482.

33. Arshinov, *Istoriia makhnovskogo dvizheniia*, pp. 171-2. Litvinov points out that the original demands of the anarchists as presented remain unknown ('O chetverstom (oktiabr' 1920 goda) voenno-politicheskom soglashenii', p. 364).

34. Arshinov, *Istoriia makhnovskogo dvizheniia*, p. 174.

35. Golovanov, *Nestor Makhno*, p. 344.

36. Azarov, *Starobel'skoe soglashenie*, p. 141; Litvinov, 'O chetverstom (oktiabr' 1920 goda) voenno-politicheskom soglashenii', p. 364.

37. Lenin, *Polnoe sobranie sochinenii*, 5th ed. (Moscow: Izdat. Politicheskoi Literatury, 1958-65), vol. 41, p. 401.

38. Lenin, *Polnoe sobranie sochinenii*, vol. 41, p. 340.

39. Trotsky, 'Chto oznachaet perekhod Makhno na storonu Sovetskoi vlasti?' in Danilov and Shanin (eds), *Nestor Makhno*, pp. 497-9. See also his *Kak vooruzhalas revoliutsiia na voennoi rabote* (Moscow: Vysshii Voennyi Redak. Sovet, 1923-25), vol. 2, part 2, pp. 210-12.

40. Trotsky, 'Chto oznachaet perekhod Makhno na storonu Sovetskoi vlasti?'

41. *Grazhdanskaia voina na Ukraine*, vol. 3, p. 644.

42. Arshinov, *Istoriia makhnovskogo dvizheniia*, p. 174.

43. *Grazhdanskaia voina na Ukraine*, vol. 3, pp. 651-2.

44. Jacobs, *Frunze: The Soviet Clausewitz*, p. 224.

45. Lenin, *Polnoe sobranie sochinenii*, vol. 51, p. 321; Meyer (ed.), *The Trotsky Papers*, vol. 2, pp. 344-5.

46. *Grazhdanskaia voina na Ukraine*, vol. 3, p. 671.

47. On 29-30 October, Budenny could have closed off access to Crimea, when White reinforcements sent to keep the route open 'got lost in the cold and darkness'. But the opportunity was lost (*Frunze: The Soviet Clausewitz*, pp. 220n-221n).

48. Jacobs, *Frunze: The Soviet Clausewitz*, pp. 211-12.

49. Jacobs, *Frunze: The Soviet Clausewitz*, pp. 212-13.

50. Jacobs, *Frunze: The Soviet Clausewitz*, p. 215.

51. *Grazhdanskaia voina, 19181921* (Moscow, 1928-30), vol. 3, p. 513. See also Belash and Belash, *Dorogi Nestora Makhno*, pp. 472-3.

52. Belash and Belash, *Dorogi Nestora Makhno*, p. 472.

53. *Grazhdanskaia voina na Ukraine*, vol. 3, pp. 707-9. See also A. V. Golubev (ed.), *Perekop i Chongar: sbornik statei i materialov* (Moscow: Gos. Voennoe Izdatel'stvo, 1933), pp. 33-5; M. V. Frunze na frontakh grazhdanskoi voiny: sbornik dokumentov* (Moscow: Voennoe izd-vo Narodnogo komissariata oborony SSSR, 1941), pp. 426-7; and *Iz istorii grazhdanskoi voiny v SSSR, 1918-1922: sbornik dokumentov i materialov* (Moscow: Sov. Rossiia, 1960-1961), vol. 3, p. 427.

54. Golovanov, *Nestor Makhno*, pp. 323-4.

55. Jacobs is scathing: 'Such a failure [to use artillery] can be blamed either on the inexperience and low professional competence of the firing batteries or on the failure of local commanders ...' (*Frunze: The Soviet Clausewitz*, p. 217).

56. Some regiments lost as many as sixty per cent of their strength (*Frunze: The Soviet Clausewitz*, p. 218; see also Lincoln, *Red Victory*, p. 447). Frunze reported to Lenin on 12 November that he had lost not less than 10,000 men (*Direktivy komandovaniia frontov Krasnoi Armii, 19171922 gg.: sbornik dokumentov* [Moscow: Voennoe Izdat. Ministerstva Oborony SSSR, 1974], vol. 3, p. 510).

57. Jacobs, *Frunze: The Soviet Clausewitz*, p. 218.

58. Arshinov, *Istoriia makhnovskogo dvizheniia*, p. 175.

59. Jacobs, *Frunze: The Soviet Clausewitz*, p. 218; Arshinov, *Istoriia makhnovskogo dvizheniia*, p. 175.

60. Luckett, *The White generals*, pp. 380–81.

61. Jacobs, *Frunze: The Soviet Clausewitz*, p. 219.

62. Jacobs, *Frunze: The Soviet Clausewitz*, p. 221.

63. Wrangel's proclamation in Luckett, *The White generals*, pp. 381–82. Frunze made an unauthorised amnesty offer (Jacobs, *Frunze: The Soviet Clausewitz*, p. 222n, quoting *Krasnyi Arkhiv* no. 6 [1935], p. 62).

64. Karetnik was an effective commander, but 'extremely cruel' and 'mentally unbalanced'. He enjoyed Makhno's favour as somebody with firm anarchist convictions (Volodymyr Chop and Ihor Lyman, *Vol'nyi Berdiansk: misto v period anarkhizms'koho sotsial'noho eksperymentu, 1918-1921 r.* [Zaporizhzhia: RA Tandem-U, 2007], p. 79–80).

65. Arshinov, *Istoriia makhnovskogo dvizheniia*, p. 175.

66. Lincoln, *Red Victory*, p. 449.

67. Golovanov, *Nestor Makhno*, p. 326.

68. Jacobs, *Frunze: The Soviet Clausewitz*, p. 225; Golovanov, *Nestor Makhno*, p. 326.

69. Litvinov, 'O chetverstom (oktiabr' 1920 goda) voenno-politicheskom soglashenii', p. 380.

70. Jacobs, *Frunze: The Soviet Clausewitz*, p. 225.

71. *Direktivy komandovaniia frontov Krasnoi Armii*, vol. 3, p. 513; *M. V. Frunze na frontakh grazhdanskoi voiny*, pp. 442–3. Mawdsley concludes that Makhno's part in the Perekop campaign 'should not be exaggerated' (*The Russian civil war*, p. 270).

72. Danilov and Shanin (eds), *Nestor Makhno*, p. 533.

73. Valerii Volkovinskii, *Makhno i ee krakh* (Moscow: Izdat. VZPI, 1991), pp. 179–80.

74. Danilov and Shanin (eds), *Nestor Makhno*, introduction, p. 26.

75. The telegram cited the 4th paragraph of the political section of the Starobel'sk agreement. Danilov and Shanin (eds), *Nestor Makhno*, p. 524.

76. *M. V. Frunze na frontakh grazhdanskoi voiny*, p. 447. See also Aleksandr Timoshchuk, *Anarkho-kommunisticheskie formirovaniia N. Makhno, sentiabr' 1917-avgust 1921* (Simferopol': Tavriia, 1996), p. 126.

77. *Grazhdanskaia voina na Ukraine*, vol. 3, p. 771.

78. M. V. Frunze, *Sobranie sochinenii*, vol. 1, p. 177. Arshinov omits the list of allegations of insurgent crimes (*Istoriia makhnovskogo dvizheniia*, p. 185).

79. Timoshchuk, *Anarkho-kommunisticheskie formirovaniia N. Makhno*, pp. 126-7.

80. Timoshchuk, *Anarkho-kommunisticheskie formirovaniia N. Makhno*, p. 127.

81. Danilov and Shanin (eds), *Nestor Makhno*, p. 534.

82. Danilov and Shanin (eds), *Nestor Makhno*, p. 534.

83. Arshinov, *Istoriia makhnovskogo dvizheniia*, p. 187.

84. Arshinov, *Istoriia makhnovskogo dvizheniia*, pp. 179–80.

85. Arshinov, *Istoriia makhnovskogo dvizheniia*, pp. 182-3, 188-9.

86. Arshinov, *Istoriia makhnovskogo dvizheniia*, p. 187.

87. *Grazhdanskaia voina na Ukraine*, vol. 3, pp. 780–81.

88. Fedor T. Fomin, *Zapiski starogo Chekista* (Moscow: Gospolitizdat., 1962) p. 76.
89. Arshinov, *Istoriia makhnovskogo dvizheniia*, p. 182.
90. The Cheka published a piece entitled 'Makhno's Treason' to justify these actions against the anarchists. Danilov and Shanin (eds), *Nestor Makhno*, pp. 536–7.
91. Arshinov, *Istoriia makhnovskogo dvizheniia*, p. 188. Maksimov says there were many arrests (*The guillotine at work*, pp. 447–8). Kubanin confirms it: 'Nabat was liquidated by the organs of the Cheka' (*Makhnovshchina*, p. 213).
92. Maksimov and Markus petitioned the Executive Committee of the Third International and the Central Committee of the RKP(b) (Maksimov, *The Guillotine at Work*, p. 452).
93. Danilov and Shanin (eds), *Nestor Makhno*, p. 535.
94. Litvinov, 'O chetverstom (oktiabr' 1920 goda) voenno-politicheskom soglashenii', p. 385, emphasis added.
95. Vasilii Golovanov, *Nestor Makhno* (Moscow: Molodaia Gvardiia, 2013), p. 326. Litvinov notes the discrepancies between the account of Frunze and later historians and advises 'wariness and the closest attention' to the matter ('O chetverstom (oktiabr' 1920 goda) voenno-politicheskom soglashenii', p. 358).
96. Chop and Lyman, *Mistsiamy pam'iati povstans'kykh peremoh u Zaporoz'komu krai*, p. 11.
97. Grain requisitioning did not stop in Ukraine until the autumn of 1921 (*Istoriia Ukrains'koi RSR* [Kiev: Vydavnytsvo Akademii Nauk Ukrain'skoi RSR, 1967], vol. 2, p. 178).
98. Moshe Lewin, 'The Civil War: Dynamics and Legacy', in Diane Koenker, William Rosenberg and Ronald Grigor Suny (eds), *Party, State and Society in the Russian Civil War: Explorations in Social History* (Bloomington: Indiana University Press, 1989), pp. 414–15.
99. Lewin, 'The Civil War: Dynamics and Legacy', p. 415.
100. See Anatolii Dubovik, *After Makhno: The Anarchist Underground in the Ukraine in the 1920s and 1930s* (London: Kate Sharpley Library, 2009); and Roger Pethybridge, *One Step Backwards, Two Steps Forward: Soviet Society and Politics in the New Economic Policy* (Oxford: Clarendon Press, 1990), p. 257. An 'insignificant' group of *makhnovtsy* was active near Kiev in 1922 (T. Hornykiewicz (ed.), *Ereignisse in der Ukraine 1914-1922, deren Bedeutung und historische Hintergrunde* (Philadelphia: Horn Berger, 1966–1969), vol. 4, p. 335. G. P. Kulchycky takes the story of attempts to maintain insurgency up to 1926 ('The Ukrainian Insurgent Movement, 1919 to 1926', [Ph.D. dissertation, Georgetown University, 1970]).
101. Orlando Figes, *Peasant Russia, Civil War: The Volga Countryside in Revolution, 1917-1921* (Oxford: Clarendon Press, 1989), p. 321.
102. Shubin, *Makhno i makhnovskoe dvizhenie*, p. 146, emphasis added; see also his *Makhno i ego vremiia: o velikoi revoliutsii i grazhdanskoi voine, 1917-1922 gg., v Rossii i na Ukraine* (Moscow: Knizhnyi Dom Librokom, 2014), p. 275 and p. 284.
103. Arshinov, *Istoriia makhnovskogo dvizheniia*, p. 189.
104. 'Iz boevoi deiatel'nosti Tov. Timoshenko v godoi grazhdanskoi voiny v SSSR'. *Krasnyi Arkhiv* no. 104 (1941), p. 101.
105. 'Iz boevoi deiatel'nosti Tov. Timoshenko', p. 102.
106. Earlier, for obvious reasons, it had been policy only to recruit armed fighters. This was probably the motive for sending 4,000 prisoners home (see Makhno, *Ukrainskaia revoliutsiia, iiul'-dekabr' 1918 g.* [Paris: Izdat Komiteta N. Makhno, 1937], p. 74).
107. Meyer (ed.), *The Trotsky Papers*, vol. 2, p. 366.

108. Arshinov, *Istoriia makhnovskogo dvizheniia*, pp. 189–90. Palij, basing his chronology on the collation of a range of Soviet and other sources, gives the sequence as being: 12 December, Berdiansk; 14 December, Andreevka; last, no date, Komar' (*The Anarchism of Nestor Makhno*, p. 235).

109. 'Rech'tov. Bukharina [19 July 1921]', *Biulleten' Pervogo Mezhdunarodnogo Kongressa Revoliutsionnykh Professional'nykh i Proizvodstvennykh Soiuzov* no. 15 (21 July 1921), p. 11.

110. Chop and Lyman, *Vol'nyi Berdiansk*, pp. 243–4.

111. Valerii Volkovyns'kyi, *Nestor Makhno: lehendy i real'nist'* (Kiev: Perlit Prodakshn, 1994), p. 201.

112. Chop and Lyman, *Vol'nyi Berdiansk*, p. 245.

113. Many of the Red troops were brought in from other fronts and had little idea about who they were fighting or why (Arshinov, *Istoriia makhnovskogo dvizheniia*, p. 199).

114. The Bolsheviks were successful because they addressed popular grievances. Robert Eideman (aka Eidemanis), 'Piataia godovshchina odnogo uroka', *Voina i Revoliutsiia* no. 12 (1926), pp. 32–9; and E. Esbakh, 'Poslednie dni Makhnovshchiny na Ukraine', *Voina i Revoliutsiia* no. 12 (1926), pp. 40–50.

115. Eideman, 'Piataia godovshchina odnogo uroka', p. 37.

116. Estimates of the actual size of the Makhno army, as always and for the reasons already adduced, vary. Palij quotes two estimates, ranging from 5,000 to 6,000 at the lower end of the scale, to an unlikely 10,000 to 15,000 at the upper end (*The anarchism of Nestor Makhno*, p. 316). Frunze put the numbers on 14 December at 7,000 fighting men (Meyer (ed.), *The Trotsky Papers*, vol. 2, p. 366).

117. Arshinov, *Istoriia makhnovskogo dvizheniia*, pp. 190–91.

118. Meyer (ed.), *The Trotsky Papers*, vol. 2, pp. 366–7.

119. Meyer (ed.), *The Trotsky Papers*, vol. 2, pp. 366–7.

120. Meyer (ed.), *The Trotsky Papers*, vol. 2, p. 367.

121. In September Lenin had told the newly-appointed Frunze that the Bolsheviks did not have the right 'to subject the people to the horrors and sufferings of another winter campaign' (S. A. Sirotinskii, *Put' Arseniia: biograficheskii ocherk M. V. Frunze* [Moscow: Voen. Izd-vo, 1956], p. 188, quoted by Jacobs, *Frunze, The Soviet Clausewitz*, p. 209).

122. Letter from Makhno, quoted by Arshinov, *Istoriia makhnovskogo dvizheniia*, p. 194, 196. See also *Revoliutsionnaia Rossiia* (31 September 1921); *Protokoly desiatyi s"ezd RKP(b), mart 1921 g.* (Moscow, 1933), p. 260, 314, 733; and Trotsky, *Kak vooruzhalas revoliutsiia na voennoi rabote* (Moscow: Vysshii Voennyi Redak. Sovet, 1923–1925), vol. 2, part 1, p. 172.

123. Arshinov, *Istoriia makhnovskogo dvizheniia*, pp. 190–91.

124. Eideman, 'Piataia godovshchina odnogo uroka', p. 38.

125. Viacheslav Azarov, *Kontrrazvedka: the story of the Makhnovist intelligence service* (Edmonton: Black Cat Press, 2009), first published in Russian as 'Makhnovskaia kontrrazvedka'.

126. M. Rybakov, 'Makhnovskie operatsii v 1920 g'. *Krasnaia Armiia* no. 12 (1922), p. 12.

127. Makhno and other *atamany* collected information and followed developments in each other's areas with close attention (Shubin, *Makhno i makhnovskogo dvizhenie*, pp. 145–6), and Landis describes ways in which spies could recognize each other; Makhno's men wore a discreet piece of black thread on their caps ('Waiting for Makhno' *Past and Present* no. 183 [2004], p. 225).

128. Litvinov, 'O chetverstom (oktiabr' 1920 goda) voenno-politicheskom soglashenii', pp. 327–8.
129. John A. Armstrong, *Ukrainian Nationalism*, 2nd edn. (New York: Columbia University Press, 1963), pp. 130–31.
130. V. K. Tukan, 'Zvuzhennia sotsialnoi bazi makhnovs'koho rukhu ta ioho zgortannia, 1921 r'. *Zbirnik Naukovykh Prats: Seriia Istoriia ta Heografiia* [Kharkiv], no. 41 (2011), p. 17.
131. Arshinov, *Istoriia makhnovskogo dvizheniia*, p. 199. For an analysis of the fighting between November 1920 and August 1921, see the chapter 'Unichtozhenie makhnovskii formirovanii, noiabr 1920-avgust 1921 g'. in Timoshchuk's *Anarkho-kommunisticheskie formirovaniia N. Makhno*, pp. 126–42.
132. Tukan, 'Zvuzhennia sotsialnoi bazi makhnovs'koho rukhu ta ioho zgortannia, 1921 r'. pp. 17–18.
133. Tukan, 'Zvuzhennia sotsialnoi bazi makhnovs'koho rukhu ta ioho zgortannia, 1921 r'. p. 18.
134. Esbakh, 'Poslednie dni Makhnovshchiny na Ukraine', p. 42.
135. Telegram dated 6 February 1921, in Lenin, *Polnoe sobranie sochinenii*, vol. 52, p. 67.
136. Littlejohn, *A Sociology of the Soviet Union* p. 52. See also Bettelheim's detailed discussion of the balance sheet of war communism and NEP (*Class Struggles in the USSR. First period: 1917-1923*, pp. 437–537). For the standard Soviet view of the relationship between 'kulak revolts' and the crisis of war communism, see I. Ia. Trifonov, *Klassy i klassovaia bor'ba v SSSR v nachale NEPa, 1921-1923 gg. Vol.1: Bor'ba s vooruzhennoi kulatskoi kontrrevoliutsii* (Leningrad: Izdat. Leningradskogo Universiteta, 1964), especially pp. 51–71, 72–115, and 270–89.
137. Chamberlin, *The Russian Revolution*, vol. 2, p. 431.
138. Quoted by Lincoln, *Red Victory*, p. 472.
139. The VTsIK decree was published in *Pravda* (23 March 1921); an English translation is printed in Chamberlin, *The Russian revolution*, vol. 2, pp. 499–501.
140. In early 1921, the Soviet writer Mikhail Sholokhov, then a 15- or 16-year-old, was captured by the *makhnovtsy* while working with a grain requisition detachment. Sholokhov describes Makhno as 'very bitter'. His comrades were shot, but Sholokhov was released (introduction to *Selected tales from the Don* [Oxford: Pergamon Press, 1967], p. x).
141. Meyer (ed.), *The Trotsky Papers*, vol. 2, pp. 386–89.
142. Meyer (ed.), *The Trotsky Papers*, vol. 2, pp. 388–91.
143. *Pravda* (17 March 1921), p. 4.
144. Meyer (ed.), *The Trotsky Papers*, vol. 2, pp. 394–5; Lenin, *Polnoe sobranie sochinenii*, vol. 52, p. 88.
145. Report dated 17 March 1921, in Meyer (ed.), *The Trotsky Papers*, vol. 2, pp. 402–5.
146. Issues for 27 and 29 April, and 1 June 1921. See also S. N. Semanov, 'Makhnovshchina i ee krakh', *Voprosy Istorii*, no. 9 (1966), pp. 59–60.
147. Makhno describes the insurgent requisitioning process during an earlier phase. Poor peasants would contribute bread according to their means. Kulaks would each contribute a sheep. If this was still the procedure in the conditions of 1921 it would have been a heavy burden indeed (Makhno, *Ukrainskaia revoliutsiia*, p. 74).
148. Arshinov, *Istoriia makhnovskogo dvizheniia*, p. 195, 197.
149. In earlier periods, women rode in some of the *tachanki* to nurse wounded men (Makhno, *Ukrainskaia revoliutsiia*, p. 74).
150. Arshinov, *Istoriia makhnovskogo dvizheniia*, pp. 196–7.

151. By 1922, Ukraine was still treated differently: taxes were not lifted there as they were in the Volga region, and the peasantry was still obliged to supply grain – although only 92 wagon loads were collected that year (Pethybridge, *One Step Backwards, Two Steps Forward*, pp. 108–9).

152. E. Hurwicz, *Staatsmänner und Abenteurer: russische Porträts von Witte bis Trotzki, 1891-1925* (Leipzig: Hirschfeld, 1925), p. 272. See also Arshinov, *Istoriia makhnovskogo dvizheniia*, p. 199.

153. Letter by Makhno quoted in Arshinov, *Istoriia makhnovskogo dvizheniia*, p. 199.

154. P. Sergeev, 'Poltavskaia operatsiia protiv Makhno', *Voina i Revoliutsiia* no. 9 (1927), pp. 122–34. See especially the map of operations on p. 131.

155. *Gnusnyi trus* or 'vile coward' is the expression used (Arshinov, *Istoriia makhnovskogo dvizheniia*, p. 199). But according to Mett, ('Souvenirs sur Nestor Makhno', p. 6), Makhno in exile spoke in terms of professional respect about both Budenny and Voroshilov.

156. Shubin, *Makhno i makhnovskoe dvizhenie*, pp. 146–7.

157. Shubin, *Makhno i makhnovskoe dvizhenie*, p. 147; see also his *Makhno i ego vremiia*, p. 286.

158. *New York Times* (18 July 1921), p. 15.

159. There is indeed a noticeable change in the level of Bolshevik hostility towards *makhnovshchina* after 1921, as commentators have noted. Makhno is increasingly portrayed as simply a bloodthirsty and uncultured bandit, a characterisation later picked up and elaborated by Joseph Kessel. Pre-war Soviet films also portrayed Makhno as simply a robber chief (Gilbert Guilleminault and André Mahé, *L'épopée de la révolution: le roman vrai d'un siècle d'anarchisme* [Paris: Denoël, 1963], p. 325).

160. 'Zaiavlenie russkoi delegatsii po povodu rechi Sirolia v zasedanii 19 iiulia 1921 g', *Biulleten' Pervogo Mezhdunarodnogo Kongressa Revoliutsionnykh Professional'nykh i Proizvodstvennykh Soiuzov*, no. 16 (July 1921), p. 10.

161. Maksimov, *The Guillotine at Work*, p. 444.

162. 'Rech' tov. Bukharina', p. 10.

CHAPTER 8   THE BITTER POLITICS OF THE LONG EXILE: ROMANIA, POLAND, GERMANY, AND FRANCE, 1921-34

1. After the collapse of the Kornilov rebellion in April 1918 'counter-revolution was no longer on the agenda', and an opportunity briefly existed for the emergence of a 'democratic coalition' of socialist parties; Lenin was briefly in favour. See Geoffrey Swain, *The Origins of the Russian Civil War* (London: Longman, 1996), especially pp. 42–3.

2. Anatolii Dubovik, *After Makhno: The Anarchist Underground in the Ukraine in the 1920s and 1930s* (London: Kate Sharpley Library, 2009), pp. 1–14.

3. V. K. Tukan, 'Suspilno-politychna diial'nist' N. I. Makhno v emihratsii, 1921–1934 rr'. *Zbirnyk Naukovykh Prats': Seriia Istoriia ta Heohrafiia*, no. 45 (2012), p. 25.

4. See Makhno's *Makhnovshchina i ee vcherashnie soiuzniki-bol'sheviki: otvet na knigu M. Kubanina «Makhnovshchina»* (Paris: Izdanie Biblioteki Makhnovtsev, 1928); also, his *Po povodu raz"iasneniia Volina* (Paris, 1929). He calls Volin a liar and a hypocrite whose politics are 'dirty and vulgar in their falsity and vile in their consciousness'. In his turn, Volin 'nurtured resentment' and thought that Makhno was a 'an ignorant, uncultivated, uneducated fellow' and a '*muzhik*' (Alexandre Skirda (ed.), *The Struggle against the State and Other Essays by Nestor Makhno* [Edinburgh: AK Press, 1996], pp. 106–13).

5. Viktor Danilov and Teodor Shanin (eds), *Nestor Makhno: krest'ianskoe dvizheniia na Ukraine, 1918-1921. dokumenty e materialy* (Moscow: Rossiiskaia Politich-eskaia Entsiklopediia, 2006), pp. 629-30.

6. Viacheslav Azarov, *Kontrrazvedka: The Story of the Makhnovist Intelligence Service* (Edmonton: Black Cat Press, 2008), p. 60.

7. Belash and Belash, *Dorogi Nestora Makhno*, p. 554.

8. Makhno's forces were moving rapidly, 'with the speed of a hawk'. They arrived at the Dnestr on 16 August. A. V. Belash and V. F. Belash, *Dorogi Nestora Makhno: istoricheskoe povestvovanie* (Kiev: Proza, 1993), p. 572.

9. Belash and Belash, *Dorogi Nestora Makhno*, p. 572.

10. Belash and Belash, *Dorogi Nestora Makhno*, p. 572.

11. There are conflicting accounts (a battle, the disarming of border guards); the Bolsheviks had no intelligence on what had happened until September 1921 (Aleksandr Timoshchuk, *Anarkho-kommunisticheskie formirovaniia N. Makhno, sentiabr' 1917-avgust 1921* [Simferopol': Tavriia, 1996], p. 142).

12. V. A. Savchenko, *Makhno* (Kharkiv: Folio, 2005), p. 381.

13. Petr Arshinov, *Istoriia makhnovskogo dvizheniia, 1918-1921* (Berlin: Gruppy Russkikh Anarkhistov v Germanii, 1923), p. 200.

14. Osip Tsebrii (Ossip Tsebry) wrote that after linking up with the Belash group and suffering defeat at the hands of the Red Army, 'along with two compan-ions I crossed into Poland and then via Austria and Jugoslavia reached France' (*Memories of a Makhnovist partisan* [London: Kate Sharpley Library, 1993], p. 17). On Tsebrii, see the notes by Nick Heath, online at libcom.org/history/tseb-ry-ossip-after-1958, accessed 3 March 2020.

15. Savchenko, *Makhno*, p. 380.

16. Perhaps as many as 1,000 cavalrymen (Savchenko, *Makhno*, p. 381).

17. Skirda, *Nestor Makhno, le cosaque de l'anarchie: la lutte pour les soviets libres en Ukraine, 1917-1921* (Paris: A.S., 1982), p. 295.

18. Michael Malet, *Nestor Makhno in the Russian Civil War* (London: Macmillan, 1982), p. 78.

19. Savchenko, *Makhno*, p. 380.

20. Savchenko, *Makhno*, p. 381.

21. Belash and Belash, *Dorogi Nestora Makhno*, p. 573.

22. Savchenko, *Makhno*, p. 381.

23. Estimates vary (Savchenko, *Makhno*, pp. 380-81).

24. Vasilii Golovanov, *Nestor Makhno* (Moscow: Molodaia Gvardiia, 2013), p. 434.

25. The two aides were the Zadov brothers, Lev and Daniil, senior intelligence officers in the insurgent movement (Golovanov, *Nestor Makhno*, pp. 435-6). While Makhno and Kuz'menko were interned at Braşov, they met Stepan Mat-venko-Sikar, who was 'astonished' at the quantity of gold and diamonds which they had about them (P. Fedenko in the *Institute for the Study of the USSR Bulletin* vol. 15, no. 6 [1968], pp. 43-4).

26. Petliurist report dated 25 November 1921 (*L'Ukraine sovietiste: quatre années de guerre et de blocus. Recueil des documents officiels d'après les livres rouges ukrai-niens* [Berlin: Puttkammer und Mühlbrecht, 1922], p. 123).

27. Makhno struggled to adapt to the new circumstances, even finding a job, but his health was fragile as a consequence of his wounds. (Savchenko, *Makhno*, p. 382).

28. Romania refused diplomatic and commercial relations with the Soviet gov-ernment. See Andrei Cusco, 'Nationalism and War in a Contested Borderland: The Case of Russian Bessarabia, 1914-1917', in Eric Lohr, Vera Tolz, Alexander

Semyonov and Mark von Hagen (eds), *Russia's Great War and Revolution*, vol. 2, pp. 137–62.

29. A report dated 13 January 1921 identified the delayed land reform, and the changeover from Russian currency as sources of discontent (*L'Ukraine sovietiste*, p. 122).

30. Some Petliurists were captured crossing the frontier with *tachanki*, normally associated more closely with Makhnovite tactics (*L'Ukraine sovietiste*, pp. 92–3). For Russian texts of this correspondence, see *Dokumenty vneshnei politiki SSSR* (Moscow: Gospolitizdat, 1957–), vol. 4, pp. 435–8, 488–91. See also *Istoriia Rumynii 1918-1970* (Moscow: Izdat. Nauka, 1971), p. 62.

31. It is not clear from the text whether these were *makhnovtsy* or not (*L'Ukraine sovietiste*, p. 91).

32. *L'Ukraine sovietiste*, p. 91; Skirda, *Nestor Makhno, le cosaque de l'anarchie*, p. 305; Michał Przyborowski and Darius Wierzchoś, *Nestor Machno w Polsce* (Poznań: Oficyna Brastwa Trojka, 2012), pp. 62–3.

33. This demand was described by later Soviet historians as 'mocking' [*izdevatel'ski*] (*Istoriia Rumynii*, p. 62).

34. *L'Ukraine sovietiste*, p. 92.

35. *L'Ukraine sovietiste*, p. 96.

36. The Odessa newspaper *Stanok* added that the Romanian government had forgotten 'the countless executions which it has carried out, for example, in Bessarabia' (quoted in *Istoriia Rumynii*, p. 62).

37. *L'Ukraine sovietiste*, p. 98.

38. *L'Ukraine sovietiste*, pp. 98–9.

39. *L'Ukraine sovietiste*, p. 99 ff.; J. Degras (ed.), *Soviet Documents on Foreign Policy* (London: Oxford University Press, 1951–53), vol. 1, pp. 274–6; *Izvestiia* (16 November 1921).

40. The period of exile is glossed over by Arshinov (*Istoriia makhnovskogo dvizheniia*) and Volin (*La révolution inconnue, 1917-1921: documentation inédite sur la révolution russe* [Paris: Les Amis de Voline, 1947]). The main accounts in English and French (Palij, *The Anarchism of Nestor Makhno*; Alexandre Skirda, *Nestor Makhno, le cosaque de l'anarchie: la lutte pour les soviets libres en Ukraine, 1917-1921* [Paris: A.S., 1982]; Malet, *Nestor Makhno in the Russian Civil War*; with the exception of Malcolm Menzies (*Makhno: une épopée. Le soulévement anarchiste en Ukraine, 1918-1921* [Paris: Belfond, 1972]), pay little attention to Makhno's political activity after August 1921. Menzies cites few sources, but mentions that he has had access to 'the personal archives of somebody who knew Makhno well in Paris' (p. 232).

41. *L'Ukraine sovietiste*, pp. 123–4.

42. Przyborowski and Wierzchoś, *Nestor Machno w Polsce*, p. 64. See also Savchenko, *Makhno*, p. 385.

43. *L'Ukraine sovietiste*, pp. 123–4.

44. *L'Ukraine sovietiste*, p. 124.

45. The agreement was concluded for the eyes of the Romanian and Polish authorities, which supported the nationalists, as the only hope for the *makhnovtsy* of avoiding extradition (Skirda, *Nestor Makhno, le cosaque de l'anarchie*, p. 309).

46. Golovanov, *Nestor Makhno*, p. 436.

47. *L'Ukraine sovietiste*, pp. 124–5.

48. Lepetchenko was later arrested and jailed for illegal possession of a firearm. Golovanov, *Nestor Makhno*, pp. 436–7.

49. Golovanov, *Nestor Makhno*, p. 436.

50. Dmitrii Nikolaevich Medvedev (1898–1954), a Cheka operative, later a partisan commander behind German lines in Nazi-occupied Ukraine.
51. Savchenko, *Makhno*, pp. 386–7; Valerii Volkovyns'kyi, *Nestor Makhno, lehendy i realnist'* (Kyiv: Perlit Prodkshn, 1994), p. 231.
52. Savchenko, *Makhno*, p. 388. The exceptions were White Guards or Ukrainian nationalist leaders. Przyborowski and Wierzchoś, *Nestor Machno w Polsce*, p. 112, 115.
53. Golovanov, *Nestor Makhno*, p. 437.
54. Makhno cooperated with the Romanian intelligence services to spread rumours that a large-scale revolt in Ukraine was imminent, causing panic in Soviet Odessa. The purpose of the disinformation was to direct attention away from his departure for Poland (V. K. Tukan, 'Suspilno-politychna diial'nist' N. I. Makhno v emihratsii', p. 25).
55. 'Since it is unlikely that any of the rebels knew how to drive a car, we will have to accept a less romantic version' of how they escaped (Golovanov, *Nestor Makhno*, p. 438).
56. Press reports quoted by Menzies (*Makhno: une epopee*, p. 217). He questions whether Makhno was expelled, or escaped from Romania. Skirda says that the group was passed back and forth from one side of the frontier to the other for the whole night of 12 April, until finally the Poles interned them (*Nestor Makhno, le cosaque de l'anarchie* p. 310).
57. 'Lev Zadov made a good career in the new service, becoming a colonel of state security ... [but] he was arrested in 1937 ... [and] confessed that he had worked for Romanian and British intelligence' (Golovanov, *Nestor Makhno*, p. 439).
58. Przyborowski and Wierzchoś, *Nestor Machno w Polsce*, p. 117.
59. A list of 17 of the internees described Makhno as 40 years old, short and dark, and lame in the left leg; Kuz'menko was described as 26 years old, and tall with brown hair. Przyborowski and Wierzchoś, *Nestor Machno w Polsce*, p. 123.
60. Report in the newspaper *Kurźer Poranny*, 2 December 1923, in Przyborowski and Wierzchoś, *Nestor Machno w Polsce*, p. 186.
61. Note dated 22 April 1922, reprinted in Przyborowski and Wierzchoś, *Nestor Machno w Polsce*, p. 110; Skirda, *Nestor Makhno, le cosaque de l'anarchie*, pp. 311–12.
62. Newspaper report, *Kurier Poranny*, 18 April 1923, in Przyborowski and Wierzchoś, *Nestor Machno w Polsce*, p. 151.
63. Volkovyns'kyi, *Nestor Makhno, lehendy i realnist'*, p. 232.
64. *Kurier Poranny* (26 May 1922), in Przyborowski and Wierzchoś, *Nestor Machno w Polsce*, p. 122.
65. Hurwicz, *Staatsmänner und Abenteurer*, p. 273.
66. Note from the Ukrainian Deputy National Commissioner for Foreign Affairs, 24 April 1922, in Przyborowski and Wierzchoś, *Nestor Machno w Polsce*, pp. 127–8.
67. Polish Ministry of Foreign Affairs, August 1922, in Przyborowski and Wierzchoś, *Nestor Machno w Polsce*, p. 131.
68. Aleksei Brusilov (1853–1926), quoted by Ronald Grigor Suny, 'Introduction: Bringing Empire Back', in Eric Lohr, Vera Tolz, Alexander Semyonov and Mark von Hagen (eds), *Russia's Great War and Revolution, vol.2: The Empire and Nationalism at War* (Bloomington: Slavica, 2014), p. 3.
69. Malet, *Nestor Makhno in the Russian Civil War*, p. 185.
70. Domashchenko and Khmara were described by another prisoner as 'always silent' while Makhno joined in political discussions 'willingly' (Przyborowski and Wierzchoś, *Nestor Machno w Polsce*, p. 158).

71. Document dated 4 October 1922, in Przyborowski and Wierzchoś, *Nestor Machno w Polsce*, p. 140.

72. Malet, *Nestor Makhno in the Russian Civil War*, p. 185. Polish reports at the time mention eight years as the likely sentence (e.g. Przyborowski and Wierzchoś, *Nestor Machno w Polsce*, p. 194).

73. Przyborowski and Wierzchoś, *Nestor Machno w Polsce*, p. 78 and 156.

74. Volkovyns'kyi, *Nestor Makhno, lehendy i realnist'*, p. 232; Aleksandr Shubin, *Makhno i ego vremia: o velikoi revoliutsii i grazhdanskoi voine 1917-1922 gg. v Rossii i na Ukraine* (Moscow: Librokom, 2013), p. 298.

75. Przyborowski and Wierzchoś, *Nestor Machno w Polsce*, p. 130. Evhen Petrushevych (1863-1940) was a minor west Ukrainian nationalist leader in Galicia.

76. Volkovyns'kyi, *Nestor Makhno, lehendy i realnist'*, pp. 232-3.

77. Hurwicz, *Staatsmänner und Abenteurer*, p. 273.

78. Report by a consular official in Danilov and Shanin (eds), *Nestor Makhno*, pp. 839-40. See also Volkovyns'kyi, *Nestor Makhno, lehendy i realnist'*, p. 234 and Savchenko, *Makhno*, p. 392.

79. Przyborowski and Wierzchoś, *Nestor Machno w Polsce*, p. 75.

80. 'Statement by G. A. Kuz'menko', in Danilov and Shanin (eds), *Nestor Makhno*, pp. 838-9. See also Volkovyns'kyi, *Nestor Makhno, lehendy i realnist'*, pp. 233-4.

81. Volkovyns'kyi, *Nestor Makhno, lehendy i realnist'*, p. 235.

82. Przyborowski and Wierzchoś, *Nestor Machno w Polsce*, pp. 132-3; Volkovyns'kyi, *Nestor Makhno, lehendy i realnist'*, p. 235.

83. Report dated 7 August 1922, in Przyborowski and Wierzchoś, *Nestor Machno w Polsce*, p. 134-5.

84. Grigorii Besedovskii, *Na putiakh k termidoru* (Paris: Izd-vo Mishen', 1930), vol. 1, pp. 63-4.

85. Skirda relies (*Nestor Makhno, le cosaque de l'anarchie*, pp. 311-14) on an account of the trial by Arshinov and Volin, '[Makhno before the Polish courts]' in the U.S. anarchist weekly *Amerikanskie Izvestiia* (28 November 1923).

86. The accused were represented by a team of three Polish defence lawyers (Przyborowski and Wierzchoś, *Nestor Machno w Polsce*, p. 159).

87. Przyborowski and Wierzchoś reprint several of these reports in full, together with other materials, in Polish, as documents 35-47 in *Nestor Machno w Polsce*, pp. 159-90.

88. Report in *Glos Narodu*, 1 December 1922, in Przyborowski and Wierzchoś, *Nestor Machno w Polsce*, p. 187.

89. Malet, *Nestor Makhno in the Russian Civil War*, p. 185.

90. The Polish authorities could not ignore the conspiracy, and so decided to bring the case to court. Przyborowski and Wierzchoś, *Nestor Machno w Polsce*, p. 77.

91. Report in *Rabotnik*, 28 November 1923, in Przyborowski and Wierzchoś, *Nestor Machno w Polsce*, p. 159. See also Besedovskii's later account (*Frankfurter Zeitung* [no date given], quoted by the *New York Times* [24 February 1924], section II, p. 7).

92. Report in *Rabotnik*, 28 November 1923, in Przyborowski and Wierzchoś, *Nestor Machno w Polsce*, p. 160.

93. *New York Times* [24 February 1924], section II, p. 7.

94. Przyborowski and Wierzchoś, *Nestor Machno w Polsce*, p. 82.

95. Seweryn Strzałkowski, *Ataman Machno: Rosja na rubieży* (Warsaw: Rój, 1923), pp. 52-7, quoted by Przyborowski and Wierzchoś, *Nestor Machno w Polsce*, pp. 194-5.

96. Report in Kurźer *Poranny* 2 December 1922, in Przyborowski and Wierzchoś, *Nestor Machno w Polsce*, p. 186.

97. Strzałkowski, *Ataman Machno*, pp. 52-7, quoted by Przyborowski and Wierzchoś, *Nestor Machno w Polsce*, p. 196.

98. Report in Kurźer *Poranny* 2 December 1922, in Przyborowski and Wierzchoś, *Nestor Machno w Polsce*, p. 183.

99. Volkovyns'kyi, *Nestor Makhno, lehendy i realnist'*, pp. 235-6.

100. Przyborowski and Wierzchoś, *Nestor Machno w Polsce*, p. 189.

101. Strzałkowski, *Ataman Machno*, pp. 52-7, quoted by Przyborowski and Wierzchoś, *Nestor Machno w Polsce*, pp. 194-6.

102. Przyborowski and Wierzchoś, *Nestor Machno w Polsce*, p. 83. However, they were released only on 4 January 1924 (Malet, *Nestor Makhno in the Russian Civil War*, pp. 185-6).

103. Przyborowski and Wierzchoś, *Nestor Machno w Polsce*, p. 84.

104. Przyborowski and Wierzchoś, *Nestor Machno w Polsce*, p. 85.

105. Przyborowski and Wierzchoś, *Nestor Machno w Polsce*, p. 85. See also Volkovyns'kyi, *Nestor Makhno, lehendy i realnist'* p. 243, who refers to 'stringent police surveillance'.

106. He was probably intending to contact anarchist comrades (Przyborowski and Wierzchoś, *Nestor Machno w Polsce*, p. 85).

107. Przyborowski and Wierzchoś, *Nestor Machno w Polsce*, p. 87.

108. It is unclear what congress Makhno wanted to attend. Two anarchist conferences had been held earlier in Berlin, in December 1920 and in June 1922, leading to the first congress of the International Workingmen's Association - also held in Berlin - in December 1922.

109. Przyborowski and Wierzchoś, *Nestor Machno w Polsce*, p. 87.

110. Przyborowski and Wierzchoś, *Nestor Machno w Polsce*, pp. 87-8.

111. Golovanov, *Nestor Makhno*, pp. 44-5; see also Savchenko, *Makhno*, p. 399.

112. Lithuanian telegraph agency report cited by Volkovyns'kyi, *Nestor Makhno, lehendy i realnist*, p. 243.

113. Przyborowski and Wierzchoś, *Nestor Machno w Polsce*, p. 89.

114. Przyborowski and Wierzchoś, *Nestor Machno w Polsce*, pp. 89-90.

115. The Free City of Danzig was established in 1920 under the Treaty of Versailles, and protected by the League of Nations. The population was overwhelmingly German.

116. This is the date given by Przyborowski and Wierzchoś, *Nestor Machno w Polsce*, p. 89.

117. Established in December 1922.

118. Malet, *Nestor Makhno in the Russian Civil War*, p. 186.

119. Przyborowski and Wierzchoś, *Nestor Machno w Polsce*, p. 90.

120. Przyborowski and Wierzchoś, *Nestor Machno w Polsce*, pp. 90-91, and Malet, *Nestor Makhno in the Russian Civil War*, p. 186.

121. Przyborowski and Wierzchoś, *Nestor Machno w Polsce*, p. 93.

122. Malet hypothesises that it 'It may have been in Berlin that Fedeli obtained the collection of Makhnovist leaflets now in Amsterdam'. These were subsequently edited and published by L. J. van Rossum as 'Proclamations of the Machno Movement, 1920', *International Review of Social History* vol. 13, no. 2 (1968), pp. 246-68.

123. Golovanov, *Nestor Makhno*, p. 477. Przyborowski and Wierzchoś give the year incorrectly as 1924 (*Nestor Machno w Polsce*, p. 94).

124. Shubin, *Makhno i ego vremia*, p. 299.

125. Menzies, *Makhno: une épopée*, p. 232.
126. 'Makhno et sa juive', *Revue Hebdomadaire* (27 February 1926), pp. 419–44 and (6 March 1926), pp. 22–4S. It later appeared as a book (Paris: Éditions Eos, 1926). It is available in English in Kessel's collection *The Pure in Heart* (London: Gollancz, 1928), pp. 199–259.
127. For an account of the assassination and trial see Yosef Nedava, 'Some Aspects of Individual Terrorism: A Case Study of the Schwartzbard Affair', *Terrorism*, vol. 3, no.1/2 (1979), pp. 69–80. A documentary history of the assassination and trial was edited by David Engel as *The Assassination of Symon Petliura and the Trial of Scholem Schwarzbard, 1926-1927: A Selection of Documents* (Göttingen: Vandenhoeck and Ruprecht, 2016).
128. Przyborowski and Wierzchoś, *Nestor Machno w Polsce*, p. 103.
129. Przyborowski and Wierzchoś, *Nestor Machno w Polsce*, p. 104.
130. Vladimir Chersakov-Georgichevskii, 'Nesgibaemyi antigosudarstvennik' in Nestor Makhno, *Azbuka anarkhista* (Moscow: Prozauk, 2013), p. 14.
131. Przyborowski and Wierzchoś, *Nestor Machno w Polsce*, p. 105.
132. L. Nikulin, 'Makhno v Parizhe', *Ogonek* (27 May 1928); extracted in Vladyslav Verstiuk (ed.), *Nestor Ivanovich Makhno: vospominaniia, materialy i dokumenty* (Kiev: Dzvin, 1991), p. 123. The report is illustrated with a photograph of Makhno with his daughter, who would have been about six years old at the time. See also Nikulin's later article 'Gibel' makhnovshchiny', *Znamia* no. 3 (1941), pp. 169–97.
133. Lucien van der Walt and Michael Schmidt, *Black Flame: The Revolutionary Class Politics of Anarchism and Syndicalism* (Oakland CA: AK Press, 2009), pp. 258–9. The subject is still sensitive: see 'Bob Black', *Wooden Shoes or Platform Shoes? On the Organisational Platform of the Libertarian Communists* (Anarchist Library, 2009), which was provoked by a 1989 Irish reprint of the Platform, described variously as a 'betrayal of anarchism', 'fundamentally false in its historical method', and 'a formula for victory conceived by losers' (p. 8).
134. Van der Walt and Schmidt, *Black Flame*, p. 257.
135. Kropotkin's funeral in February 1921 was the last of the great anarchist demonstrations on Soviet soil (Van der Walt and Schmidt, *Black Flame*, p. 38). See also Peter Marshall, *Demanding the Impossible: A History of Anarchism* (London: Fontana Press, 1993), p. 334; Paul Avrich, *The Russian Anarchists* (Princeton: Princeton University Press, 1967), pp. 227–8. On clandestine anarchist activity in the 1920s and 1930s, see Dubovik, *After Makhno*.
136. Golovanov, *Nestor Makhno*, p. 464.
137. 'Such émigré milieus are notorious for their infighting' (Van der Walt and Schmidt, *Black Flame*, p. 256).
138. Van der Walt and Schmidt, *Black Flame*, p. 239.
139. 'By the autumn of 1920, [the Red Army] had grown into a mass conscript army of five million soldiers', most of them peasants (Orlando Figes, 'The Red Army and Mass Mobilisation During the Russian Civil War, 1918-1920', *Past and Present*, no. 129 [November 1990], p. 168).
140. Skirda (ed.), *The Struggle Against the State*, p. 108.
141. Skirda (ed.), *The Struggle Against the State*, p. 110.
142. Menzies, *Makhno: une épopée*, p. 233.
143. A Red envoy had been shot by the partisans. When Volin's opinion was canvassed, he replied that if Makhno had agreed, then he did not want to discuss it further. When Makhno heard this, he demanded to know why Volin had not even asked what the man had been condemned for. 'And what if [I] were drunk when [I] had

the man shot, what then?' (Ida Mett-Lazarevich, 'Souvenirs sur Nestor Makhno' [Paris, 1948], p. 4).

144. Menzies, *Makhno: une épopée*, p. 233.

145. Shubin, *Makhno i ego vremia*, pp. 300–301, and also his *Anarkhiia mat' poradka: mezhdu krasnymi i belymi* (Moscow: Iauza, Eksmo, 2005), pp. 386–7. Compare van der Walt and Schmidt's categorisation of syndicalism, 'anti-organisationalism', and organisational dualism (*Black Flame*, p. 239).

146. Viacheslav Azarov, *Starobel'skoe soglashenie* (Odessa: DP Nabat, 2011), p. 6 is dismissive: they ceased to be real anarchists.

147. Sandomirskii was a member of the Moscow Federation of Anarchist Groups in 1918 and later worked for the Soviet People's Commissariat of Foreign Affairs. He was shot in 1937 during the purges.

148. Grossman-Roshchin, a former member of *Chernoe Znamia*, spent years in exile in Western Europe. Returning to Russia in 1917, he joined the Moscow Federation, but defended the Bolsheviks, arguing that they were libertarians at heart and that it was necessary to defend the revolution against reaction and foreign intervention. In 1919 he stayed briefly in Guliaipole: Makhno suspected that he was an agent of the Cheka, but did not care (Belash and Belash, *Dorogi Nestora Makhno*, p. 174). He died of natural causes in the early 1930s.

149. See Paul Avrich, *The Russian Anarchists* (Princeton: Princeton University Press, 1967), pp. 198–9. An account of the 'Soviet anarchist' controversy in broad outline can be found in H. Goldberg, 'The Anarchists View the Bolshevik Regime, 1918-1922', (Ph.D. dissertation, University of Wisconsin, 1973), pp. 211–47.

150. Errico Malatesta (1853–1932), an important figure in the Italian anarchist movement; a prolific article writer and pamphleteer (Marshall, *Demanding the Impossible*, pp. 345–61; see also Vernon Richards [ed.], *Life and Ideas: The Anarchist Writings of Errico Malatesta* [Oakland, Calif.: PM Press, 2015]).

151. *Umanità Nova* (4, 16, 20 and 21 May 1922), all p. 1.

152. Volin et al., 'Agents du gouvernement bolshevique: qu'est-ce que Sandomirskii?' *Le Libertaire* [Paris] (21/28 July 1922), p. 2.

153. *Le Libertaire* (1/8 December 1922), p. 2.

154. Volin, 'Données complementaires sur les agents bolchevistes', *Le Libertaire* (15/22 December 1922), p. 2.

155. 'K voprosu ob anarkho-bol'shevizme i ego roli v revoliutsii', *Anarkhicheskii Vestnik* (July 1923), pp. 59–63.

156. Arshinov, 'Anarkho-bol'shevizm i ego rol' v russkoi revoliutsii', *Anarkhicheskii Vestnik* (July 1923), pp. 56–9,

157. Available online in English at www.nestormakhno.info/english/newplatform/org_plat.htm (accessed 20 June 2019), with links to other editions and commentaries.

158. Van der Walt and Schmidt, *Black Flame*, p. 260.

159. Van der Walt and Schmidt, *Black Flame*, p. 22, emphasis in the original.

160. Marshall, *Demanding the Impossible*, p. 444.

161. Van der Walt and Schmidt, *Black Flame*, pp. 253–4.

162. 'Organisational Platform', online edition.

163. Van der Walt and Schmidt, *Black Flame*, p. 253.

164. 'Organisational Platform', online edition.

165. Volin, *Manifeste*, quoted by Menzies, *Makhno: une épopée*, p. 236.

166. Volin, *Manifeste*, quoted by Menzies, *Makhno: une épopée*, p. 236.

167. The French anarchist movement was divided into an individualist and communist wing and a syndicalist wing. *Le Libertaire* had a history of suspicion towards the anarcho-syndicalist trend (Marshall, *Demanding the Impossible*, pp. 441–4).

168. Menzies, *Makhno : une épopée*, p. 236.
169. Van der Walt and Schmidt, *Black Flame*, p. 256.
170. Shubin, *Makhno i makhnovskogo dvizheniia* (Moscow: Izdat. MIK, 1998) p. 169, quoting an account by Kuz'menko cited as *Nabat*, no. 5, 1990.
171. Shubin, *Makhno i makhnovskogo dvizheniia*, p. 169. Skirda is unimpressed by the 'solidarity' of the anarchist comrades, noting that significantly more money was collected by the 'Comité Makhno' than was passed on to the ailing former partisan (*Nestor Makhno, le cosaque de l'anarchie*, pp. 333–4).
172. Shubin, *Makhno i makhnovskogo dvizheniia*, pp. 169–70.
173. Shubin gives the date, following Kuz'menko, as 6 July 1934 (*Makhno i makhnovskogo dvizheniia*, p. 170). However, Malet says Makhno died early in the morning on 25 July (Malet, *Nestor Makhno in the Russian Civil War*, p. 192). Skirda also gives 25 July (Skirda, *Nestor Makhno, le cosaque de l'anarchie*, p. 333).
174. An English version is available online as 'Makhno in Paris' at The Nestor Makhno Archive: www.nestormakhno.info/english/personal/personal5.htm, accessed 20 June 2019.
175. 'Après la mort de Makhno, elle est devenue la femme de Voline'. Ida Mett-Lazarevich, 'Souvenirs sur Nestor Makhno', p. 3. Mett's account is cited, inter alia, by Danilov and Shanin (eds), *Nestor Makhno*, p. 889. Przyborowski and Wierzchoś suggest that an affair started when Volin and Makhno and their families all lived together in Paris, and that Mett hated Kuz'menko for marrying Volin (*Nestor Machno w Polsce*, p. 108).
176. Savchenko, *Makhno*, p. 413.
177. Danilov and Shanin say she was in a boarding school in Dzhezkazgan (*Nestor Makhno*, p. 901).
178. Przyborowski and Wierzchoś, *Nestor Machno w Polsce*, p. 109. Tian-Shan is an extensive and remote mountainous region in Central Asia, in the border area between Kazakhstan, Kyrgyzstan and Xinjiang in northwest China.
179. Przyborowski and Wierzchoś, *Nestor Machno w Polsce*, p. 109.
180. Iuri Gaev, 'Nestora Makho ne mogli poniat' ni Lenin, ni Trotskii, ni Denikin', *Fakty i Komentarii* (13 November 1998), available online at www.makhno.ru/st/89.php, accessed 25 January 2015.
181. Gaev, 'Nestora Makho ne mogli poniat'.

CHAPTER 9   WHY ANARCHISM? WHY UKRAINE? CONTEXTUALISING MAKHNOVSHCHINA

1. Aaron B. Retish, Liudmila G. Novikova and Sarah Badcock, 'Introduction: A Kaleidoscope of Revolutions' in: Badcock, Novikova and Retish (eds), *Russia's Home Front in War and Revolution, 1914-22. Book 1. Russia's Revolution in Regional Perspective* (Bloomington, Ind.: Slavica, 2015), p. 1.
2. Ronald Grigor Suny, 'Introduction: Bringing Empire Back', in: Eric Lohr et al. (eds), *The Empire and Nationalism at War* (Bloomington: Slavica, 2014), p. 1.
3. Serhii Plokhy, *Lost kingdom: A History of Russian Nationalism from Ivan the Great to Vladimir Putin* (London: Penguin, 2017), p. 192.
4. Neil Faulkner, *A People's History of the Russian Revolution* (London: Pluto Press, 2017), p. 1.
5. Luciano Canfora, *Democracy in Europe: A History of an Ideology* (Oxford: Blackwell, 2006), p. 250.

6. Alexander Rabinowitch, *The Bolsheviks Come to Power: The Revolution of 1917 in Petrograd*, new edn. (London: Pluto Press, 2017).

7. Jonathan Smele, *The 'Russian' Civil Wars, 1916-1926: Ten Years That Shook the World* (New York: Oxford University Press, 2017).

8. Maxim Gorky, 'On the Russian Peasantry' in: Teodor Shanin (ed.), *Peasants and Peasant Societies* (Harmondsworth: Penguin, 1971), p. 370.

9. Karl Marx, 'The Eighteenth Brumaire of Louis Bonaparte', in *Selected Works* (Moscow: Progress Publishers, 1969–70), vol. 1, pp. 478–9.

10. Jane Burbank, *Russian Peasants Go to Court: Legal Culture in the Countryside, 1905-1917* (Bloomington: Indiana University Press, 2004), p. xiv–xv; Badcock, 'The Russian Revolution', p. 246.

11. See Gordon Hahn, 'Did Putin Really tell Bush Ukraine is not even a state?' (26 January 2015) at gordonhahn.com/2015/01/26/did-putin-really-tell-bush-ukraine-is-not-even-a-state/, accessed 30 November 2019.

12. Joshua A. Sanborn, *Imperial apocalypse: The Great War and the Destruction of the Russian Empire* (Oxford: Oxford University Press, 2014).

13. Sanborn, 'War of Decolonisation: The Russian Empire in the Great War', in: Lohr et al. (eds), *The Empire and Nationalism at War*, pp. 50–51.

14. S. A. Smith, 'The Historiography of the Russian Revolution 100 Years on', *Kritika*, vol. 16, no. 4 (2015), p. 740. Sarah Badcock uses the expression 'the regional turn' ('The Russian Revolution: broadening understandings of 1917', *History Compass*, vol. 6, no. 1 [2007], p. 243).

15. Badcock, 'The Russian Revolution', p. 244.

16. Paul Ham, *1914: The year the world ended* (London: Black Swan, 2014), pp. 3–4. See also Barbara Tuchman's *The Proud Tower: A Portrait of the World Before the War, 1890-1914* (New York: Macmillan, 1966).

17. George Orwell, *In Front of Your Nose, 1945-1950: The Collected Essays, Journalism and Letters*, ed. Sonia Orwell and Ian Angus (San Diego: Harcourt Brace Jovanovich, 1968), p. 357.

18. Felix Schnell, 'Tear Them Apart ... and be Done with It! The Ataman-Leadership if Nestor Makhno as a Culture of Violence', *Ab Imperio*, vol. 3 (2008), p. 200, emphasis added.

19. Andy Willimott and Matthias Neumann, 'Crossing the Divide: Tradition, Rupture and Modernity in Revolutionary Russia', in: Neumann and Willimott (eds), *Rethinking the Russian Revolution as Historical Divide* (London: Routledge, 2018), p. 2.

20. Badcock, 'The Russian Revolution', pp. 243–62.

21. *The Russian Revolution, 1899-1919* (London: Fontana Press, 1990) and *Russia under the Bolshevik regime, 1919-1924* (London: Fontana Press, 1995).

22. *A People's Tragedy: The Russian Revolution, 1891-1924* (London: Jonathan Cape, 1996).

23. *Russia in Flames: War, revolution, civil war, 1914-1921* (New York: Oxford University Press, 2018).

24. Smele, *The 'Russian' Civil Wars, 1916-1926*.

25. Robert Gerwarth, *The Vanquished: Why the First World War Failed to End, 1917-1923* (London: Penguin, 2017).

26. S. A. Smith, 'The Historiography of the Russian Revolution 100 years on', *Kritika*, vol. 16, no. 4 (2015), p. 734.

27. Smith, 'The Historiography of the Russian Revolution', p. 734.

28. E. H. Carr, *The Bolshevik Revolution, 1917-1923* (Harmondsworth: Penguin, 1966), vol. 1, p. 308; W. H. Chamberlin, *The Russian Revolution, 1917-1921* (New York: Grosset and Dunlap, 1965), vol. 2, pp. 232-9.

29. See, for example, the response by Iain McKay to Jason Yanowitz's article in *International Socialist Review* in 2007 (links available at www.colindarch.info/makhnovshchina.php).

30. A *kulak* (pl. *kulaki*) or 'fist' was a wealthy peasant who owned land and hired labour to work it.

31. See the account of Lev Kamenev's visit to Makhno, in Chapter Four of this volume, and, *passim*, multiple references to the opinions of Antonov-Ovseenko.

32. See Gayle Lonergan, 'Where Was the Conscience of the Revolution? The Military Opposition at The Eighth Party Congress, March 1919', *Slavic Review*, vol. 74, no. 4 (2015), p. 832.

33. For a discussion of the significance of identification and self-identification of and by e.g. the 'greens' and other categories of rural resistance, see Erik Landis, 'Who were the "greens"? Rumor and collective identity in the Russian civil war', *Russian Review*, vol. 69 (2010), pp. 30-46.

34. Viktor Danilov and Teodor Shanin (eds), *Nestor Makhno: krest'ianskoe dvizheniia na Ukraine, 1918-1921. Dokumenty i materialy* (Moscow: Rossiiskaia Politich-eskaia Entsiklopediia, 2006), introduction, p. 5.

35. For example, *Grazhdanskaia voina na Ukraine, 1918-1920: sbornik dokumentov i materialov* (Kiev: Izdat. Naukova Dumka, 1967), 3 vols; and *Direktivy koman-dovaniia frontov Krasnoi Armii, 1917-1922 gg.: sbornik dokumentov* (Moscow: Voennoe Izdat. Ministerstva Oborony SSSR, 1971-78), 4 vols.

36. See *Soviet Studies*, vol. 31, no. 3 (1979), pp. 443-4.

37. For a short discussion of the work of these military analysts, see Aleksandr Timoshchuk, *Anarkho-kommunisticheskie formirovaniia N. Makhno, sentiabr' 1917-avgust 1921* (Simferopol': Tavriia, 1996), pp. 4-5.

38. Vladimir Litvinov 'O chetverstom (oktiabr' 1920 goda) voenno-politicheskom soglashenii mezhdu Revoliutsionno-Povstancheskoi Armiei (Makhnovtsev) i kommunisticheskim pravitel'stvom RSFSR', *International Review of Social History*, vol. 32 (1987), pp. 327-8.

39. Teper had been a member of the Nabat Confederation and fought with the *makhnovtsy*. He was captured and wrote a short book, probably under the Cheka's supervision (*Makhno: ot edinogo anarkhizm k stopam rumynskogo Korolia* [Kiev: Izdat. Molodoi Rabochii, 1924]).

40. N. V. Gerasimenko, 'Makhno', *Istorik i sovremennik*, vol. 3 (1922).

41. Vladimir Antonov-Ovseenko, *Zapiski o grazhdanskoi voine* (Moscow: Vysshii Voennyi Redak. Sovet, 1924-1933), 4 vols.

42. M. Kubanin, *Makhnovshchina: krest'ianskoe dvizhenie v stepnoi Ukrainev gody grazhdanskoi voiny* (Leningrad: Izdat. Priboi, 1927).

43. Terry Cox, *Peasants, Class and Capitalism: The Rural Research of L. N. Kritsman and his School* (Oxford: Clarendon Press, 1986), pp. 202-6.

44. V. V. Rudnev, *Makhnovshchina* (Khar'kov: Knigospilka, 1928).

45. S. N. Semanov, 'Makhnovshchina i ee krakh', *Voprosy istorii* no. 9 (1966), pp. 37-60.

46. *Pod chernym znamenem: zhizn' i smert' Nestora Makhno* (Moscow: Tovarishche-stvo Vozrozhdenie, 1991); and *Makhno kak on est': dokumental'no-istoricheskaia povest'* (Moscow: Tovarishchestvo Sovetskikh Pisatelei, 1991), parts 1 and 2.

47. *Makhno: podlinnaia istoria* (Moscow: AST-Press, 2001); and *Nestor Makhno: vozhak anarkhistov* (Moscow: Veche, 2005).

48. See the scathing review article by A. Dubovik, available, in Russian, at www. makhno.ru/st/107.php.

49. Roy Medvedev, 'Vladimir Litvinov: An Obituary', *International Review of Social History*, vol. 32 (1987), pp. 311-13.

50. 'O chetvertom (oktiabr' 1920 goda) voenno-politicheskom soglashenii mezhdu Revoliutsionno-Povstancheskoi Armiei (Makhnovtsev) i kommunisticheskim pravitel'skom RSFSR', *International Review of Social History*, vol. 32, no. 3 (1987), pp. 314-401.

51. 'Bat'ka Makhno ili oboroten' grazhdanskoi voiny', *Literaturnaia Gazeta* no. 5228 (8 February 1989), available online at a-pesni.org/grvojna/makhno/a-oboroten. php, accessed 30 November 2019.

52. Vera Tolz, 'Another Example of Rewriting Soviet History: The Re-Evaluation of Nestor Makhno', *Report on the USSR* [New York, RFE/RL], vol. 1, no. 10 (10 March 1989), pp. 18-19.

53. Smith, 'The Historiography of the Russian Revolution', p. 748.

54. V. F. Verstiuk (ed.), *Nestor Ivanovich Makhno: vospominania, materialy i dokumenty* (Kiev: RIF Dzvin, 1991).

55. Gosudarstvennyi Arkhiv Dnepropetrovsk Oblasti (ed.), *N. Makhno i makhnovskoe dvizhenie: iz istorii povstancheskogo dvizheniia v Ekaterinoslavskoi gubernii. Sbornik dokumentov i materialov* (Dnepropetrovsk: AO DAES, 1993).

56. Danilov and Shanin (eds), *Nestor Makhno*, p. 6. Stepan 'Stenka' Razin was a seventeenth century Cossack leader of an anti-Tsarist rebellion; Imam Shamil' was an anti-colonial leader in Dagestan in the nineteenth century.

57. *Tachanki s iuga: khudozhestvennoe issledovanie makhnovskogo dvizheniia* (Zaporozh'e: Dikoe Pole, 1997) and *Nestor Makhno* (Moscow: Molodaia Gvardiia, 2013).

58. Shubin's doctoral thesis on Spanish and Russian anarchism was submitted to the Institute of General History of the Russian Academy of Sciences in 1999. He has published *Makhno i makhnovskoe dvizhenie* (Moscow: Izdat. MIK, 1998); *Anarkhiia mat' poriadka: mezhdu krasnymi i belymi; Nestor Makhno kak zerkalo Rossiiskoi revoliutsii* (Moscow: Iauza, Eksmo, 2005); and most recently *Makhno i ego vremia: o velikoi revoliutsii i grazhdanskoi voine, 1917-1922 gg., v Rossii i na Ukraine* (Moscow: Knizhnyi Dom Librokom, 2014), as well as various articles.

59. Aleksandr Timoshchuk, *Anarkho-kommunisticheskie formirovaniia N. Makhno, sentiabr' 1917-avgust 1921* (Simferopol': Tavriia, 1996).

60. V. F. Verstiuk, *Makhnovshchyna: selians'kyi povstans'kyi rukh na Ukraini, 1918-1921* (Kiev: Naukova Dumka, 1991).

61. V. N. Volkovinskii, *Makhno e ego krakh* (Moscow: Izdat. VZPI, 1991), in Russian; Valerii Volkovyns'kyi, *Nestor Makhno: lehendy i real'nist'* (Kiev: Perlit Prodakshn, 1994), in Ukrainian.

62. Mark Baker, *Peasants, Power and Place: Revolution in the Villages of Kharkiv Province, 1914-1921* (Cambridge, Mass.: Harvard University Press, 2016), p. 139.

63. *Makhno i makhnovskoe dvizhenie*, p. 146; see also *Makhno i ego vremiia*, p. 275 and p. 284.

64. A. V. Belash and V. F. Belash, *Dorogi Nestora Makhno: istoricheskoe povestvovanie* (Kiev: Proza, 1993).

65. Danilov and Shanin (eds), *Nestor Makhno*.

66. Volodymyr Chop and Ihor Lyman, *Vol'nyi Berdiansk: misto v period anarkhizms'koho sotsial'noho eksperymentu, 1918-1921 r.* (Zaporizhzhia: RA Tandem-U, 2007); and Chop and Lyman, *Mistsiamy pam'iati povstans'kykh peremoh u Zaporoz'komu krai: Azovs'ka operatsiia Nestora Makhna* (Zaporizhzhia: Berdians'kyi Derzhavynyi Pedahohichnyi Universytet, 2017).

67. Viacheslav Azarov, *Starobel'skoe soglashenie* (Odessa: DP Nabat, 2011).

68. As Shubin has pointed out, for many people Makhno has become 'more of a fabulous hero than a real historical person. He is a gangster and a national hero, a noble knight and a symbol of a raging mob, an anarchist and a dictator ...' (*Makhno i makhnovskoe dvizhenie* p. 3).

69. Peter Lyashchenko, *History of the National Economy of Russia* (New York: Octagon Books, 1970), p. 730; M. P. Bazhen et al. (eds), *Soviet Ukraine* (Kiev: Ukrainian Soviet Encyclopaedia, 1969), pp. 289–90. Nicholas L. Chirovski states that up to 65 per cent of the total area of ethnic Ukraine is arable land (*The Ukrainian economy* [New York, 1965], p. 17).

70. Orest Subtelny, *Ukraine: A History* (Toronto: University of Toronto Press, 1988), p. 265.

71. Shubin, 'The Makhnovist movement and the national question in the Ukraine, 1917-1921', in: Steven Hirsch and Lucien van der Walt (eds), *Anarchism and Syndicalism in the Colonial and Postcolonial World, 1870-1940: The Praxis of National Liberation, Internationalism and Social Revolution* (Leiden: Brill, 2010), p. 148.

72. Feshchenko-Chopivs'kyi, *Ekonomichna heohrafiia Ukraini* (Kiev, 1923), p. 161, quoted in Konstantyn Kononenko, *Ukraine and Russia:A History of the Economic Relations Between Ukraine and Russia, 1654-1917* (Milwaukee: Marquette University Press, 1958), p. 238.

73. Subtelny, *Ukraine: A History*, p. 265.

74. These made up about 33 per cent of total imports. Russia continued to import chemicals and machinery from Germany even after the outbreak of war in 1914 (Maurice Dobb, *Soviet Economic Development since 1917*, 6th edn. [London: Routledge, 1966], p. 37).

75. Dobb, *Soviet Economic Development since 1917*, pp. 37–8.

76. William Blackwell, *The Beginnings of Russian Industrialization* (Princeton: Princeton University Press, 1968), p. 26, quoted by Subtelny, *Ukraine: A History*, p. 264.

77. Dobb, *Soviet Economic Development since 1917*, p. 16.

78. On high levels of peasant membership of the commune in Khar'kov province, see Baker, *Peasants, Power and Place*, pp. 11–12.

79. In the early years of the century, the peasants' reaction to the emergence of capitalist agriculture, on the right-bank at least, has been shown to have been to adopt forms of resistance usually associated with urban workers, i.e. strikes. See Robert Edelman's detailed study of the right-bank, based on archival research, *Proletarian Peasants: The Revolution of 1905 in Russia's Southwest* (Ithaca NY: Cornell University Press 1987).

80. Ral'nyi Statisticheskii Komitet MVD, *Statistika zemlevladeniia 1905 g. Svod dannykh po 50-ti guberniiam evropeiskoi Rossii* (St. Petersburg, 1907), pp. 174–5.

81. A *bedniak* was a poor peasant who had to sell his labour to survive, and was regarded by the Bolsheviks as a natural ally. A *batrak* was a landless rural labourer.

82. A *seredniak* was a middle peasant, someone who worked his own land with his own labour.

83. Subtelny, *Ukraine: A History*, p. 263.

84. K. R. Kacharovskii, *Russkaia obshchina. Vozmozhno li, zhelatel'no li ee sokhranenie i razvitie?* 2nd edn. (Moscow: Tipo-litografiia Russkago Tovarishchestva, 1906), p. 74. Figures are for 1892.

85. Lenin, *The Development of Capitalism in Russia* (Moscow: Progress Publishers, 1974), pp. 77–8.

86. V. Postnikov, *Iuzhno-russkoe krest'ianskoe khoziaistvo* (Moscow: I. N. Kushnerev, 1891). This book is the subject of a favourable review in the earliest surviving text

by Lenin, 'New economic developments in peasant life', written in 1893, in his *Collected Works* (Moscow: Progress Publishers, 1960–1971), vol. 1, pp. 11–73.

87. Lenin, *The Development of Capitalism in Russia*, pp. 72–6.
88. Lenin, *The Development of Capitalism in Russia*, p. 75.
89. Subtelny, *Ukraine: A History*, p. 262.
90. 'Most writers agree that peasants were pressured to leave the commune, though some feel that the degree of compulsion has been exaggerated' (Dorothy Atkinson, 'The statistics on the Russian land commune, 1905-1917', *Slavic Review*, vol. 32, no. 4 [1973], p. 776).
91. Atkinson, 'The Statistics on the Russian Land Commune'.
92. It also intensified the contradictions *within* the Ukrainian peasantry. In September and October 1917 one quarter of all reported seizures and destructive activity in the Empire occurred in south-western Ukraine (Dobb, *Soviet Economic Development since 1917*, p. 76).
93. On the *perelog* system, see Dobb, *Soviet Economic Development since 1917*, pp. 40–41.
94. Lyashchenko gives the ratio as 3.5-fold in 1801–10 and 3.7-fold in 1861–70 (*History of the National Economy of Russia*, p. 324).
95. Lyashchenko, *History of the National Economy of Russia*, p. 735.
96. Feshchenko-Chopivs'kyi, *Ekonomichna heohrafiia Ukraini*, p. 36, quoted in Kononenko, *Ukraine and Russia: A History of the Economic Relations between Ukraine and Russia*, unpaged introduction. The figures, in metric cwt. per hectare, are 12 to 7.8 for wheat; 10 to 8.7 for rye; 10 to 9.7 for barley; 11.8 to 9 for oats; and 85 to 80.7 for potatoes.
97. Lyashchenko, *History of the National Economy of Russia*, p. 451.
98. Kubanin, *Makhnovshchina*, p. 27; cf. Myron Kordouba, *Le territoire et la population de l'Ukraine: contribution géographique et statistique* (Berne: Suter, 1919), pp. 94–7.
99. Lyashchenko, *History of the National Economy of Russia*, p. 731 (map); *Sbornik statistiko-ekonomicheskikh svedenii po sel'skomu khoziaistvu Rossii i inostrannykh gosudarstv* (St. Petersburg, 1916), pp. 15–16, quoted by Kubanin, *Makhnovshchina*, p. 10.
100. Lyashchenko, *History of the National Economy of Russia*, p. 748.
101. In Kherson, for instance, between 1883 and 1895 the real increase in redemption payments (to acquire private land rights) was 40 per cent; land allotments diminished 27 per cent in the same period (Francis M. Watters, 'The peasant and the village commune', in Wayne Vucinich (ed.), *The Peasant in Nineteenth Century Russia* [Stanford: Stanford University Press, 1968], p. 154 ff.).
102. Lyashchenko, *History of the National Economy of Russia*, p. 371 and p. 373 (maps).
103. *Mir*, or *obshchina*, were terms for the repartitional commune, the main form of social and economic organisation of the Russian peasantry before the revolution. See, e.g., Roger Bartlett (ed.), *Land Commune and Peasant Community in Russia: Communal Forms in Imperial and Early Soviet Society* (London: Palgrave Macmillan, 1990).
104. See the account of the Potapenko uprising in Chernigov province in 1905 in E. J. Hobsbawm, *Primitive Rebels* (New York: Norton, 1965), p. 27; for a chronology of such revolts see A. V. Shapkarin (ed.), *Krest'ianskoe dvizhenie v Rossii, iiun' 1907 g.-iiul' 1914 g.* (Moscow: Izd-vo Nauka, 1966), p. 492–623.
105. Dobb, *Soviet Economic Development since 1917*, p. 81.
106. Lenin, 'Imperialism, The Highest Stage of capitalism', in his *Selected Works in Three Volumes*, rev. edn. (Moscow: Progress Publishers, 1975), vol. 1, p. 635.

107. Lenin, 'Imperialism, the Highest Stage of Capitalism', p. 678 ff.

108. Dobb, *Soviet Economic Development since 1917*, p. 38.

109. Dobb, *Soviet Economic Development since 1917*, p. 38.

110. S. I. Potolov, *Rabochie Donbassa v XIX veke* (Moscow: Izdatel'stvo Akademii Nauk, 1963), pp. 88–9.

111. From 250,000 tons in 1870 to 10.8 million tons in 1900. In 1885 only 32,000 tons of iron were smelted, but by 1900 the figure had increased to 800,000 tons, one quarter of the total output of the Russian Empire. Potolov, *Rabochie Donbassa v XIX veke*, pp. 80–81.

112. Lyashchenko, *History of the National Economy of Russia*, pp. 688–9.

113. *Statisticheskii ezhegodnik za 1914 g.*, p. 199, quoted by M. Gordon, *Workers before and after Lenin* (New York: Dutton, 1941), p. 354; cf. Isaac Deutscher in the *New Cambridge Modern History*, vol. 12, 2nd edn. (Cambridge: Cambridge University Press, 1968), p. 405.

114. *Materialy po raionirovaniiu Ukrainy* (Khar'kov, 1923), p. 136, quoted by Kubanin, *Makhnovshchina*, p. 23.

115. *Materialy po raionirovaniiu Ukrainy*, p. 136, quoted by Kubanin, *Makhnovshchina*, p. 24.

116. Tsentral'nyi Statisticheskii Komitet, *Pervaia vseobshchaia perepis' naseleniia Rossiiskoi Imperii, 1897 g.* (St. Petersburg, 1905), vol. 2, p. 23. Demographic trends for the period 1900–1930 are described in *Ukraine: A concise encyclopedia* (Toronto: University of Toronto Press, 1963–), vol. 1, pp. 214–22.

117. That is, in a large number of small strikes (Iu. M. Kir'ianov, *Rabochie iuga Rossii, 1914-fevral' 1917 g.* [Moscow: Nauka, 1971], p. 282).

118. Lyashchenko, *History of the National Economy of Russia*, p. 693.

119. I. Merinkov et al., 'Brianskii zavod v 1905 g'. *Litopys revoliutsii* nos. 3–4 (1926), p. 126, quoted by D. Lane, *The roots of Russian communism* (Assen: Van Gorcum, 1969), p. 172n.

120. Kir'ianov, *Rabochie iuga Rossii, 1914-fevral' 1917 g.* p. 286.

121. *Istoriia Kommunisticheskoi Partii Sovetskogo Soiuza* (Moscow: Gospolitizdat, 1966), vol. 2, map facing p. 588.

122. Lyashchenko, *History of the National Economy of Russia*, pp. 765–6.

123. Lyashchenko, *History of the National Economy of Russia*, p. 767.

124. Harold Fisher, *The Famine in Soviet Russia, 1919-1923: The Operations of the American Relief Administration* (New York: Macmillan, 1927), p. 259.

125. Vsevelod Holubnychy, *The Industrial Output of the Ukraine, 1913-1956: A Statistical Analysis* (Munich: Schubert, 1957), p. 32.

126. Holubnychy, *The Industrial Output of the Ukraine*, pp. 8–9, 14, 20, 22.

127. Kubanin, *Makhnovshchina*, p. 63; cf. Lenin, 'Report on Work in the Countryside, March 23, 1919', [to the 8th Congress of the RCP(b)] in his *Selected Works*, vol. 3, p. 148. The *sovkhoz* or *sovetskoe khoziaistvo* was a state-owned farm, often a large confiscated estate, and distinct from a *kholkhoz* or collective farm.

128. D. Mitrany, *Marx Against the Peasant* (New York: Collier 1961), pp. 231–2.

129. Shubin, 'The Makhnovist Movement and the National Question in the Ukraine', p. 147.

130. Shubin, 'The Makhnovist Movement and the National Question in the Ukraine', p. 153.

131. Oscar Wilde, 'The Soul of Man Under Socialism,' in his *Works* (London: Spring Books, 1963), p. 924.

EPILOGUE: THE REFRAMING OF MAKHNO FOR THE TWENTY-FIRST CENTURY

1. 'Interviu z Oleksandrom Ishchenkom: pro likarniu, perepokhovannia prakhhu Nestora Makhna ta dorogu na Polohi', *Guliaipole City* (27 February 2019), available at https://tinyurl.com/y3e63kq9, accessed 10 March 2019.
2. Formerly Aleksandrovsk (Ukrainian: Oleksandrivs'k).
3. 'Interviu z Oleksandrom Ishchenkom'. The move to secure the return of Makhno's ashes was subsequently widely reported in the Ukrainian and international press. There seems to have been some opposition from exiles in France.
4. Lucien van der Walt and Michael Schmidt, *Black Flame: The Revolutionary Class Politics of Anarchism and Syndicalism* (Edinburgh; AK Press, 2009), p. 20.
5. Volodymyr Ishchenko, 'Ukraine's Fractures', *New Left Review*, no. 87 (May–June 2014), pp. 16–17.
6. 'National-Makhnovism' (29 June 2017), available at nonstateactorblog.wordpress. com/2017/06/29/national-makhnovism/, accessed 30 November 2019.
7. Report by Sergey Shevchenko of the FAD-RKAS (Federation of Anarchists of the Donbass-Revolutionary Confederation of Anarcho-Syndicalists), 12 January 1999, available at http://www.hartford-hwp.com/archives/63/354.html, accessed 30 November 2019.
8. Report by Sergey Shevchenko, emphasis added.
9. Casey Michel, 'The Last Time Ukraine Was Truly Free', *Roads and Kingdoms* (5 March 2014), available at https://roadsandkingdoms.com/2014/the-last-time-ukraine-was-truly-free/, accessed 30 November 2019.
10. Nikolai Kozloff, 'Note to Ukraine: Time to Reconsider Your Historic Role Models', *Huffington Post* (27 May 2016), available at https://www.huffpost.com/entry/ note-to-ukraine-time-to-r_b_7453506, accessed 30 November 2019.
11. Volodymyr Ishchenko, *The Ukrainian Left During and After The Maidan Protests*, 2016, available at https://www.academia.edu/20445056/The_Ukrainian_Left_ during_and_after_the_Maidan_Protests, accessed 29 February 2020, and Ishchenko, 'Ukraine's Fractures', p. 17.
12. Michel, 'The Last Time Ukraine Was Truly Free'.

Index

Thanks to our Patreon Subscribers:

Abdul Alkalimat
Andrew Perry

Who have shown their generosity and comradeship in difficult times.